ASIAN TEXANS

OUR HISTORIES *and* OUR LIVES

Edited by Irwin A. Tang

The it Works | Austin, Texas

Asian Texans: Our Histories and Our Lives

Copyright © 2007 by Irwin A. Tang

Cover and book design by Angela Pan.

All cover photos appear in the body of the book except upper-right photo of M.J. Khan, courtesy of Mr. Khan (see Chapter 14).

All questions and requests should be addressed to Irwin A. Tang, The it Works, by email at asiantexans@hotmail.com. Comments, corrections, and opinions are welcome.

Additional copies of this and other books published by The it Works may be purchased at *www.irwinbooks.com*.

Second Edition, First Hardcover Edition.

First Printing, March 2008.

Library of Congress Cataloging-In Publication Data

Tang, Irwin

Asian Texans: Our Histories and Our Lives / edited by Irwin A. Tang

ISBN 978-0-9679433-7-4

Printed in the United States of America

CONTENTS

ASIAN TEXANS

OUR HISTORIES *and* OUR LIVES

★

INTRODUCTION

Irwin A. Tang

Over one million Asian Americans live in Texas. Some were born in Asia. Some were born in America. Some were born in Texas. Asians have been in Texas since the days of the republic. We, the Asians and Asian Americans of Texas, whether young or old, citizen or not, mixed blood or not, dark-skinned or light, short or tall, rich or poor, we are the Asian Texans. This book represents the first effort to chronicle a comprehensive history of Asian Texans.[1]

I hope that this book serves three purposes. I hope that it will enrich the lives of Asian Texans and Asian Americans by providing for some a sense of their place in the struggles, glories, and progress of history. Second, I hope that this book helps researchers of history—Asian American, Asian, Texan, and American history. Third, this book has been written for the general reader, for that reader's enjoyment, enlightenment, and education.

Previous books chronicling pan-Asian American histories only gloss over specific events and characteristics of Asian Texan history. The two most prestigious volumes on general Asian American history—Ronald Takaki's *Strangers from a Different Shore* and Sucheng Chan's *An Interpretive History of Asian Americans*—rarely mention Asian Americans in Texas. The same can be said about books that are dedicated to only one Asian American ethnic group. Henry Tsai's *The Chinese Experience in America* and Iris Chang's *The Chinese in America* both make little mention of Chinese Americans in Texas or the South. Certain books offer more on Asian Texan history because of their topic. Erika Lee's *At America's Gates: Chinese Immigration during the Exclusion Era, 1882–1943* concentrates on Texas and Arizona because Texas was a major entry point for Chinese immigrating into the United States during the sixty-one years of Chinese Exclusion.

Takaki's and Chan's books covered vast periods of time and vast swaths of geography. They did so, necessarily, at the sacrifice of the histories of some of the less populous Asian ethnic groups. This volume devotes time to groups whose histories have rarely been written about in book form: Pakistani Americans, Bangladeshi Americans, Sri Lankan Americans, Burmese Americans, Tibetan Americans, Nepalese Americans, Singaporean Americans, Malaysian Americans, and Indonesian Americans. Also, this book dedicates an unusual amount of space to the histories of ethnic groups mostly written about in sociological terms: Cambodian Americans, Laotian Americans, Thai Americans, and Pacific Islanders living on the U.S. mainland.

This book draws from all of the major academic works on Asian Texan history. The first of these was the short volume, *The Chinese in El Paso*, by Nancy Farrar, published in 1972 by Texas Western Press. Her book relies largely on newspaper stories and archival photographs. Historian Dr. Edward J.M. Rhoads is best known for his research on the history of China, but in 1977, he published a seminal article on the history of Chinese Texans in *Southwestern Historical Quarterly* entitled, "The Chinese in Texas," which covered the history of Chinese Texans from 1870 to 1970. This work is considered a major contribution to Asian American history and has been reprinted and cited in Asian American history books. Dr. Rhoads contributed all of his extensive research materials on Asian Texans to this book project.

Dr. Edward C.M. Chen and Dr. Fred R. von der Mehden wrote *The Chinese in Houston*, a 19-page book published by the Houston Center for the Humanities in 1982. The book was part of a series that included histories of the Japanese and Vietnamese in Houston. Dr. Chen also wrote an unpublished history of Chinese and Japanese in Houston, which he contributed to the research efforts for this book.

Thomas K. Walls published *The Japanese Texans* in 1987 through the Institute of Texan Cultures, an organ of the University of Texas system. This book concentrates on the history of Japanese Texans from the turn of the 20th century through the end of World War II. The book gives special attention to the Japanese Texan owners of rice farms and truck farms in East and South Texas. Dr. Walls holds a Ph.D. in Sociology from UT-Austin and serves as the Chief of Staff of the Oklahoma State Senate. Dr. Walls wrote the chapter on the pre-World War II Japanese Texans and co-wrote the World War II chapter for this book.

A tremendously useful book on the history of Korean Texans was Victoria Kwon's *Entrepreneurship and Religion: Korean Immigrants in Houston, Texas*, published by Garland Publishing in 1997. Kwon interviewed numerous Koreans on two of the most important aspects of their community: business and church affairs.

Other recent books on Asian Texans have included *First of Many* by Julian Mardock (Eakin Press), about the life of Julian's father, Sam Mardock, an early Chinese Texan; *Chinese Heart of Texas: The San Antonio Community, 1875–1975* by Mel Brown (Lily on the Water Publishing) and *The Asian Texans*, a book for young readers by Marianne Del Brady (Texas A&M University Press).

The writers of this book also utilized a dozen or so very useful master's theses, Ph.D. dissertations, and books on very specific topics or individuals. Most of these works dealt with Chinese and Japanese Texans.

The organization of this book matches the identities and organization of Asian Texans throughout most of their history. The book is organized primarily by ethnic group, time period, and geography. Three "pan-ethnic" chapters act as bookends to the fifteen "ethnic-specific" chapters. The first chapter of this book is a historical overview of the entire history of Asian Texans; it also provides historical context for many of the laws, terms, and time periods mentioned in the chapters that follow. The next six chapters chronicle the history of Chinese and Japanese Texans from 1870 through World War II; before 1946, most Asian Texans were of Chinese or Japanese descent. The following nine chapters chronicle the histories of all Asian Texan ethnic groups from World War II into the 2000s. Six ethnic groups—the Filipinos, Indians, Koreans, Chinese, Japanese, and Vietnamese—were assigned individual chapters because of the size of their population and the length of their history. For the sake of space, and due to common elements, three chapters chronicle the histories of more than one ethnic group.

Ethnic identity, historical period, and geography overlapped in such ways that made organization of the information difficult. For instance, the first known Asian Texan was a Filipino named Francisco Flores who came to Texas while it was still an independent republic. However, few Filipinos lived in Texas until after World War II, and therefore, the Filipino Texans chapter is in the second half of this book.

For the vast majority of Asian Texan history, the voices of Asian Texans were ignored, suppressed, and generally omitted from mass media or history books. Like Takaki, the writers of this volume pay special attention to the lives and the voices of individual Asian Americans. Like Erika Lee's *At America's Gates*, this history does not take a condemning tone towards the illegal immigration of Asians.

Although books like Takaki's and Chan's are multi-ethnic, they are written by one author. I purposefully sought out writers and researchers who belonged to the communities they were to write about; I sought contributors and interviewees who were "insiders" to those communities, especially community leaders. Hence, rather than using a subtitle such as Takaki's "A history of Asian Americans" or Chan's "An Interpretive History," this book carries the subtitle, "Our Histories and our Lives." This book embraces a pluralism of views, voices, and interpretations in both its process and its final result. It was only after all of the ethnic histories had been written that I began writing the historical overview, which attempts to create a common historical structure for the ethnic histories presented herein. This process allowed for the writing of individual ethnic histories without any pressure to relate them to other histories. What was stressed in the process was the chronicling of events, developments, turning points, and characteristics important to the respective ethnic groups rather than the pan-ethnicity of Asian Texans.

I am the editor and co-author of this book. Besides writing or co-writing chapters, I conducted research for most of the chapters. I also helped revise chapters for content and length. In 1995, I earned an M.A. in Asian Studies from UT-Austin, for which I wrote a thesis chronicling the history of the politics surrounding cases of anti-Asian violence in the United States since the murder of Vincent Chin. My thesis advisor was the aforementioned Dr. Ed Rhoads. I have been speaking with Asian Texans about their lives and experiences since the mid-1990s, and I began research for this book in 2002. Since then, I have written numerous magazine articles concerning Asian Texans.

The co-writers of this volume, along with many of the interviewees, include top experts on their respective areas of Asian Texan history. The following is a list of most of the co-writers, along with their works, experiences, and backgrounds.

Dr. Thomas K. Walls wrote both a master's thesis and a Ph.D. dissertation on Japanese Americans as part of his graduate work for the sociology department at UT Austin. His book, *The Japanese Texans*, is a major contribution to Japanese American history.

Dr. Arthur Sakamoto is a professor of sociology at UT-Austin and has published numerous academic articles concerning Asian Americans, race, and demographics.

Dr. Harishini Ernest holds a Ph.D. in applied linguistics from UT-Austin. An early Sri Lankan immigrant to Texas, she was one of the founding members of the social service agency, Saheli for Asian Families.

Sam Kannappan has been a leader of the Indian Houstonian community since the 1970s. He was instrumental in the establishment of the Sri Meenakshi Temple in Pearland, Texas.

Rakesh Amaram conducted several interviews to chronicle the history of Indian Americans in West Texas.

Thao Ha, a second-generation Vietnamese Houstonian working on her Ph.D. in Sociology at UT-Austin, has presented and published numerous papers on Vietnamese Americans, including work on the sociology of Vietnamese nail salons.

Anna L. Fahy wrote her UT-El Paso master's thesis on the history and community development of the El Paso Chinese community. Her work involved numerous interviews with Chinese of El Paso and Juárez, Mexico and archeological findings concerning Chinese El Pasoans of the 19th and 20th centuries.

Vynarack Xaykao holds a master's degree in Information Sciences from UT-Austin. She is of both Hmong and non-Hmong Laotian descent, and her father is an ethnic community leader. She interviewed numerous Hmong and Laotians for her two chapter sections in this book.

Naoko Kato is currently pursuing a Ph.D. in History from UT-Austin. She holds an M.A. in the history of education from the University of British Columbia and an M.S. from the School of Information at UT-Austin.

K.L. Yap is currently writing a Ph.D. dissertation on Singaporean and Malaysian Americans.

Yvonne Lim Wilson is a professional journalist who grew up in San Antonio, Texas as a second-and-a-half generation Chinese American. Her father emigrated from Hong Kong and her mother was born in San Antonio, where they own the historic Golden Star Café.

Rebecca Teng, a third-generation Chinese Dallasite and descendant of one of the oldest Chinese Dallasite families, conducted twenty-four interviews with community representatives to write "The Chinese Experience in Dallas, Texas: 1900–2000," which was chosen as a 2005 Model Thesis for UT-Austin's Plan II Honors Program.

Pat Charnveja is a long-time leader of the Thai American community of Houston and hails from one of the oldest Thai families in Texas.

Sophia Hong is a registered nurse and a second-generation Cambodian Texan.

Lucy Lee and Michelle Lee are both second-generation Korean Americans of Dallas.

I am proud of the process by which this book was researched and written, and I believe it is a process that can be reproduced to write other histories. First, this process stressed the viewpoints of particular "insiders," meaning members of the community who lived through, or whose ascendants lived through, the specific history in question. This group includes community leaders, elder members of the respective community, and particularly observant or well-placed members. Some of them were oral historians, and some were formally trained historians and researchers. Second, the book embraces multiple viewpoints and disciplinary influences without abandoning a general historical structure. Third, each chapter stresses important events, turning points, and problems. As a result, some chapters may deal with problems and issues that many Asian Texans would prefer to forget. Only by addressing these problems can we seek to understand the struggles undertaken in overcoming them. Fourth, certain individuals' lives were spotlighted. Fifth, common sense assumptions by knowledgeable insiders were balanced by a conservative academic approach.

Our research and writing process drew from few secondary sources, as few exist. Many interviews and newspaper articles were utilized. The later the history and the smaller the ethnic group, the more the history relied on interviews with community leaders. Taking into account that all of the writers were essentially working in their "spare time," a tremendous amount of time was spent in writing these histories. Our research budget was more than $3000, and some of us invested our own money. Two thousand dollars was donated by Dr. Vijay Mahajan, who is the UT-Austin John P. Harbin Centennial Chair in Business.

While we, the writers, have attempted to make this volume as comprehensive as possible, we acknowledge and hope that this history is only the beginning of the writing of more Asian Texan histories. Discussion, clarification, and expansion of issues, stories, and assertions made herein are highly encouraged. We hope that those who feel dissatisfied with this history or lament what was left out write their own histories to add to the ones we have chronicled here. We hope all interested Asian Texans consider adding to this history. For this purpose, I plan to make the publishing company's website, *www.irwinbooks.com*, a clearinghouse for the publishing of letters, articles, oral histories, and photographs sent to me for the purpose of enriching the written history of Asian Texans.

I would like to thank the following people without whom this book would not exist: all of the writers and researchers directly and indirectly involved in the production of this book; all of the interviewees and providers of research materials; my parents, Dr. Yi-Noo and Eugenia Tang; my sister, Irene Tang; Dr. Ed Rhoads; Dr. Vijay Mahajan; Dr. Art Sakamoto; UT Austin's Center for Asian American Studies; Dr. Mia Carter; Dr. Rowena Fong; Dr. Madeline Hsu; Dr. Evelyn Hu-DeHart; Dr. Dale Baum; Debbie Chen; Organization of Chinese Americans, Greater Houston chapter; Jerome Veilman; Amy Wong Mok; the Teng family; Wei Luo; Monica Wong of El Paso Community College; Barbara Jann; Vincent Lozano; Monica Rios; Wea Lee; Martha Wong; Gordon Quan; Rogene Gee Calvert; Angela Pan; Tiffany Marshall; Elizabeth Smith; Mel Brown; the Institute of Texan Cultures; the UT Center for American History; the UT-El Paso Library Special Collections; El Paso Public Library; Houston Public Library's History Center; and University of Texas Press. My heart swells for all who have helped me with this book, both the living and those who have passed on.

ENDNOTE

1 Based on 2000 census figures, population growth rates, and population estimates by community leaders made in the early 2000s. Some ethnic leaders' population estimates were several times those of the 2000 Census, indicating that many Asian ethnic groups were undercounted to the extreme. Estimates were based on numbers attending local events, numbers belonging to local organizations, numbers of businesses owned by members of the ethnic group, church and temple congregations, ethnic neighborhood sizes and so forth.

————————— ★ —————————

HISTORICAL OVERVIEW

Irwin A. Tang

This overview serves two main purposes. The first is to place the arc of Asian Texan history into larger historical contexts of immigration, race relations, Texas history, American history, economics, military activities, war, and international relations. The second purpose is to structure Asian Texan history into three overlapping periods.

The first period of Asian Texan history was the "racial-caste period." It began with Texas gaining independence in 1836 and ended in 1947 with the closure of Japanese internment camps in Texas. In the first period of Asian Texan history, Asian Texans lived in a distinct racial-caste system structured by racist laws; social hierarchy; segregation of residence, sexual relations, and marriage; and the separation of Asian family members from each other.

The lives of all Asian Americans during this period were constricted severely by a set of federal laws. The 1790 Naturalization Act established that only free white persons were allowed to naturalize, excluding Asians from that right. The vast majority of Chinese women were prohibited from immigrating through the 1875 Page Act. Chinese immigration was

1

almost completely prohibited through the Chinese Exclusion Act of 1882. The main exception for the exclusion act was the class of immigrants labeled "merchants," which was vaguely defined; those planning to open a business were not necessarily allowed merchant status. The 1888 Scott Act prohibited Chinese Americans who visited China from returning to the United States. The 1892 Geary Act required Chinese to carry registration papers proving their legal status in the nation. A 1907 executive order prevented Japanese from entering the United States from Mexico, Hawaii, or Canada, and most Japanese immigration was prohibited through the "Gentlemen's Agreement" of 1907–1908. In 1917, the Asiatic Barred Zone was established, prohibiting the immigration of Asian Indians. The 1924 Immigration Act attempted to shut out immigration from all Asian nations except the Philippines, which was considered a ward of the United States. However, the 1934 Tydings-McDuffie Act limited Filipino immigration to fifty per year.

In addition to these exclusions were the sexual and marital restrictions. Most Asians in America, as a result of federal legislation and other circumstances, were men. Texas prohibited marriage between people of different races (known as "miscegenation") in 1837, and this law was not rescinded until 1970. It is unclear, however, how strictly anti-miscegenation legislation was applied against Asian men in Texas. Certainly the *social* sanction against a white woman marrying a man of Asian descent was heavy in Texas. It seems from the marriage patterns of Asian Texan men from 1870 to 1970, though, that the social sanction against Mexican, Mexican American, and black women marrying Asian men was much less than that applied against white women. In addition to state legislation, the federal Cable Act of 1922 stipulated that an American female citizen who married an "alien ineligible to citizenship," a category encompassing most Asian Texan men, would lose her U.S. citizenship. Ignoring or shirking these laws, Filipino, Chinese, and Japanese men in Texas married and sired children with Hispanic, black, and white women.

Another layer of the racial-caste system dealt with land ownership and residency. Local residents and governments prevented Asians from living in certain neighborhoods, and some even discouraged Asians from living and working within city limits. Texas passed an alien land law in 1921 designed to prohibit Japanese in Texas from owning farm land. In 1937, some Texas legislators attempted to pass an *urban* alien land law aimed at prohibiting Chinese in Texas from owning and operating groceries.

Educational segregation applied to Asian Texans, but the way it applied varied. Asian Texans with black ancestry attended black schools. Other Asians were likely forced to attend black or predominantly Mexican American schools as well. But many were allowed to attend white schools. Asian Texans began attending universities in small numbers in the 1920s.

The fact that Asians could not naturalize prevented most Asian Texans of this period from voting. Other factors in preventing voting were simple intimidation and Texas's law that only whites could vote in primary elections.

The influence of Mexican culture, language, and politics on Asian Texans during the racial-caste period was immense. This influence was a result of the large population of Mexicans/Mexican Americans in Texas, the state's proximity to Mexico, and the immigration of Asians from Mexico. Two types of Asians migrated from Mexico: 1) those who lived in Mexico and then decided to move to the United States and 2) those who traveled to Mexico with the sole intent of migrating to America. Many Asians who entered from Mexico did so illegally, breaking the exclusion laws mentioned above. A major portion of those Asians who entered Texas through Mexico did not stay in Texas for longer than weeks or months—only long enough to prepare to travel, say, from El Paso to the West Coast. A majority of those Asians who lived in Texas *for some time* (be it weeks, months, or generations) also lived for some time in Mexico. This assertion is based on the fact that in many years, hundreds or thousands of Asians entered Texas from Mexico, and the total Census count of Asians in Texas did not surpass 1000 until 1920.

In contrast to those Asians living in Texas for less than a year were those who chose to live in Texas "permanently." Major portions of the permanent Chinese, Filipino, and Japanese populations of Texas spoke Spanish and lived and worked within local Mexican American communities. Among the Asians who married *in Texas*, the most common combination was that of an Asian man and a Mexican American woman. The largest Asian Texan communities, located in El Paso and San Antonio, were in many ways more "Mexican" than "American."

Although it was illegal for most Asians to immigrate, make return trips to Asia, bring their wives to the United States, naturalize as citizens, marry white women, live in certain places, or own certain real properties, some Asian Texans did live completely lawfully. They worked in legitimate businesses, and they married American women so that they did not have to travel between Texas and Asia. They were born in the United States or immigrated legally.

On the other hand, most of the Asian Texan population in the 19th century lived some aspects of their lives "underground." They utilized "underground" networks to immigrate or to make return trips to visit family in Asia. Asians helped other Asians, including blood kin, to immigrate illegally. Some Asians gambled or operated gambling parlors; smoked opium or operated opium dens for non-Asians and Asians; or belonged to tongs, merchants associations, and family associations. These were all mutual aid organizations in which members collectively helped each other politically and economically. *Some* tongs organized underground activities and "policed" themselves. In as much as Texas was seen as the "Wild West," Asian Texans were as Texan as any group.

Chinese settlers were sent deeper underground by national and local campaigns to deport illegal immigrants, to close down opium dens, and to eliminate gambling. In its efforts against illegal immigrants, government officials arrested, detained, and deported Asians to Asia or Mexico. They conducted highly invasive searches of homes, requested registration papers, monitored movements, required permission for inland travel, and photographed and measured Asians for monitoring purposes. Some local political and economic efforts were aimed at shutting down Asian-owned businesses. For such purposes, media representations of Asians were often brutally racist.

Furthermore, Asians sometimes had multiple identities and names, depending on where they lived. They had the names they were born with, the names they used to immigrate, English names, and Spanish names. Some Chinese Texan men had a wife and children in North America,

and another family in China. Finally, Chinese American burial practices—such as the disinterment of bones for re-burial in China—likely
forced Chinese Texans to bury their dead in areas other than white cem-
eteries. Being pressured underground was often very literal—as Chinese
built often-elaborate underground rooms and tunnels beneath their
homes and businesses in Texas, Arizona, Oklahoma, and Mexico.

Asians, despite their relative success in running farms, laundries,
restaurants and groceries, lived, in many ways, in a lower racial caste
than Mexican Americans in Texas. This was due in large part to three
issues. The vast majority of Mexican Americans, until the 1930s, could
freely travel and migrate both between nations and throughout the United States. Mexican Americans' high numbers gave them political power
and allowed them, at certain times and places, to be considered "white."
Because of Texas's history and because of the familiarity of Mexican culture, Mexicans seemed much more "Texan." Overall, blacks were treated
with the highest degree of oppression and malice. Blacks and whites were
thought to be at far ends of the racial-caste spectrum, and Asian Americans and Mexican Americans were positioned somewhere in between.

There were several ways in which Asian Texans could climb the
social hierarchy during the racial-caste period. They could increase their
wealth by saving their wages or growing their businesses. Additionally,
some Asians improved their citizenship status from illegal to legal; from
laborer class to merchant class; or from legal resident to citizen. They
did so by increasing their wealth, serving in the U.S. military, lobbying, or other means. Finally, association leaders, informal "mayors of
Chinatown," and Japanese plantation owners often represented Asians
in local affairs and improved Asians' status. Asian leaders developed relationships with government officials, contributed to charities, and built
edifices for local use.

The population growth of Asian Texas in this early period resulted
from various factors: the hiring of large numbers of Chinese Americans
from the West Coast to work on the Houston & Texas Central Railroad
and the Southern Pacific Railroad; the finishing of the first transcontinental railroad and the general need for Asians on the west coast to find
employment; the end of slavery and Southern capitalists' search for new

sources of inexpensive labor in the 1860s and 1870s; the general migration of Asians eastward from the west coast and, later, westward from the Deep South, as they sought better lives and unexploited markets for their small businesses; the funneling of Asian migrants through El Paso as a result of immigration laws; the recruitment of Chinese, Korean, Japanese, and Asian Indian laborers to Mexico beginning in the 1870s; the Mexican Revolution and Pancho Villa's hatred for Asians; and the desire of Asians and Pacific Islanders living in China, Japan, the Philippines Islands, Korea, India, the Pacific Islands, Mexico and Latin America, and the Caribbean Islands for better lives for themselves and their families.

Considering the numerous anti-Asian expulsions, riots, and lynchings in the far western United States, Texas was, in general, far less violent towards its Asian American residents. Nevertheless, the final spasm of the racial-caste era was, in essence, violent. Although most Japanese *Texans* were not imprisoned in internment camps during World War II, most of these Texas families were investigated, their adult males detained, and their lives highly regulated. Thousands of Japanese from the West Coast and Latin America were imprisoned for months or years in three internment camps in Texas. In 1947, the last of the Japanese interned in Texas were freed. After this last mass violation of civil and human rights, both the state and the nation moved steadily towards respecting the equal rights of Asian Americans. Thus, 1947 marks the end of the racial-caste era.

The population of Asian Texans during the racial caste period climbed from zero, or near-zero, in 1836 to about 850 in 1900. Almost all were Chinese; the Census counted only thirteen Japanese that year. Because of Chinese Exclusion, the number of Chinese Texans fell to under 600 in the 1910 Census, but because the Japanese had enjoyed several years of unfettered immigration (until 1907), their population grew to 340 by that year. Similarly, unfettered immigration allowed the Filipino Texan population to grow to 288 by the year 1930, while the Chinese population, at 703, was essentially equal to its 1890 size. By 1930, the Japanese population had leveled off at 519, and there were small numbers of Indians (49) and Koreans (17). Because of reproduction and migration from other states, Chinese Texans finally broke the 1,000 mark in

1940. Meanwhile, due to immigration policies, the Japanese and Filipino populations shrank to 458 and 219, respectively.

The second period of Asian Texan history was largely defined by military activities and war, so it will herein be known as the "military period." This period overlaps both the first and third periods of Asian Texan history. World War II both ushered out the racial-caste era of Asian Texan history and commenced the military period. When, in 1937, Chinese forces fought back against the invading Japanese military, World War II began, and the violence prevented or discouraged Chinese Texans from returning to their homes in China and continuing with their generations-long system of supporting a family in China while working in the United States. Escaping from the war, some Chinese Texans returned from China to Texas; some family members—especially the wives and children of Chinese Texan men—migrated to Texas for the first time. Even the bodies of dead Chinese Texans, as evidenced from the tombstones at El Paso's Chinese cemetery, began accumulating in Texas, instead of being disinterred and shipped back to their homeland, as had been the custom. In 1943, the federal government, allying itself with China in the war, abolished the Chinese Exclusion Act; the stringent prevention of Chinese immigration was relaxed; and Chinese were also allowed to naturalize. Thus, Chinese Texans lost, to a great degree, the air of illegality. Texans felt a greater affinity to all Chinese and Filipinos as they fought for the Allied nations both as soldiers in Asian nations and as American GIs. And when the Japanese American 442nd Regimental Combat Team rescued the Texas "Lost Battalion" from Nazi German siege, the Japanese Texans certainly improved their status as well.

In addition to the abolishment of Chinese Exclusion, the relevant political activity that ended the racial-caste period and ushered in the military period included the 1945 War Brides Act that granted citizenship to foreign-born women who married American servicemen and the 1947 amendment to this law that allowed women who married Chinese American soldiers the same rights; the 1946 Luce-Celler bill allowing for a small quota for Indian and Filipino immigration; the granting of citizenship to Asian and Asian American soldiers serving in the U.S. military; the 1949 granting of refugee status to 5000 well-educated Chinese so that they could immigrate to the U.S. during the Chinese Communist Revolution; the 1952 McCarran-Walter Act granting Japanese Americans the right to naturalize and Japanese a small immigration quota; and the general relaxation of measures designed to keep Asians out of the nation. Still, the number of immigrants allowed to migrate from Asian nations under the national quota system was so low as to be measured by the hundreds.

In Texas, World War II resulted in rapidly expanding war industries and quickly growing and proliferating military bases. With shipbuilding and manufacturing spurring Houston's economic growth, the city grew more than any other in Texas. Military installations were established or expanded in San Antonio, El Paso, Austin, Dallas-Fort Worth, Houston, Killeen, Corpus Christi, Kingsville, and Beeville. And while some military bases shrunk after World War II, others, like Killeen's Fort Hood, grew tremendously to meet the needs of the Cold War, the Korean War, and the Vietnam War.

Much, if not most, of the Asian immigration to Texas from 1937 to 1980 was directly related to war and U.S. military activities. There were four basic categories of war and military-related immigrants. The first group consisted of those serving in the military and military veterans. These included Asian American veterans—mostly Filipino Americans, Chinese Americans, and Japanese Americans—who were stationed in or retired in Texas. While Chinese Texan soldiers were enlisted and stationed in Fort Bliss as early as World War I, Asian soldiers first began moving to Texas in large numbers during World War II. Besides U.S. servicemen and -women, the "soldiers" category also includes those who served in foreign military units and citizens of foreign nations who joined the U.S. military. Prominent among this latter group are former members of the Philippines Scouts, who fought alongside U.S. forces in World War II; Filipino nationals recruited into the U.S. military; veterans of the South Vietnamese military who left Vietnam after the fall of Saigon; Laotian and Hmong war veterans immigrating from Laos after the Communist takeover of Laos; and veterans of the Cambodian military immigrating after their government fell to the Khmer Rouge. Oftentimes, foreign veterans spearheaded a wave of immigration from their nation; their working relationship with the U.S. government and its military and their access to the means of escape (ships, routes, guns) often allowed them to be the first to seek refuge in America.

The second category consists of Asian "war brides." These Asian women met, and eventually married, U.S. servicemen stationed abroad during times of both war and peace. The servicemen or military contractors were usually living and/or working on U.S. military bases. These "war brides" included Chinese women, Japanese women, and Filipina women who married American (including Asian American) soldiers during or directly after World War II; Japanese women who married American servicemen based in Japan, from the occupation of Japan after World War II to the present; Korean women who married American servicemen from the onset of the Korean War, through the expansion of U.S. military bases in Korea, to the present; Filipino "war brides" who married from the end of World War II to the closing of U.S. military bases in the Philippines in 1992; Vietnamese "war brides" from the period of the Vietnamese War; and Thai women who married American men based in Thailand since the start of the Vietnam War.

Asian immigration to the U.S. through the national quota system— between 1943 and 1965—was relatively low. Asians mostly immigrated through other means—military status, marriage, adoption, illegal entry, special status, and refugee status. Because Texas was home to an unusually large number of U.S. military bases, U.S. servicemen, military contractors, and veterans, Asian immigrants to Texas during these years were disproportionately associated with the U.S. military.

"War brides" made up a major portion of Asian immigrants settling in the state. In 1940, before American involvement in World War II, Japanese men outnumbered Japanese women in Texas by a ratio of 141 to 100. Just twenty years later, the imbalance was reversed, and Japanese women outnumbered Japanese men by a ratio of 100 to 58.[4]. From 1940 to 1970, the Japanese Texan population increased from 458 to 6,537. Of that increase of 6,079, females made up 4,036 and males were just 2,043, a ratio of two to one. Considering that some of the increase resulted from reproduction and migration from other U.S. states, it appears that the single-most important source of Japanese immigration to Texas during the "military" period of Asian Texan history were "war brides."[1]

A similar phenomenon occurred among Korean immigrants between 1950 and 1970, during which time the Korean Texan population was highly associated with U.S. soldiers, veterans, and military bases. Before the Korean War (1950-1953), the population of Koreans in Texas was small. Korean "war brides" and Korean "war orphans" constituted most of the immigration from Korea to Texas in the 1950s and early 1960s. After 1965, female Korean nurses began arriving in Texas. By 1980, as a result of the immigration of these two groups, female Koreans outnumbered male Koreans in Texas two to one.[2]

The Filipino Texan community had maintained strong ties with the U.S. military since the beginning of the U.S. war in the Philippines in 1898. Many Filipino and Filipino American soldiers immigrated to Texas through the U.S. military directly after World War II, but the arrival of their Filipino wives, Filipino "war brides," and Filipino nurses balanced the sex ratio. In 1960, the ratio of Filipino males to females in Texas was 122 to 100, but by 1970 that ratio was virtually even. The Filipino Texan population in 1970 was 3,442. Over 13.3% (459) of that population lived in U.S. forts and towns and cities associated with the military, including Corpus Christi (279), Killeen (134), Kingsville (109), Beeville, Copperas Cove, and those residing within four military bases. Another 22.8% (785) of Filipino Texans lived in El Paso (361) and San Antonio (424), where they were closely associated with Fort Bliss, Fort Sam Houston, and the Brooke Army Medical Center. Among this 36% of the population (1244) living in or near military bases, Filipino males outnumbered females by 876 to 368 (about 2.4 to 1). In Houston, however, the balance favored women 326 to 254 (about 1.3 to 1). Thus, despite an even balance between Filipino Texan men and women, they lived to a great degree in separate communities. This tendency of men and women to live in separate communities was not unique to Filipinos. In some Asian ethnic groups, especially before 1975, men tended to concentrate around universities while females tended to concentrate around military bases and hospitals.[3]

The immigration of large numbers of nurses and "war brides" maintained a great gender imbalance in Texas as late as 1990, when the Census counted 67.1 Korean males per 100 Korean women; 66.5 Japanese men per 100 Japanese women; and 72 Filipino men per 100 Filipino women.

The third and fourth categories of Asians immigrating during the military period consist of war refugees and those escaping political persecution. The first of these refugees were the relatively small numbers of Asians settling in Texas after escaping the 1949 Chinese Communist Revolution and the Korean War. The largest groups of refugees consisted of those fleeing Vietnam, Cambodia, and Laos during and after the Vietnam War. On April 17, 1975, the Communist "Khmer Rouge" seized power in Cambodia. On April 30, 1975, South Vietnam fell to Vietnamese Communist forces. On December 2, 1975, the Communist Pathet Lao forces took control of the nation of Laos. During the respective wars leading up to these Communist takeovers, very few refugees came to the United States. But as the Communist forces seized power, initial waves of refugees arrived in the United States. These initial refugees were often members of Asian militaries. Others worked for, or were associated with, the American military, the U.S. government, and U.S.-based companies. They tended to be people with some connection to the means of escape. This initial wave was dwarfed by the next wave of Southeast Asian refugees, which began arriving in large numbers in the United States in 1978. These refugees ran from political persecution, genocide (committed by the Khmer Rouge), and extreme poverty in Vietnam, Cambodia, and Laos.

The 1975 Indochina Migration and Refugee Assistance Act granted refugee status and legal immigrant status to more than 130,000 Vietnamese, Laotian, and Cambodian refugees of wars and persecution.[4] The 1975 act accommodated only a fraction of those Southeast Asian refugees attempting to reach America. The federal government took incremental measures to receive a portion of the refugees fleeing into Thailand, Malaysia, and other nations, and in 1980, the United States passed the Refugee Act, which established a more systematic way of coordinating and funding refugee resettlement in the United States. In 1980, the number of Southeast Asian refugees topped 166,000, but the number steadily declined from there, as the Refugee Act capped refugee arrivals at 50,000 and shifted control of refugee policy to the legislative branch. While the numbers of Vietnamese refugees arriving in Texas declined after 1980, the numbers of Laotian and Cambodian refugees did not, as many of them languished in refugee camps for years before arriving in the United States. Nevertheless, because of the sharp drop in the number of total refugees arriving in Texas and because of the increase in non-refugee immigrants, the end of the military period is set at 1980.[5]

Refugees of war and persecution immigrated to Texas from almost every Asian nation. In many years during the military period, a majority of the Asian Texan population belonged to the above-mentioned four categories. Even those who were not, by definition, members of these categories were, in essence, war refugees. For instance, Koreans who survived World War II and the Korean War and then endured the poverty following these wars struggled with, and were motivated by, the same issues as those who immigrated immediately after the wars. The survivors of war and persecution had common experiences and attitudes. They believed they had no other choice than to come to the United States *and* remain here. They often suffered both shell-shock and culture shock upon arrival. They often felt depression concerning the past and anxiety concerning the future. Having experienced war, poverty, and homelessness, they often worked hard, saved a great deal of their earnings, emphasized education with their children, and shied away from politics. More so than other groups, refugees succeeded spectacularly—literally going from rags to riches—or failed spectacularly.

Military activities, war, the Cold War, and Texas's economic growth fundamentally changed the face of Asian Texas. In 1930, thirteen states in the West, Northeast, and Midwest were home to more Asians than Texas. By 1960, only five states had Asian populations greater than Texas. This development was, in part, a result of immigration to Texas from the Cold War-allied nations of the Philippines, Japan, and Korea. Between 1950 and 1960, the Japanese Texan population more than quadrupled in size, from 957 to 4053, essentially reaching parity for the only time with the Chinese Texan population, which only increased 71% in those same years. The Korean Texan population grew from two in 1930 to 201 in 1960 to 2,090 in 1970. Similarly, the Filipino Texan population, having dipped to 219 in 1940 multiplied sevenfold after World War II to 1,623 in 1950 and then more than doubled to 3,442 by 1970.

By 1980, California and Texas were by far the two most popular states for the resettlement of Southeast Asian refugees. Refugees sought jobs in a growing Texas economy fueled by oil and oil services; refugees also sought opportunities to work in the seafood industry along the Texas coast. The 1980 U.S. Census counted nearly 30,000 Vietnamese in Texas; California was home to nearly 90,000 Vietnamese, and the third most populous state was Louisiana with about 11,000 Vietnamese. Before 1975, the Vietnamese were essentially nonexistent in Texas, but by 1980, Vietnamese Texans constituted the largest Asian ethnic group in the state. In 1980, the Chinese and Indian Texans numbered 25,000 and 22,000 respectively, and the second-tier populations of the Filipino, Korean, and Japanese Texans numbered over 15,000, nearly 14,000, and over 10,500 respectively. In contrast, the census figures for California show that their largest Asian ethnic groups in 1980 were the Filipinos, the Chinese, and the Japanese, numbering, respectively, more than 357,000, more than 322,000, and nearly 262,000. In California, the second-tier Asian populations, size-wise, were the Koreans and the Vietnamese, who numbered nearly 104,000 and nearly 90,000 respectively. Thus, while California's population reflected the historical growth of the Asian American population, Texas's population reflected the demographics of post-1965 Asian immigration.[6]

The third period of Asian Texan history is the "diversification period," which overlaps the military period and begins with the 1965 Immigration Act. The period is defined by a wide diversification of the ethnic groups making up Asian Texas. Most of these new ethnic groups mark the beginning of their presence in Texas at or around the implementation of the 1965 immigration reform. These groups include the Pakistani Texans, Bangladeshi Texans, Nepalese Texans, Sri Lankan Texans, Thai Texans, Vietnamese Texans, Laotian Texans, Hmong Texans, Cambodian Texans, Burmese Texans, Indonesian Texans, Singaporean Texans, Malaysian Texans, and Tibetan Texans.

One of the major features of the diversification period was the steep increase in immigration of Asian professionals. The first wave of Asian professionals to immigrate to Texas came under the allowances of the Exchange Visitors Program (EVP), which was established in 1948 in part as a Cold War measure to introduce people from other nations to America's system of republican democracy and mixed economy. Scholarly visitors and professionals were allowed to study, train, and work in the United States, and before 1956, there were no measures to prevent or place conditions upon their becoming permanent residents of the United States. Nurses and doctors were among the early Asian "visitors" to train in Texas, and they constituted some of the early post-War Filipino, Korean, and Japanese immigration unrelated to the military. The program was adjusted in later decades, sometimes increasing and sometimes decreasing the number of "exchange visitors."[7]

The 1965 Immigration Act opened widely the doors for the immigration of Asian nurses and doctors by giving special status to both professional immigrants and to those working in occupations in short supply in the United States. The number of nurses migrating to Texas from the Philippines, Korea, Japan, India and other nations grew tremendously after 1965, and so did the numbers of doctors from India, Pakistan, Korea, the Philippines, and other nations. The medical migrants made up major portions of certain Asian ethnic groups, especially the Korean, Indian, and Pakistani populations in the 1970s, and the Filipino population from 1965 to the present. It is safe to say that the majority of the Filipino population in some Texas communities consisted of nurses, doctors, and their families. Bolstered by Texas hospitals that recruited foreign-born nurses and doctors, Asian medical personnel formed the foundations of some local Asian Texan communities in the 1960s and 1970s.

The 1965 Immigration Act allowed the federal government to grant 170,000 visas to Eastern Hemisphere nations, with a maximum of 20,000 visas per nation. The act gave preference to seven categories of immigrants, including the unmarried and married children, 21 years or older, of U.S. citizens; siblings of U.S. citizens; spouses and unmarried children of permanent residents; professionals, scientists, and artists of exceptional ability; types of workers in short supply in the United States;

and refugees.[8] The Immigration Act produced burgeoning new Asian communities in the 1960s and 1970s, especially around the state's numerous, growing universities. All Asian ethnic groups were well-represented among the students of Texas universities, but because Chinese and Indian immigrants were underrepresented among refugees and "war brides" and overrepresented among graduate students and professors, these two ethnic groups, more than others, expanded around universities in the 1960s and 1970s.

University neighborhoods were home to many of the highest concentrations of Asians in Texas. During the late 1960s through the early 1980s, the centers for cultural activity for these Asian ethnic groups tended to be university student associations (such as the Indian Students Association). Not only were cultural rituals and celebrations carried out through these organizations, they also served as major social venues and the arena of sometimes contentious political activity. After a critical mass of population had been formed, first- and second-generation Asian Texans formed community organizations and independent churches outside of the universities. Many of these entities could apply for financial grants and provide services, such as day care.

The diversification period was shaped by the tremendous economic and population growth of Houston and Dallas-Fort Worth, as well as the rise and fall of certain industries such as oil and "high technology." By 1930, Houston had become the state's most populous city. During World War II, Houston became home to the state's largest Asian population. The growth of the Asian population was driven by the city's economic growth. World War II jump-started Houston's oil, oil service, chemical, natural gas, and ship-building industries. Even before the Japanese attack on Pearl Harbor, oil drilling and the establishment of the Houston Ship Channel had fueled quick growth in the local economy. The economic expansion provided opportunities for thousands of Chinese Americans to move to the city, as the market for their groceries expanded exponentially. The 1965 Immigration Act, the growth of the Texas Medical Center in the decades after World War II, the establishment of NASA in nearby Clearlake in 1962, and the oil boom years from 1973 to 1981 combined to attract hundreds of thousands of Asians to Houston, especially the largest occupational groups—small business owners, engineers, computer scientists, and medical personnel.[9]

The combination of the U.S. recession of the early 1980s and a drop in oil prices led to a recession in the Texas economy. The recession hit Houston and east Texas especially hard because of the area economy's concentration in oil and energy. In the spring of 1982, oil and petrochemical companies Shell, Texaco, Exxon, Dow, and DuPont began asking employees to retire for severance packages. The recession hit its height in December 1982, when Houstonians filed 237,000 claims for unemployment benefits. While the rest of the nation's economy was recovering, low oil prices sent Texas into another recession in 1986–1987. In May 1986, Houston's unemployment rate hit 10.7% and Texas's reached 9.6%. The recession reached its lowest point in 1987, and Houston did not fully recover until 1990, when employment equaled the March 1982 peak of nearly 1.6 million. During the worst of the recession years, tens of thousands more people left the state each year than entered. Houston suffered population swings. Because the Asian Texan population was so dependent upon employment by energy, engineering, chemical, and manufacturing companies, laid-off workers and unemployed graduate students left Texas, especially Houston, at a tremendous rate. The exodus from Houston beginning in spring 1982 was likely the largest of any Asian population from a major city since World War II. However, the diversification of Texas's economy provided hundreds of thousands of new jobs for Asians in the 1990s and 2000s.[10]

In the 1980s, a major portion of the Asian Texan population opened businesses. Some were professionals not wanting to rely on the hiring and firing cycles of corporations and large companies. The small business boom among Asian Texans, however, was fueled mostly by the "family reunification" immigration of the siblings, spouses, and parents of Asian professionals, "war brides," and others. The opening of restaurants, retail stores, gas stations, convenience stores, laundries, dry cleaners, alteration shops, textiles firms, seafood businesses, and others was made possible by the employment of family members, loans by families and friends, the availability of low-wage immigrant laborers who spoke the same Asian language as the employer, and the availability of

Mexican immigrant labor. Asians often sought out low property prices for their homes and businesses. By doing so, they sometimes revived run-down neighborhoods and expanded suburbs outward. Asian Texans opened so many businesses that a 1988 study found that Dallas-Fort Worth and Houston ranked first and second in the national ratings for Asian American business ownership. According to the study, over 9% of Asian Americans in Dallas-Fort Worth and about 8.5% of Asian Houstonians owned businesses.[11]

Between 1980 and 1990, the Asian population in Texas increased by 168%, from 116,399 to 311,918. Many Asian community leaders stated specifically that the 1980s was the decade of family reunification—that population expansion was largely fueled by immigrants arriving in the 1970s and 1980s deciding to bring to Texas their relatives still in Asia, or even in other states. Several community leaders also specifically tagged the 1980s as the decade in which Asian Texans opened businesses. These two factors, more than others, defined the 1980s in Asian Texan history.

In the 1990s, the numbers of "high-tech" Asian and Asian American workers in Texas increased tremendously, and the smallest Asian Texan ethnic groups grew and formed more local communities. The 1990 Immigration Act established the H-1B Visa. Foreign employees holding H-1B Visas could work in the U.S. for a maximum of six years. The worker must then remain outside of the United States for at least one year before applying for another H-1B Visa. The annual cap for these visas was set at 65,000 and was temporarily increased to 115,000 for the years 2001 through 2003 only. The H-1B Visa was designed to allow U.S. companies to recruit highly educated foreign workers to fill shortages of qualified Americans. These foreign workers tended to be engineers, computer programmers, scientists, nurses, and doctors. Additionally, the 1990 act increased the numbers of visas for immigrants with permanent jobs in the United States. Finally, it established 55,000 "diversity visas" for those people in countries usually granted few visas. These visas were granted through "lotteries" in which applicants were chosen randomly.

Several factors coalesced to produce an influx of tens of thousands of Asian immigrant professionals to Texas to work for telecommunications, computer, software, and internet companies. There was a shortage of American engineers; for instance, the number of electrical engineering college graduates peaked in 1989 and declined over the next decade, even as demand for them soared. Texas universities continued to expand quickly between 1970 and 2000, opening their doors to thousands of international students from Asian nations earning engineering, computer, and other technical degrees. Furthermore, thousands of American-born Asian students and professionals sought education and jobs in Texas. Among other major factors, the availability of qualified workers in Texas encouraged high technology companies to establish manufacturing, research and development, and administrative campuses in the state. In the 1970s and 1980s, various telecommunications, electronics, and computer firms established branches and headquarters in the Dallas-Fort Worth area, concentrating their campuses in what became known as Telecom Corridor in the northern suburb of Richardson. By 1989, Dallas's 115,613 high-technology jobs made up nearly 48% of the state's total high-tech employment. Austin was home to 12.7% of the high-technology jobs but would increase its share in the 1990s, as companies moved to that city and Dell Computers expanded its production there. In the 1990s, Texas became home to the second-largest number of high-technology jobs in the nation, second only to California. The number of high-technology jobs increased between 1994 and 2000 by 151,500 and peaked at nearly 500,000 in 2001. High-tech jobs declined thereafter in what was termed the "tech bust," a contraction in high-technology production. Texas lost 11% of it high-technology jobs in 2002.[12]

The high technology boom brought tens of thousands of Asians and Asian Americans to Texas. For example, the number of Indians in Texas doubled in the 1990s largely due to the immigration and migration of Indian and Indian American high-tech workers and entrepreneurs. But a major portion of the newly arriving Indians also opened mainstream or ethnic businesses. In May 2001, Taiyab Kundawala, president of India Association of North Texas, told the *Dallas Morning News* that in the past three years high technology jobs had helped fuel an increase in the population of Indians in the Dallas area from about 55,000 to about 80,000. Because of its "telecom corridor," according to Kundawala, the Dallas suburb of Richardson became the center for Indian life in North Texas.[13]

The Asian Texan population during the diversification period was made up of many more ethnic groups and large numbers of recent immigrants. From 1965 to 2005, Asian Texans steadily organized themselves into communities. Their community and social organizations evolved and proliferated. They simultaneously diversified and consolidated. And as the population evolved, so did the perceptions of Asian Texans by other Texans.

In 1970, Asian Texans comprised only 0.16% of the total Texas population and were in some ways a "novelty" population. Increasing to 116,399, or 0.8% of the total population, the Asian Texan population in some ways "emerged" by 1980 as a substantial racial group, especially in certain localities. For instance, the populations of some coastal cities and towns were over 5% Vietnamese. In military towns and college towns, Asian populations were also major components of local communities. But for the most part, Asian ethnic groups did not have a collective identity. By 1990, the Asian Texan population had grown to 311,918 or 1.9% of the total population, according to the Census. By then, a collective identity as "Asian Americans" had formed, and Asian Texans, taken as a whole, emerged as a minority group alongside blacks and Hispanics. The populations of Asian Texans living near universities and military bases continued to grow. Asians comprised 6.5% of College Station's population and 5.8% of Killeen's population. Because of the large Vietnamese presence on the coast, some of the "most Asian" places were coastal towns such as Seadrift and Palacios, whose populations were 13.4% and 6.4% Asian, respectively. The "most Asian" big city was Houston, with Asians making up 4.1% of its population. The Asian populations of Houston's southwestern suburbs were growing at an even faster rate, as Sugar Land was nearly 13% Asian, and Stafford was over 8%. Dallas and Fort Worth had about average Asian population "densities" for Texas, at just above 2% for both cities. That area's Asians tended to concentrate in its northern suburbs, as Richardson and Plano had Asian "densities" of 6.6% and 4.0%, respectively. During the 1990s, the fastest growing Asian populations (by population densities) were in Dallas, Houston, and their suburbs. By 2000, Richardson and Plano were both well over 10% Asian, and Sugar Land and Stafford were both well over 20% Asian. Both Dallas and Houston increased their Asian population "density" by about 50%, as the total city populations were just over 3% and almost 6% Asian, respectively.

By 1980, five ethnic groups emerged as by far the largest Asian ethnic groups in Texas: the Vietnamese, Chinese, Indians, Koreans, and Filipinos. They remained the "big five" ethnic groups to the present (2007). But by 1990, the Laotian Texans (population 9,332), Pakistani Texans (7,627), Cambodian Texans (5887), and Thai Texans (5816) joined the Japanese Texans (14,795) to round out the next five largest Asian ethnic groups. Texas was a favorite destination for Southeast Asian immigrants in the 1980s; comparing the sum of Laotian, Cambodian, and Thai populations for each state, only California surpassed Texas in 1990. By 2000, the Census counted 25,324 total Pakistanis in Texas. Both the quickly growing Pakistani Texans and the slowly increasing Japanese Texans had broken the 20,000 population threshold in the 1990s.

In the year 2000, the census counted 572,253 "full-blooded" Asians and 657,664 total Asians in Texas. Thus, there were less than 82,000 "mixed-blood" Asian Texans. Unlike Asians from the previous two periods of Asian Texan history, the vast majority of adult Asian immigrants in Texas after 1965 married and lived with Asian spouses. Thus, the "mixed blood" Asians, which made up about 13% of the census total for all Asians, were comprised largely of the grandchildren of the post-1965 Asian immigrants, the children of American-born Asians, and the children and grandchildren of foreign-born "war brides."

A basic class structure has existed for some time within the Asian Texan community. Before World War II, most Asian Texans belonged to three basic classes: laborers, small business owners, and those associated with the U.S. armed forces. Around the time of World War II, another major class took form: the class of professionals. Immigration status, visa types, levels of acculturation, and education tend to reinforce class differences. In many instances, these classes represent separate communities *within* ethnic communities; for instance, Korean Dallasites associated with the military may not interact much with Korean Dallasite professionals.

Because immigration laws were designed to encourage the immigration of professionals and not laborers, members of the laborer class often immigrated through family reunification or as refugees. They were the least likely to hold university degrees. Immigrants of this class are likely to save money and work with other family members in order to become small business owners. It is common for the U.S.-born generation of this class, through education, hard work, and intra-family cooperation, to move into one of the other classes.

The military class often included members of all three other classes. Military wives often opened businesses or took on a profession. Retired soldiers sometimes worked as civil servants or laborers. Members of this class tended to have immigration statuses based on their marriages to U.S. citizens, their own service in the U.S. armed forces, or family reunification. As a result, Asians in the military class tended to have the "highest" immigration statuses as they may have earned "automatic" citizenship or legal residency through military service or marriage.

The small business class was extremely diverse and included those who arrived through family reunification, as refugees, through the U.S. military, through their professional status, or through other means. Opening a small business was extremely attractive to Asian Texans who were born in Asia. Individuals could make a good living, be their own boss, avoid dealing with employment discrimination, and succeed with little or no U.S.-based education or fluency in English.

Those immigrants who arrived to the United States through an H-1B visa, through the EVP program, and through preference as a professional worker were almost all members of the professional class. Almost all of the immigrants who arrived originally as international students strived to become part of the professional class. The professional class was also the class of preference for American-born Asian Texans. With an American education and native skills in the English language, the second-generation was better suited to succeed in American universities. Asian Texan parents typically hoped for their children to work in the professional class. Unlike the immigrant professionals, who were likely to have trained in America in the areas of engineering, computer sciences, medicine and hard sciences, the second generation was more diverse in its vocations, including law, liberal arts, humanities, fine arts, education, and other areas.

The arc of Asian Texan history, like the arc of Texas history has been driven by population growth, a diversification of ethnic origin, diversification of class and occupation, the growing Texas economy, the heavy association of Texas with the U.S. military, war, political persecution, the close proximity of Mexico, relations with other racial groups, racism, hard work and dedication to family. The term "Asian Texan," though coined very recently, is both a historic term and a current and ongoing reality. We, as Asian Texans, continue to grow, and our histories and our lives continue to evolve, defining and influencing each other.

ENDNOTES

1 U.S. Censuses, 1940, 1950, 1960, 1970.

2 U.S. Census, 1980.

3 U.S. Censuses, 1960, 1970.

4 Chan, Sucheng, *Asian Americans: An Interpretive History* (New York: Twayne Publishers, 1991), pp. 192–199.

5 Chan, pp. 145–165.

6 U.S. Census, 1980.

7 *http://www.minoritynurse.com/features/other/06-06-06-5.html* (minority nurse site accessed October 16, 2006); *http://www.srwlawyers.com/J-1.asp* (immigration law firm site accessed September 8, 2006); *http://www.uscis.gov/lpbin/lpext.dll/inserts/ afm_redacted/afm-95-redacted-494-1/afm-95-redacted-10874?f=templates&fn=docu ment-frame.htm* (federal INS site accessed September 17, 2006)

8 Chan, pp. 142–148.

9 "Houston," *Handbook of Texas Online, http://www.tsha.utexas.edu/handbook/on-line/articles/HH/hdh3.html* (accessed October, 2006).

10 "Houston History Timeline," *http://www.texasbest.com/houston/history.html* as retrieved on Oct 13, 2006; King, Wayne, "Despite success, sun belt oil patch is finding it's not immune to recession," *New York Times*, Jul 9, 1982; Tutt, Bob, "More Folks leaving than coming: decline in Texas economy blamed for net exodus of

90,000," *Houston Chronicle*, Feb 13, 1986; Halkias, Maria, "Jobless rate in Texas hits 9.6%," *Dallas Morning News*, Jun 7, 1986; Britt, Bonnie, "Houston's growing number of unemployed: what some are saying about their situations," *Houston Chronicle*, Jul 6, 1986.

11 Barnett, John, "Asian-owned firms flourish," *Houston Chronicle*, Aug 3, 1988.

12 Frieden, Kit, "Dallas' 'Silicon Prairie' feels downturn in high-tech jobs," *Houston Chronicle*, Nov 24, 1985; Blackistone, Kevin, "The lowdown on high technology," *Dallas Morning News*, Aug 24, 1989; Mabin, Connie, "Study: Texans taking on new high-tech jobs in Austin area," Jul 3, 2000; Engibous, Tom, "Texans must prepare for high-tech jobs," *Dallas Morning News*, Oct 15, 2000; Fest, Glen, "Texas second in nation in tech jobs, payroll," *Fort Worth Star-Telegram*, Jun 7, 2001; "Report: High tech job loss slowing," *The Victoria Advocate*, Nov 20, 2003. High tech jobs include manufacturing, communications services and software and computer-related services, according to the American Electronics Association.

13 Horner, Kim, "Right at Home: Asian Indians make distinctive mark on culture as jobs attract them to area in soaring numbers," *Dallas Morning News*, Dec 21, 1999; Harrison, Crayton, "Growth Spurt: Indian businesses mushroom to serve rapidly expanding immigrant community," *Dallas Morning News*, May 19, 2001.

CHAPTER ONE

★

THE CHINESE TEXAN EXPERIMENT

Irwin A. Tang

Galveston, Texas, January 10, 1870. About 250 Chinese Americans and Chinese immigrants stepped off a train. Almost all of the group were men aged 25–30. Most had been born in the Guangdong province of southern China. Just a few in the group were young boys, and a few were men over forty. Only one was a woman.[1]

Most or all of the men of the group had recently helped complete the first transcontinental railroad of the United States, the Central Pacific Railroad. Some of the best railroad builders in the world, they helped complete the railroad seven years ahead of schedule. For three years, they built track through the solid granite of the Sierra Nevada Mountains. At one point, they struck for better pay and better working conditions, and Central Pacific rail executive Charles Crocker cut off their food supply and threatened to replace them. They still won a raise of two dollars per day. About 1,200 of the 11,000 Chinese workers died building the Central Pacific from avalanches, dynamite blasts, and the elements. The Chinese American men who arrived in Texas on January 10, 1870 were among the hardened survivors, some of the toughest men America had ever known.[2]

They needed work. In May 1869, they finished building the final mile of the first transcontinental railroad, uniting the nation by rail and allowing for the speedy settlement of the West. Having finished their work, they lost their jobs. Thousands of them returned to San Francisco, where they first landed on American soil. In November 1869, labor contractor Chew-Ah-Heung of San Francisco negotiated a contract with John G. Walker for a group of these Chinese American laborers. Walker was an agent of the Houston and Texas Central (H&TC) Railroad—Texas's second railroad and one of its most important commercial lines. Construction had begun in 1853 at Houston's Buffalo Bayou on the Gulf coast, and by January 1870, the railroad ran north through the cotton plantations of the Brazos River Valley. The H&TC railroad allowed for the efficient shipment of raw cotton to port. The Chinese Americans were to extend the railhead further north in rural northeast Texas, from Bremond to Corsicana.[3]

The labor contract Chew negotiated with Walker committed the Chinese American rail builders to three years of work on the H&TC at twenty dollars of silver coin per month, which consisted of 26 working days. Chew himself would serve as the group's leader and interpreter for $100 gold per month. In exchange, the Chinese would live and work in the unknown territory of Texas, where very few Chinese had ever visited. While there had not been any anti-Chinese riots in Texas, as there had been in California, there were discussions that the Chinese could be the new slaves of the South.

Those 250 or so Chinese American workers left San Francisco on December 19, 1869 by rail. The train stopped in Council Bluffs, Iowa where the Chinese Americans crossed the frozen Missouri River by walking on wooden planks laid across the cracked ice. They arrived in St. Louis on December 30, via the North Missouri rail line. From there, they took the steamship *Mississippi* down the Mississippi River. They stopped in Memphis, Tennessee for a day and then steamed down to New Orleans.[4] Upon their arrival in Galveston, a journalist described these new Texans to his readers, many of whom had never encountered people of Chinese or Asian descent:

Considering the length of time those who passed through yesterday had been cooped up on the deck of a vessel, they were much cleaner and neater in their clothing and persons than could have been expected. Though small in stature they were robustly formed, and from the ease with which they handled heavy packages of plunder they are both strong and active.[5]

According to the *St. Louis Republican*, the Chinese each carried with ease a pole on the ends of which hung bundles of belongings weighing about 150 or 200 pounds. They were described as having "dark, almond eyes and olive colored countenance, a whitish hue, tinged with orange and vermilion."[6] The Galveston reporter wrote that the Chinese dressed in traditional garb, such as shoes that resembled "canoes," turning upwards at the toes, hats like "inverted washbowls," blue cotton shirts, and wide-legged pants. Some wore boots and overcoats, and all seemed "comfortably clad." The men wore their hair in the tradition of the Qing Dynasty in China; their hair was long and braided and coiled up underneath their hats.

If they saw anything new or unexpected in Galveston they did not manifest it by word or sign, neither did they appear conscious of being the centre of attraction for crowds of strange people.

After their arrival at the depot preparations were made for cooking breakfast. Fires were lighted, kettles were brought out, pans and bowls were placed in the hands of each, and every thing was conducted systematically and decorously. The principal ingredient of the cuisine was rice, though we noticed that some of them placed small pieces of pork that had been browned to a crisp, over the tops of their pans of rice. The chop-sticks were the only instruments used in carrying their food to their mouths [...] After breakfast was over we noticed that most of them took a good big drink of the hot water in which the rice had been boiled. Carefully putting aside the wood which remained after the cooking was done, they washed their bowls and chopsticks, packed away their pots, &c., lighted their pipes and enjoyed a smoke with as much philosophical composure as the most devoted lover of the weed among the ouside [sic] barbarians could have done. Several of them spoke English indifferently well but did not evince any disposition to be communicative.

There was but one woman in the lot; she was small in size and by no means attractive in personal appearance, having undergone the usual process for rendering the feet disproportionally small; her walk was anything but graceful . . .

About one o'clock yesterday afternoon the train left for Calvert with these, the first Mongolians ever brought to the State. The success of this experiment will be watched with anxiety by a very large proportion of the people of the State . . . [7]

The migration of these 250 Chinese to Texas may have doubled the Chinese population of the American South. Only 217 Chinese lived in the South in 1870, twenty-five of them residing in Texas. In fact, these 250 Chinese pioneers represented the first major eastward migration of Asians away from the West Coast. In 1870, there were more Chinese in Calvert than in New York State. Thousands followed their lead in the subsequent months and years, establishing the first Chinese American communities throughout the East, South, and Midwest.[8]

The Chinese Experiment in the American South

Although the Emancipation Proclamation went into effect on January 1, 1863, it was not made public in Texas until Union General Gordon Granger read it in Galveston on June 19, 1865 (a day now known as Juneteenth). Gradually, the 250,000 African American slaves of Texas were freed from bondage by their proprietors. Although there was now an abundance of freed black laborers available to work on Texas farms, some of these men and women preferred to live in cities, in part for the urban social environment and in part for their own safety. Throughout Texas, and particularly in the Brazos River Valley, many whites attempted to keep African Americans in a state of semi-slavery through racist state laws and violence. Others sought alternatives to black labor. Just weeks after the announcement of emancipation in Texas, the Galveston *Daily News* suggested that Chinese contract laborers could replace black slave labor. A "model minority" image was immediately created as the Chinese were described as "docile and thrifty, taking good care of themselves, and doing their work without reluctance." Unfortunately for plantation owners, though, "[the Chinese] will never go in debt to the proprietor and, of course after the contract has expired, the planter has no lien on the laborer, and cannot compel him to remain."[9]

Despite protests that the Chinese were "heathens" and that introducing the Chinese might once again upset race relations in the South, commercial conventions in 1869 decided that Chinese be brought to work in the South. Southern capitalists and planters voted to form a joint stock company that would bring to the United States "as many Chinese immigrant laborers as possible, in the shortest time." One such employer, J.W. Clapp, stated that the South preferred labor managed "as of old," meaning as slaves, and one well-known labor contractor, Cornelius Koopmanschaap, stated that in the South, "nothing but coerced labor will bring about prosperity."[10]

Some Southerners opposed the Chinese "experiment." *The Dallas Herald* stated in unambiguously racist terms, "We want neither nigger nor Mongolians—we want white men . . . men created in their Maker's image." In a later editorial, the paper stated that it opposed "the mad scheme of introducing the Chinese into the country to take the place of negro labor in the South and to supplant white labor in the North." The paper stated that the Chinese would "lower the standard of labor, demoralize society and vote the Radical [Republican] ticket."[11]

Many of the first Chinese laborers in the South were coolies—slave-like laborers who were mostly employed by coercion and almost entirely in Latin America and the Caribbean. Most of these coolies of the South worked in Louisiana and Arkansas, and many of them died under the harsh conditions of their work and life. In contrast, the Chinese American railroad workers of the South were free laborers doing far less work under much better conditions for much more money; many planned on returning to their villages in Guangdong with substantial savings. Many whites and blacks nevertheless saw the Chinese as "replacement workers." As the Chinese rail workers traveled by train and steam ship from San Francisco to Galveston, they were met by African American protestors in St. Louis, Memphis, and New Orleans. A Memphis reporter wrote that African Americans standing before the steamship were "open in their threats to demolish any of the usurpers who might step upon shore." The *St. Louis Democrat*, utilizing racial stereotypes, explained the animosity by writing that protesting African Americans "regard them [the Chinese] as interlopers who work for half pay, keep all they earn, despise fat bacon, and never indulge in whiskey and poker." The railroad moguls were adept at playing ethnic groups against each other. Central Pacific railroad owner Charles Crocker had threatened during the Chinese railroad workers' strike to replace them with newly emancipated African Americans. In the early 1870s, some factory own-ers on the East Coast also contracted Chinese American labor as a way to subdue white workers. While some Chinese workers during this time certainly knew that they were pawns in a war against all laborers, they needed the work and sought jobs wherever they could, much like black and white workers.[12]

Upon arrival in Calvert, Texas, the Chinese American rail work-ers headed directly to the end of the rail line around Bremond and began constructing towards Thornton; the rail line would eventually reach Corsicana and then Dallas. The Chinese lived in huts and tents in a large work camp. They ate rice, pork, dried fish, and vegetables, and they drank hot tea, even in the Texas heat. They spoke mostly Chinese, although Chew-Ah-Heung was fluent in English. At least one Chinese foreman was in charge of each group of one hundred men, and one in-terpreter represented the group to English speakers. A writer for the *Calvert Enterprise* observed that "they all speak at once, and reminded us of a covey of blackbirds." The Texans observed that the Chinese work-ers were thrifty with their silver because, after all, they were in Texas to make money, not spend it. The *Galveston Tri-Weekly News* editorialized that the Chinese would bring the newly enfranchised blacks back under the control of planters and capitalists. "When the Negro once finds out it is work or starve he will not hesitate long between the two. Welcome then, John Chinaman." The *Calvert Enterprise* stated, "We hope they [the Chinese workers] will rouse the negroes to work . . . Outside of this we see no particular need of them." In March, the *Centreville Experi-ment* reported that some black freedmen watched the Chinese Ameri-cans, who were "habited in the lightest kind of cotton," laying track dur-ing a Texas norther.[13]

Texas's first Chinese New Year celebration occurred on January 30, 1870 in Bremond, Texas. "In full Chinese costume, including large umbrellas, they promenaded the streets, 'to the delight of the juveniles without distinction of race or color.'" The Chinese Americans drank whiskey during their celebration and returned to their work camps by noon.[14]

The Chinese railroad workers sometimes rode the H&TC train down to Houston and picked up supplies. The *Houston Telegraph* observed just such a man named Yo Wykee, about 28 years of age and dressed "in his best clothes," walking the streets of Houston followed by a crowd of onlookers. "Under the circumstances, his manner was rather instructive to us barbarians, and speaks volumes for the finish given in one branch of Celestial education anyway—politeness." Another paper marveled that "the poorest day laborer that arrives here from that country can write and cipher." Yo Wykee bought a ten gallon hat, a Bowie knife, two holsters, and two guns. According to the *Telegraph*, the Chinese had been told that the Arapaho Indians had awaited the arrival of the Chinese "with anticipation of intense enjoyment in lifting their scalps."[15]

By all early accounts, the Chinese Texans of the H&TC railroad were great workers. The railroad company claimed that Chinese labor was the "only labor" they could rely on. A group of Swedish workers had already quit working on the Texas rails and left for Minnesota, saying that they could not endure the Texas heat. Local planters also were considering hiring the Chinese as farm workers.[16]

By July 1870, this glowing opinion of Chinese workers reversed. The *Calvert Enterprise* reported that "The Chinese at work on the Central Railroad are said to be very lazy and trifling, requiring constant watching." Had the Chinese suddenly quit working hard? It is more likely that the railroad company wanted to rid itself of Chinese workers to appease its white workers and the white communities that would utilize their rail lines. The *Enterprise* continued its rant later in July, "We are determinedly opposed to the Chinese coming here; we protest against it, as a laboring man . . . We would rather see every railroad in Texas abandoned, than that one man from the Celestial Empire should be imported in their construction." As early as February 1870 the *Waco Register* had noted "the jealousy of the Irishman towards the pig-tailed Chinese."[17]

By August, the *Calvert Enterprise* reported that "the Chinese laborers on the Central road are said to be worthless, and the company would like to get rid of them." The H&TC rail company evidently stopped paying the Chinese their wages. By September 1870, according to the *Bryan Appeal,* the Chinese "have all quit work, and have entered suit against their employers for wages and for a failure of compliance with contract."[18]

The Chinese American workers' suit against the H&TC railroad was one of the first among a series of petitions and protests for fair labor relations by Chinese workers throughout the South. In the summer of 1870, Chinese field workers on a Louisiana plantation known as the Millaudon estate kidnapped a Chinese labor contractor to protest working conditions. This led to the imprisonment of sixteen Chinese "ringleaders." The other Chinese attempted to break these leaders out of jail and refused to work until conditions had improved. In December, a white overseer on the plantation pushed a Chinese worker, who retaliated. The overseer shot the Chinese, and by some accounts, killed him. The Chinese workers rebelled by taking up clubs and knives and demanding that the overseer be handed over to them. In 1871, Chinese workers at W. L. Shaffer's Cedar Grove plantation in Louisiana protested the whipping of a Chinese servant. Three Chinese workers were shot—killing one of them. Throughout 1870 and 1871, hundreds of the 960 Chinese rail workers on the Alabama and Chattanooga Railroad left their jobs in Alabama for higher wages in Louisiana. The three hundred who stayed on were left in a lurch by the railroad when it went bankrupt in June 1871, owing six months' of wages. In protest, the Chinese, black, and white workers took over the trains and refused to let them run. The H&TC rail workers' lawsuit for lost wages may have spearheaded a series of Chinese American actions for fair treatment throughout the South. The Chinese labor protests of the American South coincided with worldwide Chinese coolie desertions, escapes, protests, mutinies, and rebellions of that time. Their sense of justice spurred them to organize and fight for better conditions.[19]

Southern capital attempted to cast Chinese Americans as a "model minority" to punish African Americans, but the Chinese Americans shirked this role in their struggle to improve their work conditions and to gain economic independence. By the mid-1870s, Southern capital stopped contracting with Chinese and Chinese American laborers. With the end of Reconstruction, Southern plantations also abandoned the system of contract labor in favor of the system of sharecropping.

The Early Chinese of The Brazos River Valley

Upon quitting their rail jobs, the Chinese Americans of the H&TC were in limbo in rural East Texas, far away from any other major population of Chinese. Chew-Ah-Heung traveled to New Orleans in November 1870 and advertised in the newspaper that he had "under his control Two Hundred and Forty (240) CHINESE LABORERS (now in Calvert, Texas) in need of employment, and whose services he offers to the community at large." While some of the H&TC workers may have worked in or opened hand laundries in various Texas cities and towns, and some may have returned to China, the largest single portion worked as field hands or sharecroppers on Brazos River Valley farms around Calvert and Hearne. One sharecropping contract of 1872 stipulated that Sin Yong and John See farm thirty acres of James Scott Hanna's land near Calvert. The cotton and corn grown on the land would be split evenly between the two Chinese and Hanna. In 1874, the Hanna plantation "imported" fifty-nine more Chinese farm laborers either directly from China or from Cuba, upon expiration of their coolie labor contracts there. Still more Chinese may have been "imported" to Calvert in the 1880s.[20]

One Alabama man, in recalling the harvesting of the 1874 Calvert area cotton crop, wrote that "the country was full of negroes and Chinamen." The African Americans and Chinese Americans were almost all sharecroppers, farm hands, and servants. What did the Chinese do besides work? An 1875 invoice charged James Scott Hanna $9.75 for a pound of opium, which he likely purchased for his workers.[21]

The Chinese also actively sought American citizenship and all its rights and responsibilities. By the fall of 1874, radical Republicans had gained power in Robertson County. In the liberating environment of Reconstruction, fifty Robertson County Chinese, including Ah Cong, Ah Chop, and Johnnie Williams, "personally appeared in open court" to request naturalized citizenship. The fifty Chinese declared that it was

The State of Texas,
COUNTY OF ROBERTSON.
} **Know all Men by these Presents,** That James S. Hanna, of the first part, and

Ah Geow, Ah Yong, & Ah Bao of the second part, have this day agreed, as follows: Said _Ah Geow- et al_ agree to cultivate _Sixty (60)_ acres of land on said Hanna's Plantation, in State and County aforesaid, in a farmerlike manner, for the year 18_74_, (_Ten (10)_ acres in Corn; _Fifty (50)_ acres in Cotton), under the superintendence of said James S. Hanna, or his authorized agent: And further agree to crib the Corn, pick, gin and pack the Cotton, upon the following terms—viz: The Corn to be divided by the wagon load, _One Load_ for said Hanna, _Two Loads_ for said _Ah Geow, Ah Yong & Ah Bao._ The Cotton to be sold on joint account, or divided, at _Calvert_ _One fourth_ for said Hanna, _Three fourths_ for said _Ah Geow et al_. James S. Hanna, on his part, agrees to furnish all necessary team and tools to cultivate the land, and corn to feed the team until the corn crop of 1874 can be used; and further agrees to make such advances as he may deem necessary, throughout the year. Each party furnishes his own Bagging and Ties. Said _Ah Geow, Ah Yong & Ah Bao_ also agree to DO AND KEEP in good repair, the fences and ditches around and about _their_ crop, and to take proper care of all work animals and implements used by _them_ in making the crop, and not remove them from the place without permission; and to return them at the end of the year, in good order and condition, and not to ATTEMPT TO MOVE any portion of the crop until said Hanna HAS BEEN PAID for all advances made to said _Ah Geow, Ah Yong & Ah Bao. Said Ah Geow agrees to furnish one horse or mule to cultivate 'im all the land throughout the season until the crop is made. Said Hanna agrees to pay Ah Geow et al Eight Dolls per acre for forty acres of the cotton, to be paid at the time of first Cotton picked out of the forty acres_

For the faithful performance of the stipulations of this contract by each party, each party gives the other a lien on his share of the crop.

Signed by us, this _29_ day of _December_ 187_3_.

WITNESS:

J. W. Atkinson   _James S. Hanna_

M. B. Taylor   亞蓋農   亞添   照保

A sharecropping contract between sharecroppers Ah Geow, Ah Yong, and Ah Bao and plantation owner James S. Hanna. The contract stipulates that the Chinese Texans grow and process cotton and corn in exchange for payment and use of land. Signed Dec. 29, 1873.

Texas's first Chinese New Year celebration occurred on January 30, 1870 in Bremond, Texas. "In full Chinese costume, including large umbrellas, they promenaded the streets, 'to the delight of the juveniles without distinction of race or color.'" The Chinese Americans drank whiskey during their celebration and returned to their work camps by noon.[14]

The Chinese railroad workers sometimes rode the H&TC train down to Houston and picked up supplies. The *Houston Telegraph* observed just such a man named Yo Wykee, about 28 years of age and dressed "in his best clothes," walking the streets of Houston followed by a crowd of onlookers. "Under the circumstances, his manner was rather instructive to us barbarians, and speaks volumes for the finish given in one branch of Celestial education anyway—politeness." Another paper marveled that "the poorest day laborer that arrives here from that country can write and cipher." Yo Wykee bought a ten gallon hat, a Bowie knife, two holsters, and two guns. According to the *Telegraph*, the Chinese had been told that the Arapaho Indians had awaited the arrival of the Chinese "with anticipation of intense enjoyment in lifting their scalps."[15]

By all early accounts, the Chinese Texans of the H&TC railroad were great workers. The railroad company claimed that Chinese labor was the "only labor" they could rely on. A group of Swedish workers had already quit working on the Texas rails and left for Minnesota, saying that they could not endure the Texas heat. Local planters also were considering hiring the Chinese as farm workers.[16]

By July 1870, this glowing opinion of Chinese workers reversed. The *Calvert Enterprise* reported that "The Chinese at work on the Central Railroad are said to be very lazy and trifling, requiring constant watching." Had the Chinese suddenly quit working hard? It is more likely that the railroad company wanted to rid itself of Chinese workers to appease its white workers and the white communities that would utilize their rail lines. The *Enterprise* continued its rant later in July, "We are determinedly opposed to the Chinese coming here; we protest against it, as a laboring man . . . We would rather see every railroad in Texas abandoned, than that one man from the Celestial Empire should be imported in their construction." As early as February 1870 the *Waco Register* had noted "the jealousy of the Irishman towards the pig-tailed Chinese."[17]

By August, the *Calvert Enterprise* reported that "the Chinese laborers on the Central road are said to be worthless, and the company would like to get rid of them." The H&TC rail company evidently stopped paying the Chinese their wages. By September 1870, according to the *Bryan Appeal*, the Chinese "have all quit work, and have entered suit against their employers for wages and for a failure of compliance with contract."[18]

The Chinese American workers' suit against the H&TC railroad was one of the first among a series of petitions and protests for fair labor relations by Chinese workers throughout the South. In the summer of 1870, Chinese field workers on a Louisiana plantation known as the Millaudon estate kidnapped a Chinese labor contractor to protest working conditions. This led to the imprisonment of sixteen Chinese "ringleaders." The other Chinese attempted to break these leaders out of jail and refused to work until conditions had improved. In December, a white overseer on the plantation pushed a Chinese worker, who retaliated. The overseer shot the Chinese, and by some accounts, killed him. The Chinese workers rebelled by taking up clubs and knives and demanding that the overseer be handed over to them. In 1871, Chinese workers at W. L. Shaffer's Cedar Grove plantation in Louisiana protested the whipping of a Chinese servant. Three Chinese workers were shot—killing one of them. Throughout 1870 and 1871, hundreds of the 960 Chinese rail workers on the Alabama and Chattanooga Railroad left their jobs in Alabama for higher wages in Louisiana. The three hundred who stayed on were left in a lurch by the railroad when it went bankrupt in June 1871, owing six months' of wages. In protest, the Chinese, black, and white workers took over the trains and refused to let them run. The H&TC rail workers' lawsuit for lost wages may have spearheaded a series of Chinese American actions for fair treatment throughout the South. The Chinese labor protests of the American South coincided with worldwide Chinese coolie desertions, escapes, protests, mutinies, and rebellions of that time. Their sense of justice spurred them to organize and fight for better conditions.[19]

Southern capital attempted to cast Chinese Americans as a "model minority" to punish African Americans, but the Chinese Americans shirked this role in their struggle to improve their work conditions and to gain economic independence. By the mid-1870s, Southern capital

The offspring of Tom and Moriah Yepp: (clockwise on left) Frank, Johnny, Mary Jane, and Callie. On the right are pictured Lou Virgie and her husband.

CHINESE COOLIES CROSSING THE MISSOURI RIVER.—[Sketched by Leavitt Burnham.]

Chinese crossing the frozen Missouri River. Carrying their possessions in bundles hanging from poles balanced across their shoulders, they walked on wooden planks laid on the ice. This drawing was published in Harper's Magazine in 1870.

Robertson County soon after they came. The Chinese of this time could have worked as subsistence farmers in China. By coming to the United States, they sought to open their own businesses or work as laborers to earn gold, silver, and American currency. The moment they had an opportunity even to toil at a laundry house, the Chinese likely left Robertson County for one of the growing Texas cities—Galveston, San Antonio, Dallas, El Paso, or Houston. Of those fifty Chinese granted citizenship in 1874, very few show up on the 1880 Robertson County census rolls just six years later. This suggests that Robertson County was most likely the first stop for most of the Chinese who lived there. This also suggests that there are many more "Robertson County Chinese" than the Census figures suggest, as Chinese came and went from the county briskly.[26]

Chinese men helped build many of the Texas rail lines of the 1870s and 1880s, including parts of the Texas and Pacific built from Longview (in East Texas) to Dallas in 1873 and from Fort Worth to Sierra Blanca (in West Texas) in 1881. Some Chinese, rail workers and not, settled along this rail line, from Dallas to small towns like Denison, Sanderson, and Toyah. Brothers Joe Fong and Joe Lung came from Hoiping of the Guangdong province to California at the ages of fourteen and twelve in the year 1876. Joe was their surname. In the first half of the 1880s, Joe Lung likely worked on the Texas & Pacific railroad. He told his son, Sam Lung, that he came with 300 Chinese rail workers, but he was the only one to remain in Texas. Joe Lung settled in Calvert, living among the Chinese community that had developed there. By the early 1890s, Joe Lung had moved to Waco, and then to Austin, where his brother had established himself. Joe Lung opened a grocery store on East 5th Street, and in 1897, he opened the Joe Lung Café at 6th and San Jacinto. He served "businessmen who wanted a clean, tasty lunch, and farmers who brought their produce to town and were glad to get a vegetable and steak dinner for twenty-five cents." On the weekends, Joe Lung sometimes traveled to San Antonio to gamble with other Chinese, and there he met Dora Wong. Dora had been orphaned at the age of four or five and spent a lot of time on the streets before a Jewish woman known as "Miss Hannah" adopted her. After a courtship, Joe and Dora married. They raised nine children in Austin, Texas, where the family established, across two generations, several popular and successful American, Chinese, and Mexican restaurants.[27]

Joe and Dora Lung. The chain of American, Chinese, and Mexican restaurants operated by the Lungs and their children and grandchildren fed many Austinites.

Double wedding day, June 25, 1959. The couple on the right are Inez Lung and Wah Foon Lee. The couple on the left are Ching Wei Wong and his bride (name unknown).

"My father was a kind and hard-working man," remembered their son, Sam, "He was always ready to feed the hungry who seemed to be out of funds." Lung also lent cash out of a "big red box" to African Americans, Mexican Americans, and others who had difficulty procuring loans from the white-owned banks. In the 1920s, son Sam and daughter Inez became some of the earliest Chinese American students at University of Texas-Austin. When his father died, Sam quit college to run the Joe Lung Café, but Inez Lung went on to earn a master's degree from UT-Austin and for thirty-one years served as a Baptist missionary in south China and Hong Kong for the First Baptist Church of Austin. The nine Lung children married five white Americans, two Mexican Americans, and two Chinese. Sam Lung married Lorene Dismuke, a white woman from Lee County, and they raised three children, including Joe Lung (the second), who in the 1960s became the president of the Austin Restaurant Association. The Lung family phased out of the restaurant business in the early 1970s.[28]

Just months after some African Americans had protested the 1870 arrival of the Chinese to the South, Chinese Texans began to live, work, and raise families with African Americans. Segregation and the taboo of miscegenation had thrown Chinese Texans and black Texans into overlapping racial classes. The intermarriage of Chinese men with black women demonstrated that the Chinese Americans of Robertson County had integrated at least in some ways with the black community. The marriage of Chinese men with white women and the bucking of white capital demonstrated that, as early as the 1870s, Chinese Texans challenged racial segregation and the myth of white supremacy.

Early Chinese Dallas
By Stanley Solamillo with Irwin A. Tang

Sam Shong was apparently the first Chinese and the first Asian to live in Dallas –having been listed in the city directory in 1874. He, like most of the Chinese Dallasites before 1900, ran a laundry. By 1880, thirty-three Chinese lived in Dallas County, and by 1890, sixty-three Chinese were counted—the vast majority being laundrymen. Others appar-

Charlie Lung (left) was the brother of Sam Lung, with whom he managed Lung family restaurants. He poses with two kitchen workers (possibly cooks) at the Joe Lung Café in downtown Austin (507 San Jacinto). Circa 1930s.

Sam Lung was one of the first Asian Texans to attend a Texas university. Pictured here in his dorm room, Sam dropped out of the University of Texas at Austin in the 1920s when his father died.

ently worked in white homes, and in 1891 one man was listed as a doctor. In that year, the Chinese were at their height in dominating the Dallas laundry market, running 41 of 49 of the city's laundries.[29]

But just as local businesses had campaigned against Chinese laundrymen in other Texas cities, a campaign transpired in 1894 to close down Chinese laundries. One white laundry, Eureka Steam Laundry, published an advertisement in a city directory depicting a caricatured Chinese man being chased back to China. The slogan, borrowed from the anti-Chinese movements of California, was "The Chinese Must Go!" That same year, *The Dallas Times Herald* opined that "the people should give white laundries a chance." Utilizing racist propaganda of the time, the newspaper claimed that Chinese laundries spread diseases and that the Chinese were taking business from honest white women and girls.[30]

By 1900, there were only eleven Chinese laundries and twenty-two Chinese living in Dallas County. The Chinese had begun running restaurants and groceries. Signaling their prosperity and perhaps their acceptance, some business owners began living in residences separate from their business. While the Chinese primarily lived and worked in the central business district, they were not confined to it. Jim Wing, who lived in Dallas for 44 years, started in the laundry business in 1891 and opened the first Chinese-owned restaurant in 1894. In 1900 he opened a grocery named Jim Wing & Co., and in 1905 he began advertising on the front cover of the city directory. His "Star Café" remained in service until 1935. Wing was apparently one of the very few Chinese who lived in Dallas continuously through the first three decades of the 20th century, as the continuing effects of the Chinese Exclusion acts caused the Chinese population in Dallas to dwindle to three by 1913. Some of the Chinese Dallasites likely left Dallas to return to their families in China, and others returned to China in a coffin. Charlie Sing, who worked as a cook for a Chinese-owned restaurant in 1899, established his own butchery in a black neighborhood by 1905. He died in 1909, and his home, which was valued at $1,250, was sold along with his belongings to pay for his body's return trip to China. A man named Sam Choi was executor of his estate, along with the estates of other Chinese.[31]

Galveston Chinatown

Chinese from the west coast and from Mexico took the railroads or built the railroads to cities and towns throughout Texas. They achieved great geographical diversity, opening laundries in places big and small, in east, north, and west Texas. By 1882, San Antonio, Houston, El Paso, Austin, Dallas, Galveston, and many small Texas towns were home to Chinese Texan communities. Before the Great Storm of 1900, Galveston was the state's major seaport of immigration and trade. The first major urban Texan Chinatown was formed in its downtown. From the 1870s to the early 1900s, most of the Chinese of Galveston were involved with the laundry business; at their height in 1893–1894, Chinese Galvestonians ran thirty-two of the thirty-five local laundries. While white business-men ran steam laundries, which required special equipment, the Chinese washed only by hand.[32]

Other Chinese Galvestonians worked in Chinese-owned restaurants and groceries, and some worked as house servants. In the first decades of the twentieth century, some worked as cooks in Galveston's extravagant gang-run casinos. Perhaps the most famous casino was located on the pier and originally had the Chinese name of Sui Jen before it became The Balinese Room. Chinese American men worked in the kitchen, and according to one story, an old Chinese American cook used a trap door in the kitchen floor to fish the Gulf Coast waters. Once, upon catching a fish too big to fit through the trap door, he had to be restrained from taking a hatchet to the floor.[33]

While white American capitalists pitted race against race, so did some labor leaders, as seen in the Galveston strike of July 1877. On July 30, 1877 most of the African American workers of Galveston struck for a wage increase from $1.50 to $2.00 per day. A man named Martin Burns (race unknown) led the strike, and in a speech to workers the next evening railed against Native Americans (whom he labeled "scalp takers") and Chinese Americans. According to Burns, the nation had been "built up by the Irishman, the negro and the mule" and if the Chinese and foreign-ers were to benefit from their hard work, the nation "should be knocked to pieces, so that the Chinese and others could build it over again."[34]

In the first recorded labor strike by Texas women, black women laundry workers of Galveston joined the general strike on the morning of July 31. Twenty-five African Americans, including a few men, asked white women employees of a white-owned steam laundry to join the strike for higher wages. After keeping laundry workers out of J.N. Harding's steam laundry and nailing the entrance shut, the group headed toward the Chinese American laundries. These "California laundries," as the *Daily News* called them (implying that the Chinese Americans who opened them came from California), were located in a contiguous line "beginning at Slam Sing's, on Twentieth street, between Market and Postoffice, and ending at Wau Loong's, corner of Bath avenue and Postoffice street." The Galveston Chinatown, then, was substantial in size and only a few blocks south of the great port.[35]

According to the *Galveston Daily News*, "At these laundries all the women talked at once, telling Sam Lee, Slam Sling, Wau Loong and the rest that 'they must close up and leave this city within fifteen days, or they would be driven away.'" These Chinese American men were neither the strikers' employers nor their co-workers, but were seen as competition in the laundry business. The men agreed to leave, saying, as quoted by the *Daily News*, "yees, yees," "Allee rightee," and "Me go, yees." They closed their shops for the day, but there is no evidence that they closed their shops for good. The strike ended the next day, with the requested increase in wages, and the city went back to work, no one apparently forced to leave.[36]

One event that brought Galvestonians together was the Chinese American funerals of the nineteenth century, during which a roasted pig would be placed at the grave of the deceased. After the mourners left the cemetery, non-Chinese feasted on the pig—a common phenomenon throughout the nation. One such funeral occurred in 1898, for Sam Lee, a Galveston laundry owner who was most gruesomely murdered by a Chinese "hatchetman" working for a tong. "Tong" literally means "hall" but refers to brotherhoods, secret societies, mutual aid societies, and local community organizations and their international networks of similarly named organizations, most of which helped Chinese immigrants with immigration and settlement, and some of which committed crimes and/or violence.[37]

Two years later, on September 8, 1900, Galveston suffered one of the deadliest natural disasters ever to strike North America. The Galveston Hurricane of 1900 killed 6000 of Galveston's 37,000 residents and so thoroughly destroyed the city that it "called into question the location of the city itself." Although many or most of the Chinese Galvestonians moved away from Galveston after the storm (their businesses likely destroyed), and though no Chinese apparently died, one journalist recorded that the Chinese American men of the city acted heroically during Galveston's darkest days. According to the *Galveston Daily News*, the Chinese Galvestonians "called on the authorities and asked to be put to work without pay, at anything that could relieve the sufferings" of others.

> The work assigned them was not of the sort for which "heroes" are detailed. They were told that the desolate men would need a change of clothing, and that the wounded in the improvised hospitals would require clean linen, bed clothing and bandages, and it was suggested to them that they do the washing for the afflicted survivors. They acquiesced gladly, and in a few hours a club of them was formed, which, as long as was necessary, did the unheroic work of keeping the garments of the sufferers clean. It was never necessary to tell them they were needed. They volunteered for any service that would bring relief—and in the performance of every duty, no matter how arduous, they were apt, efficient and earnest.

The news story concluded that "the conduct of the Galveston Chinese during the late horror will give much comfort to those who are ever looking forward to an establishment of the 'universal brotherhood of man.'"[38]

ENDNOTES

1   Etta B. Peabody, "Efforts of the South to Import Chinese Coolies, 1865–1870," (M.A. Thesis, Baylor University, 1967), pp. 57–65, citing *Houston Telegraph*, Jan 13, 1870.

2   *Harper's Weekly*, "Coolies for Texas," Jan 22, 1870, p. 53; Stan Steiner, *Fusang: The Chinese Who Built America: The Chinese Railroad Men* (New York: Harper & Row, 1979); Geoffrey C. Ward and Dayton Duncan, *The West* (New York: Back Bay, 1999), pp. 230–233.

3   Peabody, 57–65; Norman L. McCarver and Norman L. McCarver, Jr., *Hearne on the Brazos* (San Antonio, Texas: Century Press of Texas, 1958); Edward J.M. Rhoads, "The Chinese in Texas," *The Southwestern Historical Quarterly* 81 (July 1977).

4   Rhoads, p. 3; *St. Louis Republican*, Dec 29, 1870, reprinted in *Houston Telegraph* Jan 6, 1870 as "The Coming Chinaman"; *Harper's Weekly* 1/22/1870; *Galveston Tri-Weekly News*, Jan 7, 1870; Peabody, 57–65.

5   *Houston Telegraph*, Jan 13, 1870.

6   *Houston Telegraph*, Jan 6, 1870.

7   *Houston Telegraph*, Jan 13, 1870.

8   See Peabody for population figures of the South. On New York, see Benson Tong, ed., Asian American children: a historical handbook and guide (Greenwood Press, 2004), p. 38.

9   Alwyn Barr, *The Black Texans: A history of African Americans in Texas, 1528–1995*, second edition (Norman, Oklahoma: University of Oklahoma Press, 1996), 40–41; Barry A. Crouch., *The Freedmen's Bureau and Black Texans* (Austin, Texas: University of Texas Press, 1992); Lucy M. Cohen, *Chinese in the Post-Civil War South: A People Without A History* (Baton Rouge: LSU Press, 1984), p. 46.

10 Cohen, 67, 72; *Harper's Weekly*, "Coolies," Aug 14, 1869, pp. 514–515.

11 *Dallas Herald*, Feb 12, 1869, p. 2; *Dallas Herald*, Jul 30, 1869, p. 2.

12 *Houston Telegraph*, Jan 4, 1870; Peabody, 58–59; Ward and Duncan 232; Edward J.M. Rhoads, ""White Labor" vs. "Coolie Labor": The "Chinese Question" in Pennsylvania in the 1870s," *Journal of American Ethnic History*, Winter 2002, pp. 3–32.

13 Rhoads, "Chinese in Texas," p. 3; *Galveston Tri-Weekly News*, Jan 19, 1870, p. 3 (Reprint of story from *Calvert Enterprise* of Jan 13, 1870); *Galveston Tri-Weekly News*, Jan 10, 1870, p. 4; *Galveston Tri-Weekly News*, Mar 9, 1870, p. 3 (Reprinting story from *Centreville Experiment*).

14 *Galveston Tri-Weekly News*, Feb 18, 1870, p. 2. Reprint of *Waco Register* story.

15 *Galveston Tri-Weekly News*, Feb 18, 1870.

16 Cohen, 87; *Galveston Tri-Weekly News*, Feb 4, 1870, p.3.

17 *Galveston Tri-Weekly News*, Jul 3, 1870, p. 3 (reprint of *Calvert Enterprise* editorial); *Galveston Tri-Weekly News*, Jul 25, 1870, p.1 (Reprint); *Dallas Herald*, Feb 3, 1870, p. 3 (Reprint from the *Waco Register*).

18 *Dallas Herald*, Aug 20, 1870, p. 1 (Reprint from *Calvert Enterprise*); Rhoads, 6;

Galveston Tri-Weekly News, Sep 2, 1870, p.2 (Reprint from *Bryan Appeal*).

19 Cohen, 94, 111.

20 Cohen, 89; Rhoads, "Chinese in Texas"; Pauline Burnitt, interview, as summarized in the file "Chinese Farmers of 1870's," Robertson County, Texas Historical Commission (obtained from the notes of Dr. Ed Rhoads).

21 Rufe O'Keefe, *A Cowboy Life* (San Antonio: The Naylor Company, 1936), p. 10; 1880 U.S. Census; on Hanna, see Rhoads, "Chinese in Texas."

22 McCarver, and McCarver, on p. 57 claim that 150 Chinese voted in the 1874 elections; "RE: Robertson County Chinese Immigrants," an email to the author from Dr. Dale Baum, Texas A&M University Dept. of History, Oct 7, 2006; "The Naturalization of Ah Cong … " Minutes of the Robertson County District Court, Book M, pp. 241–242.

23 Rhoads, 7; Frank X. Tolbert, "Tolbert's Texas" column, "The Black Chinese of Calvert Town," *Dallas Morning News*, Jun 25, 1972.

24 Burnitt; Johnnie Yepp, notes of interview by Edward J.M. Rhoads, in Calvert, Texas, Feb 22, 1974 and then by phone on Mar 2, 1974; Tolbert, Frank X., "Tolbert's Texas" column, *Dallas Morning News*, Jun 20, 1981.

25 Sadberry, Charles, phone interview by Irwin Tang, Jan. 25, 2007; Lucille Wiser, phone interview by Irwin Tang, Feb 9, 2005; *yahoo.com* people search for the names "Yepp" and "Chopp," 2004; also see Tolbert, above.

26 Sadberry; Lazarus, Cathy, conversation with Irwin Tang, Feb 7, 2007; 1880 Census info from "Re: List of the 70 men in Robertson Co. in 1880 who were born in China," an email to the author from Dr. Dale Baum, Feb. 8, 2007; according to Sadberry, some Black Chinese were counted as blacks in the 1880 Census (see also Benson Tong).

27 Frances Alexander, *Miss Chou: The Biography of Inez Lung Lee: Missionary-Teacher in China, 1927–1958* (Austin, Texas: self-published, 1974), preface, 1–2, 14; Joe Lung (the second), interview by Irwin Tang, Austin, Texas, Feb 22, 2005.

28 Alexander.

29 Stanley Solamillo, "The First Chinese in Dallas, 1874–1913," unpublished article; based largely on research using city directories and public records. Solamillo, formerly of Dallas, lives in Hawaii.

30 Solamillo; Dallas City Directories, 1886 to 1894; *Dallas Daily Times Herald,* May 11, 1894, p. 5.

31 Solamillo paper, see above; Dallas City Directories, various from 1891 to 1935; Dallas County, Probate Records, Apr 23, 1909.

32 Galveston City Directories, various from 1880 to 1910.

33 Alan Waldman, "Isle of Illicit Pleasure, Part III: The Casinos," *In Between* #53, August 1979, pp. 7–57, esp. 7, 8, 54-55. On Galveston casinos, brothels, and Chinese cooks.

34 *Galveston Daily News*, "The Strike," Jul 31, 1877, p. 2; *Galveston Daily News*, "Another Raid," Aug 1, 1877, p. 2.

35 Ruthe Winegarten, *Black Texan Women: 150 Years of Trial and Triumph* (Austin: University of Texas Press, 1995); *Galveston Daily News*, Aug 1, 1877.

36 Ibid, see also *Galveston Daily News*, "The Strike at An End," Aug 1, 1877, p. 4; *Galveston Daily News*, "The Strikers in Council," Aug 1, 1877, p. 2.

37 See articles from *Galveston Daily News*, "Jim Gouy's Funeral," Jan 20, 1908; "A Chinaman Assassinated," Feb 15, 1898; "A Chinaman's Funeral," Jun 30, 1892, p. 8; "Chinese Funeral Services," Feb 16, 1898.

38 Ralph A. Wooster with Robert A. Calvert, *Texas Vistas: Selections from the Southwestern Historical Quarterly* (Austin, Texas: Texas State Historical Association, 1986), p. 245; "The Chinese are Leaving," *Houston Chronicle*, Apr 28, 1902; *Galveston Daily News*, "The Chinese in Galveston," Oct 4, 1900, p. 4.

CHAPTER TWO

★

CHINESE EL PASO, 1881–1941

Irwin A. Tang and Anna L. Fahy

May 13, 1881. It was the most important day in the history of El Paso, Texas. Sam Mardock, born Mar Yum Eh, drove a steel spike into the rail line with his sledgehammer. Sam and about three thousand other Chinese men pounded spike after spike into the desert floor as they built the Southern Pacific Railroad eastward toward El Paso. Sam had come a long way. Born in a village in the Toishan district of China's Guangdong province, Sam was told by his father one day, "Now, Yum Eh, you are thirteen years old, a man. Would you be willing to go to the land of the Gold Mountain (the United States)?" Sam said, "Yes." Though some of his cousins and uncles had died on the long, crowded ship voyage to the United States, Sam arrived alive at California where, until the age of seventeen, he worked on farms and ranches.[1]

The Southern Pacific Railroad, which ran southward from San Francisco, renewed construction eastward from Yuma, Arizona in November 1878. Sam joined the primarily Chinese work force. Upon reaching Tucson, Arizona, a military attachment escorted the workers through the territory of the Apaches, who were engaged in a war with the United States government. There, Sam witnessed an Indian massacre of the majority of a crew of thirty Chinese American workers. The Chinese and white workers lived in separate camps to prevent violence. The Chinese Americans had few alternatives to sleeping under the desert sky, as many hotels and restaurants in the Southwest refused to serve Chinese customers. The arrival of the Southern Pacific and, soon thereafter, four other U.S. rail lines and two Mexican rails, transformed the small border town of El Paso into the major railroad hub of the Southwestern United States. Within years, the city grew into a major center of international commerce, transport, and cultural interaction, as well as a major entry point and stopping point for Chinese immigrants.[2]

But the railhead did not stop at El Paso. The Chinese American workers built the rail southeastward toward the confluence of the Rio Grande and the Pecos River, where the Southern Pacific was to connect with the Galveston, Harrisburg & San Antonio rail line (the GH&SA), which was being built westward from San Antonio by white and Mexican men along with some Chinese men. The Chinese of the Southern Pacific worked under J.H. Strobridge, the same man who oversaw their amazing and deadly work on the Central Pacific. Noted the *San Antonio Light*, "The Chinese are treated more like slaves than anything else, they are drove round and sometimes used severely, if they don't work to suit the bosses." The Chinese American rail workers sometimes fought off hostile white and even Mexican American rail workers, but again, Apaches dealt the deadliest blow. On the last of day of 1881, a surveying gang of eleven Chinese Americans were killed at Eagle Pass.[3]

As the two railheads converged, according to West Texas historian C.L. Sonnichsen,

> the tension in the camps rose. Work and vice speeded up together. As more jobs were finished and more men laid off, the devil found more work for idle hands to do. Greater numbers of corpses per day were buried in the rocky ground. The dance halls grew noisier and the human leeches grew plumper.

The rail construction managers asked the Texas Rangers to bring order to the lawless desert and its shack-towns. In response, the Rangers on August 2, 1882 appointed a man named Roy Bean to the office of Justice of the Peace of Pecos County. Not long afterward, Roy Bean made one of his most famous proclamations, as first reported by *The El Paso Daily Times*:

> Here is the latest on Roy Bean:
>
> Somebody killed a Chinaman and was brought up standing before the irrepressible Roy, who looked through two or three dilapidated law books from stem to stern, and finally turned the culprit loose remarking that he'd be d----d if he could find any law against killing a Chinaman.[4]

On January 12, 1883, the Southern Pacific and the GH&SA railroads were connected, uniting the West Coast and the Deep South. The second transcontinental railroad of the United States was completed two and a half miles west of the confluence of the Pecos and the Rio Grande. Several years later, some of the Chinese rail builders of the Southern Pacific, including Sam Mardock, helped build the Pecos River High Bridge. By replacing the circuitous Loop Line railway bridge with a 2,180 foot-long bridge across the Pecos River canyon, rail workers enabled trains to travel much more quickly. Again the Chinese worked from the west end, and the Irish, Mexicans, and Germans worked from the east. The two groups risked their lives in constructing 321-foot tall steel girders. Upon completion, this, the highest bridge in North America, was a source of wonder, vertigo, and beautiful scenery for wide-eyed train passengers.[5]

Birth of a Community

In Spanish, "El Paso" means "The Pass," and this name could not have been more appropriate for the Chinese of old El Paso. Between 1881 and the end of Chinese Exclusion in 1943, tens of thousands of Chinese, Chinese Mexicans, and Chinese Americans spent time working, living, or waiting in El Paso, but only a fraction of these Chinese retired and died in El Paso. Sam Mardock first came to El Paso at the age of nineteen, and he made the city his home base for the next ten years as he served as an

An unidentified man in El Paso, probably in the 1890s. He is almost certainly a Chinese El Pasoan. He carries a gun in a holster next to his thigh, and a metal chain hangs across his chest.

interpreter for the U.S. government, worked in laundries and restaurants, and did cowboy work on a ranch. Mardock eventually settled in Tyler in east Texas and ran a chain of restaurants that served American food, including the "soul food" associated with African American cuisine.[6]

Enough Chinese Americans did spring roots, though, to make El Paso's Chinese community one of the nation's most cohesive and vibrant and to forever alter the landscape and culture of El Paso. El Paso writer Owen White recalled that when Chinese began arriving in El Paso, even before the arrival of the Southern Pacific, locals felt their "cleansing and civilizing influence."

> Prior to May 13, 1881 a laundry and a restaurant or two were already in operation, but after that date signs bearing such names as Soo Wah, Sun Lee, Hop Woo and Ah Sin began to be hung up all over the town. Laundries and eating places became almost as common as saloons and gambling houses, and the residents of El Paso, especially the bachelor residents, could now get something besides chile and frijoles with which to satisfy the inner man, and they could, also, if they wanted to, put on a clean shirt and a fresh pair of socks every Sunday.[7]

The first one hundred or so Chinese to live in El Paso slept in a single adobe building, which happened to stand across the street from the city dump. Their first major act was to erect a grocery store to supply their need for Chinese food.[8] On the first day of 1882, *The El Paso Times* offered this population review:

> El Paso, like all frontier cities, has a large floating population, which changes rapidly and largely from various causes, frequently making a difference of from 500 to 1000 per week. In the TIMES estimate, secured from the best possible authority, we have placed the permanent population at 2800, classified as follows: American, 1600; Mexican, 600; Chinese 500; colored, 100. The Chinese are engaged principally as servants in various hotels, restaurants, and private families. Many others have laundries, while a large number are working on the Southern Pacific railroad. As a class they are peaceable and inaffensive [sic]. Those who have lived any length of time in the country are

gradually giving up their national style of dress and assuming that of the American.[9]

Chinese Americans, then, made up 18% of the El Paso population. But as the El Paso population grew steadily from less than 1,000 in 1880 to over 100,000 in 1930, the Chinese El Pasoan population bounced between 200 and 1,000. Fluctuations were driven by influxes and exoduses of Chinese immigrants, U.S. immigration policies, and war. The Chinese formed a major U.S. Chinatown in downtown El Paso. While they lived and worked in many places throughout El Paso and its rural outskirts, a dense concentration of Chinese businesses and homes existed on South Oregon Street between Overland and Second or Third Street. During these early decades, most Chinese El Pasoans lived at their workplaces or in modest homes, usually one-story adobe structures. One major Chinese lodging house was home to many Chinese, mostly newcomers, and its front portion served as a "Chinese Information Bureau." Some Chinese El Pasoans worked as train wipers or engine cleaners for the rail lines, and some of them slept in camps in the rail yards.[10]

Most Chinese Texans started their own businesses or worked for Chinese Texan employers. The Chinese of El Paso dominated the hand laundry business. According to El Paso city directories, Chinese El Pasoans owned thirteen out of fifteen laundries in 1886 and twelve out of sixteen in 1907. Because everything was done by hand and little monetary investment was required, cash-strapped laborers could, with hard work and frugal living, survive and even save money. According to lifelong El Pasoan Leigh White Osborn, Chinese laundry workers "kept a big vessel of water with a dipper, with a cup. They'd fill their mouths full of water and then they'd blow the water out on the clothes and then they'd iron. Yes. Then the clothes were delivered." Although the Chinese made up a small portion of the population, they owned, between 1890 and 1910, most of El Paso's restaurants. These restaurants served mostly American food, and many were quite popular places. Around the turn of the century, the Chinese-owned English Kitchen was described as "the" place to dine after taking in a show at Myar's Opera House.[11]

Truck farming was, for some time, nearly monopolized by Chinese El Pasoans. Beginning in 1882, Chinese El Pasoans bought and leased land along the outskirts of El Paso and Juárez, the Mexican town on the opposite bank of the Rio Grande. They grew vegetables and fruits (including grapes, apples, and peaches) and raised hogs and horses. El Pasoan Leola Freeman recalled the Chinese farms as "beautiful gardens with arrow-straight rows without a weed." She watched the Chinese cultivate the land:

> All day stooped figures worked along the rows or irrigated the fields. Night failed to discourage them. They continued by lantern light, conversing in a musical sing-song which we kids tried to imitate.

Each morning, Chinese men led horse-drawn wagons filled with produce from Juárez and local farms into El Paso, where they delivered their goods door-to-door to housewives. In later years, some growers sold their produce wholesale to grocers while others supplied their own stores, such as the original Big 8 Grocery Store. Beginning around the turn of the century, owning and managing grocery stores became a major occupation among the Chinese. In addition to groceries, some Chinese stores specialized in Chinese and Japanese goods, medicines, firecrackers, kites, toys, and teas.[12]

The El Paso Chinese community became known for its traditional Chinese doctors. For years Dr. Ng Che Hok advertised in the *El Paso Daily Herald* that he cured "Men and Women's diseases. All Female complaints instantly cured. Coughs, chronic stomach trouble, heart disease, liver, kidney and bladder trouble. All rheumatism and blood poison eradicted [sic] immediately. Cancer cured without a knife." Ng dressed in a traditional high-collared shirt and a cylindrical hat for the ad, while his competitor, Wo You Ching, sported a full beard, western suit, and a bowler hat. Margo Gutierrez of Austin remembered her maternal grandmother telling the story of how, in 1910, her first husband Luis Lomeli "broke out with boils all over his body." The childless couple moved from Ray-Sonora, Arizona to the El Paso-Juárez area to receive treatment from a traditional Chinese doctor. The doctor cured Luis of his boils and, without the use of scientific equipment, also informed Luis that he was sterile. It turned out to be true.[13]

The Chinese of El Paso and their Detractors

The hard work of the Chinese paid off, and many of their businesses flourished. Especially during their first few decades, Chinese successes drew the envy of whites. In February 1889, the *El Paso Daily Herald* published an especially resentful series of editorials. "An active exportation of the American Dollar is carried on by the flourishing and lavishly patronized Chinese of the city," wrote the *Herald* on the second of February. Indeed, because federal immigration laws prevented the Chinese from bringing their families to El Paso, many Chinese men sent money to their families in China. On the fifth of February, the *Herald* declared derisively that "El Paso is the Chinese Mecca of the Southwest. They are liberally patronized much to the detriment of the American." White-owned businesses fretted publicly about Chinese commercial success and sought ways to siphon business from them. On February 8, the *Herald*, implying that the Chinese carried diseases, suggested that the Chinese be forced to live in a segregated ghetto.[14]

Overcoming cultural, language, and racial barriers, the Chinese earned a reputation for industriousness and honesty. Chinese Juárez resident Enrique Woo said the mid-twentieth century Chinese shopkeepers of Juárez worked twelve hours a day for 362 days a year. In 1936, the *El Paso Herald Post* wrote that the Chinese of the city were "highly respected for their honesty." The newspaper recalled that in the early 1880s, the postmaster dumped all Chinese mail in one box, and "there was never a case of a Chinese disturbing the mail of another."[15]

The Wild Chinese West

El Paso was known, from the arrival of the railroads to the onset of World War II, as "Six-Shooter Capital" and "Sin City." El Paso Chinatown was surrounded by a sea of gambling, prostitution, shoot-outs, and alcohol. South Oregon and Utah (now South Mesa) Streets were occupied by both large whorehouses and smaller "cribs." At all hours, two big dance halls—the Monte Carlo on South Oregon Street and the Red Light Dance Hall on Utah Street—spewed drunken people onto the streets of the homes and businesses of Chinatown. From the 1890s to 1915, the city-sanctioned red light district ran straight through the heart of Chinatown. Daily, the streets saw shootings and brawls over gambling disputes, women, and the illegal business of helping Chinese immigrants enter Texas from Mexico. The city government, rather than rid the city of vices, only contained them and profited from a steady stream of "fines." All ethnic groups contributed to the hell-raising. The city's reputation was such that Sam Mardock, in his first days in El Paso, bought a Colt revolver and used it to protect himself after winning large sums of money at cards, as he often did. According to Owen White, the Chinese were known for having "no equals" at the gambling table.[16]

On August 15, 1884, Chinese El Pasoans Sing Lee and Ah Choy posted the following in the *Daily Herald*:

Look Out!

This is to warn all people that a Chinaman named Ju Ah Zeu (English name is Jim) is a bad man and carrying arms to kill Lem Ah Chong. Jim is the man who worked for "Gypsie" a couple of weeks ago and was yesterday discharged by Kate Clark for fighting.

When the Chinese secret societies, or tongs, decided to eliminate their enemies, they posted a declaration of their intentions on one of several trees in Chinatown, naming the man to be killed and the bounty on his head. The Chinese El Pasoans were able to "administer their own brand of justice without interference from the police." When some Chinese El Pasoans "decided to make a bonfire of Moy Jim," killing him on the night of February 8, 1893, Moy Jim was likely being punished by tong leaders. Besides tong violence, Chinese El Pasoans and Chinese Texans sometimes dealt with racial violence. It made front page news in 1901 when Fred Himmel stabbed El Pasoan Woo Bing with large clippers and then went on to "Kim Wee Wa's place where he threatened to exterminate another bunch of Celestials."[17]

Like most Chinatowns throughout the nation, El Paso's Chinese community ran its share of opium dens and gambling houses. In the 1910s, the "mayor" of Chinatown, Charlie Sam, ran a "fan tan" parlor in his own living quarters, upstairs from an herbalist's shop. Clifford Alan Perkins, an immigration official of the time, described the operation:

> At the [herbalist's] back was a solid woodfaced wall of small drawers containing herbs and dried items, better unidentified, from which he supposedly selected remedies for the ailments of a sizeable clientele who were actually patronizing the gaming tables. No whites were allowed at the two ten-foot-long oval tables where twelve or fifteen or more Chinese would gather to play fan-tan. Chain smoking cigarettes or cigars, they would shuffle up to the table, make their bets on how many white markers would be left under the small cup when the dealer had finished removing them four at a time, then win or lose, walk away.

In El Paso, several opium dens ran brisk business in the late 1800s. Some of the patrons were Chinese, but an August 19, 1885 *Lone Star* study found, in the span of a single hour, sixty-three white opium smokers entering a popular opium joint, indicating that most patrons at this joint were white. Some white patrons were prostitutes, and some were "good citizens." In efforts to prevent opium use, three anti-opium city ordinances were passed between 1882 and 1885. Religious leaders such as one Reverend Barnes crusaded against the opium joints, and newspapers complained about them. Although the city assessed fines for opium smokers, especially Chinese smokers, the dens operated well into the twentieth century.[18]

A Unique Community Grows

The Chinese El Pasoan community was culturally very Mexican. Many or most of the Chinese El Pasoans had lived in, or immigrated through, Mexico. Many married Mexican or Mexican American women, and most did business with Mexicans and Mexican Americans. The El Paso and the Juárez Chinese communities were conjoined twin communities, united by common cultures (Chinese and Mexican), commerce, and common political and immigration issues. Communication, cooperation, and travel between the two communities were common. Some

Chinese El Pasoans, especially those who dealt with whites, spoke fluent English. Before 1965, most Chinese Texans, including those of El Paso, spoke the Toishan dialect of the Chinese language.

Until 1943, the Page Act of 1875 prevented immigration of almost all Chinese women. Additionally, Chinese women may not have wished to live in El Paso. As a result, few Chinese women lived in El Paso before 1965. Only two Chinese women could be found in the city directory in 1883, and a special U.S. census reported only four in the city in 1916. Most Chinese men who married women in El Paso, then, married Mexican and Mexican American women, though some married white and black women. Most Chinese children born in El Paso, then, were biracial or multiracial. Many of the Chinese El Pasoans and Chinese Texans had wives and children in China, whom they visited at various intervals. Sometimes these men brought their wives to Texas, but more often one or more of their sons made the journey to Texas and helped them work at their business. Those able to bring their wives or their entire families to Texas tended to be well-established and wealthier business owners who could more easily arrange to have their wives and children immigrate legally or illegally. While some men rarely saw their families in China, other Chinese Texan men had two wives and two families—one in Texas and one in China.[19]

The most famous Chinese El Pasoan of the 1880s—Sam Hing—married a Creole woman (name unknown) from New Orleans. Sam Hing made most of his wealth contracting Chinese laborers for the Southern Pacific railroad, and he built a mansion on East San Antonio Street. In 1885 the couple brought a son into the world. The *El Paso Daily Herald* dubbed the newborn "probably the first Chinaman ever born in the state of Texas" and called Hing "the happiest man in El Paso today." Because Hing was a wealthy labor contractor, a tong leader, a community banker of sorts, a store-owner, and "probably the most influential Chinese in El Paso," the *El Paso Herald* claimed that Sam Hing's son was "not one of the class that 'must go.'" Hing's wife had two sisters who both married prominent white El Paso men. Because Sam Hing was Chinese, Mrs. Hing felt "ostracized" by the rest of El Paso high society. She left Sam, and Sam left for Mexico, where he made another fortune.[20]

The biracial children of the Chinese El Pasoans, like their fathers, tended to be of three cultures—Chinese, Mexican, and American. But unlike the Chinese-Black community of Calvert and Hearne, in which the Chinese were essentially absorbed genetically into the Black community, the Chinese-Mexican community of El Paso was large enough to maintain a more equally biracial genetic make-up through a dozen decades of intermarriage. Many biracial Chinese-Mexicans married other Chinese-Mexicans or married full-blooded Chinese.

The early Chinese Texans held dearly to their culinary heritage. Some ate Chinese food daily, and Chinese fathers even taught their biracial children to cook Chinese food. A major contract stipulation of the Chinese rail workers of the Houston & Texas Central was that the workers be provided with a supply of dozens of specific Chinese foods, from dried fish to tofu. Southern Pacific rail workers cooked Chinese food and ate it with Chinese utensils. Archaeological digs in both El Paso Chinatown and rail line campsites revealed large numbers of Chinese tea cups, rice bowls, soy sauce bottles, and opium bottles.[21]

As in China, rituals paying tribute to the dead were extremely important. Chinese funerals were often major events in Texas cities. Man Tuck was the head of the brotherhood and mutual aid association called "Chee Kung Tong," or the "Chinese Masons," and when he died in 1892, almost half of the Chinese in El Paso belonged to the local branch. As a result, Man Tuck's funeral was "the most imposing that ever took place in the city." Every available carriage and buggy in the city, sixty in all, was contracted by the Chinese Masons for the funeral procession. One of the four Chinese American women in El Paso rode in her own carriage, while Woey Gee, Man Tuck's successor, rode on a pony. Both a Chinese and a mainstream band played dirges as hundreds of Chinese walked from the Masonic Lodge to Concordia Cemetery, where 500 El Pasoans watched the mourners place a feast of two hogs and a goat at the grave and set ablaze a miniature house, which Man Tuck could utilize in the afterlife.[22]

In the early decades, most of the Chinese buried in Concordia Cemetery were later disinterred and reburied near their ancestral homes in China. Although El Paso's Concordia cemetery was divided into sec-

Students and teachers of an English class for Chinese, 1905 in El Paso. The teachers are white women, and almost all of the students are Chinese men. A Chinese woman, rare in the city at that time, sits in the center. Most, if not all, of the men wear their hair in a queue (long braid), and four wear Western suits.

tions such as "colored" and "Mormon," the Chinese section was apparently the only section that had been walled-off from the rest of the cemetery. The walls were likely erected after 1937, when the Japanese invasion of China made reburial in China more difficult. Of the more than one hundred gravestones at Concordia's "Chinese Cemetery," the vast majority date from 1936 to the early 1960s, while several are too old to read. The most common names among the gravestones are Mar, Wong, and Yee, and almost all of the deceased came from the "four counties" region of Guangdong province. Over half of the deceased were from Toishan county, another 30% hailed from Hoiping county, and the rest were evenly split between Yanping and Sunwui counties.[23]

In 1892, some Chinese of El Paso detonated chains of firecrackers in public in honor of Guan Yin, the Goddess of Mercy, demonstrating that traditional Chinese spiritual beliefs were very much alive in El Paso in the 1890s. Four years later, in 1896, one of the first major Chinese Christian organizations in Texas—a Baptist Chinese Mission—opened in downtown El Paso. The mission co-existed with Chinatown's Chinese Masonic Temple, likely established in the 1880s and rebuilt and opened with fireworks and music in January 1904. At the temple, Chee Kung Tong members paid respect to deities and mythical figures. One newspaper wrote that this temple was "beautifully decorated inside and on the walls are pictures of various prominent men of the Celestial empire, while the altar is covered in the richest tapestries and burns the costliest perfumed joss sticks [incense]."[24]

In their free time, the Chinese El Pasoans could choose among an assortment of diversions besides gambling and smoking opium. Chinese American bands played traditional instruments at funerals and public events. A group of Chinese musicians played Chinese instruments within the often-goofy McGinty's Band, a club for El Paso musicians which played concerts, funerals, and weddings. In the years leading up to World War I, the Chinese El Pasoans organized a baseball team that competed against other teams in Washington Park and wore pin-striped uniforms labeled simply, "Chinese." Chinatown even had its own theater.[25]

The Mexican Revolution

During the Mexican Revolution of 1910-1920 revolutionary leaders such as Francisco "Pancho" Villa led mobs and armies in attacking Chinese merchants and workers, killing hundreds of Chinese, their Mexican wives, and their children. Those who were not killed often had their stores destroyed. The May 15, 1911 massacre at the city of Torreón, Coahuila resulted in the deaths of about half of the Chinese community of the city, the final death toll totaling 303 Chinese and 5 Japanese. The massacre, which utilized particularly sadistic methods, was an act of racial hatred.[26]

El Paso became a beacon of hope for Chinese, whites, Mexicans, and all who were displaced or persecuted in Mexico. But for the Chinese, crossing the border suddenly became more difficult during the Mexican Revolution. Chinese were generally not allowed to enter the United States from Mexico, and the number of U.S. forces on the border increased tremendously as a result of the war. Nevertheless, hundreds, likely thousands, of Chinese succeeded in crossing the Rio Grande. Clifford Alan Perkins described the "tradesmen, cooks, laundrymen, and gardeners" who escaped into the El Paso area: "Each fugitive brought whatever he could with him, especially food, clothing and household goods, with some miscellaneous livestock and pets." Some Chinese, upon crossing the border, simply walked along rail lines until U.S. immigration officials arrested them and deported them to China.[27]

In 1913, when Pancho Villa led his forces northward toward Juárez, a flood of war refugees preceded him toward the Texas border. Eighteen- or nineteen-year old Herlinda Wong of Juárez was the daughter of store- and hotel-owners Carlos Wong and Francis Perez, an Aztec woman. Upon learning from one of Villa's scouts (who was a patron of the Wong store) that Villa planned to seize Juárez, and that it was "going to be a bad one," she knew that her family had to escape to El Paso. Herlinda's daughter, Herlinda Leong, recalled how her mother helped save many Chinese of Juárez:

> So she went to the [U.S.] Immigration and talked to some of her
> friends there and told them and said, "I'd like to have permission to

bring my family and some of my people [to El Paso] and I'll guarantee you that I'll see to it that they'll come back [to Juárez] after the battle." So they said, "Well, I think they could arrange that. Just tell us how many people will come across?" And she said, "Oh, about 200." [...] So finally they agreed that [the Chinese from Juárez] could wait at the border and after the first shot was fired they could go across but not until after that. So she got the people and got them across. And when they got across the border they were looking for some place to stay. And she said the only hotel that would take them in was the Gateway Hotel. And they always felt very, very close to them because they were the only ones that would take them in.[28]

Herlinda married Antonio Chew, a Chinese Mexican who had wooed her by serenading her with mariachis, a traditional Mexican band. The couple ran a grocery store in Juárez called La Garantía. Like many Chinese Juárezians, the Chew family moved to El Paso. Arriving by the early 1920s, they opened the New China Grocery in downtown El Paso. Acting as liaisons between the Chinese of El Paso-Juárez and U.S. immigration officials, Herlinda and Antonio Chew helped many Chinese Mexicans immigrate to the United States. They also acted as escorts in the 1920s and 1930s for Chinese traveling from Mexico to San Francisco, from where they sailed to China. In the 1930s, the Chews visited China, where Herlinda discovered that some of the Chinese men who had brought their Mexican wives back to China had abandoned them. These men may have had Chinese wives in China. Around Canton City, Herlinda Wong Chew found seventy Mexican women and helped them return to Mexico with the aid of the Mexican consulate.[29]

Upon returning to El Paso, Herlinda Wong Chew continued her community activism in helping women find health care and organizing small grocers against the growing strength of chain groceries. She had eight children, including immigration attorney Wellington Chew, who often represented mistreated women and minorities. Wellington's son, David Wellington Chew, became one of Texas's first Asian American elected officials, serving West-Central El Paso on the City Council from 1989 to 1991. Chew was elected in 1994 to serve on Texas's Eighth District Court of Appeals and was appointed the court's Chief Justice in 2007.[30]

Josephine Wong Chew, Antonio and Herlinda's daughter and one of the first women at UT Law School, returned to El Paso in 1939 after her parents' deaths to care for her sisters and brothers as her oldest brother, Antonio, Jr., joined the U.S. Army Air Corps. She and husband Ernest Wong ran an insurance agency in Los Angeles. Photo taken in 1938. See Casasola Project supplement, El Paso Times, June 6, 2004.

C. S. Tong served as a U.S. soldier in World War I. He enlisted at El Paso's Fort Bliss and his name appears in El Paso's city directories, 1920-1922. This postcard photo was labeled "C.S. Tong, Battery A 52nd F.A., U.S.A., Camp Travis." Camp Travis was located in Austin, and the "F.A." indicated that Tong served in field artillery. Circa 1917-1918.

World War I, The Great Depression, and a Transformation

Benjamin "Ben" Mar (Chinese name, Mar Sum) was born in 1888 in San Francisco while his parents were on a business trip from the Guangdong Province. Ben Mar grew up in China and returned to the United States at the age of eighteen. In 1908, he settled in El Paso, where some cousins lived. In partnership with a man known as Ah Bing, Ben Mar opened the Pan American restaurant. In 1915, Ben Mar consulted on the design of the main building of the Texas College of Mines, later renamed the University of Texas at El Paso. At that time, the three Chinese families of Mar, Ing (Eng or Ng), and Wong constituted most of the 500 Chinese El Pasoans, and among the older men of these families were several highly respected businessmen. Numbering 175 at one point during Ben Mar's life, the Mar family "sponsored" in the late 1910s "a number of" the city's fifty or sixty illegal Chinese whom the federal immigration office "ignored because they created no problems." All of these men enlisted in the National Guard to defend the United States against Pancho Villa's army. Perhaps in part because of General John J. Pershing's presence at El Paso's Fort Bliss, at least eighteen Chinese El Pasoan men volunteered or were drafted into the Army during World War I. Ten of the eighteen men were inducted into the military on September 20–21, 1917, indicating a concerted effort on their part to join the war effort. The men served as combat soldiers and as cooks, and several died. After the war, the federal government granted Chinese American veterans citizenship. During World War I, Ben Mar may have served as a personal cook for General Pershing. After the war, Ben Mar returned to El Paso to marry his sweetheart and first wife, Maria. Over the next twenty years, the couple had nine children and adopted one child. The children attended Chinese language classes and spoke both English and Spanish.[31]

The Chinese Masons survived into the twentieth century, and Ben Mar became one of its leaders. This tong "served as a police force" to "defend and protect the people of the Chinese colony, and, on occasion, the surrounding Hispanic community." But the Great Depression brought other dangers to the Chinese El Pasoan community—hunger and unemployment. While many Americans sought help from the government, the Chinese American communities of El Paso and San Antonio preferred to remain independent from the government. The El Paso Chinese community had established a system in which one of the best-educated Chinese was chosen as the unofficial "mayor" of Chinatown. With a Chinese university education, Ben Mar was chosen to lead the Chinese during the Great Depression. Ben Mar organized what was known as the "Chinese WPA," a system of distributing food from better-off Chinese El Pasoans to unemployed Chinese El Pasoans. Chew Din, a World War I veteran and a grocery store owner, said that the Chinese were

> too damn proud. We all helped each other then. When a relative was out of work with a family to feed, I'd take groceries once a week—no money. They would have never have accepted money anyway. But the food, well, it helped them survive just one more day.[32]

In the early 1930s, James Yee Garbern (Yu Gah Bun) and his wife Grace Toy Garbern came to El Paso from San Francisco after their printing business failed. One morning in 1935, Grace Garbern sat down for Sunday School at First Baptist Church. The woman next to her stood up and said, "I'm not sitting next to a Chinese." Mrs. Garbern realized then that some Chinese might feel more comfortable in their own church. The Garberns established what became the Chinese Baptist Church. Indicative of the evolving Chinese community, the church attracted members because of its Chinese language school for children rather than English classes for Chinese adults, as had been common at Texas churches in earlier decades. An early Chinese Texan Christian community grew around this new church.[33]

In the late 1930s, Chew Din's wife, Sit See, and their teen-aged daughter lived in China. Sit See's small, mutilated feet (a result of footbinding) and immigration laws prohibited her from living in the United States. Meanwhile, Chew Din and his son Ralph kept their noses to the grindstone, working at their grocery store. During his off-hours, Chew Din and other Chinese leaders organized the Chinese Colony Association, amassing 400 members by 1938. The Chinese Colony Association aimed to unite all Chinese El Pasoans, eliminate opium smoking and Chinese lotteries, and promote political participation. Chew announced publicly that the days of the tong wars were "gone forever." Paralleling the reforms of the Chinese, the city of El Paso outlawed prostitution and gambling. Such political changes and the replacement of the largely immigrant male society by a community of Chinese families sounded the final death knell of the El Paso Chinatown. Lily Love Chew Soo Hoo, born in 1932, remembered being taken to the old Chinatown as a child: "It was not fancy. Old Chinese men gathered on the street corners where they gossiped and smoked long pipes. Many didn't have their wives with them." Further isolating the formerly bustling Chinatown was the movement of Chinese grocery stores to various parts of the expanded city, the marriage of Chinese men to Mexican women, and the arrival to El Paso of more Chinese women.[34]

After World War II, the numbers of full-blooded Chinese families continued to increase, but as late as 1956, the membership of the Chinese Baptist Church was about one-third Chinese-Mexican families. Chinese Mexicans continued to immigrate to El Paso over the years, in part because of the large numbers of Chinese Mexicans living in Juárez and Northern Mexico. Francisco Wong and Eva Enriques de Wong first met in the Mexican town of Nuevas Casas Grandes, Chihuahua, where Wong and other Chinese men settled to open stores in the 1890s after working as farm laborers. Francisco converted to Catholicism in his 30s, and at the age of 40 he married Eva, who was 20. Eva and all of her friends married these Chinese men in part because they were "good workers and they had money." Francisco and Eva had four children. Eva cooked Mexican food for the family, while Francisco made Chinese food every New Year, including an entire chicken with vegetables. Running a meat market, Francisco often ate T-bone steaks rather than traditional Chinese food. Eva died in 1956, and two years later Francisco Wong, missing his wife, died at the age of 85 of no apparent illness. Daughter Evangelina, born in 1929, married a Mexican man named Clemente Arvizo, and they attempted in 1957 to immigrate to El Paso. While it was relatively easy for Mexicans to immigrate, Evangelina was denied entry because she was one-half Chinese. After immigration regulations eased, Evangelina's family, including her four children, immigrated to El Paso in 1973. In the early 2000s, she had ten grandchildren in El Paso, and one of her sons had married an-

Maria Dolores Lopez Chong (See Ch. 3) holding up pictures of her two daughters, 2003. Maria's parents are of Mexican and Chinese blood, a combination locals say produce attractive offspring. She met her husband in Juárez, where a large Chinese merchant community lived in the mid-20th century.

This tomb, about four feet tall, was built in 1993. In the background stands the front arch, and beneath it the front gate labeled "Chinese Cemetery" in English and Chinese. To the right of the arch are the vast majority of the graves.

other mixed-blood Chinese Mexican; such marriages were not uncommon among Chinese Mexicans through their history.[35]

From 1881 until the U.S. entry into World War II, the El Paso Chinese community slowly transformed from a society of "sojourners" and
brotherhoods living in a downtown Chinatown to a community of wide-
ly-dispersed families. In those sixty years, it was one of the nation's most
unique and dynamic Chinese American communities.

ENDNOTES

1   Julian Mardock, *The First of Many* (Dallas: self-published by Mardock, 1998), pp.
    1–16.

2   Erle Heath, *Seventy-Five Years of Progress: Historical sketch of the Southern Pacific*
    (San Francisco: Southern Pacific Bureau of News, 1945), pp. 13–15; Alton King
    Briggs, "The Archaeology of 1882 Labor Camps on the Southern Pacific Railroad,
    Val Verde County, Texas," Master's Thesis, Anthropology, UT Austin, January
    1974; Mardock, 14.

3   Heath, 15; Charles Leland Sonnichsen, *Roy Bean: Law West of the Pecos* (New York
    City: The Devin–Adair Company, 1958), p. 78; *San Antonio Light*, Oct 10, 1882;
    Edward Rhoads, "The Chinese in Texas," *The Southwestern Historical Quarterly* 81
    (July 1977), p. 10.

4   Sonnichsen, 78–80.

5   Heath, 15; Mardock, 20–22.

6   Mardock, 21. The restaurant had a "soul food" night every week to cater to black
    patrons.

7   Owen White, *The Autobiography of a Durable Sinner* (New York: G.P. Putnam's
    Sons, 1942), p. 155.

8   Anna Louise Fahy, *Chinese Borderland Community Development: A Case Study of
    El Paso, 1881–1909*, Master of Arts Thesis, University of Texas at El Paso, July 2001,
    pp. 38–40.

9   *El Paso Times*, January 1, 1882, p. 2.

10 Nancy Farrar, *The Chinese in El Paso* (El Paso: Texas Western Press, 1972), pp. 4,
    5, 44, *El Paso Herald Post* May 28, 1936, p. 7; Fahy, 49–50; Rhoads, 13; Second St. is

now Paisano St.

11 Fahy 79, 85, 88–89; see also Rhoads.

12 Fahy, 90–91; Farrar, 10; *El Paso Herald-Post*, Leola Freeman letter to "Ask Ann Carroll," Aug 4, 1977; Soo Hoo, Lily Chew, interview by Anna L. Fahy, Nov 25, 1995.

13 *El Paso Herald* newspapers, 1904; Margo Gutierrez of Austin, interview by Irwin Tang, Aug 15, 2003; emails September 8, 2003.

14 Editorials, *El Paso Daily Herald*, Feb 1889.

15 Enrique Woo, interview by Anna L. Fahy, Oct 28, 1995; *El Paso Herald Post*, May 28, 1936, p. 7.

16 Charles Leland Sonnichsen, *Pass of the North* (El Paso: Texas Western Press, 1968), pp. 283–84, 338–340; Leon C. Metz, *Turning Points in El Paso, Texas*, (El Paso: Mangan Books, 1985), p. 76; Mardock, 17–19; White, 156.

17 Farrar, 6, 25; Sonnichsen, *Pass*, 249–250; *El Paso Herald*, Feb 10, 1893; *El Paso Daily Herald*, Aug 15, 1884; *El Paso Herald*, Aug 10, 1901, p. 1. "Celestials" was an informal term referring to Chinese people.

18 Clifford Alan Perkins, *Border Patrol: With the U.S. Immigration Service on the Mexican Boundary 1910–1954* (El Paso: Texas Western Press, 1978), p. 51. *Lone Star* Aug 19, 1885; Farrar, 16–19.

19 Farrar, 5; Woo, interview; Jose Fong, interview by Irwin Tang, El Paso, 2003.

20 *El Paso Herald–Post*, May 28, 1936, page 7 column 8; *El Paso Daily Herald*, Oct 14, 1885, page 3, column 2; White, 93–96.

21 On the Southern Pacific, see Briggs; on the H&TC, see Rhoads; on the Chinatown dig, see Staski, Edward, *Beneath the Border City, Volume 2* (a bound report prepared for City of El Paso), University Museum Occasional Papers No. 13, (Las Cruces, New Mexico: New Mexico State University, 1985), pp. 96–130.

22 *El Paso Herald-Post*, Nov 12, 1973, reprinting Nov 14, 1892 article; see also Rhoads.

23 Rhoads, 14.

24 *El Paso Daily Herald*, Mar 17, 1892, p 1; *El Paso Daily Herald*, Jan 14, 1904.

25 Sonnichsen, *Pass of the North*, 265; photos at center of Farrar book.

26 Grace Delgado, "In the Age of Exclusion: Race, Region and Chinese Identity in the Making of the Arizona-Sonora Borderlands, 1863–1943," University of California at Los Angeles History Ph.D. dissertation (2000), p. 244.

27 Perkins, 34, 26.

28 Perkins, 32–33; Herlinda Leong, Josephine Wong, and Grace Got, daughters of Herlinda Wong Chew, interview by Richard Estrada, El Paso, July 28, 1978, Transcript #257, UTEP Institute of Oral History.

29 Sarah John, "Herlinda Wong Chew: El Paso Trailblazer," *Password* 37 (Spring 1992), pp. 41–46.

30 John, 45–46; *http://www2.8thcoa.courts.state.tx.us/Chew.htm* as retrieved on Dec 24, 2004.

31 Maria de los Angeles Mar Skates, interviews by Anna L. Fahy, Dec 1997 and Nov

24, 1998; Perkins, 49–50; Mar Skates; number of dead from Perkins, 50; Skates. On the 18 stat, see Mary Elizabeth Bush, "El Paso County, Texas, in the First World War," Master's Thesis, UT-Austin, 1950, Appendices.

32 Mar Skates; Sue Ann Carpenter, "Gold Mountain, Texas: From China to El Paso in 1915," *Paseo del Norte*, Nov 1983, p 50–53.

33 Damon Ernest Lee Garbern, interviews by Anna L. Fahy, May 7, 1999 and May 28, 1999.

34 Carpenter; *El Paso Herald Post*, Feb 1, 1938, p. 5; Soo Hoo, Lily Love Chew.

35 Sonny Lew, residing in San Antonio, phone interview by Irwin Tang, Jun 11, 2004; Evangelina Wong de Arvizo, interview by Irwin Tang, El Paso, Texas, Mar 8, 2003.

★

CHAPTER THREE

THE ASIAN AMERICAN
UNDERGROUND RAILROAD

Irwin A. Tang

White politicians and unions led a series of anti-Asian American movements in the western United States in the latter half of the 1800s and the early 1900s. These movements spurred riots, massacres, and expulsions that resulted in the violent deaths of hundreds of Chinese Americans, Filipino Americans, Japanese Americans, and Indian Americans. Segregation and violence limited Asian Americans to certain occupations, residences, and marriages. Simultaneously, a series of federal bills outlawed the immigration of the vast majority of Asians (see Historical Overview). Ostensibly for the purpose of enforcing immigration, opium, and gambling laws, government officials systematically monitored, searched, punished, and deported Asian Texans, forcing much of their life underground, sometimes literally.

Radiating from California, anti-Chinese movements spread into Arizona and New Mexico. Naco, Arizona, a border town west of El Paso, had an "unwritten law" that "no wearer of the queue shall abide or be employed" in the town. When Chinese El Pasoan High Ling attempted in 1903 to work at a Naco hotel, locals cut off his queue and ran him out of town. In 1885, the "anti-Chinese faction" of Silver City, New Mexico attempted, through political means and economic boycott, to drive the town's Chinese residents away. In Texas, organized movements attempted to close Chinese laundries in various cities.[1]

Bolstering local racism was the federal Chinese Exclusion Act, enacted on May 6, 1882. Signed into law just one year after Chinese American rail workers built the Southern Pacific through El Paso, the law prohibited the vast majority of Chinese from immigrating to the United States. It also prohibited Chinese Americans from naturalizing as U.S. citizens. The Chinese Exclusion Act was the first U.S. law to outlaw a race or ethnic group from immigrating to the U.S., and many Americans considered the law plainly racist and unjust. The exclusion was based on race, not national citizenship; although most Mexicans were free to enter the U.S. before 1924, *Chinese* Mexicans, and even the mixed-race children they fathered in Mexico, were categorically excluded until the abolition of Exclusion in 1943.

After 1882, Chinese immigrants landing in San Francisco, their main port of entry, were forced by immigration officials to prove the legality of their immigration. Because the vast majority of Chinese did not qualify to immigrate, Chinese immigrants began landing by the thousands each year in Mexico and Canada. From these nations, they entered the United States overland, crossing from British Columbia into Washington State, or from Ontario to Buffalo, New York. Some jaunted from Tijuana, Mexico into San Diego, California. Many risked death by dehydration by crossing the Arizona desert to reach Phoenix or Tucson. Crossing the Rio Grande from Ciudad Juárez (in Mexico) into El Paso, Texas was a favored entry point into the United States. A passageway through the mountains ran through El Paso (hence its name). Located on the Mexican border, Chinese immigrants did not need to travel through miles of empty desert to reach a major city. They could blend in to a vibrant El Paso Chinatown. Being the largest railroad hub on the Mexican border, immigrants could hop on a box car to any region of the nation. And in the wild border town of El Paso, there were many who, for a fee or for free, helped the Chinese abridge the law. Those who abetted illegal Chinese immigrants were known, whatever their race, as "Chinese smugglers." Because federal laws prohibiting Japanese, Koreans, and

Indians from immigrating were enacted, those Asian ethnic groups also began immigrating through El Paso, albeit in much smaller numbers.

Some immigration officials compared the underground network of helpers, Asian organizations, and paid illegal smugglers to the "Underground Railroad" of the days of slavery. One immigration official wrote that "El Paso was the largest Chinese smuggling center on either border," and both local and national officials wrote similarly. By 1943, fifty thousand Chinese had entered the United States legally through the immigration station on Angel Island, off the coast of San Francisco. During the period of Exclusion (1882-1943), tens of thousands of Chinese likely entered the U.S. through El Paso, making it comparable to Angel Island. Many others stopped in El Paso to buy immigration papers, stay in a "safe house," or board a box car in their illegal journey through the states. These two entry points—Angel Island and El Paso—likely attracted different types of immigrants. Immigrants holding proper immigration papers (counterfeit or not) tended to enter through Angel Island, while those without such papers likely entered at El Paso. Further, a major portion of those entering at El Paso had lived in Mexico, or other parts of Latin America; some had been born in these places. Immigration officials often detained Chinese for weeks, months, or years at Angel Island to question them about their past and ensure their legality. While detained, immigrants earned no money for their families, so those seeking immediate work may have preferred the southern route.[2]

Hopping the border was a cakewalk in the early years, requiring only some vegetables. "The Law restricting Chinese immigration is a dead letter in El Paso, and, so far as we know, along the Mexican border," wrote *The Lone Star* newspaper of El Paso in 1885, "The celestial gardeners of Paso del Norte keep the residents of this city supplied with vegetables, crossing back and forth [from Mexico] daily without any restrictions whatever."[3] In February of that same year, the *Lone Star* had warned that El Paso's Chinese population "seems to increase as it rolls on," and that the Chinese might soon cross over the Mexican border in "herds and droves." Border guards were few and inconsistent in and around El Paso.[4]

The Mexican route only got busier after Canada strengthened its anti-Chinese immigration legislation. The Canadian campaign to tax and then stop Chinese immigration began in 1885 with a $50 head tax on all Chinese immigrants and eventually led to a law prohibiting Chinese immigration to Canada. By the late 1880s, patterns of covert entry into the El Paso area were well-established. In a spring 1890 report, the El Paso Custom-House's "Chinese Inspector," the person in charge of monitoring and controlling Chinese immigration, wrote that Chinese immigrants entering at El Paso or Nogales, Arizona boldly attempt to walk across the border, and when turned back, simply tried again when and where immigration officials were absent. Entry was easy, as the 960 miles from Presidio, Texas to Yuma, Arizona were guarded by only eight mounted customs inspectors and one mounted "Chinese inspector." Although Chinese easily crossed from the town of Juárez, Mexico into the El Paso area, the federal government in the 1880s and 1890s was more concerned about Chinese immigration from the province of Baja California, Mexico into the San Diego area. Intensified efforts in Southern California further funneled Chinese immigration through the El Paso region, helping make El Paso the most popular illegal entry point for Asian immigrants.[5]

In 1892, the federal government passed the Geary Act, requiring every Chinese American to carry a certificate of residence, proving they resided legally in the United States. Those without proper papers were deported to China. Although the Chinese Six Companies, a national Chinese American organization based in San Francisco, asked Chinese Americans to *not* register for certificates of residence, and although many Chinese American communities complied with this request, the *El Paso Herald* reported that "El Paso seems to be about the only exception where the Chinamen as a whole have registered." Days later, the Six Companies' test case went to trial, and the Geary Act was ruled constitutional. El Paso registered about 500 Chinese Americans in 1893 and about 450 the next year. Interestingly, though, in 1895, only 210 Chinese Americans were counted in the city directory. Another apparent halving of the Chinese El Pasoan community occurred between 1902 and 1905, when population estimates fell from 700 to 350. Such fluctuations in population counts were caused by different counting methods, but movements of large numbers of Chinese into and out of the city likely also played a a part.[6]

Deportation also played a role in population fluctuations. By July 1895, two years after the implementation of the Geary Act, the federal government had deported sixty Chinese El Pasoans, possibly 10% of the total permanent Chinese population. Government-organized harassment also made Chinese El Pasoans want to leave. In September 1893, city officials charged sixteen of the eighteen Chinese laundries with violating safety standards. This ostensible concern for safety occurred in a city which ignored every conceivable vice. In July 1895, federal agents rounded up, apparently, the entire Chinese population of El Paso. Among 500 Chinese, they discovered only two without certificates of residence. As a result of such harassment, the *El Paso Herald*, in its own racist manner sympathized with the Chinese:

> In El Paso the Chinese as a rule is a peaceable citizen, obeying laws as far as he can understand them and engaged in occupations which least compete with white labor. The withdrawal of this class of persons from our city would be a serious inconvenience, to say the least, to the comfort of our residents, and would for a while cause the expenses of living to be increased.[7]

Because El Paso was a stopping point for hundreds, or thousands, of immigrants each year, its Chinatown was an anomaly among American Chinatowns. As other Chinese communities in small cities depopulated and became neighborhoods of old men, El Paso's community received a constant stream of young men, and the population fluctuated both down and up. The heavy Chinese immigration to El Paso between 1890 and 1910, however, barely changed the size of the permanent Chinese population. This permanent population was substantially smaller than the total Chinese population at any given point. Thus, while population estimates were as high as 700, only between 200 to 300 Chinese felt comfortable answering the U.S. Census. The U.S. Census counted 312, 299, and 228, and 243 Chinese in El Paso in the years 1890, 1900, 1910, and 1916.[8]

The Asian American Underground Railroad

Chinese immigration into the United States, legal and illegal, had always relied on networks of family, fellow villagers, and friends. With the onset of Chinese Exclusion, that network incorporated underground commercial and non-commercial elements, which helped Chinese enter the United States safely and with immigration documents. Because of the intensifying enforcement of Exclusion in the 1890s and 1900s, the methods and routes of Chinese smuggling evolved into sophisticated systems and subcultures. When, in the first decade of the twentieth century, Japanese immigrants began utilizing Mexican routes to enter the United States both legally and illegally, and when some Korean and Indian immigrants followed this trail as well, these covert passages became a *multi-ethnic* Asian American underground railroad.[9]

Often the first (but sometimes the last) items an Asian immigrant secured on his attempt to enter the United States were immigration papers allowing him to reside or visit the nation. Authentic or counterfeit papers could be purchased in China, Mexico, Canada, or the United States. A young Chinese apprehended while crossing the border at El Paso on February 6, 1906 was asked about his history. He said that it was his first attempt to enter the United States, and that, "my father had procured me a section 6 certificate purporting to be traveling for curiosity in the United States." The certificate cost his father over a hundred dollars. His father was to be "the president of one of the societies," and he was to be his father's assistant.[10]

The long, crowded ship ride to the United States from Hong Kong or other Chinese ports often killed some of the passengers. The survivors usually saw their first glimpse of America at the port of San Francisco. But San Francisco Bay's Angel Island immigrant detention center was hardly beatific. Immigrants lived in a place compared to zoos and prisons for months or years before they were accepted or rejected. Although most were allowed to enter the United States, many were deported to China. Wang Zhongang, who came to El Paso in the early 1930s explained, "Instead of going to San Francisco, many Chinese went to Mexico. They thought it really worthy of trying their luck at the border rather than to tolerate the misery and humiliation at the Angel Island." Many long-time Chinese residents of the United States, after visiting China, preferred to return through Mexico. Immigration official Clifford Alan Perkins recalled:

> As a matter of practice, few Chinese who left the country [the United States] tried to qualify for reentry. If they had a fairly good stake here [in the U.S.] and wanted to go back to China for a visit, they just went. Legally, they could not return without a certificate of identification, so those who did come back shipped to Mexico and were smuggled into the country with the idea of making our government prove they had been away.[11]

To travel from San Francisco to Mexico, some Chinese rode a train with permission from the U.S. government, and most simply continued their steamship rides southward to Mexican cities like Enseñada, Mazatlán, Guáymas, and Manzanillo. From there, many Chinese traveled by rail to cities like Chihuahua, Torreón, and Mexico City, or they headed directly to Juárez. As one example of this phenomenon, the steamship Persia arrived at Manzanillo, Mexico on July 3, 1910 with 822 Chinese passengers. Within ten days, 155 new Chinese arrived by rail in Juárez; most held certificates of U.S. residence or affidavits stating that they were merchants—making them an exception to the exclusion law. While in Mexico, according to one U.S. immigration report, Chinese traveled within a "system of stations," most of which were called "restaurants," where both Chinese and non-Chinese helped them, for free or a fee, to reach the U.S. border.[12]

While in Mexico, Chinese and Japanese immigrants often entered education programs in which they learned both English and Spanish. These schools were located in Mexico City, Chihuahua, Tampico, Guáymas, and other cities. In Mexico City, H. Wah Lin's English school taught basic spoken English and American geography. The geography lessons helped immigrants find their way through the country and fool immigration officials who tested them on U.S. geography. In the early twentieth century, nine or so Japanese firms in Mexico produced false passports and bribed immigration officials. Letters from friends, family, or smugglers instructed Chinese immigrants on the routes, say, from El Paso to Tucson. Immigrants also sought American money, Chinese-English dictionaries, Chinese American newspapers, American railroad maps, specialized immigrant guidebooks, and fake immigration documents that were sometimes made in Mexico and even mailed through the El Paso post office.[13]

With their counterfeit papers, immigrants took on new identities, pretending to be born in cities like New Orleans or Chicago. Because the 1906 San Francisco earthquake destroyed tremendous numbers of government records kept on Chinese Americans and immigrants, many of the Chinese who crossed the border after 1906 claimed to be born in San Francisco. The Chinese immigrant sometimes memorized a widely-distributed chart describing San Francisco Chinatown, its history, and its geography. To prepare for questioning by immigration officials, the Chinese immigrant "would also memorize a complete description of the house where he supposedly had been born and an account of who his parents were, who the neighbors were, who lived upstairs and down, the school he attended, the names of his teachers, and the names of children he could claim to have played with." If the government attempted to deport an immigrant brought to the United States by the Chinese Six Companies, the organization sometimes helped the immigrant with bail, with delaying his trial, and with Americanizing himself. During deportation trials, "witnesses, including a few Anglos, would be brought in from San Francisco to swear he was the child born to Mr. and Mrs. So-and-So, who lived in the apartment next to them, and it would be almost impossible to disprove their stories."[14]

Chinese often waited in Juárez for weeks or months for their opportunity to cross into El Paso. In 1903, an American immigration inspector reported that 800 Chinese were in the town of Juárez; most of them planned to cross into El Paso, and several could be arrested everyday on the American side. In 1905 regional immigration chief T. F. Schmucker reported that "from 150 to 200 unemployed Chinese coolies are in the detention quarters of the smuggling firms in Juárez, at all times." Meanwhile, only forty-six Chinese lived and worked permanently in Juárez.[15]

Jon Juey Chong, who renamed himself Juan Chong, arrived in 1900 at Tampico, Tamaulipas on the northeast coast of Mexico. Shortly after arrival, he attempted to enter the United States and was turned back. Years later, Chong married Rebecca Rodriguez, the daughter of a rancher, and moved the family to Juárez. Juan Chong, embittered by his experience with U.S. immigration officials, remained a proud Mexican citizen the rest of his life even as many of his children and grandchildren immigrated legally to El Paso. Since the abolition of Exclusion, however, Juárez-El Paso has continued to serve as an alternate route for Asian immigration. Juan Chong's granddaughter, Dolores Lopez Chong (now of El Paso) grew up in Juárez in the 1950s and 1960s. She recalled a Chinese woman named Ampano who came from Asia to Juárez in 1960 and lived with Chong's family for a year and a half. She knitted quilts to pass the time. Eventually, a Chinese El Pasoan man agreed to marry her, and she moved to El Paso.[16]

In crossing the Rio Grande, the Chinese had options. One Chinese-owned operation charged immigrants twenty-five dollars to be smuggled across the Rio Grande east of El Paso and seventy-five dollars for crossing west of El Paso. Mexican smugglers offered guided crossings by boat, ferry, or swimming. Some immigrants simply walked across the international bridge and dealt with El Paso immigration officials. Asian immigrants often disguised themselves as non-Asian Mexicans. *The El Paso Daily Herald* in 1895 wrote that dressing in Mexican clothes was the favorite method of crossing the border, "as those [Chinese] who have resided in the sister republic [Mexico] for any length of time speak the language fluently." When Chinese dressed as Mexicans told immigration officials, "Yo soy Mexicano," the officials found it "exceedingly difficult" to distinguish them from native-born Mexicans. Chinese crossing the Canadian border sometimes dressed as Native Americans, and Chinese entering the South sometimes painted their faces black.[17]

Legend has it that in the early twentieth century Chinese reaching the northern bank of the Rio Grande had the option of crawling into a half-mile long tunnel that opened up into an underground compound in a building known as "The Turtle House" in El Paso. To this day, multiple tunnels of unknown origin lead into these underground quarters, which include a kitchen and three other rooms. The tunnels may have been utilized by immigrant Chinese men, Chinese women entering El Paso to meet prospective Chinese husbands, and Mexican revolutionaries.[18]

When a Chinese arrived in El Paso, help could be sought from any number of smuggling firms run by local Chinese. Regional immigration chief T. F. Schmucker reported in 1905 that "it is believed that the handling of Chinese [immigrants] is the sole occupation of perhaps one-third of the Chinese population of El Paso." Business owners and even some of the "mayors of Chinatown" provided jobs and housing, which included attics and underground rooms. Immigration officials of the early 1900s reported that underground tunnels, through which immigrants could evade officials, ran between Chinese-owned properties in El Paso. In recent decades, construction crews excavating downtown El Paso have discovered beneath old Chinese establishments underground rooms and tunnels leading between these rooms. A set of five "secret" underground bedrooms fitted with bunk beds and connected by passageways was discovered in 1909 in San Antonio. The sheriff and constable's "department on Chinese" arrested seven Chinese men apparently living in the rooms on gambling charges. Tunnels running between several Chinese-owned "shacks" were discovered in Tombstone, Arizona in 1907. In 1912, custom officials searched for opium in El Paso Chinatown homes. Wrote the *El Paso Herald*, "The raid was not relished by the Chinese denizens of the quarter, and several protested loudly at being interrupted in their work and their affairs pried into by the American officers. But the older Chinese, accustomed to these visits from the customs officers, submitted to the search of their premises and unlocked secret doors, hidden trunks and chests and showed where the passageways were to the underground chambers."[19]

During the 1920s, myths circulated Oklahoma City about an underground Chinese "city." In 1969, downtown construction crews there discovered beneath a Chinese property a set of living quarters for families and single men, an opium den, a temple, and a cemetery. An extensive network of underground bedrooms, casinos, and tunnels were actively used in the twentieth century by Chinese living in Mexicali, Mexico (south of San Diego), home of Mexico's largest Chinatown. For

Chinese living in the Southwest and Mexico, underground life may have increased privacy and security and helped them avoid immigration officials, police, and Mexican revolutionaries.[20]

Most American cities could be reached by riding box cars out of El Paso. Organized into commercial smuggling rings, white train conductors and Mexican and black rail workers guided Chinese immigrants into box cars parked in El Paso train yards. The Chinese would ride these cargo cars to their cities of destination. The cars were sometimes empty, sometimes locked, sometimes left open for ventilation, and sometimes loaded with cargo. As many as twenty-eight Chinese rode in a cargo car. Immigration authorities discovered north of El Paso in 1905 one box car holding thirteen Chinese men who were traveling with thirty-five gallons of water, a dozen canteens, bologna sausage, crackers, and other foods. Chinese also stowed away between the ceiling and roof of baggage cars, tool compartments, ice chambers of dining cars, and, dressed as Mexicans, in the comfort of passenger cars.[21]

The Chinese rode from El Paso to all regions of the nation. New York City laundrymen, upon visiting their wives and children in China, returned home through El Paso. Chinese rode to Texas cities, settling in their Chinese communities. One underground firm, run by Greek Americans, helped Chinese settle in Bay St. Louis, Mississippi. The busiest leg of the Asian American underground railroad ran back and forth between El Paso and Arizona, from where many travelers rode trains to California. A man named Choi King, detained by immigration officials while on board a ship to Mexico in 1901, held "addresses of a firm in El Paso, Tex., and a firm in San Francisco, also marked copy of New York Sun of Monday, April 2, 1900, containing death notice marked with Chinese characters." King probably planned on living in El Paso until he secured employment and legal status in San Francisco or New York.[22]

Crackdown on Asian Immigration

In 1902, President Theodore Roosevelt appointed Frank P. Sargent to head the Immigration Bureau; a friend of white organized labor, Sargent enforced the Chinese Exclusion laws with an iron fist. The new stringency required more deportations, making life for Chinese Americans even more difficult. In 1902, Lue Yom was arrested and ordered deported. According to the *El Paso Herald*, his wife and four children were "starving" in China and needed his income. He attempted suicide in his jail cell, but was stopped. He said he would kill himself before he reached China.[23]

Also in 1902, the Chinese Six Companies asked that each Chinese in America contribute one dollar to help prevent the renewal of the Chinese Exclusion Act. The Chinese of El Paso contributed about $1500, a sizable amount for the estimated 700 Chinese. Asked about the Six Companies' campaign to end exclusion, Lee Chee, the owner of the Baldwin Restaurant, replied with one of the few recorded statements of Chinese El Pasoans of that time:

> I guess the big companies ask the Chinamen to pay one dollar to help fight all right but I no hear of it yet. They want us to help them keep the law from passing. The companies will make big fight this time and they want lots of money to do it. The rich Chinese they give lots of money for this and the poor boys help all they can. I think the law bad and should not be any more. The Chinese come here and work hard and want to be left alone. The Chinaman always pays his bills and never like American want time and make trouble when asked to pay what they owe. Chinaman never try to make laws in this country and never want to take what is not theirs.[24]

The Six Companies' campaign failed, and Roosevelt signed a bill in 1902 making Chinese Exclusion permanent. Meanwhile, the Six Companies continued to help finance and organize the Asian American underground railroad.

In 1903, the Immigration Bureau began deporting Chinese who had lived in Mexico for more than a year back to Mexico, rather than placing them on a ship to China. This policy prevented Chinese Americans from securing free trips back to China by traveling into Mexico and then purposely getting caught crossing into the United States. In 1904, the Immigration Bureau tried to frustrate these deportees by taking pictures of all those deported and matching them with the faces of those returning to the United States through Mexico. Also in 1904, the Immigration Bureau established the Chinese Division within its organization and began stationing "spies" in cities throughout Mexico in order to count, photograph, and track Chinese men. The federal spying was bolstered by the 1903 policy of recording the physical measurements of Chinese Americans in order to prevent counterfeiting of residence certificates. Because in 1903, Canada, at the behest of the American government, increased the head tax on Chinese immigrants to $500 and because a new Chinese steamship line ran directly to Mexico, Chinese immigration across the Mexican border likely increased despite stringent new policies.[25]

In the first decade of the twentieth century, Immigration Bureau inspections of railroad cars increased tremendously. Nevertheless, inspectors could not or would not inspect every car of every train. In 1909, the federal government began giving cash rewards to Americans who captured Asians crossing the border. Also in the first decade of the century, the number of mounted border patrolmen increased to at least sixty. These "line riders" were dedicated to stopping Chinese immigrants and evolved into the modern U.S. Border Patrol. From 1907 to 1909, U.S. officials arrested 2,492 Chinese illegally crossing the Mexican border; the immigration service also recorded arrests of Japanese and Asian Indians crossing the border.[26]

Between 1900 and 1910, thousands of Japanese immigrants entered the United States via Mexico, Canada, and Hawaii. At one point, as many as 500 each month applied for entrance at the El Paso immigration office. Most of these Japanese were rejected, so many of them entered the U.S. illegally. Tokujiro Oyama in 1904 stowed away on a ship from Japan to Vera Cruz, Mexico. He survived the early years of the bloody Mexican Revolution, during which he lived in the mountains, surviving on bananas. In 1912, he crossed the border into Eagle Pass, Texas. He married in San Francisco, worked as a farm worker in San Pedro, California, and around 1920 made his way to the Rio Grande Valley in Texas, where he raised his family and spoke to his farm workers in fluent Spanish. Mitsuo Fujimoto remembered his father's story of being lost at sea for fifty-eight days after a typhoon hit his North American-bound boat. He landed in Mexico and lived in Guadalajara and studied law at the home of a millionaire Mexican attorney. During the Mexican Revolution, Fujimoto worked on the Mexican railroads and made his way to El Paso. Upon crossing the border, he worked at a nursery in Corpus Christi before working as an office manager for Harris County flood control.

In March 1907, President Theodore Roosevelt issued a decree prohibiting Japanese from immigrating to the United States through Mexico, Hawaii, or Canada, and in 1908, the government banned Japanese laborers from immigrating to the U.S.. The two policies severely curtailed Japanese immigration to Texas.[27]

Undercover operations both in the United States and Mexico yielded Chinese, white, and Mexican counterfeiters, river guides, smuggling railroad men, and smuggling chiefs. Even a former chief of police of El Paso was implicated as a Chinese smuggler. Raids on homes and businesses discouraged El Paso smuggling firms but did not stamp them out. According to Immigration Inspector Clifford Alan Perkins, one mayor of El Paso's Chinatown was a notorious Chinese smuggler. While the impeccably-dressed, cigar-smoking Charlie Sam represented the Chinese community at local events and made public donations to El Paso charities, he also quietly helped Chinese immigrate illegally. His smuggling business was no secret, but he never got caught in the act. Perkins often kidded Charlie Sam about how many immigrants he had helped enter El Paso, and Charlie Sam "never took offense." Upon retiring, Sam confessed his activities to Perkins. That day, Sam and Perkins drank "rice whiskey" in Charlie Sam's house and reminisced about the old days. Charlie Sam returned to China to live his final years.[28]

In 1908, after six years of intensified border patrols, a federal secret service agent investigating Japanese immigration from Mexico reported that Chinese and Japanese immigrants could still simply wade across the Rio Grande while guards were absent or not looking. Efforts at control tightened, and by 1910, all Chinese El Pasoans were required to check in with the immigration office before traveling inland into the United States. Beginning in 1910, the Mexican Revolution sent many Chinese across the border but also likely discouraged Chinese travel and immigration to Mexico. Chinese immigration from Mexico continued, however, likely spiked by such events as the Mexican government's expulsion of Chinese from Mexico in 1932 and the onset of World War II in China in 1937. Kong

Woo, a Chinese American native of San Antonio, described how in 1938 one of his paternal uncles crossed from Mexico into Laredo, Texas. The uncle arrived at the Woo family grocery in the bed of a pick-up truck. "They wheeled a pickle barrel in and he just popped out of the barrel."[29]

Regional Immigration Chief T.F. Schmucker wrote in 1905 that El Paso Chinatown was "banded together as one man" in helping their brethren settle in the United States.[30] Although Asian El Pasoans were breaking the law, the law they were breaking was both racist and unjust. Some broke the law to help family and friends. Some did so for money. Out of pride and out of shame, few Asian Americans admitted to crossing illegally from Mexico into the United States, and thus, although the story of the Asian American underground railroad constitutes a major chapter in Asian American history, much of this history has passed away with the passing of those who took and organized those underground routes. Some may remember the Asian immigrants of the underground railroad as the first "wetbacks" of America. But others see these Asian Americans as men, women, and children willing to break the law in order to re-unify with, and provide for, their families.

ENDNOTES

1 *El Paso Herald*, Aug 3 and Aug 7, 1903, p. 8 and p. 2; *Lone Star*, Nov. 28, Dec 2, Dec 5, and Dec 26, 1885 and Jan 6, 1886.

2 G.C. Wilmoth, district director of immigration and naturalization, El Paso, "Asiatic Labor Once Problem," *El Paso Herald Post*, May 28, 1936, A5; see also Daniel Keefe to Ng Poon Chew, July 25, 1910, located in folder 1, box 3, Ng Poon Chew Collection, Asian American Studies Library, University of California, Berkeley; Clifford Alan Perkins, *Border Patrol: With the U.S. Immigration Service on the Mexican Boundary 1910–1954* (El Paso: Texas Western Press, 1978); Ronald Takaki, *Strangers from a Different Shore*, (New York: Little, Brown, 1989, revised and

updated 1998), p. 238.

3 *Lone Star*, Aug 29, 1885, p. 2.

4 *Lone Star*, Feb 7, 1885, p. 3.

5 "Letter from the Secretary of the Treasury," U.S. Senate, 51st Congress, 1st Session, Ex. Doc. 97, Part 5, includes report from H.H. Schell, Chinese Inspector; Leon Metz, *Border: the U.S.-Mexico line*, (El Paso: Mangan Books, 1989) pages 364–365, citing U.S. immigration reports; see "Chinese Immigration," U.S. House of Representatives, 51st Congress, 2nd Session, Report No. 4048, March 2, 1891.

6 For "only exception" quote, see *El Paso Herald*, May 9, 1893, page 1, col. 4; on registration numbers, see *El Paso Evening News*, May 3, 1893; Cleofas Calleros, *El Paso Then and Now*, (El Paso, 1954), p. 51; Nancy Farrar, *The Chinese in El Paso* (El Paso: Texas Western Press, 1972), p. 44.

7 On deportations, see *El Paso Herald* Jul 22, 1895, p. 4, col. 2; Edward J.M. Rhoads, "The Chinese in Texas," *The Southwestern Historical Quarterly* 81 (July 1977), p. 17; on long quote, see *El Paso Herald*, Apr 5, 1893, p. 2, col. 1.

8 Farrar, 44.

9 For a mention of Hindu immigration through Mexico, see Erika Lee, *At America's Gates: Chinese Immigration During the Exclusion Era, 1882-1943*, (Chapel Hill: University of North Carolina Press, 2003), p. 82.

10 "Facts Concerning the Enforcement of the Chinese Exclusion Laws," U.S. House Doc 847, 59th Congress, 1st Session (Serial 4990), Compilation from the Records of the Bureau of Immigration (Washington: GPO 1906), pp. 54–55.

11 Zhao, Xuezhong, "Chinese Immigration and American Business Interest," Master's Thesis, University of Texas El Paso, Department of History, 1995, p. 46; Perkins, 8.

12 Metz, 365; Keefe to Ng, 3; "Facts Concerning ..." p. 83.

13 "Facts Concerning ..." p. 107; Zhao, 51, 54–55; Lee, p. 60.

14 "Facts Concerning ..." p. 9; Perkins, pp. 12–13.

15 *El Paso Herald*, Nov. 21, 1904, p. 1; Zhao, 54; *El Paso Herald*, Dec 16, 1905.

16 Socorro Chong de Coronado, and Maria Dolores Lopez Chong, interview by Irwin Tang, El Paso, Mar 9, 2003.

17 Zhao, 56, 41–64; *El Paso Daily Herald*, Jan. 15, 1895; Lee, 61–62, in regards to Braun, quoted by Lee, see footnote 19 on page 62.

18 *El Paso Herald-Post*, May 9, 1984.

19 David Romo, *Ringside Seat to a Revolution: An Underground Cultural History of El Paso and Juárez, 1893-1923* (El Paso: Cinco Puntos Press, 2005), p. 199.

20 *Annual Report of the Commissioner-General*, Bureau of Immigration, Washington, D.C., 1905, pp. 95–96; Fahy, p. 41; *San Antonio Light Sun*, Mar 14, 1909; *El Paso Herald*, Jan 17, 1907, p. 6; Alice Lee Marriott and Carol K. Rachlin, *Oklaho-*

ma: the forty sixth star (Garden City, New York: Doubleday & Co., Inc., 1973), pp. 123–125; William T. Vollmann, "They came out like ants!" *Harper's Magazine*, Oct 2004, pp. 47–60.

21 *El Paso Herald* Jan 9, 1909, p. 1; *El Paso Herald* Dec 8, 1906, p. 3;. *El Paso Herald*, Dec 8, 1906, p. 3; *El Paso Daily Herald* Jul 28, 1905, p. 1; also Nov 21, 1904, p. 1; *El Paso Herald*, Nov 27, 1911, p. 1; *El Paso Herald* Feb 28, 1912, p. 2; *El Paso Herald*, Jan. 30, 1906, p. 1.

22 *El Paso Herald* Jan. 9, 1909, p. 1; Lee, p. 62; also footnote 21 in Lee; Grace Delgado, "In the Age of Exclusion: Race, Region and Chinese Identity in the Making of the Arizona-Sonora Borderlands, 1863–1943," University of California at Los Angeles History Ph.D. dissertation (2000), pp. 205–225.; "Facts Concerning ..." p. 82.

23 Shih-Shan Henry Tsai, *The Chinese Experience in America* (Bloomington and Indianapolis: Indiana University Press, 1986), p. 76; *El Paso Herald*, Feb 9, 1902.

24 *El Paso Herald*, Feb 26, 1902.

25 *El Paso Herald*, July 24, 1903, p. 8; *El Paso Herald*, June 14, 1904, p. 1; *El Paso Herald*, Jan 20, 1904, p. 1; see also Lee, 81; *El Paso Herald*, March 18, 1903, p. 1; *El Paso Herald*, Oct 12, 1903, p. 1; *El Paso Herald*, Apr 7, 1903, p. 3.

26 *El Paso Herald*, Jan. 30, 1909; Zhao, p. 47; Lee, pp. 81–82.

27 *El Paso Herald*, Mar 22, 1907, p. 1; Mary Oyama Hada, phone interview by Irwin Tang, July 2003; Mitsuo Fujimoto, interview by Thomas K. Walls, Houston, Feb 27, 1979.

28 Lee, 63; Perkins, pp. 50–53.

29 *El Paso Herald*, Jan. 16, 1908; Ng Poon Chew to Daniel Keefe, on travel regulation, unknown when this policy started; Kong Woo, interview by Yvonne Lim and Irwin Tang, Jan 11, 2003.

30 *Annual Report of the Commissioner-General* (1905), pp. 95–96.

CHAPTER FOUR

★

THE EARLY JAPANESE TEXANS

Dr. Thomas K. Walls

In April 1902, Seito Saibara was sailing aboard the Japanese battle-ship *Takasago*, en route to London, England, to represent the Japanese government at the coronation of King Edward VII. Slender and distinguished-looking in his wire rim glasses, Saibara had just finished serving a four-year term in the Japanese House of Representatives as the representative of his home area around Kochi Prefecture on the island of Shikoku, one of the four main islands comprising Japan. Earlier, in 1877, at the age of 16, Saibara had attended the Risshisha English School in the capital city of Kochi. The school was run by a political group calling themselves *Risshisha*, or the *Free Thinkers Society*. This group opposed what they believed was an autocratic central government in Tokyo.[1]

Saibara continued his association with Risshisha's founder, Taisuke Itagaki, who in 1881 organized a political party called the Liberal Party. Saibara joined the group and followed Itagaki to Tokyo, where he attended Shigematsu Law School and was later admitted into the Japanese bar. He married, and at the age of 23 became a father when his wife Motoko gave birth to son Kiyoaki. Seito needed all of his legal skills in 1886 and 1887 when he was arrested for allegedly participating in a plot to assassinate the local prefecture governor. Saibara proved his innocence, but not before appearing before four separate courts in four cities. Confinement, trials, and travel left Saibara exhausted and in ill health. But upon his return to Kochi, he was greeted by his friends and associates as a true champion who stood up against what they saw as an unjust prefectural government.[2]

Over the next ten years Seito Saibara honed his political skills and became known as an eloquent and engaging public speaker. Prior to the first national election of the Japanese Diet in 1890, Saibara traveled from village to village in Kochi Prefecture, helping to educate the populace concerning the upcoming elections and the role of the people in a constitutional monarchy, which was to be Japan's new form of government. Later on, Saibara was called upon to travel around Japan to make speeches on behalf of the Liberal Party. From there it was but a short step for him to run for national office from his home prefecture, which Saibara did in 1898. He won in a landslide.

For the next four years Saibara served in the Japanese House of Representatives. In his spiritual life Saibara became a Christian, joining the Congregational Church. Christianity had few followers in Japan at the time, since most Japanese were active practitioners of the more traditional religions of Buddhism and Shinto. Still, it is not surprising that Saibara would be drawn to this foreign religion, much the same way he seemed drawn to other foreign ideas and customs. The church that he joined also operated a university in Kyoto, called Doshisha University. In 1899 Saibara became the fourth president of Doshisha and emerged within the Japanese Diet as a strong defender of the rights of the Christian minority in Japan.

Aboard the battleship *Takasago*, Saibara looked forward to attending the coronation of King Edward VII, but his final destination was Hartford Theological Seminary in Connecticut, where he planned to study theology. Why Saibara chose this path rather than continue his political career is uncertain. Perhaps he was tiring of the rough and tumble of Japanese politics. The death of his wife, Motoko, and his subsequent remarriage could certainly have been factors. Whatever the reasons, Saibara settled into his studies at Hartford in the 1902–1903 academic year. Some time during that period, Saibara became intrigued with the idea of leading a group of Japanese immigrants to farm rice in either Texas or California. Most Japanese immigrants favored the more accessible state of California, but with the completion of more and more railroad tracks crisscrossing the nation, Texas was suddenly within reach of any Japanese who could afford a ticket. Saibara obviously knew this, and in July 1903 began looking for employees for his rice colony, as demonstrated by this diary entry:

> July 8, 1903—Sent letters to hire helpers for my enterprise. Besides board, a helper will be paid 500 yen yearly and his wife will be paid 180 yen, while a laborer will be provided 1 yen and 50 sen [*100 sen equals one yen*] a day and board, etc. Wrote to Mr. Ogasawara if he were willing to come for $8.00 a month.[3]

Over the next five weeks Saibara wrote at least twenty more letters to arrange the immigration of potential colonists and explain his work to political colleagues. Saibara also asked his new wife, Taiko, to join him in Texas. When she responded in early August that she was willing to come, Saibara wrote in his diary, "I was very much relieved and felt that I attained more courage." But in the same entry Seito noted that his son, Kiyoaki, was entertaining thoughts of his own. Kiyoaki, eighteen at the time, dreamt of studying engineering in Japan in preparation for a career in the shipbuilding industry. Saibara, the father, asked his son to put aside his personal plans and come to Texas. Kiyoaki, the dutiful son, obeyed.[4]

By August 25th, 1903, Saibara arrived by steamship and train in Houston, where he was met by Japanese Consul General Sadatsuchi Uchida's friend, Oswald Wilson, and two Japanese gentlemen, Hosho Inoue and Kaname Inoue, who earlier that year had leased land near the Rio Grande in Del Rio in an attempt to grow rice. They hired local field hands, but the venture was unsuccessful. They were now in Houston raising money for another attempt. The only other Japanese rice farming venture in Texas at the time was led by Junzo Fujino and four colleagues. Together in 1903 they leased some ninety lowland acres along the Gulf near Port Lavaca, but when a dam broke and let salt water into their fields, the whole crop of rice was ruined. Consul General Uchida himself had encouraged Japanese rice cultivation in Texas after surveying Texas farmland in 1902 and writing a report that was well-publicized in Japan.[5]

Undeterred by previous failures, Saibara spent the next three weeks crisscrossing a ten-county region around Houston seeking out the perfect piece of land on which to establish his rice colony. At three weeks' end, Consul General Uchida joined Saibara in Houston. Saibara escorted Uchida to view land around the small town of Webster, which was well situated on a rail line halfway between the port of Galveston and Houston. Although he took Uchida to inspect property at numerous other locales, Saibara within two weeks purchased 304 acres near Webster, close to the railroad tracks.

Saibara's next step was to send for his family and the other colonists he had recruited. Helping him was Rihei Onishi, a Japanese journalist who had also come to Texas to farm rice. With Rihei was his cousin, Toraichi Onishi, a wealthy wine merchant who provided most of the financing for his and Rihei's venture. After Saibara purchased his land near Webster, the two cousins bought 300 acres of farmland nearby. Having secured the property, Rihei Onishi left for Japan to escort a group of fifteen immigrants back to Texas. Among that group were Saibara's wife and son and Rihei's own wife, Hisa, and his young daughter, May. The traveling party was met in San Francisco on January 20th, 1904 by Seito Saibara, who escorted the group back to their new home in Texas.

During the time that Rihei Onishi was gone, Saibara and Toraichi Onishi were busy preparing their respective properties for the colonists' arrival. With the help of Japanese immigrants already in the area, land was surveyed and fences erected. Saibara plowed a small field and planted green onions, leeks, horseradish, and several other vegetables used in Japanese cuisine. He also planted pear and fig trees. He bought mules and agricultural equipment and perhaps most importantly, drilled a 600-foot well on the Saibara property. A reliable source of water would be needed for irrigation throughout the rice cultivation process. Still, there was much more work to be done. A complex system of canals and side ditches needed to be constructed to deliver the well water to the fields, and the fields themselves needed to be cleared and plowed.

The enormity of the task confronting the colonists might have been overwhelming but for the expertise of the individuals that Saibara had recruited from Japan. Of particular value to the group was Tadao Yasui, who had worked at an agricultural experiment station on Hokkaido, the northernmost large island of Japan. There he had learned large-scale rice growing techniques using large machines, a somewhat novel method in Japan since rice there was typically grown on small plots. But on the large tracts of land available to farmers in southeastern Texas, machinery was needed to make rice growing a profitable affair.

In the United States the first large-scale efforts at farming rice occurred in the mid-1880s when wheat farmers from the Midwest brought their reapers and threshing machines to Louisiana. Their success led others to follow, and soon the cultivation of rice had spread westward into Texas, where it was noticed by men like Consul General Uchida and Seito Saibara. Experimentation with different strains of rice was common, including the introduction of several types from Japan. Rihei Onishi himself brought special seed rice to Texas when he returned with the colonists. Called *Shinriki*, or God Power, this strain of rice was known for its hearty nature. When it was planted in the rich soil around Webster, it also proved to be exceptionally prolific. That first year, the Saibara and Onishi farms yielded two to three times the amount of rice per acre typically grown on other farms in the area. So successful was the harvest that the local milling company sold the rice to area farmers as seed rice for the following year.[6]

Shinriki rice was not the only thing the Saibara and Onishi colonists brought with them from Japan. When working the fields, a few of the new immigrants, at least in the early years of the colony, sported large-brimmed conical shaped hats that were common in Japan at the time. These hats were made from rice straw, as were the sandals that were preferred by many of the workers. The Saibara and Onishi colonists also grew and ate some of the same vegetables, beans, and legumes they had in Japan. When Seito Saibara's father, Masuya Saibara, came to Texas to live in 1907, he brought with him equipment to process soybeans, a common ingredient in Japanese food.

The Saibara and Onishi families and other Japanese immigrants to Texas also brought with them many traditional values and beliefs. Kiyo-aki Saibara's desire to please his father by joining him in Texas reflected the strong bond between a patriarch and his son. Matrimony was also important. But as with many migrations, men were disproportionately represented. To deal with this gender imbalance, a "picture bride" system developed in which single women in Japan and immigrant Japanese men would exchange photographs. Once each prospective spouse had approved the other, a marriage ceremony would be held in Japan with only the bride in attendance. After signing the appropriate documents, the new bride would travel to America to meet her new husband.

Although himself married, Rihei Onishi in 1909 helped his rice colony's single men by traveling to Japan to escort at least three picture brides and four or five other Japanese women back to Texas. But when they reached San Francisco, the authorities turned the women away. Not to be deterred in his mission, Onishi took his female charges by ship to Mexico and then overland to Eagle Pass, Texas, where they successfully entered the United States.

In this manner the number of Japanese in Texas slowly increased, with a total of 340 being counted by the 1910 census. Having husbands, wives and children together also made for a more stable settlement and increased the odds of a colony's success. The lack of such families contributed to the instability of some Japanese rice farming projects in the area. Dissension among workers, inexperience with large-scale farming equipment, and simple bad luck were other problems. Despite the difficulties, at least thirty Texas rice farming ventures were attempted by Japanese within six years of Consul General Uchida's first visit to the state. Near the Saibara and Onishi colonies was a 300-acre farm financed by Shotaro Nishimura, a wealthy tea merchant from Yokohama who had been living in Canada before moving to Texas. A smaller farm of 160 acres near the town of Garwood, about 75 miles west of Houston, was operated by Junzo Hashimoto, who was Consul General Uchida's brother-in-law. The 20-year old Hashimoto initially employed local workers to farm his rice. Later, he leased 500 acres of land near Bay City in Matagorda County with two Japanese partners and hired four Japa-

Kiyoaki Saibara (front) and two workers in the rice fields in 1906. The shorter worker is a boy, and the shallow canal in the center is filled with water.

Kiyoaki Saibara (far left) and friends in the early 20th century.

nese immigrants to help in the fields. By all accounts Hashimoto's first harvests, like those of the Saibara colony, were bumper crops.

Another young Japanese who was attracted to Texas was Shinpei Maekawa (also spelled Mykawa). In 1904 he was an official delegate to the Louisiana Purchase Centennial Exposition held in St. Louis. On Maekawa's return trip to Japan he traveled through Houston, almost certainly stopping at the Saibara colony for a tour. In 1906, Maekawa returned to Texas with five other young investors. Together they paid a down payment on 520 acres of land near the small railway station at Erin, just south of Houston. Assisting them in their enterprise was Garret A. Dobbin, a colonization agent for the railroad who had befriended the group. Dobbin recommended which piece of land to buy and even helped with the purchase of farm equipment and supplies. The project was moving forward until Maekawa was crushed and killed beneath a piece of his own farm machinery. In memory of the young man, Dobbin arranged for the railway station at Erin to be renamed Mykawa Station. Although the station is no longer there, the railroad tracks remain, and the road that parallels the tracks is a major road in far south Houston called Mykawa Road.[7]

In 1905 after Japan defeated the Russian military in the Russo-Japanese war, the two nations signed the Treaty of Portsmouth, which gave Japan greater control over both Manchuria and Korea. After thousands of Japanese soldiers were discharged from duty, many of them traveled to North America. Upon arrival, unsympathetic immigration officials turned away Japanese who had little or no money on the grounds they were "likely to become public charges." Those denied entry at San Francisco often entered the United States through Mexico or Canada, but by March 1907, this type of immigration, which often went through El Paso, was officially outlawed by President Theodore Roosevelt. The *El Paso Herald* estimated that the new rule would prevent some 500 Japanese a month from coming to the U. S. via El Paso. Further, working class whites resented that former Japanese railroad workers in Mexico were being recruited to work on rails in Sacramento and Seattle. When anti-Japanese sentiment in San Francisco peaked in 1906–1907 over the issue of Japanese children attending grammar school with white children, a compromise between Washington, D.C. and Tokyo was reached which resulted in Japan agreeing to stop issuing passports to "laborers" traveling to the United States. Although this was a significant restriction, this "Gentlemen's Agreement," not only gave Japanese children in San Francisco the right to attend local schools, but more importantly allowed for continued immigration of Japanese businessmen, students, and relatives of Japanese already in the United States.[8]

A majority of Texans at this time remained relatively positive toward the Japanese in Texas. This was in part because the Japanese were viewed not so much as competitors, but as economic allies in developing the farm economy to the benefit of all Texans. Many Japanese rice farms were actually creating jobs for non-Japanese workers rather than competing with them for scarce work. They were also investing considerable sums of money in the local economy by leasing or buying land and by purchasing expensive farming equipment. It probably helped too that some of the Japanese immigrants, like the Saibara family, were converts to Christianity who attended church regularly. Also, men like Seito Saibara were very serious about establishing permanent settlements in Texas. Saibara had even applied for naturalization papers to become an American citizen shortly after arriving in Texas. Although his application was denied because of the 1790 naturalization law allowing only "free white men" citizenship, Saibara was unwavering in his efforts to be accepted into the larger community. Such an attitude was no doubt instrumental in convincing Texans that the presence of Japanese immigrants in the state actually enhanced their quality of life rather than threatened it, as so many on the West Coast believed.[9]

The connection between Japanese immigration and local economic development was clearly evident, at least for a short time, near the town of Dacosta, a small community situated between Victoria and Port Lavaca. In 1906 two Japanese men created the Nippon Farming Company and invested $155,000 in a 5,200-acre farm they named "Deepwater." Pump stations and canals for irrigation were already located on the property, as were warehouses, a barracks and a two-story house. The two partners, S. Kurabayashi and Major Oshimaru Takayama, hired 27 Japanese men to work 500 acres of the land, and leased 2,000 additional acres to local farmers. Takayama, a former artillery officer, had recently been released from the Japanese army following the 1904–1905 war with Russia. He and Kurabayashi attracted local attention by attempting to grow rice using traditional, labor-intensive techniques taken from Japan. Because they wanted their harvest to be of such high quality that it could be used as seed rice, they carefully transplanted their rice seedlings by hand instead of using a mechanical drill. A friendly rivalry even developed between the local American and Japanese farmers as to who could produce the highest yield.[10]

As different as their farming techniques were, so too were some of the Japanese customs these immigrants brought to Deepwater. Of particular note was the refusal of the Japanese to bathe in the shallow, galvanized metal tubs that were provided at the local hotel where many of them lived. They insisted instead on using deep wooden tubs that were common in Japan. More curious still, at least to the local people, was their daily habit of thoroughly washing themselves prior to sitting in the tub, which was filled with steaming hot water. Such frequent bath taking was so unusual in Texas at the time that some speculated it must be part of an exotic religious ritual, rather than the more mundane but accurate explanation that the Japanese were enjoying a relaxing hot soak after a hard day in the fields.

Despite Takayama and Kurabayashi's hard work, less than three years after they established the Nippon Farming Company at Deepwater, the company went bankrupt. A bad growing season in 1907 led to unpaid bills for the fuel that was necessary to run the irrigation pumps. When the oil company demanded payment of the colonists, they were forced to liquidate their holdings, taking an estimated loss of $100,000.

The spectacular failure of the Deepwater colony stands in contrast to a rice farming venture further east in Orange County around the small town of Terry, near Beaumont. This colony's founder, Kichimatsu Kishi, was the son of a well-to-do banker and businessman. He attended college at the prestigious Hitotsubashi University in Tokyo, where he studied business. During the Russo-Japanese War, he won the Japanese Order of the Kite for his service as a military quartermaster in Manchuria. After the war, Kishi left the army. He considered farming in Manchuria, but land prices there were nearly as high as in Japan. He had heard that land was cheap and plentiful in the United States, so in 1906 he obtained financial backing from business associates of his father and surveyed land in California, Texas, Louisiana (where the state's alien land law deterred him), Mississippi, and the Carolinas. In the center of Orange County, near the border with Louisiana, was a piece of flat prairie land with a nearby water source. It was here that Kishi would fulfill what his son, Taro, would later describe as his father's "natural urge to own land."[11]

In 1907 Kishi returned to Texas to buy the 3,500 acres of property he had inspected earlier. Traveling with him were sixteen Japanese men to help work the land, along with his wife, Fuji, and his four-year-old son, Taro. As their train neared Houston, Taro was badly burned when hot water from a small portable stove accidentally spilled on his legs. In Houston Kichimatsu Kishi sought medical attention for his son, who was treated by Dr. Eskridge, a woman physician who took an immediate interest in Taro and the family. When she noticed that Taro was small for his age and was in generally poor health, she recommended for him a diet with more vitamins and protein. In the ensuing years Dr. Eskridge and her husband visited the Kishi colony frequently, and when Taro was older, they invited him to live with them in their Houston home while he attended grammar school. By the time Taro became one of the first Asian American students to attend Texas A&M University, the doctor's care had worked wonders. A fit and fast Taro majored in agricultural administration, and as a running back for the football team helped the Aggies win the 1925 Southwest Conference Championship during his senior year.[12]

Taro had come a long way since the Kishis first arrived in Terry in 1907. The son of Sataro Kondo, who was one of the original sixteen men to make the journey with Kichimatsu Kishi, recalled stories his father told about that first year in Terry:

> They plowed all winter long. They used a single blade sulky plow pulled by three mules or a two blade gang plow with four mules. The drill and binder too were pulled by mules.[13]

The Kishi family with servant. Front row, left to right: Toki, Fuji, Kichimatsu, Moto (wife of Hachitaro) and Taro. Back row: a maid, Hachitaro, Tora, and a cousin.

Rae Sayoko Jingu poses with fan and umbrella at the Japanese Tea Garden in San Antonio. This photo was taken before World War II, when the Jingus still lived in the Garden.

That winter the men also dug irrigation canals with a steam-powered dredging machine and constructed levees to hold in the water. The following spring they planted a total of 1,600 acres and were rewarded at harvest time with nearly 16,000 sacks of rice, each one weighing 200 pounds. Although most of the men were working individual tracts of land as tenant farmers or sharecroppers, they came together at harvest time to help one another. The success of the first harvest led to a quick doubling in size of the colony population the following year. Most of those who came were from Niigata Prefecture, the area from which the initial immigrants had originated. Included in the new arrivals the next year were four women and three children, as well as Kichimatsu's younger brother, Hachitaro Kishi. In 1911 Sataro Kondo was joined by his wife Fumi and their three children. At least five picture brides would also come to Terry, Texas, making the colony more and more a family affair.

More children were born at the rice colony. One observer in 1924 noted that there were twenty-seven Japanese children in Terry. As the colony grew, so did its needs. Terry had a schoolhouse where Japanese studied side by side with children of the other workers in the area, many of whom were of Louisiana French and Mexican descent. Because the small community lacked a church, Kishi donated three acres of land and helped build a small chapel, where all were welcome to worship. Like Seito Saibara in Webster, Kichimatsu Kishi was a Christian and wanted to provide his fellow colonists with an opportunity to learn more about his adopted religion. Kishi even paid one-half the salary of the Methodist minister who came every Sunday to preach, and he also taught Sunday school to the children. Upon request, he helped the county home demonstration agent, Susie Thompson, form an agricultural club for the Japanese boys and girls in the community. During meetings every other Saturday the club members not only learned practical skills such as sewing, gardening, and food canning, they were also taught basic civics lessons and American history. Such efforts at "Americanization" were ultimately quite successful in assimilating the children of the colonists into the wider community. Years after the colony ceased as a viable enterprise, those children and their descendants were still found scattered throughout the state, working, living and playing alongside their fellow Texans.[14]

As the Kishi colonists grew in number, Kichimatsu Kishi increased his land holdings from 3,500 acres in 1907 to a total of around 10,000 acres by 1927. During those twenty years the Kishi colony went through many other changes, the greatest of which occurred in 1916 when the nearby ship channel to Orange was straightened and dredged. The operation allowed salt water to invade the inland waterways used by the colony for irrigation. Two years in a row, brackish water destroyed the rice fields when water was pumped in. At a time when rice prices were soaring due to the disruption in food production brought about by World War I, the Kishi colonists were forced to switch to crops requiring less irrigation. Soon, much of the land around Terry was planted with vegetables, including cabbage, potatoes, cucumbers, spinach, celery, tomatoes, lettuce, carrots and beets.[15]

Following the end of World War I in 1918 the supply of food staples increased dramatically. The price of rice dropped, severely cutting revenues for Texas rice farms. Fortunately the Kishi colony's earlier diversification into other crops enabled them to prosper even as other Japanese farming efforts in Texas struggled. The Saibara colony in Webster branched out into cotton and oranges in response to the market change, yet their efforts brought limited success. Heavily in debt and faced with low rice prices, Rihei Onishi sold his acreage near Mackay, Texas, causing his workers to disperse to other farms, including Kishi's. A few of his colonists found work in nearby plant nurseries that fellow Japanese Texans were developing, but many others simply moved away. Rihei Onishi himself returned to Japan in 1920 to continue his journalism career. That same year the U.S. Census counted 449 Japanese living in Texas, an increase of only 109 from ten years earlier.

The small Japanese Texan population owned large farms. The 1910 Census showed that Japanese Texans owned 15,735 acres of farmland, an amount greater than the Japanese owned in any other state except California. Furthermore, Japanese Texan farms were an average of 357.6 acres—making them by far the largest Japanese American farms in the nation. Japanese Texans owned 7.7% of the farm land in Orange County—again, by far the largest percentage in any county in the nation. The Japanese Texans were far more of a rural population than the highly urbanized Chinese, who owned in 1910 only 163 acres of farmland. While the 1910 Census counted between 36 and 40 Japanese each in Orange, Galveston, and Dallas counties, they numbered 92 in Harris County, where they farmed over 3,500 acres. In addition to agriculture, the early Japanese also ran various businesses in Texas cities, from nurseries to restaurants.[16]

Japanese began settling in El Paso as early as the 1880s. The number of Japanese there likely fluctuated upwards in the first decades of the 20th century due to increased Japanese immigration from and through Mexico; Japanese immigrating during and after the Russo-Japanese War (1904–1905); and Japanese escaping from the Mexican Revolution (1910–1920) by entering Texas. In 1916, a special war-time El Paso census showed that the Japanese population there had increased from 14 in 1910 to 41. In the early 1920s, Japanese began purchasing large tracts of farmland on the outskirts of El Paso. The Japanese in El Paso numbered 150 by 1921, but their numbers dwindled to 34 by 1941 in large part due to the sudden spillover of anti-Japanese sentiment from the West Coast.[17]

In 1920, California passed strict legislation prohibiting Japanese immigrants from owning land in the state. Central in this effort was the American Legion, an organization of military veterans that had long been at the forefront of anti-Japanese activity. Reacting to Japanese purchases of land near El Paso, and also to the arrival in Texas, beginning in 1920, of small groups of Japanese from the West Coast seeking a friendlier political climate, American Legion leaders called on Texans to discourage Japanese from migrating to the state. In January 1921 vigilante action surfaced when a small group of Japanese consisting of two men, two women and two children arrived at the Harlingen railway station in the Rio Grande Valley. A newspaper story described how they were met by a "committee of citizens" who informed them that "their presence was undesirable in Harlingen" and that "they could remain over night, but were 'expected to leave' Thursday." A similar "welcoming committee" had accosted a Japanese immigrant family earlier that week, giving them the message that they should "move on."[18]

The American Legion in Texas then sought a statewide "alien land law" similar to the one recently enacted in California. Their efforts led

Senator Richard M. Dudley of El Paso to introduce a bill in the Texas Legislature prohibiting land ownership by resident aliens who were not qualified to become citizens. Because Japanese immigrants were barred from U.S. citizenship, the bill would effectively keep them from buying land. In Senate hearings before the Committee on State Affairs in 1921, the American Legion and representatives of the Japanese Texan community locked horns. Herbert Davenport of Brownsville testified to the committee that the American Legion supported the legislation and that, "We were there first and we propose to keep our Valley for Americans and not for Japanese." Proponents of the bill argued that the Japanese were "unassimilable" and could never become part of the larger "white" community.[19]

The Japanese already residing in Texas would not give up without a fight. Calling themselves the Japanese Association of Texas, Japanese rice farmers in southeast Texas and Japanese businessmen from Dallas cotton firms banded together and hired several attorneys. These lobbyists appeared before the Senate committee and presented written briefs as well as letters of support from white neighbors of Japanese immigrants already living in the Rio Grande Valley. Also present was Saburo Arai, a respected Japanese businessman and owner of a large nursery in Harris County. As Arai stood before the committee and assembled audience in the Senate chamber, he spoke about how the alien land bill would be seen as an affront to all Japanese and how that fact could harm the cotton business in Texas, since Japan purchased one million bales of cotton each year from growers in the state. Senators asked about "picture brides" and how they were chosen. Arai described the practice and went on to explain how this method of matrimony was a natural fit with traditional, Japanese-style courtship. When asked, he assured the committee that the brides were not sent by the Japanese government and that in any case the practice had already been halted. Arai told his own story of how he had come to Texas in 1904 to farm rice and how he had applied for U.S. citizenship, only to be turned down because the law did not permit it. Arai submitted a written statement summarizing his feelings and the feelings of those he represented[20]:

I am here to work, to live and to die. I have a wife and children. My money is all invested in real property. I have hopes for the future; so have the members of my family. But should this bill pass what a blow it will be to us. The means of agricultural expansion will forever be closed to me.[21]

After the hearings, *The Dallas Morning News* was quick to editorialize against the alien land bill by commenting that "even if there is any need of this legislation, there is certainly no urgent need of it." When the Texas House of Representatives later took up the bill, Representative Pope of Nueces County easily amended the measure to exclude from its provisions "bona fide inhabitants of this State on the date this act becomes law." This "grandfather clause" allowed Japanese immigrants currently living in Texas to keep their land, and equally important, it preserved their right to purchase additional land in the future. Although watered down, the bill was supported by the American Legion and Senator Dudley, who knew that stricter legislation simply would not pass. And even though the Japanese Texans opposed the restrictions on land ownership, they could at least be pleased that their collective voice had been heard and their individual interests protected.[22]

Without any prospect of owning or leasing land, few Japanese newcomers would now be attracted to the state. The final blow, however, came in 1924, when the United States Congress passed the Johnson-Reed Act halting any further immigration of Japanese into the country. This law was incredibly devastating to the Texas Japanese who had worked so long and hard to prepare the way for others. Seito Saibara was so disappointed that he and his wife resettled in Brazil, where they farmed rice and established another Japanese colony. He did return to Texas in 1937, but only to be with his son and family after his health had begun to fail. Seito Saibara died two years later at the age of 78, and was buried in a family plot near Webster.[23]

In addition to the Japanese farms around Webster, Terry, and El Paso, Japanese immigrants also established many farms on a seventy-mile stretch of farmland north of the Rio Grande between Brownsville and McAllen. When the railroads were established in the Rio Grande Valley in the early 1900s, the opportunities for irrigated agriculture must have seemed limitless. The first Japanese to settle there came around 1909. Some had already worked in rice colonies, while others such as Uichi Shimotsu came from outside the state. Shimotsu was a student at the State Agricultural College in Ft. Collins, Colorado when a professor told him how land development companies were turning south Texas brush land into productive farmland by means of irrigation. So upon graduation in 1909 Shimotsu moved to the outskirts of McAllen, Texas, and began farming. He traveled to Japan in 1916 and returned with a wife, Takako, who would later tell their children what an adventure it was to journey to the Rio Grande Valley. Being a border area it naturally had its share of lawlessness, and the system of roads was underdeveloped. For the young bride, "It was like going into darkest Africa!"[24]

Nonetheless, the opportunity to work and raise a family was a powerful attraction for anyone with a pioneer spirit. Uichi Shimotsu felt obligated to assist other Japanese drawn to the Valley, including Saburo Kitamura, a Californian who, in 1920, was disturbed by that state's recent racial incidents and its newly-passed alien land law. After reading in a Japanese language newspaper about Shimotsu's success in raising cantaloupes in the Texas Valley, Saburo wrote to Uichi, who encouraged him to leave California. On New Years Day, 1921, at the same time the American Legion was meeting other Japanese at other rail stations in the Valley, Saburo, his wife and their four-year old son arrived on the Shimotsus' doorstep. Uichi and his family welcomed the Kitamuras into their farm home and later helped them find a place of their own. In this way, one family at a time, Japanese immigrants increased their presence in south Texas. But rather than congregating in a colony, they dispersed along the length of the wide river valley, making good use of irrigation waters provided by the Rio Grande.[25]

One exception to the pattern of scattered settlements in the Valley was a 1917 colonization effort by seven Japanese near Brownsville. Together they purchased 700 acres of farmland to grow sugar. Although the sugar grew well, the same post-World War I depression in the commodities market that drove down the price of rice also sunk the price of sugar. By 1921 the colony had disbanded, but at least one couple, Minoru and Toku Kawahata, stayed in the area to continue farming. The Kawahatas had originally come to Texas in 1917 from Santa Fe, New Mexico, where they had operated a restaurant. By 1924 they were growing crops on 1,000 acres of land next to the Rio Grande, and by 1926 they had opened a packing and shipping business to handle their produce and that of their Japanese neighbors. These successes were followed in quick succession by a hailstorm in 1929 that destroyed much of their crops and by the stock market crash in the same year. To make matters worse, Minoru Kawahata suffered an extended illness and was unable to run the farm for four years. The family lost its packing and shipping business and by 1933 was farming less than 40 acres of land. Despite these setbacks the Kawahata family persevered. Like most farmers in the Valley, they suffered considerably from the Great Depression during the 1930s. But as long as they could grow food for themselves, they were in better shape than many others.[26]

From 1930 to 1940 the population of Japanese in Texas decreased from 519 to 458. The Great Depression was clearly a factor in this decrease, but so too were the long-term effects of the alien land law and the exclusionary immigration laws. Through all this the Japanese who had made Texas their home continued to live, work and play, much the same as other ethnic groups in Texas at the time. But all this changed dramatically for them when even greater forces brought about World War II, a devastating struggle between the homeland these immigrants had left and the homeland they had adopted—the birthplace of their Japanese Texan children.

ENDNOTES

1 Kiyoko T. Kurosawa, "Seito Saibara's Diary of Planting a Japanese Colony in Texas," *Hitotsubashi Journal of Social Studies* 2, no. 1 (1964): 54–55.

2 Kurosawa, 56.

3 Kurosawa, 68–69.

4 Kurosawa, 69; Nelson Antosh, "Son Obeyed Japanese Father's Wish in 1904," *Houston Chronicle*, Feb 5, 1967.

5 Kiyoshi K. Kawakami, "Japanese on American Farms," *The Independent*, October 26, 1905, 963.

6 Thomas K. Walls, *The Japanese Texans*, San Antonio, TX: The University of Texas Institute of Texan Cultures at San Antonio, 1987, 53–54.

7 Walls, 59–61.

8 *El Paso Herald*, "Turning Back Japs in Large Numbers," Dec 27, 1906.
   El Paso Herald, "Japs Are Turned Back from Border; Sweeping Order to Take Effect," Mar 22, 1907.

9 Kawakami, 964; Kurosawa, 74.

10 George S. Bruce, "Japanese Colony in Texas," *Farm and Ranch*, Aug 25, 1906.

11 Gwendolyn Wingate, "The Kishi Colony," in *The Folklore of Texan Cultures*, ed. Francis Edward Abernethy, 327–337 (Austin, TX: The Encino Press, 1974).

12 Taro Kishi, interview by Thomas K. Walls, May 16, 1979, tape recording, The Institute of Texan Cultures, San Antonio, TX.

13 Wingate, 18.

14 S.C. Hoyle, "How Orange County Solved the Jap Question," *Farm and Ranch*, May 17, 1924.

15 Lillie Mae Tomlinson, "The Japanese Colony in Orange County," *Texas History Teachers' Bulletin*, Dec 1927: 143.

16 United States Census, 1910, "Bulletin 127: Chinese and Japanese in the United States," (Washington: GPO, 1914).

17 David Romo, *Ringside Seat to a Revolution* (El Paso, Texas: Cinco Punto Press, 2005): 201–202.

18 *El Paso Herald*, "Japanese Threaten El Paso Valley, Asserts This Man," July 20, 1920; *Austin American Statesman*, "Jap Colonists Warned Away from Harlingen," Jan 6, 1921.

19 *San Antonio Express*, "Texas Japanese in Rice Belt Protest Alien Land Bill; Rio Grande Valley Send Men from Legion," Feb 4, 1921.

20 *San Antonio Express*, "Texas Japanese Plan Fight on Exclusion Act; Confer in Ft. Worth," Jan 11, 1921; *Dallas Morning News*, "Alien Exclusion Bill Reported Favorably," Feb 11, 1921; *San Antonio Express*, "Texas Jap Argues Against Exclusion," Feb 6, 1921.

21 *Dallas Morning News*, "Alien Land Bill Causes Agitation; Many Reasons Given," Feb 6, 1921.

22 *Dallas Morning News*, "Premature and Perhaps Superfluous," Feb 7, 1921.
San Antonio Express, "Pope Bill to Bar Japanese from Texas Lands Passes; Present Ownership by Orientals Not Involved," Mar 10, 1921.

23 *Dallas Morning News*, "Seito Saibara, Jap Colonizer in Texas, Dies," Apr 12, 1939.

24 Walls, 107.

25 George and Tonia Kitamura, interview by Thomas K. Walls, May 14, 1979, tape recording, The Institute of Texan Cultures, San Antonio, TX.

26 Henry Kawahata, interview by Thomas K. Walls, May 13, 1979, tape recording, The Institute of Texan Cultures, San Antonio, TX.

CHAPTER FIVE

THE SAN ANTONIO CHINESE COMMUNITY, 1880–1949

Irwin A. Tang and Yvonne Lim

Four Chinese lived in San Antonio in 1877. Sam Choi ran one of the three Chinese-owned laundries in San Antonio during these early years. Choi married a German woman and may have been the first Chinese to serve on a jury in Texas. In 1883, the second transcontinental railroad, which ran through San Antonio, was completed, and the 1883–1884 city directory listed twelve Chinese-owned laundries. For the next decade, the Chinese owned a majority of the city's laundries, and by 1893, they ran many of the city's restaurants, the directory listing ten Chinese-owned restaurants. In these early decades, they also ran shops selling Chinese curiosities and grew and peddled vegetables.[1]

Chinese San Antonioan Ching Ah Kow apparently grew wealthy running a Chinese bazaar. Ching told the *San Francisco Examiner*, "I was admitted as a member of the Social club and became extensively acquainted." He then ran away with orphan Annie Freese, whose guardian opposed her being courted by Ching. The couple married and returned to San Antonio, where Annie Freese revealed to her husband her 1000 acres of land. The couple raised cattle and bought 5,000 more acres, making Ching "the Chinese Cattle King." After giving birth to two daughters, the couple visited Ching's father in China, and upon their return in 1888, Ching said that he had come back to look after his business and "to become a white man, or as nearly pass." Asked how San Antonio whites treated him, he said, "Things are all right now—you see, I have money, and that makes a difference."[2]

Indeed, the common Chinese were harassed over immigration issues, opium, and gambling. In a 1909 San Antonio newspaper article about Chinese arrested for gambling, they were openly referred to as "Chinks." While Chinese Texans often endured such indignities, the Chinese in Mexico suffered much greater political and social persecution. Resented for their economic successes as owners of stores and factories, Chinese men, including the poor, were persecuted during the early decades of the twentieth century through the combined efforts of Mexican politicians, writers, and revolutionaries. To raise the ire of common Mexicans, Chinese men "were stereotyped as filthy, disease-ridden, money-grubbing, parasitic, and sexually threatening."[3]

When the Mexican Revolution began in 1910, fewer than 40,000 Chinese lived in Mexico, many concentrated in the northern provinces of Sonora and Chihuahua. In May 1911, Mexican revolutionaries killed over 300 Chinese in the Mexican city of Torreón. Chinese Mexicans were thus alerted to their likely fate at the hands of revolutionaries. Little is written in English concerning the origin of Mexican revolutionary Pancho Villa's hatred of Chinese. While it fit within the revolution's anti-foreigner thrust, one *San Antonio Express* reporter learned of another possible reason. The Mexican government organized a company of Chinese Mexican soldiers in Chihuahua City, northwest of Torreón. The Chinese likely joined the *federalistas* in response to the Torreón massacre:

The Chinese proved apt scholars in this grim art of war and in a month they were ready to fight, as fighting goes in Mexico. So one fine day, when the Villista commissary was running low and there was a scarcity of the "dinero" of the realm they set out on a voyage to levy tribute, loot and kill. [...] the Orientals were elected to take the lead in going against the invaders. The Chinese are not given to wasting anything, not even ammunition. They permitted the Villa contingency, which outnumbered them about six to one, to come within easy range. Then they opened up, and just kept on pumping hot bullets into Villistas until two-thirds of their number had been wiped out. [...] From that day on Pancho Villa has had a price on every Chinaman's head in Mexico.[4]

On the night of March 8, 1916, Pancho Villa killed seventeen Americans during a raid on Columbus, New Mexico. On March 15, General John J. Pershing, who had been stationed in El Paso's Fort Bliss, led 6,000 U.S. troops (later increased to a force of 11,000) into Mexico's Chihuahua province (south of El Paso) to capture Pancho Villa. By March 18, Pershing, who had recently lost his wife and three of his four children to a fire, had set up a base of operations in Colonia Dublán, a Mormon village north of Casas Grandes. Pershing's men then advertised for cooks in Casas Grandes, and many Chinese men, apparently needing the work, offered their services. Others set up shops, restaurants, and laundries around the Dublán camp. Their prices fixed by the U.S. Army, the Chinese even sold goods at mobile U.S. military camps where soldiers were actively pursuing Pancho Villa:

> Many a soldier without soap obtained his first good wash by buying a cake [of soap] from a Chinaman. In the desert, wherever a truck train was likely to stop for water, there was a Chinaman. Doughnuts, pies, candy, tobacco, matches, and fruit, which comprised about all the luxuries known to the men during this campaign in a poverty-stricken country, were furnished by Chinese, and by them only.[5]

The Chinese working with Pershing's army became known as the "Pershing Chinese." Many were likely unemployed or underemployed before Pershing invaded. Among the Pershing Chinese was the father of Kong Woo, a native of San Antonio. Woo's father rarely mentioned his life in Mexico but did say that he was a poor person in a poor country and that he rode the trains looking for work until he began working at the U.S. military camps. The U.S. Army had difficulty supplying their own men in part because they were prohibited by the Carranza government from using the Norteoeste de Mexico railroad leading south from Juárez. The Chinese Mexicans obtained goods for the U.S. Army in part by working with Chinese in El Paso, Texas and utilizing the railroads leading out of Juárez. By July 18, 1916, about 300 Chinese worked at the Army's Dublán camp, some of them as laborers for the U.S. Army. The leader of the Chinese was Charley Tien, who envisioned the Chinese following exiting U.S. forces to the American border, whereupon they would remain in Mexico but flee into the United States if Pancho Villa's army attacked. The federal Chinese Exclusion Act prohibited most Chinese from immigrating to the United States. In late summer, the Chinese constructed and ran a large laundry for the U.S. Army. Army officers were impressed by the Chinese men's industriousness and attention to detail in all their occupations.[6]

Within the first month of Pershing's expedition, the Carranza government wounded Pancho Villa and dispersed many of his forces. But by September, Villa had regrouped in Chihuahua and "in any place he captured, the Chinese were murdered in cold blood." When ethnically "clearing" an entire district between Parral and Jiminez, Villa's men killed Chinese men, their Mexican wives, and their children. Some were burned alive on a bonfire. On November 23, Villa attacked Chihuahua City again, this time battling for three days. Upon taking the city, his men "stalked" the Chinese launderers and restaurant owners "and shot them where they stood," killing over a hundred Chinese. Some escaped, perhaps going northward to Pershing's Dublán camp. In total, Villa's violence against the Chinese sent hundreds, or thousands, of Chinese running for the American border (especially Juárez-El Paso) or into the safety of American military camps. Descendants of Chinese survivors, now living in Texas, still recall their parents and grandparents' stories of Villa torturing and hunting down Chinese civilians.[7]

At some point, the Chinese asked General Pershing to allow them to enter the United States for their own safety. Because the Chinese Exclusion Act prohibited Chinese from entering the United States, Pershing requested special permission for their entrance. The Army granted it. After an exhausting journey through the desert, 3,800 Chinese and Mormon refugees arrived in Columbus, New Mexico in early February 1917. Among them were 527 Chinese, including both those Chinese who served the U.S. Army and others from Parral and Chihuahua City

This photo features Chinese men in a Chinese-owned store in Mexico during Pershing's "punitive expedition" into that nation. Many Chinese merchants, workers, and unemployed men provided supplies to the U.S. Army.

This old postcard, labeled "Chinese Refugees," likely shows refugees fleeing the Mexican Revolution. They may be Pershing Chinese serving food at a makeshift restaurant.

who had escaped attacks. General Pershing, occupied with preparing for World War I, asked his long-time friend, William Tracy Page, to help the Chinese legally remain in the United States. Some bureaucrats spoke of deportation to China.[8]

By March 1917, another group of about 500 Chinese refugees had gathered in Juárez, Mexico. They attempted to cross into El Paso, but federal officials denied them entry. Chinese Chief Consul T.K. Fong, supported by the Chinese government, set up an office in El Paso, and Fung Ching of the Chinese Benevolent Association of San Francisco organized efforts to feed and support both the Chinese in Juárez and the group in Columbus. The fate of the Chinese in Juárez is unclear; some likely found safe harbor in Northern Mexico, and some likely migrated to the U.S.

Meanwhile, at a self-organized meeting in Columbus, the Pershing Chinese committed themselves to never trying to escape from the military camp, to never lying to each other, and to avoiding any rough treatment of each other. They agreed that they would discipline their own community. One hundred Chinese were allowed to leave the camp to return to China or to Baja California, Mexico—likely to the city of Mexicali, where a large Chinese community lived. Another forty left the camp by qualifying under the exception to Exclusion allowing Chinese merchants to reside in the United States. Some of these merchants, including Lew Moon, opened grocery stores and restaurants in San Antonio. The old men among the group were asked to return to China.[9]

To prevent a Pancho Villa attack on the Columbus camp, the U.S. Army stationed extra guards, and the Chinese built a protective trench. Eventually, the military and the Pershing Chinese agreed that they should be moved to San Antonio's Fort Sam Houston, where they arrived on June 7:

> The refugees came here with an unblemished record, and no sooner had they struck town than their industry was making itself apparent in and about the military reservation. They lost no time laying out their camp and they did that well, followed so closely along engineering lines and never lost sight of sanitation and hygiene that this particular corner of the reservation has attracted wide attention. It has

been held up as an example of what can be done in the way of building a canvas city.[10]

Engaged in World War I, the U.S. military needed reliable labor. The day after setting up camp, 350 Chinese refugees, led by Mon Lee Chew (also a refugee), began clearing dense growth for the erection of Camp Travis, which would be used to train the 90th and 18th Divisions for World War I. The Chinese seemed to enjoy work and were determined to prove their usefulness to the Army. Paid twenty cents an hour and nothing for overtime, some Chinese volunteered to continue working under moonlight. The clearing of the grounds was completed in five weeks rather than the projected three to four months. It was estimated that each Chinese refugee got as much done as three typical civilians. After the Chinese built a railroad into the camp, William Tracy Page and the Army began in August to put the Chinese to work at other Texas military installations. A San Antonio paper described the Chinese as "painfully" polite with a healthy sense of humor, having fun with the American word "slacker." They highly regarded hygiene and sanitation, and only three died in the influenza epidemic of 1918–1919. Just one month after their arrival, the Chinese refugees organized a Chinese feast to benefit the Red Cross, and in April, 1918, they raised 600 dollars to endow a bed in an American army hospital in France.[11]

Almost all of the Chinese were unmarried and the majority were younger than 31 years. All of them spoke a dialect of Chinese and at least some Spanish. Few spoke English; some took night school English classes. Although the Army did not guard the Chinese camp, none of the Chinese deserted, except for Jung Hoy, who was later discovered serving as a member of a U.S. Army artillery regiment fighting in World War I in France. The U.S. armed forces in the war were led by none other than General Pershing.[12]

After the war, General Pershing returned to Washington a hero. Utilizing his immense popularity, Pershing, along with William Tracy Page, in November 1919 began lobbying and writing letters to Congress and federal officials to allow the Pershing Chinese to live freely and legally in the United States. While congressional hearings dragged on for more than two years, some Chinese Americans saw the Pershing Chinese as indentured servants of the U.S. military. The Chinese Benevolent Association and Chinese Americans appealed to the U.S. government on behalf of the Pershing Chinese.[13]

Four and a half years after the Pershing Chinese first entered the United States, President William Harding on November 23, 1921 signed Public Law No. 29 granting the Pershing Chinese legal status to live in the United States. While Chinese born outside of the United States were generally denied both legal residency and the right to naturalize, the Pershing Chinese, born outside of the United States, were granted status as legal residents. Thus Public Law No. 29 seemed to set a precedent in immigration law. Through this law, the U.S. government recognized that politically persecuted immigrants must be given special consideration. In later decades, the U.S. and other nations systematically provided asylum to war refugees and the politically persecuted, saving innumerable people from violent deaths.

In January 1922, on the heels of Public Law No. 29, Pershing visited the Chinese at Camp Travis. He encouraged the one hundred or so Chinese men there to "learn the American language" and to be "good Americans." The Chinese, happy to see him, thanked him for his efforts in helping them. In February 1922, the 365 remaining Pershing Chinese were free to leave their military camps and live legally in the United States. When Qu Song, a large man, received his papers, he smiled and said, "Uncle Sammy mighty fine man."[14]

After being released, some of the Pershing Chinese opened restaurants at the San Antonio army camps, where "the soldiers had grown fond of the Chinese food." By 1940, each camp in San Antonio hosted one or two Chinese-owned restaurants. Many Pershing Chinese used the money they had saved working for the U.S. military to open businesses; twenty-four had saved over 1,000 dollars by the time of their release. In El Paso, some Pershing Chinese opened groceries, establishing the local Chinese in that business. In San Antonio, their presence helped increase the number of Chinese-owned groceries from nine in the 1921–22 city directory to twenty-four in the following directory (after the Pershing Chinese were released). By 1926, local Chinese owned thirty-three grocery stores, seventeen restaurants, and nine laundries. By 1941, the number of Chinese-owned groceries had more than doubled. The city's Chinese population quadrupled from 63 in the 1910 Census to 283 in the 1920 Census. In 1923, the Chinese Baptist Church estimated 500 Chinese San Antonians, and by World War II, they numbered over 1,000.[15]

In addition to the release of the Pershing Chinese, economic opportunity drove population increases. Many newly-arriving Chinese were brothers, sons, and "paper sons" (sons only on immigration papers) of Chinese San Antonioans. Most started out working for, or with, relatives in San Antonio. Moon Fong Lew (surname Lew) was a Pershing Chinese who worked for a Chinese-owned grocery store on the West Side. He borrowed money from his employer to help his younger brother, Mon Ben Lew, buy "paper son" papers and a ticket to sail to the United States. Upon arriving in San Antonio, Mon Ben Lew worked three years to pay off his travel expenses while learning Spanish to better communicate with the Mexican American patrons and neighbors. Mon Ben Lew then worked another five years to pay for a return trip to China to marry Chin Toy (surname Chin, both born around 1910 in Toishan). The couple had nine children in San Antonio.[16]

In 1910, there may have been only two dozen full-blooded Chinese women in the state of Texas. With the arrival and release of the Pershing Chinese, there seemed to be a sudden influx of Chinese women over the next decade or so. Some of these women, like Chin Toy, were brought to San Antonio by Chinese San Antonian men. Their migration to Texas from China, Mexico, or other states was likely made easier by the sterling immigration status and reputation of the Pershing Chinese, as well as the Asian American underground railroad.[17]

Some women were full-fledged American citizens. Mary Eng was born and raised in Shreveport, Louisiana, where her parents ran a *steam* laundry rather than a hand laundry, the type that Chinese had been associated with historically. She married Chinese San Antonioan Joseph Eng in 1940, and they ran three grocery stores in San Antonio. The influx of Chinese women helped create Texas's first major community of Chinese men, Chinese women, and their "full-blooded" Chinese children. Not long after the release of the Pershing Chinese, San Antonio certainly surpassed El Paso in population of "full blooded" Chinese. San Antonio also replaced El Paso as the epicenter of Chinese culture and Chinese Texan political power. While El Paso had been the Chinese "mecca" of the American Southwest, San Antonio became in the interwar years a Chinese "boomtown" of the American South.[18]

Overall, the San Antonio Chinese community was much less transient and more family-oriented. Because the community included many more Chinese-Chinese couples than previous Chinese Texan communities, this community produced institutions that Texas had never seen before. While Chinese San Antonians formed organizations typical of earlier Chinese Texan communities—a major On Leong Merchants Association, a smaller Hip Sing Association, a Chee Kung Tong, and an affiliate branch of the Kuomintang (Chinese Nationalist Party)—the Chinese also built churches and schools for a burgeoning population of Chinese families and children.

While the Pershing Chinese languished in Fort Sam Houston, some Chinese apparently languished on the streets of San Antonio looking for work during the economic downturn that followed World War I; some who migrated to San Antonio in the 1910s were likely refugees of the Mexican Revolution. According to the Chinese Baptist Church historians, "in 1919, an unknown Christian woman met a young Chinese man walking aimlessly down the streets downtown." This man was apparently shabbily dressed, and when asked how he could be helped, the Chinese man answered, "If you wish to help my people, help my people learn English."[19]

Thirty-four men and children began meeting to learn English at the old Spanish Governor's Palace, which local farmers used as a poultry and livestock market. The Chinese cleaned out the excrement and feathers, and white Christians, such as Baptist minister John Milton, used the Christian Bible to teach the Chinese both English and Christianity. After two years of having their classes interrupted by drunkards, the class moved to a room above the Woo Lee Café on West Commerce Street. At first, the classes were non-denominational and organized by Presbyterians, Methodists, and Baptists. But at the insistence of the Chinese, they were baptized by immersion in water at the Baptist church, and a commitment to the Baptist denomination was made. In 1923, a year after the release of the Pershing Chinese, the Chinese Baptist Church was formally established. San Antonio's Chinese Baptist Church was the only Chinese church in the South until another one was founded in 1934 in Mississippi. The nine charter members included four Chinese—Ng Lee, Ng Jan, Y.J. Wong, and Lee Bock Lung—and five whites, including Olive Lewellyn.[20]

During the interwar years, Olive Lewellyn (known as Miss Ollie) managed the church and gave many Chinese babies their English names. The church and its English classes served to teach Chinese immigrants both American mores and the Christian religion. Lewellyn recalled one of the older Chinese merchants telling his workers, "I want you to go to that school on Commerce Street because they're Christian and they teach you to be good and honest." Restaurant workers attended a daily late afternoon English class, and grocery store workers took a daily evening class. By 1940, most of these men had wed and had Texas-born children, and English became more common at the church. Because the Chinese tended to live behind or above their grocery stores, their residences were scattered throughout the city. Thus, the Chinese Baptist Church became the place where the Chinese children could gather and socialize.[21]

With the establishment of a Chinese Baptist church in El Paso in 1935, the establishment of one in Houston in 1953, and the continued association of Austin's First Baptist Church with missionary work in China, Chinese Texan Christians were almost all Baptists. Further, with three churches, Texas was now tied with Pennsylvania for the third highest number of Chinese Christian churches. Texas attracted Chinese Baptists to teach and preach at its churches and schools. Rev. I. P. Wan became the first pastor born in China to serve in the South, when he served as pastor of the San Antonio Chinese Baptist Church for two summers in 1925–1926. However, most of the pastors at the church before 1952 were white.[22]

Less than ten years after the aforementioned English lessons began, the Chinese San Antonioans found a need for Chinese language classes. Chinese parents wanted their children not only to speak Chinese but to internalize Chinese culture. The desire for quality education applied to both sons and daughters. Two Chinese schools were formed in the 1920s for the quickly growing population of Chinese San Antonioan children.

Students and teachers of classes held at the Chinese Baptist Church, circa 1925. The young men likely learned English, and the children may have learned both Chinese and English. Olive Llewellyn stands at the far right.

One was a school on West Houston Street run by the Chinese Masonic Lodge (Chee Kung Tong) while the other was founded in 1928 on San Saba Street. Associated with the Chinese Baptist Church, the San Saba school was founded by Louie Hing and other community leaders. "They just got together and figured the kids need to learn Chinese," recalled Hing's grandson, Sam Ng. Chinese families donated according to their wealth (as much as $500) to purchase a $10,000 two-story building which had served as a convent.[23]

By 1928, Sun Yat-Sen's Republican Revolution had, seventeen years previous, overthrown the Qing (Ching) Dynasty and imperial rule in China. The founders of the San Saba school were apparently still loyal to the imperial government, as they wished to honor the old flag at an elaborate ceremony dedicating the new school. The schoolchildren apparently felt no loyalty to the Qing Dynasty and decided to hide the old flag. The flag of the Republic had to be used, and the teacher, Benjamin Kwok, resigned in disagreement, as a result of which, Moy Yack Wun won the teaching position. The Chinese community chose the members of the board of trustees that ran the school, and five dollars tuition was collected to pay for expenses. The teachers were all men until 1935, when Sophie Fong (unmarried) began teaching the younger children.[24]

The Chinese parents wanted their children to excel in school. While many Chinese children did excel in public school, many were also required to attend the San Saba school from 5 p.m. to 8 p.m. On weekends, lessons were taught from 9 a.m. to noon. Using a traditional Chinese learning method, the children recited passages from Chinese history, Confucian texts, classics, and illustrated books until they mastered and memorized them. The classroom was loud, as children of all ages recited simultaneously. Many kids appreciated the extra schooling because "as long as we go to Chinese school, we didn't have to work." While many worked hard at speaking Toishanese and reading and writing Chinese, some students mostly socialized. Remembered Sam Ng:

When I went through, Moy San Seng [was a teacher] and there was a Gee San Seng and then we had a lady teacher. And that's when I was a "kai doy" [naughty boy] and I got expelled from the Chinese school.

125

So when I went home, my daddy gave me a whipping and my grandfather said, "No use for you to go to school anymore. You're too bad."[25]

Sam Ng's family ran the Sang Yuen grocery store, and the family of twelve lived in two rooms in the back of the store, where Sam Ng was born in 1923. "We never had a real home," remembered Sam. "The store was our home." This was common among Chinese struggling in a segregated society and economy. Counterbalancing racism and economic instability were Chinese community organizations, churches, formal and informal family name organizations, and two-parent families. The tightly-knit community cared for its own, feeding the hungry and clothing the needy during hard times like the Great Depression. The Chinese even ran a dining hall for the hungry. Benefiting from stability previously absent in the lives of most Chinese Texans, the Chinese Texans born in the 1920s and 1930s in San Antonio, El Paso, and Houston were among the first wave of Chinese Texan college graduates in the 1930s and 1940s.[26]

The Chinese combined traditional Chinese practices with Western practices. As late as 1940, Chinese funeral rites, including the burning of items for use in the afterlife, were still practiced. Some Chinese San Antonioans had their remains disinterred and re-buried in Guangdong Province, while others were buried in a special area in Mission Burial Park. Newspapers reported on the mixed-culture weddings of local Chinese Americans. In the wedding of Chinese Vice-Consul Edward K.T. Chen of Houston and Guan How Ng of San Antonio, a Christian minister married the couple, but traditional Chinese rituals were also performed before and after the Christian wedding. The desire for good Chinese food remained strong, and most Chinese families maintained gardens for Chinese vegetables.[27]

Before World War II, no Chinese women married outside of their race, but some Chinese men married women of Mexican and white origin. Many Chinese parents preferred that their children marry Chinese rather than "foreigners." Youth social groups helped to bring Chinese teens together; they were also a great way for Chinese youth to have fun. Amidst the tragedy of World War II, in 1944, Mary Eng, known among the Chinese as "Aunt Mary," organized a Chinese youth organization independent of the Baptist church known as the Chinese Youth League,

Bing Ng and Kim Quon at their wedding reception, 1950. Bing served as an engineer in the U.S. Air Force in World War II. Bing returned home from the war and met Kim Quon at San Antonio's Chinese Baptist Church. A graduate of Texas A&M University, he served in the Air Force for forty years.

Mer Leung, one of the Pershing Chinese, read of General Pershing's death on July 16, 1948. Mer owned the New Asia Café on Broadway. Leung had worked as a cook for the U.S. Army.

which saw its heyday from the 1940s to the 1960s. Although some of the Baptists considered dancing taboo, Chinese youth met for "sock dances," where they danced on living room floors in their socks. Formal dances were held on Saturdays and Sundays, alternating between San Antonio, Houston, and New Orleans. The San Antonio dances were held on Sundays, as those were the only evenings during which grocery stores were not open. In both San Antonio and Houston, the bowling alley was also an important social institution. Mary Shem of Houston remembered, "When any visitor from out of town came to Houston, they went to the bowling alley and that's where they found the crowd. We were all bowlers." In San Antonio, Mary Eng remembered how, after closing their stores at 10 p.m., a hundred Chinese men, women, and children gathered to participate in midnight bowling leagues.[28]

By 1940, the Chinese community had grown larger and more complex. The Chinese concentrated in the largely Mexican/Mexican American west side of San Antonio. By the mid-1940s, the Chinese ran over one hundred grocery stores, especially among the Hispanic and black communities; they also ran restaurants throughout the city. The 1949 Chinese Communist Revolution brought an end to the practice of Chinese Texans returning to China to reproduce or retire. Jim Eng was conceived on one of his father's return visits. Born in 1923 in a Toishan County village, Eng came to San Antonio to join his father and uncle in the grocery business at the age of seven. While only in his fifties, Jim's grandfather returned to China in 1936 to retire. Jim's father wished to do the same, but World War II and then the Communist take-over "killed any idea of going back." Considered a wealthy land-owner by the Communist government, Jim Eng's grandfather was imprisoned, tortured, and likely executed.[29]

The Communist Revolution cut off Chinese Texans from their ancestral villages in Guangdong. Furthermore, Chinese immigrants between 1949 and 1980 came mostly from Taiwan and Hong Kong, and very few of them spoke Toishanese or hailed from the same villages as the older Chinese Texans. Chinese Texan college graduates tended to move to Houston to take professional jobs, thus draining second- and third-generation Chinese Americans from San Antonio. The Chinese

San Antonioan community was in danger of losing its particular character. The Chinese immigrants who arrived after the 1965 immigration reform, however, needed Chinese American organizations, too. So, although the San Saba Chinese School closed down in 1947, it re-opened in 1971 for a re-vitalized Chinese community. The Chinese Baptist Church, too, stood tall into the new millennium.

ENDNOTES

1 Stryker McGuire, "Around the Plaza," *San Antonio Light*, Apr 12, 1974, p. 8B; *San Antonio Daily Express*, Nov 22, 1881, p. 4; San Antonio City Directories, 1877–78, 1879–80, 1885–86, 1887–88, 1889–89, 1892–93, 1894, and 1901–1902.

2 *Fort Worth Daily Gazette*, Jan 3, 1888, p. 6, reprinting an article from the *San Francisco Examiner*.

3 "Chinatown Scene Here," *San Antonio Light*, Mar 14, 1909; Alan Knight, "Racism, Revolution, and Indegenismo: Mexico, 1910–1940," *The Idea of Race in Latin America*, ed. Richard Graham (Austin: University of Texas Press, 1990), 96.

4 "Planting the Celestial Republic in San Antonio," *San Antonio Express*, June 17, 1917; the Chinese in Chihuahua City likely joined the government forces in response to the Torreón massacre. That city is 168 miles northwest of Torreón, making it one of Torreón's nearest major cities. Villa's effect on the Chinese cannot be overstated. Chinese descendants of those who survived the Revolution spoke passionately in the early 2000s to the author of their distaste for Villa, who would torture and kill Chinese.

5 Frank Vandiver, *Black Jack: the life and times of John J. Pershing* (College Station: Texas A&M University Press, 1977); Wellington Chew, interview by Dr. Edward Rhoads, in El Paso, Jun 21, 1977; *New York Times*, Jul 18, 1916, 4.

6 Kong Woo, interview by Yvonne Lim and Irwin Tang, Jan 11, 2003; Vandiver; Briscoe; *New York Times*.

7 Clarence Clendenen, *Blood on the Border: The United States Army and the Mexican Irregulars* (New York: MacMillan, 1969), 331; *New York Times*, Nov 20, 1916; Vandiver, 663.

8 Vandiver, 667; Amy Elizabeth Nims, "Chinese Life in San Antonio," (M.A. Thesis, Southwest Texas State Teachers College, 1941), 13; Briscoe, Edward Eugene, "Pershing's Chinese refugees: an odyssey of the Southwest," (Master's thesis, St. Mary's

University, 1947); on friendship with Page, see Gene Smith, *Until the Last Trumpet Sounds: The Life of General of the Armies John J. Pershing* (New York: John Wiley & Sons, 1998), 109.

9   Briscoe; Nims, 6; *San Antonio Express*, June 17, 1917.

10   *San Antonio Express*, June 17, 1917.

11   Quote from *San Antonio Express*, June 17, 1917; Nims, 8–10; Briscoe, 54–55, 64,70; Edward Rhoads, "The Chinese in Texas," *Southwestern Historical Quarterly*, 81 (July 1977), 21.

12   Briscoe 63, 78, 92–94, 102–103.

13   Ibid.

14   Briscoe, 63, 78, 92–94, 102–103, 133–134, 136; Rhoads, 23.

15   Nims, 14; Rhoads, 20–21; Esther Wu, "Church tells 60 years of history," *San Antonio Express-News*, Sep 3, 1983; McGuire.

16   Sonny Lew, interview by Irwin Tang, 2004.

17   This estimate of 24 Chinese women was arrived at by multiplying four—an approximate number of Chinese women in El Paso at the time (based on Farrar's *Chinese in El Paso* (see Ch. 2 of *Asian Texans*))—by six, representing the major population centers of El Paso, San Antonio, Dallas, Houston, Galveston, and Austin.

18   Mary Eng, interview by Yvonne Lim and Irwin Tang, 2003. On Eng, also see Mel Brown, *Chinese Heart of Texas: The San Antonio Community, 1875–1975* (Austin: Lily on the Water Publishing, 2005), pp. 181–184.

19   Nims; Wu; Lew, interview.

20   Lew, interview. Wu; Nims, 50.

21   Lew, interview; Nims, 49–59.

22   Betty Sung, *Mountain of Gold* (New York: MacMillan, 1967), 216; Sam Ng, interview by Yvonne Lim, 2004; Nims, 49–59; Lillie Mae Hagner, *Alluring San Antonio Through the Eyes of an Artist* (San Antonio: The Naylor Company, 1940); Mary Eng, interview by Esther MacMillan, San Antonio, Aug 5, 1988; Mary Eng, interview by Lim and Tang; Kenny Woo, "The Chinese Colony in San Antonio," *The Junior Historian*, January 1955.

23   Ng, interview; Nims.

24   Nims, 41–49.

25   Ng, interview; "San Seng" means "Mister."

26   Ng, interview; Nims, 41–48; Sophie Lim, interview by Irwin Tang, 2004; dining hall fact in Hagner.

27   Nims, 19–40.

28   Nims, 19–40; Eng, interview by Lim and Tang; Mark, Diane Mei Lin and Ginger Chih, *A Place Called Chinese America*, revised edition (Dubuque, Iowa: Kendall/ Hunt Publishing Company, 1985).

29   Eng, Mary; Hagner; Jim Eng, interview by Laurie Gudzikowski, San Antonio, May 20, 1997; Lim, interview;. The county of Toishan is also known as Taishan, and is pronounced "Hoy Sun" in the Toishan dialect, which is closely related to Cantonese.

CHAPTER SIX

★

CHINESE TEXANS AND JAPANESE TEXANS DURING WORLD WAR II

Irwin A. Tang and Dr. Thomas K. Walls

In 1931 Japan began its invasion of China, planting the roots of World War II. By then, the Great Depression had hit Tyler, Texas, where Chinese Texan Sam Mardock had run the popular Cotton Belt Restaurant since 1902 (see Chapter 2). Like many Chinese Texan small business owners, Sam helped people in need. At night, Sam allowed twenty or thirty unemployed men to sleep around the 24-hour restaurant's wood-burning stove, feeding them at midnight. President Franklin Roosevelt's New Deal brought more trains through Tyler—some carrying scrap iron. His son Julian noticed that "Sam would cuss loudly that these loads of iron were going to Japan." Indeed, the iron was going to Japan, that is, until December 7, 1941. On a "warm spring-like day" in Tyler, Julian, now a pre-med student at UT-Austin, was playing baseball with Tyler townsfolk:

> We heard the news on the radio! Japan had attacked Pearl Harbor. Where was Pearl Harbor? It was in the Hawaiian Islands, thousands of miles away. [...] This time sticks in our memories because it was the last time we were all together.[1]

In the following weeks, both of Sam's sons, Julian and Sam, Jr., volunteered as Aviation Cadets for the U.S. armed forces. Meanwhile, Sam and his wife, Wong, were both ordered by the government to register with the Immigration Service as aliens. The infirm and octogenarian Sam had lived in the United States for over sixty years, but he and his wife had never been allowed to naturalize as citizens because of the Chinese Exclusion Act. "It was all sort of bewildering," wrote daughter Lucille, "here we had two fellows in the U.S. Army Air Corps, -two blue stars on our door and we had to 'register.'" Julian called the alien registration "a deep, hurting, demeaning indignity."[2]

When Texas-born Japanese American Betty Akagi, then 11, heard about Pearl Harbor on the radio, she and her siblings ran out and told their parents and grandparents, working in the fields. The family was in shock, and Betty's father, Torata, became preoccupied with what American officials might do to his family. At the dinner table, Torata's mother simply repeated, "Oh, that can't be. That just can't be." The first-generation Japanese Americans, or *Issei*, of Texas were ashamed of Japan's attack on the U.S. and considered it a "loss of face" for them. Second-generation Japanese Americans, or *Nisei*, felt less connected with Japan. Draft-aged George Kitamura of San Benito admitted, "I was kind of depressed, but I had never seen Japan, and I was born and raised here, so it didn't faze me too much." Although the U.S. government prohibited Japanese Americans from joining the U.S. military until a policy change in January 1943, Mutsuo Kawamura of San Benito secured an exception to the rule and joined the U.S. Army in San Antonio in January 1942, just weeks after Pearl Harbor.[3]

On the day after the Pearl Harbor attack, the *Houston Post* announced that the federal government was "rounding up" Japanese Texans and Japanese nationals. All Japanese Texan homes were searched and often ransacked. Federal agents took guns, cameras, binoculars, and all items with Japanese writing on them, such as books and letters. Heads of Japanese Texan families were arrested and questioned, some of them being sent to an internment camp in Kenedy, Texas. They were detained and questioned along with Japanese nationals and other Japanese Americans whom the government considered potentially dangerous, even though, to this day, no evidence has been found that a single Japanese Texan was disloyal to the United States. From the Kishi family memoir:

> Following Pearl Harbor, [Toki] Kishi did not wait to be 'rounded up.' On the Monday after Pearl Harbor, he and Kaname Susuki, president of the Orange Petroleum Company, showed their loyalty by offering themselves to the FBI in Port Arthur. [Toki Kishi] spent two months of internment at Camp Kenedy, before he was able to have a hearing before a board headed by Steve M. King, the U.S. Attorney for the Eastern District of Texas. When asked, "If he was ordered by the Emperor [of Japan] to bomb the oil refinery in Port Arthur, would he do so?" His reply was, "First, I am a farmer and businessman and know nothing about explosives. Suppose I was adopted into another family and my biological parent ordered me to harm my adopted family. I can not do so." The U.S. Attorney told his son Taro that Kishi answered the questions magnificently. The family had to surrender firearms and cameras but otherwise were free.

Kaname Susuki, on the other hand, was accused by the U.S. government of being an agent of Japan and taking a secret census of Japanese living in the Orange-Beaumont-Port Arthur area. Susuki was repatriated to Japan but survived the war.[4]

Even before the attack on Pearl Harbor, the FBI had been monitoring Japanese Texan community gatherings and parties. After Pearl Harbor, the government limited the movements of Japanese Texans, especially Issei. One month after Pearl Harbor, FBI agents and local police ransacked Torata and Beatrice Akagi's farm home near Sheldon, Texas. The agents smashed the Buddhist family altar on the floor and asked Beatrice if she wasn't sorry for marrying a "Jap." "No," replied Beatrice, a Mexican American. "Of course not." She explained that she and her husband had "a home, children, property, and we're very comfortable. And I'm very happy." When the FBI agents asked the Akagis how much money was in their house, the two young Akagi daughters, Betty and Nellie, retrieved their bowl of pennies and counted them loudly and slowly, in an act of defiance.[5]

Torata Akagi, Torata's uncle, and Torata's 63-year-old father, Fu-kutaro, were arrested and taken to Houston for questioning. Fukutaro was imprisoned for three months in Houston before he went before the enemy alien hearing board. With the help of a local café owner, the family collected ten affidavits from (non-Japanese) neighbors attesting to Fukutaro's loyalty, and he was released. As the FBI continued for months to arrest ordinary citizens and close down Japanese Texan-owned businesses, affidavits and petitions from local communities shortened the detainment and business closures of Japanese throughout Texas.[6]

Some whites and Hispanics were not so friendly to their Japanese neighbors. One anti-Japanese activist in the Rio Grande Valley circulated a petition to intern all of the Valley's Japanese Texan residents. This same man, a Justice of the Peace, started a fistfight with Kumazo Tanamachi of San Benito because Kumazo was Japanese. Four of Kumazo's sons served in the U.S. Army during the war.[7]

The Jingu family of San Antonio sent two sons to battle as American soldiers. In 1918, after helping to create the Japanese tea pavilion at the city's Japanese Garden, Kimi Jingu and his family were invited to live at the garden in order to make it more authentic. Kimi died in 1938, leaving his wife Alice with eight children. In the wake of Pearl Harbor, the city of San Antonio twice cut off the Jingu family's water supply to force them out of their home. Because few were willing to rent to a Japanese family, a local Methodist church had to intervene to find the Jingus a place to stay. The city renamed the Jingus' home of twenty-four years "The Chinese Sunken Garden," and a Chinese couple lived in the garden house until the early 1960s.[8]

While Japanese American businesses such as Houston's Japan Café and Japanese Restaurant changed their names to Kay's Café and U.S. Café, some Chinese American businesses sought to distinguish themselves from Japanese American businesses in part to avoid anti-Japanese harassment. Dr. Edward M.C. Chen, just a child during World War II, remembered how his uncle, architect Charles Chan, designed a "China-USA V" victory insignia which was pinned to clothes and hung up in storefronts. One week after Pearl Harbor, the *Houston Post* featured a photo of Wilson Chu and George W. Lee standing before a storefront window upon which was written, "Hell with the Japs. We're Chinese." Lee held up a butcher knife, and the photo was captioned, "Houston Chinese Are Ready!" After being mistaken for a Japanese and threatened by a large man, Hawaiian-born Chinese Houstonian and World War I veteran Stanley Ani Kaiulani wore a sign on his hat saying, "I am not a Japanese. I am a loyal American." The local naval station refused to allow this 47-year old, disabled orchestra leader to volunteer for World War II combat.[9]

During the war, most Japanese Texans lived in rural areas and almost all Chinese Texans lived in urban areas, so there was little interaction between the two groups. Although Chinese Texans felt extremely bitter about the deaths of family and friends at the hands of the Japanese military, there was little friction between Chinese Texans and Japanese Texans. Ann Quan already had seven siblings in her struggling Chinese Texan family when her parents unofficially "adopted" a Japanese American teenaged boy who had made his way from the West Coast to San Antonio. By passing the boy off as their Chinese son, Ann Quan's parents protected him from being sent to an internment camp.[10]

Chinese Texans Overseas

In April 1938, Ben Mar of El Paso took his wife Maria and his children to the ancestral "Mar Village" in the Guangdong Province of China. According to Maria de Los Angeles Mar Skates (Ben's daughter from his second marriage), in late 1938 the Japanese army

> marched through the village. My uncles and my aunts were executed, and the village was burnt to the ground. My brothers and sisters had brought their passports showing that they were U.S. citizens so they were spared.[11]

The Japanese imprisoned the family and Ben Mar's wife died during childbirth in prison. His nine children stayed in a Japanese prison camp for four years. The Red Cross then brought them to a Hong Kong hospital where they stayed for a year or longer before they finally returned to El Paso.[12]

Around this time the Japanese also attacked Bing Eng's village in the Toishan district of Guangdong Province. Bing Eng lived in a pagoda-styled house built by his grandfather, who had earned gold by working on American railroads. Because of the federal Chinese Exclusion Act, Bing, his mother, and his siblings were prohibited from living with Bing's father, Frank Fung Wah Eng, in Austin, Texas. During the Japanese invasion, Bing's mother was killed, but Bing and brother Wayne Sam were able to escape to Hong Kong, where they jumped on a British ship. The ship was raided by the Japanese military. The Japanese, by policy, removed from European ships every tenth Chinese. Upon being lined up and counted off, Bing was number nine and thus he was spared slavery or death. When Bing made it to Austin, he worked as a dishwasher in his father's diner, learning English out of a Charlie Brown comic strip book and asking customers to pronounce words for him (also see Ch. 10).[13]

Learning of Japanese atrocities, some Americans sought to defend China, even before Pearl Harbor. Claire Lee Chennault, born in Commerce, Texas, was an Army air force officer who had worked for the U.S. Border Patrol from 1919 to 1923. On July 4, 1941, as an advisor for Chinese Nationalist General Chiang Kai-shek, Chennault officially inaugurated the now-legendary Flying Tigers. They were a group of some 300 American fighter pilots and mechanics who flew air missions as an official branch of the Chinese air force, taking on the Japanese air force in deadly dogfights. They were not a part of the U.S. military and were known as the "American Volunteer Group."

Among the Flying Tigers were a handful of Chinese American mechanics, including George Leo Wingshee of Houston, Texas. These Chinese American mechanics worked wonders under terrible conditions. "The engine knocked down, fuselage knocked down, they couldn't find a part, they still find a part and fixed it," said Army airplane mechanic Lewis Yee of Houston. After the Flying Tigers were disbanded on July 4, 1942 and replaced by the 14th Air Force of the U.S. Army (also nicknamed the Flying Tigers), George Leo Wingshee returned to Houston to teach warplane mechanics at the Aero Engine School. Chinese Houstonian community leader Albert Gee had founded the school to train young Chinese Americans in plane mechanics to help defend China.[14]

Chinese Texans and Japanese Texans rushed to join the war effort. Sam Wong and Morley Miyake speak with a recruiting officer in February 1942 in San Antonio, Texas.

On the day after the attack on Pearl Harbor, these Japanese pledged alliegiance to the United States at a general meeting of the American Legion and civic and military leaders in San Antonio.

One of George's students was Lewis Yee, who served throughout China as a mechanic in the 14th Air Force. For two years, until the end of the war, Yee built, repaired and prepared war planes for combat. The well-decorated soldier's closest brush with death occurred while helping to maintain an airstrip in the first echelon of defense in northern China. "Terrible. We got twelve or twenty of us. We take care of airplanes and base operations. [The Japanese warplanes] were bombing for seven, eight months ... We escaped in a C-47 before the enemy got to us." Yee used his ability to write Chinese to coordinate operations between the U.S. Air Force and the Chinese Air Force.[15]

While Yee served in China, Julian Mardock flew over 100 photo reconnaissance missions in four years throughout Europe. Mardock was one of the first Chinese American combat pilots. Perhaps his most important mission was on Christmas Day, 1944, when he scouted in preparation for the Battle of the Bulge. By the end of the war, Lieutenant Mardock had earned the Distinguished Flying Cross, the Air Medal with nine Oak Leaf Clusters, and six Battle Stars. He had become a good soldier, just as his father, Sam, Sr., had wanted him to be. Sam, Sr., died in 1942 while Julian was still training to fly.[16]

As the war drew on, the U.S. military allowed more Chinese Americans to participate in combat, rather than work in service positions. Chinese Americans fought mostly in Europe to avoid their being mistaken for enemy Japanese soldiers. Nevertheless, many Chinese Texans, such as Homer Ng of Houston, fought in deadly battles. Sam Wong of San Antonio fought in Italy and was captured by German forces because an American comrade lit a cigarette, revealing their hidden position. Wong spent months in a German POW camp and returned to San Antonio "all skin and bones." Of the 1031 Chinese Texans counted in the 1940 U.S. census, 137 were drafted by the U.S. military, and two of them were killed in action. An unknown additional number of Chinese Texan volunteers served and possibly died. A total of about 200 Chinese Texans likely served in World War II.[17]

The Chinese Texan community was proud to serve its nation during war. The Chinese Houston community threw a banquet for George Leo Wingshee upon his return, and when Wingshee gave his Flying Tigers patch to a young Edward Chen, Chen quickly became the envy of all his cohorts. "I was very proud of that Flying Tigers patch," he remembered.[18]

Lost in the Pacific

In 1940, President Roosevelt mobilized the Texas National Guard into the U.S. Army as the 36th Infantry Division. In March 1942, the Second Battalion, 131st Field Artillery of the 36th Division was captured by Japanese forces in Java and became known as the "Texas Lost Battalion." Most of these soldiers came from West Texas. Over the next three and a half years, the Lost Battalion was starved, beaten, tortured, and forced to do slave labor. Eddie Fung had been training to work as a cowboy in West Texas when he joined the army. He was already a diminutive young man when the battalion was captured and fed worm-laced rice and not much else. At less than eighty pounds, Fung was forced to carry sacks of rice weighing 225 pounds and 55-gallon drums of oil. "We learned to do it," he explained at a 1964 reunion, "It was simply a case of not getting jabbed by a Jap bayonet." Fung was the only Chinese American soldier captured by the Japanese military during World War II.[19]

Battalion sergeant Frank "Foo" Fujita, Jr. was the son of Frank Fujita, Sr. of Nagasaki, Japan and Ida Pearl Elliot Fujita of Oklahoma. The biracial Frank, Jr. told his Japanese captors that he was "half-Jap and half-American, and glad of it." Upon learning of Fujita's Japanese heritage, the prison camp administrators tried to convince Fujita to switch sides and join the Japanese military. "Are you ashamed to be a Japanese?" he was berated. "I'm an American!" he shot back. "But you have Japanese blood. Are you ashamed of that?" Fujita was asked. He answered, "I have seen many things that your soldiers have done that make me ashamed." Japanese prison camp guards beat Fujita until he was unrecognizable. During the beating, Fujita refused to fall to the ground. "I pulled myself up rigid to attention, threw my chest out and held my head up high," he wrote later. "I would show these native Japanese what a Japanese-American was made of." Fujita also took beatings for stealing food for his American and British comrades.[20]

The Imprisoned and the Free Japanese of Texas

In the several months after Pearl Harbor, some Japanese Texan heads of households voluntarily offered themselves up to the FBI for questioning. Some were arrested. The vast majority of Japanese Texans cooperated with the FBI. Nevertheless, many Japanese Texans (mostly men) were detained for weeks or months. Some were interned for nearly the duration of the war. Most of the interned Japanese Texans were held in Kenedy Alien Detention Station in Kenedy, Texas, southeast of San Antonio.[21]

The Immigration and Naturalization Service (INS) of the Justice Department operated internment camps at Kenedy, Crystal City (southwest of San Antonio), and Seagoville (near Dallas). These camps were operated under a federal bureaucracy not connected with the War Relocation Administration (WRA) camps of the War Department. Whereas the WRA camps held mostly Japanese Americans, the INS camps of Texas held Japanese Americans, Japanese residents of Latin American nations, Japanese nationals temporarily in the U.S. or Latin America, German nationals, and a small number of Italian nationals. Interestingly, Camp Kenedy was organized with the help of the U.S. Border Patrol, an organization originally founded to arrest and deport undocumented Asian immigrants entering from Mexico. Spanish-speaking Japanese comprised a plurality of those imprisoned in the Texas INS camps. Even before Pearl Harbor, the U.S. government had made arrangements, in case of war, to capture Japanese and German civilians in Latin America to be used in "hostage exchanges" for American prisoners in Japan or Germany. Peru, in an attempt to rid its nation of its Japanese citizens, handed over the largest number of Japanese to the United States, while Mexico, just south of the Texas internment camps, did not arrest its Japanese citizens. [22]

On January 6, 1943, Ginzo Murono of Lima, Peru spent a day at the seashore with his wife, two children, and business partner. Upon returning to his partner's home, two Peruvian plain-clothed policemen arrested Murono and his business partner "by order of the United States." Murono spent about six months at Kenedy, which housed mostly Japanese men, before he reunited with his family at the Crystal City internment camp.[23]

Tatsuo Manabe was a Japanese soldier in 1937-38, when his regiment "was almost totally annihilated" by the Chinese Army around Nanking, China. Deserting the Japanese military, Manabe traveled to La Paz, Bolivia, where he worked at an import-export company until he heard a rumor that Japanese would be forcibly sent into the Amazon jungle. In May 1944, Manabe was arrested by Argentine police and shipped to the United States along with thousands of other Japanese Latin Americans. On July 4, Manabe and other Japanese were transported to San Antonio by Pullman coach while served by African American porters, for whom Manabe passed a hat to collect a tip. Manabe spent the rest of the hot, dry summer at Camp Kenedy, where he and other Japanese men were put to work. "And at the request of my fellow internees," Manabe wrote, "I made it a rule to give my comment on war news in the shade of a big tree."[24]

By the time the federal government ordered all of the Japanese Americans on the West Coast relocated to WRA and INS camps in March 1942, many of the Japanese Texans had already been released from detention by the FBI. Among the Japanese American men from California imprisoned at Kenedy was Yasuo Kenmotsu. Since Camp Kenedy housed only men, Kenmotsu was separated from his wife and children. He was, as daughter Sue Ann described, "all alone, with men he didn't know . . . in barracks . . . and not knowing why he was being interned . . . . . away from family and away from work, which was the great wide open sea. He was a fisherman in California."[25]

The most exciting event to hit Camp Kenedy came in the summer of 1942, when a violent hurricane flattened many of the men's "victory huts," downed power lines, and ruptured gas pipes. Led by a group of German seamen, the camp internees refused to repair the camp. After the German group was dissolved, the internees cooperated. The few problems that arose at Camp Kenedy seemed to originate from organized groups of alleged German Nazis. The Japanese men were largely peaceful and were also "superb gardeners," according to one guard, growing vegetables and flowers "in abundance."[26]

During the first twenty months of operation, Kenedy averaged 819 men per day. The camp population peaked in October 1943, and by the time the camp closed on October 1, 1944, it had held over 3,500 aliens and Japanese Americans. During Kenedy's two and a half years of operation, at least 433 Japanese were repatriated in exchange for American prisoners. Camp Kenedy received its first internees on April 21, 1942 and was converted to a German prisoner of war camp on October 1, 1944, its remaining Japanese internees transferred to other internment camps, released, or repatriated to Japan. Few Japanese Latinos interned in Texas were returned to their Latin American homes.[27]

If a prison can be considered comfortable, the Seagoville internment camp, southeast of Dallas, may have been the most comfortable internment camp in the United States. Built in 1940 as a minimum-security women's reformatory, most internees lived in dormitory rooms furnished with carpeting, beds, desks, and bathing and cooking amenities. Before housing Japanese from Latin America, Seagoville held fifty female Japanese Americans arrested by the FBI; these women taught Japanese language and culture to Japanese American children in California. At its peak, Seagoville held 647 people, including Japanese from Latin America and married Japanese couples without children. The camp closed in June 1945.[28]

In 1942, as growing numbers of internees from Latin America forced the Seagoville camp to build fifty huts on its premises, the INS took ownership from the Farm Security Administration of a migrant farm worker camp on the outskirts of Crystal City. Upon conversion to an internment camp, it held entire Japanese American families and Japanese and German families from Latin America. Japanese men languishing in Camp Kenedy and others throughout the United States were reunited with their families at the Crystal City camp. The government tried to foster a community spirit at the camp, and it succeeded, even though the Japanese and Germans interacted minimally. A federal school system was established, the vast majority of its students being Japanese American children. The "American schools" (elementary and high school) served at their peak a total of 300 Japanese American children. The internees themselves established separate "Japanese schools" and "German schools," wherein Japanese and German language and culture were taught in addition to normal classes. Teachers at the Japanese schools taught in both Japanese and Spanish, as their students came from both the United States and Latin America.[29]

While at other U.S. internment camps, political conflict erupted over the Loyalty Oaths imposed by U.S. officials, the most intense conflict at the Crystal City camp involved the American high school's 1944 prom dance. One of the Japanese leaders against the prom, Ryuchi Fujii, wrote to the U.S. Commissioner of Immigration that

> According to time-honored Japanese customs social dance has been condemned morally and religiously and prohibited by law. A dance girl is despised as much as a prostitute. Any girl of a well-to-do family never attends a social dance.[30]

Camp Commander Joseph O'Rourke decided that INS policy must override the objections of the Japanese camp council, which consisted of 350 first-generation Japanese American men. The prom took place, and only thirty Japanese American high school students attended. Sachi Sasaki, who loved to dance, stayed home because she did not want to "bring shame to my father." In protest of the prom, Japanese teachers resigned *en masse*. To some, the prom incident may seem surreal, but the most jarring scenes at Crystal City occurred when Japanese American soldiers of the U.S. Army, giving life and limb to liberate Europe, came home to visit their families, confined behind barbed wire.[31]

At its peak in May 1945, Crystal City held 3,326 internees in its over 650 huts, cottages, and other buildings, more than 500 of which had been newly constructed at an expense of one million dollars. The 290-acre camp, like the other INS camps, provided a wealth of jobs and revenues for the small local community. Hundreds of babies were born at the camp, hundreds of internees were repatriated to Japan and Germany, seventeen people died in camp, and more than a hundred people were released or paroled.[32]

While many Japanese Texan young men fought for the U.S. armed services, others stayed on their Texas farms and grew food for the war cause. One was Henry Kawahata, a 1940 graduate of Texas A&M College, where he was not allowed, because of his Japanese ancestry, a military education beyond the first two years of mandatory military classes. In contrast, a Chinese American cohort was allowed to take advanced military classes. While many Japanese Texan men were detained or served in the U.S. military, some Japanese Texan women went to college during the war.

The census counted only 458 Japanese Texans in 1940. During the war, the government interned thousands of Japanese in Texas and nearby states, multiplying the total number of Japanese in the region. The number of unmarried Japanese in the region increased tremendously, and many Japanese Texans met their future spouses through the matchmaking efforts of relatives and friends in internment camps.

While most of the Japanese Texan women from the San Benito area attended Mary Hardin Baylor College, Mary Oyama attended Texas Women's College in Denton, Texas.[33] During the war, Mary Oyama met George Hada, who was interned in Poston, Arizona. The couple married.[34]

Kikuko Nakao of Long Beach, California was a teenager when she and her family were forced into an internment camp in Rohwer, Arkansas. There, she met and married Jiru "Jerry" Tanamachi, who was visiting relatives at the camp. Upon marriage, Kikuko was allowed to return with Jerry to join his father Kumazo at their San Benito farm. While Kikuko was pregnant with Sandra (her first child), Kikuko's younger brother Sadao, who was extremely depressed by life in the internment camp, hung himself. Meanwhile, like Japanese Texans throughout the state, Jerry and Kikuko dealt with anti-Japanese hostility. While dining at a hamburger joint, a group of whites shouted at Jerry, "Get out! Jap, you get out from here! You don't belong here." Kikuko recalled that five Mexican Texan soldiers on leave who had worked for Jerry "really got mad" at the whites and prevented any escalation of hostilities.[35]

Abolition of Chinese Exclusion

In 1943, Congress considered the abolition of Chinese Exclusion. Three bills were being studied by Congress, and all three would allow for immigration of Chinese according to the national quota system. This system would allow for 105 Chinese immigrants from throughout the world to immigrate each year to the United States. Many politicians believed that abolition of Chinese Exclusion would further solidify the alliance between the U.S. and China. One of the three nearly identical bills was sponsored by Congressman Ed Gossett of Wichita Falls, Texas. Gossett argued that a solid relationship with China would mean a huge market for American goods after the end of the war. Trade with China would provide jobs for the hundreds of thousands of returning American GI's. In September 1943, a gathering of seventy young Chinese Americans in San Antonio, Texas called Chinese Exclusion "the stumbling block between China and America." The Chinese youth called for an immediate repeal of exclusion, rather than waiting until the end of the war. On December 17, 1943, President Franklin Roosevelt repealed Chinese Exclusion.[36]

Although the immediate impact of the repeal of Exclusion on legal immigration was essentially imperceptible, the repeal did help lift the stigma of illegal immigration associated with Chinese Texans. Furthermore, Chinese Texans born in China rejoiced at their newly established right to naturalize as American citizens. The first Chinese Houstonian to be naturalized was Choi Yu Chu, and it made front page news. Mr. Chu, a 43-year old grocer took the oath of citizenship at the Houston federal building. "I like the United States because it is a country of free men," said a smiling Chu, "and I like Houston because it is a great business city."[37]

The improvement in status for Chinese Texans coincided with an increase in economic opportunities, as they found work unrelated to laundries, grocery stores, and restaurants. In 1941, Charles Chan was hired as a draftsman for E. Burns Roensch, making him the first Chinese Houstonian professional employed by a white-owned firm. Many Chinese Houstonians worked in military factories during the war and used their experiences to gain employment in new arenas after the war. John Eng was the first Chinese to work for the city of Houston. Wallace Gee was one of the first Chinese Texans to work as a salesman in Houston. And Richard Eng was the city's first Chinese American insurance salesman.[38]

The Japanese American 442nd Regimental Combat Team marching in France. Saburo Tanamachi (left) and his buddy George Sakato march in front.

The graduating class of a Crystal City internment camp high school. These Japanese students were apprehended in the United States and Latin America before being imprisoned at Crystal City, Texas.

Japanese Americans Rescue Texas's Second Lost Battalion

In October 1944, as the United States armed forces fought to liberate France from German forces, the First Battalion of the 141st Infantry Regiment of the Texas-based 36th Division was sent to take a high ridge overlooking La Houssiere near Bruyéres, France. The Battalion was trapped for several days on a forest hilltop by the German army and radioed for help. "Hold on," they were told, "heavy force coming to relieve you." The all-Japanese American 442nd Regimental Combat Team, which had been fighting alongside the Texan 36th Division, was sent to rescue this "lost" battalion of 275 troops.[39]

Among the Japanese American 442nd were Japanese Texan soldiers, including Saburo Tanamachi, son of Kumazo Tanamachi of San Benito. During the campaign to save the Texas battalion, Private Tanamachi led his squad over Hill 617 near Biffontaine, France. He and his squad

> began sweeping down the hill, exerting terrific pressure on the enemy. After accomplishing the squad mission, the squad was in the process of reorganizing when a counter attack by the enemy severely wounded one of the men of Pvt. Tanamachi's squad. In the face of four enemy machine guns and about 12 riflemen, Pvt. Tanamachi crept forward to aid his wounded comrade after the squad was deployed to hold back the counter attack. Even as he was creeping forward, he kept directing his men's fire. When he reached his comrade, he began to give the wounded soldier first aid when an enemy bullet fatally hit him.[40]

"He died in my arms," recalled Tanamachi's buddy George Sakato. With tears blurring his vision, an enraged Sakato led the charge against the Nazis, who were "unnerved" by the Japanese Americans' furious retribution. The Germans attempted retreat, but all were captured or killed. Tanamachi was posthumously awarded the Silver Star for his bravery. He was one of the first two Japanese Americans buried in Arlington National Cemetery.[41]

On the next day, October 30, the 442nd fought through German resistance to reach the Texas battalion, which had been trapped for five days. A Texan of the lost battalion spotted a Japanese American rescuer and

> raced down the hill like crazy, yelling and laughing and grabbing the soldier and hugging him. Pfc. Matt Sakamoto of the 442nd Combat Team (Japanese Americans) just looked at him with a lump in his throat and the first thing he could think of to say was: "Do you guys need any cigarettes?"[42]

Some of the Texans broke into sobs at the sight of the Japanese American soldiers. The 211 survivors of the Texas lost battalion had been rescued at a cost to the 442nd Combat Team of 800 wounded or killed in action. In 1963, the rescued Texan soldiers successfully lobbied Texas governor John Connolly to bestow upon the soldiers of the 442nd the title of "Honorary Texans." Some, like Saburo Tanamachi and Benjamin Franklin "Benny" Ogata of Dallas, both killed in action, were already Texans.[43]

The sacrifices of Japanese Texan soldiers helped their families back home. Although Mary Oyama suffered from employment discrimination during the war, "people couldn't push me down too much," she recalled, because she had three brothers—Takeo, George, and Sigenore—serving in Europe. George Oyama was awarded the bronze star for his service and was haunted for the rest of his life by war-related nightmares.[44]

The Atomic Bombings of Hiroshima and Nagasaki

On August 6, 1945, the United States military dropped an atomic bomb on Hiroshima, Japan, destroying the city and signifying an end to the war. "I was so happy," remembered Lewis Yee. "I couldn't believe it. The radio man told me, 'We got some kind of bomb, real powerful.' Finally a couple days later, we found out it was the atomic bomb." Both Chinese Texans and future Chinese Texans living in China celebrated the atomic bombings, believing that the Japanese occupation of China, which had resulted in millions of deaths, would soon end.[45]

Frank Fujita, Jr. and his Texan comrades were imprisoned in Tokyo when they learned from their captors of the atomic bombing:

> The blood drained from my face and the hair on my neck stood up, as I read worldwide communications about the Hiroshima atom bomb and its destruction. We all were dumbfounded. I could not imagine how that much awesome power could be contained in one bomb and one plane.[46]

Three days later, the United States dropped an atomic bomb on Nagasaki, Japan, the hometown of Frank Fujita, Sr. When asked about how she and the Japanese Texan community reacted to the atomic bombings of Hiroshima and Nagasaki, Kikuko Nakao Tanamachi became quiet and said in a shaky voice, "It was very devastating."[47]

The End of the War and Beyond

On August 14, 1945, Japan surrendered. Frank Fujita, Jr. and the Texas Lost Battalion were "found" in Tokyo by the United States armed forces. "Foo" returned to Texas, married, and worked as an Air Force illustrator.[48]

In Crystal City, Texas, a long siren sounded at 6 p.m. on August 15, signifying the end of the war. Residents of the town celebrated by ringing bells, honking car horns, and hanging an effigy of Tojo. By this time, the majority of Japanese at the Crystal City internment camp were Latin Americans. Among these, there were some who were pro-Japan and refused to believe that Japan had lost the war, shouting "We won! We won!" Peru would not accept the Japanese Peruvians, so in December 1945, 660 of them were forcibly sent to war-ravaged Japan. About 600 Japanese that same month returned to their homes in the Hawaiian territory, leaving by the new year about 650 of the original 2,100 Japanese.[49]

Among those who resisted deportation to Japan was Ginzo Murono. He, along with Paul Shuhei Katsuro, who had taught Japanese in Lima, Peru, and 176 others were eventually hired by Seabrook Farms in New Jersey. The other Peruvians were also freed from Crystal City, and on

November 1, 1947, the longest running U.S. internment camp was finally closed. Katsuro returned to Texas in 1952, after having married a Japanese American woman. The couple established a plant nursery in Houston.[50]

Yasuo Kenmotsu and wife Mieko, after their release from Crystal City, farmed in Los Ebonos and San Benito before settling in Rio Grande City, where the youngest of four, Sue Ann, was born. Lewis Yee returned to Houston and married Roberta Woo of San Antonio. They had four children and ran two Chinese restaurants and a barbecue. Jiru and Kikuko Tanamachi raised three children on their San Benito farm, and George and Mary Hada raised two children in the same area. George Leo Wingshee married Anita Moy, a Chinese Venezuelan, and they produced two children before Wingshee passed away in 1966. Julian Mardock married Ruth Wilhelm during the war, and afterwards the Mardocks, both doctors, ran a clinic in Dallas. They raised five children. In 1984, San Antonio's Chinese Sunken Garden was renamed the Japanese Tea Garden. Surviving members of the Jingu family attended the dedication ceremony, and so did Alan Taniguchi, designer of the new garden archway.[51]

To this day, Ann Quan and other Chinese Texans who grew up in San Antonio during World War II still stand up or put their hands over their hearts whenever they see an American flag.[52] Through symbolic acts such as a simple salute, through sacrifice of life and limb, and through hard work, activism, and legislation, Asian Texans, in the minds of many Texans, "became," through the war, what most of them already were: loyal Americans and proud Texans. Through their wartime sweat, blood, and death, Asian Texans gained greater rights, responsibilities, and respect.

ENDNOTES

1   Julian Mardock, *The Levee* (Texas: self-published, date unknown), 9; Julian Mardock, *The First of Many* (Dallas: self-published, 1998), 109.

2   Ibid, 109–113.

3   Betty Akagi Coker and Nellie Akagi Camacho, interview by Thomas K. Walls, Dallas, Texas, March 31, 1979; Beatrice and Torata Akagi, interview by Thomas K. Walls, Sheldon, Texas, May 18, 1979; George Kitamura, interview by Thomas K. Walls, southwest of San Benito, May 14, 1979; Thomas K. Walls, *The Japanese Texans*, 2nd ed. (San Antonio: Institute of Texan Cultures, 1996), 164.

4   Walls, *The Japanese Texans*; George J. Hirasaki, Thomas K. Walls, and Kazuhiko Orii, "The Kishi Colony"; Vicki Parfait, "With War, you get internment threats," *Penny Record*, Jan 27, 1999; both accessed at *http://jacl-houston.org* in 2004.

5   Betty Akagi Coker and Nellie Akagi Camacho, interview by Thomas K. Walls, Dallas, Texas, Mar 31, 1979. Also see Beatrice and Torata Akagi, interview.

6   Ibid.

7   Walls, *The Japanese Texans*, 161–162. See also Jiru "Jerry" Tanamachi, interview by Thomas K. Walls, San Benito, Texas, May 15, 1979.

8   Walls, *The Japanese Texans*, 156–157. San Antonio Museum Association, "WWII Times," 1991–1992; *http://www.sanantonio.gov/sapar/japanhis. asp?res=1024&ver=true*, San Antonio city website, retrieved on Mar 4, 2007.

9   Walls, *The Japanese Texans*; Edward Chen, interview by Irwin Tang, Houston, Texas, Feb 1, 2004; "Houston Chinese Are Ready!" *The Houston Post*, Dec 14, 1941; "Ex-Navy Man Wears Sign ... He's Chinese and Not Japanese," *Houston Press*, Dec 15, 1941.

10 Timothy Eng, telephone interview by Irwin Tang, May 10, 2004.

11 Maria "Mae" de los Angeles Mar Skates, interviews by Anna L. Fahy, Dec 1997 and Nov 24, 1998.

12 Ibid.

13 Eng, interview.

14 Dave Leo Wingshee, telephone interview by Irwin Tang, Apr 18, 2004; Lewis W. Yee, telephone interview by Irwin Tang, Apr 23, 2004.

15 Yee, interview.

16 Mardock, *The First of Many*.

17 Eng, interview; (on Wong) Mitchel Wong, interview by Irwin Tang, Austin, Texas, May 26, 2004, see also p. 232; Shih-Shan Henry Tsai, *The Chinese Experience in America* (Bloomington: Indiana University Press, 1986), 195; Estimate of Chinese veterans based on the estimate that about 20% of the Chinese American population served in the war, the highest percentage of any ethnic group.

18 Chen, interview.

19 Judy Yung, ed., *The Adventures of Eddie Fung: Chinatown Kid, Texas Cowboy,*

Prisoner of War (Seattle: University of Washington Press, 2007); Eddie S. Hughes, "Grim War Stories Told at Reunion of the 'Lost,'" *Dallas Morning News*, Aug 16, 1964.

20 Hughes; Frank "Foo" Fujita, *Foo: A Japanese-American Prisoner of the Rising Sun; The Secret Prison Diary of Frank 'Foo' Fujita* (Denton, Texas: University of North Texas Press, 1993), 174–178.

21 Walls, *Japanese Texans*; see also interviews by Walls, some referenced here, available at the Institute of Texan Cultures, San Antonio.

22 Robert Thonhoff, *Camp Kenedy, Texas* (Austin: Eakin Press, 2003), 67–68, 118–119.

23 Ginzo Murono, "Testimony of Mr. Ginzo Murono Provided to The Commission of Wartime Relocation and Internment of Civilians Act Nov 24, 1981," *http://www.wfu.edu/users/muroaf1/asia-pacific/page5.html.*

24 Thonhoff, 266–271.

25 Sue Ann Kenmotsu, telephone interview by Irwin Tang, May 8, 2004.

26 Thonhoff, 121.

27 Thonhoff, 69–70, 77, 89; Emily Brosveen, "World War II internment camps," The Handbook of Texas Online. *http://www.tsha.utexas.edu/handbook/online/articles/view/WW/quwby.html.*

28 Walls, *The Japanese Texans*; Brosveen.

29 Karen Lea Riley, "Schools Behind Barbed Wire: A History of Schooling in the United States Department of Justice Internment Camp at Crystal City, Texas, During World War II, 1942–1946" (Ph.D. dissertation, University of Texas at Austin, August 1996), 243.

30 Riley, 283.

31 Riley, 283–284.

32 Brosveen.

33 Henry Kawahata, interview by Thomas K. Walls, Hidalgo, Texas, May 13, 1979; Mary Oyama Hada, telephone interview by Irwin Tang, Apr 21, 2004.

34 Oyama Hada, interview.

35 Kikuko Nakao Tanamachi, interview by Irwin Tang, League City, Texas, Mar 28, 2004.

36 Xiaohua Ma, "A Democracy at War: The American Campaign to Repeal Chinese Exclusion in 1943," *The Japanese Journal of American Studies*, No. 9 (1998), 137; Ronald Takaki, *Double Victory: A Multicultural History of America in World War II* (New York: Little, Brown, 2000), 120.

37 "Grocer is First Chinese Made U.S. Citizen Here," *Houston Chronicle*, 1944, as reprinted in Edward Chen, "Into the Future Together: Two Lunar Centuries of Progress, 1877–1997; Houstonians of Asian Heritage," unpublished manuscript, 112.

38 Edward C. Chen, "The Chronology of the History of the Chinese in Houston: Business & Professions," Apr 15, 1981, available in "Chinese" vertical file, Houston Public Library.

39 Bill Jary, "Salerno To The Danube: The Battle Story of Texas 36th Division, Chapter 5," *The Fort Worth Press*, Sep 14, 1945.

40 Capt. Thomas W. Akins, "Subject: Recommendation for Award," letter to Commanding General, Seventh Army, APO 758, U.S. Army, Nov 16, 1944.

41 George T. Sakato to Thomas Kuwahara, November 23, 2003; Akins; *http://www. homeofheroes.com/moh/nisei/index7_cc.html*, site on war heroes, accessed 2003.

42 Jary.

43 Takaki, 166; *http://www.homeofheroes.com/moh/nisei/index8_cc.html*; Thomas K. Walls, *The Japanese Texans*, 166–170.

44 Oyama Hada, interview.

45 Yee, interview.

46 Fujita, 300.

47 Tanamachi.

48 Fujita, 306, 357–358.

49 "Public Rejoices Over Jap Capitulation: Hopes Turn to Securing Lasting Peace," *Zavala County Sentinel*, Aug 17, 1945; Riley, 189; Walls, 200.

50 Walls, *Japanese Texans*, 200–203, also Brosveen.

51 See interviews with Sue Ann Kenmotsu, Kikuko Nakao Tanamachi, Lewis Yee, and Dave Wingshee; also Mardock, *The First of Many*, 162; Walls, 212.

52 Eng, interview.

★

CHAPTER SEVEN

THE FILIPINO TEXANS

Irwin A. Tang

Francisco Flores was born in February 1809 on the island of Cebu in the Spanish-ruled Philippine Islands. One of his great granddaughters described his convoluted journey to Texas.

> At the age of thirteen years, he left Cebu as a cabin boy on a large schooner. He took some clothing, and his only other possession, a smoking pipe that he had carved from a piece of wood at the age of ten when he started smoking. While working on different cargo vessels and schooners, he was able to make several trips to Africa.[1]

Flores worked on ships that brought both cargo and African slaves to the United States. He saved his money and learned the ways of business, and he eventually bought two commercial schooners and fished the Gulf Coast from Port Isabel, Texas to Alabama and Georgia. It is unclear when he settled in Texas, but in 1849, Flores, then 40, married Augustina Gonzales, a teenaged Mexican American of Port Isabel. Thus, it is possible that Flores first set foot in the state while it was still part of Mexico (before 1836), and it is very likely that he settled in Texas while it was still an independent Republic (before 1845).[2]

Francisco and Augustina Flores had two sons and a daughter: Agapito, Josefina, and Antonio (nicknamed "Manila"). The family lived in Corpus Christi for a brief period before settling in Rockport, Texas, where Francisco and Agapito continued fishing for "many years." In 1898, the same year the United States acquired the Philippines from Spain through the Spanish-American War, Josefina Flores married a Mexican American man named Estolano Ramirez. After Francisco sold his fishing business and retired, he lived with Josefina, Estolano, and their three children. Francisco died in 1917 at the age of 108, and his son, Agapito died in 1918, a victim of the influenza epidemic. In 1919, Rockport was hit by a "violent hurricane" which destroyed most of the family's possessions. Antonio Flores served in World War I and suffered gas poisoning, which he self-medicated through alcohol—eventually causing him to die in Rockport in 1952. In 1979, still alive were Francisco's ten grandchildren, all born to Josefina, including Ester R. Babida and Berth R. Ramirez.[3]

Francisco Flores was the first Asian Texan. He was fishing the Texas coast during the Civil War, and he was in Texas as hundreds of Chinese railroad workers arrived in 1870. But according to great granddaughter Carmel Babida, Flores would say, with tears in his eyes, that he never met another Filipino during all his travels or during his life in Texas. Francisco did, however, go with his granddaughter, Ester, to a carnival where he met the famous original Siamese twins, Chang and Eng.[4]

Some Filipinos may have come to Texas even before Francisco Flores did. Between 1565 and 1805, Spanish galleons and other colonial ships carrying Filipino workers landed regularly in Acapulco, Mexico; Louisiana; and California. Some of these Filipino workers settled in Mexico and Louisiana, and it is likely that some Filipinos may have ventured into Texas or even lived there before Flores did. Interestingly, the area of Texas above the Medina River was known by the Spanish government and settlers as Nuevas Filipinas and Nuevo Reino de Filipinas. In 1716, Franciscan missionaries from Spain, seeking to establish missions in East Texas, saw the area as a "New Philippines," meaning that, like the Philippines Islands, this land would be a domain incorporated into the Spanish Empire by a King Philip. The Philippines were colonized under

King Philip II, and the territory now known as Texas would be colonized by the forces of King Philip V. However, by the 1800s, the name "Nuevas Filipinas" was rarely used on Spanish documents, having been replaced by the name "Texas." The Spanish provinces of Texas, Nuevo Santander, Nuevo Leon, and Coahuila were known as Provincias Interas *de Oriente* (as opposed to "de Occidente") because these provinces were on the eastern side of New Spain.[5]

In December 1898, the United States purchased the Philippine Islands from Spain, but the Philippines had already declared independence in June. The United States conquered the Philippines Islands in an extremely bloody war that lasted from 1898 to 1913. Before the outbreak of war, the only Filipinos in Texas may have been Francisco Flores and his descendants. During the war, thousands of U.S. soldiers, officers, and government officials based in San Antonio's Fort Sam Houston and El Paso's Fort Bliss served in the Philippines. These Americans hired numerous Filipinos as workers in the Philippines, and they sometimes brought these workers back to the United States. Also brought back from the Philippines was the understanding that a new source of inexpensive Asian labor was now available to American capitalists. During the war, at least one Texas farmer experimented with Filipino labor. In 1902, a "squad" of Filipinos arrived in Lytton Springs in central Texas to work on J.T. Priest's farm. They had apparently been recruited directly from the Philippines. In 1904, Philippines War veteran Edward Morgan suggested that large numbers of the "little brown people" of the Philippines be brought to Texas so that they may benefit from American education and work on American farms, especially Texas rice farms. Probably because of the numerous white, black, and Hispanic workers in Texas, Filipinos never worked on Texas farms in large numbers like they did on the West Coast.[6]

In the early twentieth century, Filipino houseboys working for American military officers in the Philippines were sometimes brought back by officers to the United States to continue working for them. In 1905, a Filipino houseboy (name unknown) about twelve years of age arrived with Captain J.A. Hulen of the 33rd Regiment in Gainesville, Texas and was described by the *Dallas Morning News* as the same size of a white boy of the same age, "remarkably good looking, with a bright black eye and an intelligent countenance." Teodolfo Dizon, originally of San Fernando, Pampanga in the Philippines, was fourteen years old when his employer, a Lieutenant Redhorse of the U.S. Army, prepared Teodolfo to work for a Sergeant-Colonel Sibly:

> Lt. Redhorse turn to me. [He said,] My boy here we part. I go back to Camp Stetsenberg. "You go with him and you wait for Col. Sibly!" [I said,] Lt. "please don't leave me here I want to go back with you!" Lt. said you cannot go back with me "Searge. Col. Sibly sent for you and you go with him to America." And so the Bell boy talk to me in Filipino and took me up stair where's all the boys are staying a short time until their Bosses parting or leaving to America, or to other part of the island.[7]

In 1912 fourteen-year old Teodolfo "Dolfo" Dizon ended up in San Antonio working at Colonel Henry L. Ripley's home, where he looked after Col. Ripley's uniforms, waited on meals, and helped around the house. He worked with a cook, a laundress, and a yard man, and he took over the cooking chores at the age of twenty. He perfected his Mexican dishes and served a Filipino adobo dish that was known as the best in the San Antonio Filipino community. Teodolfo himself was known as a proper and conservative man; Virginia San Luis Dizon, who would marry his son Freddie many years after Teodolfo's death in 1975, remembers how as a child of eight, she caught Teodolfo in his under-shirt, and Teodolfo immediately ran into his room to put on a proper shirt. In 1918, Teodolfo married a Mexican San Antonioan named Estella Muñoz. The couple established their own home and produced four sons, all of whom served in the U.S. military. Teodolfo was one of the founders of the Filipino American Association of San Antonio.[8]

The Great Depression and World War II

The U.S. Census counted six Filipinos in Texas in 1910 and thirty in 1920. A leap in population occurred in the 1920s, as the 1930 Census counted 288 Filipinos, paralleling a steep national increase that resulted from

U.S. immigration policies which allowed for relatively unmitigated Filipino immigration. In 1930, the Filipino Texan population consisted of 246 males and 42 females, an imbalance not unusual among Filipino Americans at that time. Some of these Filipino men in Texas were single and most, it seems, were in some way associated with the U.S. military. Largely because of the social sanction associated with marrying white women, the tendency of Filipino men to be Catholic, their familiarity with Spanish culture, and similarities in appearance between Filipinos and Mexicans, most Filipino Texan men before World War II married Mexican and Mexican-American women. A small minority of Filipino Texan men were married to white women, and in San Antonio, these men tended to come from northern states. Before World War II there were no Filipino women in San Antonio. Virginia Dizon, born in 1936, remembered how exciting it was when the first full-blooded Filipino woman arrived in San Antonio. Virginia, still a minor, along with other mixed-blood children and their Mexican American mothers, flocked to meet, and simply look at, Tomasita Perez.[9]

From about 1910 until about 1950, the Filipino community of San Antonio consisted mostly of Filipino-Mexican families. Some men were unmarried. During the 1930s and 1940s, at any given time, there were likely more than twenty Filipino families, including single men as family units. In those early decades, most of the Filipino men in San Antonio worked as servants and cooks for local families and the U.S. military. Some worked as civil servants. The men maintained a sense of Filipino community by hosting dinners and by cooking Filipino foods. Because they spoke various Filipino dialects, they used either Pilipino (Tagolog) or English with each other. They taught their children only English, so that they would speak the language well. Besides, the children's Mexican mothers were not fluent in Filipino languages. At weekly poker games, Filipino San Antonioan men socialized and talked politics. Living through the Great Depression, Filipinos in San Antonio voted straight Democratic tickets because of the party's provision of jobs and support for working-class Americans.[10]

Filipino families were well-accepted within the Mexican community of San Antonio, where the Filipinos learned to speak Spanish.

Filipinos often worked alongside Mexicans in the homes of the wealthy. Nevertheless, the Dizon boys went to white high schools, rather than black or Hispanic high schools. The Filipino families did interact with the sizable Chinese community in San Antonio. Chinese grocery stores were the only places to find some ingredients for Filipino foods, and some Filipino men gambled at a Chinese gambling parlor. Gambling was technically illegal, but city officials allowed local Asians to play mah-jongg for money.[11]

Filipinos lived in various Texas cities and towns. While a major storm in 1932 forced the remaining descendants of Francisco Flores to leave the coastal town of Rockport, granddaughter Ester Ramirez returned to the coast after her husband, Brigidio Babida (a Filipino man who had mi-grated from a northern U.S. state), won a large sum of money in a poker game while living in San Antonio. In Corpus Christi, Babida opened the Black Cat Café, where patrons, including politicians, ate food prepared by a Chinese cook, drank alcohol, and played billiards. During the Great Depression, Babida gave the needy free beans and rice and coffee grinds. The success of the café allowed for the family to travel in a chauffeured Rolls Royce, and Babida enjoyed high stakes poker games. Local officials apparently disliked Babida's wealth and bravado and accused him in 1935 of various crimes. While being arrested, Babida hit an immigration of-ficial in the neck with a billiards ball. His daughter Carmel (born in 1928) remembered seeing her father, days later, attempting to blow her a kiss while he was handcuffed and standing on the deck of the ship on which he was being deported to the Philippines. There, he fought the Japanese as a guerilla during World War II and eventually died a poor man. Babi-da's deportation was likely related to the passage of the Filipino Repatria-tion Act of 1935, designed to encourage and pressure Filipino Americans to return to the Philippines Islands and not come back.[12]

The children of the San Antonio Filipino men tended to marry non-Filipinos, and some of the sons continued family traditions of military service. Teodolfo Dizon's youngest son, Freddie Dizon (born in 1931), was an early Filipino in the Marine Corps, fighting in both the Korean and the Vietnam Wars. Manuel Dizon was a champion Golden Gloves boxer with a "more scientific style of boxing." Daniel Dizon, more of a

The 1946 Rizal Day gathering of the Texas Filipino Club. Teodolfo Dizon is seated in front. Among the sixty-two pictured here were many men born in the Philippines, their predominantly Mexican American and white wives, the couples' children, and a few white military officers.

slugger-type boxer, served as an officer in the 1st Division of the Philippines Scouts during World War II. The oldest son, Dolfo (born in 1919), married in the 1940s and was one of the first Texas-born Filipino men to marry a white woman. He graduated from St. Mary's College in 1951 with a B.S. in Physics. He began working as a technician at NASA's School of Aerospace Medicine at Brooks Air Force Base in San Antonio, and in 1960 he was promoted to the position of research physicist. One of the first Asian Americans working in the U.S. space program, Dolfo researched the possible effects of space travel on the bodies of early astronauts, including Alan Shepard. Among other discoveries, Dizon developed the open-chest heart massage, which could revive hearts that had stopped beating. Later in life, Dolfo Dizon married Carmel Babida, uniting the descendants of Francisco Flores and Teodolfo Dizon.[13]

The 1930 to 1940 drop in the Filipino population, from 288 to 219, may be explained by the sudden drop in Filipino immigration occurring around the onset of the Great Depression in 1929; the Tydings-McDuffie Act of 1934 limiting Filipino immigration to the U.S. to fifty per year and re-classifying Filipinos as "aliens"; and the aforementioned Filipino Repatriation Act of 1935. Nevertheless, a 1937 U.S. Census estimate put the population of Filipinos in Texas at 354, indicating a large rise in the Filipino population. The 1930s anti-Filipino riots on the West Coast may have discouraged immigration from the Philippines but encouraged migration from other states into the state of Texas. The most prominent of these riots was the Watsonville, California riot of 1930. Like the Chinese and Japanese in previous decades, Filipinos may have sought refuge from violence, expulsions, and intense segregation by moving to Texas, where no anti-Asian riots had been recorded. Furthermore, anti-Filipino sentiment was fueled by the popularity of Filipino men among white women. With few Filipino women available, Filipino men may have been encouraged to move to Texas, where they could court Mexican American women without the fear of being assaulted by groups of white men. Immigration status became a factor after 1934. As in previous decades in Texas, though, immigration laws were applied unevenly. In 1940, when 230 non-citizens registered as aliens at the Dallas Federal Building, a group of Filipinos showed up and were not given a clear answer as to whether they were citizens or aliens.[14]

The Census counted only two Filipinos living in Dallas in 1930, but by 1932, W.N. Sabater founded the Texas Filipino Club and the local newspaper recorded the organization's Rizal Day celebration as a "dinner-dance" at the Jefferson Hotel. The Dallas organization was active, holding regular meetings, lectures, receptions for visiting Filipinos, and celebrations of Filipino holidays. At the 1933 Rizal Day celebration, Sabater declared his opinion, and likely the opinion of Filipino Texans, on the issue of Filipino independence from the United States. He stated publicly that the people of the Philippines would only be satisfied with full and unconditional independence from the United States. By the late 1930s, about twenty-five Filipinos lived in Dallas, all of whom worked in domestic service.[15]

In 1937, Philippines Islands President Manuel Quezon made a tour of the United States to campaign for Philippines independence in Washington, D.C., New York City, and other places. In April, before taking the train for an official visit to Mexico, President Quezon stopped in both San Antonio and Laredo. In San Antonio, he met with Gen. Douglas MacArthur, Gen. Herbert J. Brees, and Mayor Charles K. Quin. Also, a group of local Filipinos greeted him.[16]

Within 24 hours of the attack on Pearl Harbor, Filipinos in Texas already felt the effect of anti-Japanese sentiment, even though the Japanese military had attacked the Philippines Islands simultaneously with the Pearl Harbor attack. "Because of the war we ask citizens of this city to remember that our islands are taking the first brunt of this attack," said Filipino Dallasite Resti N. Paulo to the *Dallas Morning News*. "Some Filipinos here are almost afraid to go out on the street." In the immediate aftermath of Pearl Harbor, a Filipino yo-yo expert was wrongly jailed along with a local Japanese American farmer.[17]

Filipinos in the Philippines suffered tremendously during World War II. Alfredo Quijano was born January 8, 1916 in Zamboanga City in the Philippines. His father, Alfonso Quijano (1886–1965), had served as a Philippines Scout sergeant under Colonel Arthur McArthur in quelling the Moro insurrection during the U.S. war in the Philippines. The Philippines Scouts were an ethnic Filipino arm of the U.S. forces in the Philippines. Alfredo joined the Philippines Scouts in October 1933, and

Alejandro Atienza San Luis and his wife, Adela Sustaita San Luis some time before 1936. Adela is holding Alejandro's military cap.

Alfredo Quijano stands before a portrait of himself as a young man in his military uniform. This photo was taken in 2004.

by the time the Japanese invaded in 1941, he was a specialist in person-nel. Many of the Scouts were not well-educated, but Alfredo was high school-educated and had learned American slang and culture by watch-ing American films around Fort William McKinley south of Manila.[18]

When the Japanese military invaded, the Philippines Scouts dem-onstrated extreme valor; Alfredo Quijano earned a Silver Star, a Bronze Star, and two Purple Hearts for his gallantry. In 1942, when the United States surrendered the Philippines, the Japanese took both the Filipino and the American soldiers as prisoners and forced them on what became known as the Bataan Corregidor Death March, a one to two week march to concentration camps where thousands died. Quijano recalled:

> You know there are things that are hard to [speak of] if you don't want to remember, right? So, I do not say much what happened . . . We were in concentration camps. Have no food. People were dying by the hundreds every day. About four hundred every day. We can't help it. There's no sanitation, no nothing. People were dying of dysentery, beri-beri, influenza.[19]

Beri-beri and malaria reduced Alfredo to a mere seventy pounds. His father sneaked into camp the boiled bark of the shichona tree for temporary relief for malaria victims. After Japan's defeat in 1945, a U.S. judge visited military camps in the Philippines to grant immediate U.S. citizenship to any Philippines Scout willing to join as a regular member of the U.S. military. Alfredo Quijano and thousands took their oaths of citizenship, and thousands were shipped to military bases throughout the United States, including Texas.[20]

On July 4, 1946, the federal government granted the Philippines in-dependence from the United States. Independence was "no big deal" for Filipinos long-settled in San Antonio, as they had "already American-ized."[21] Nevertheless, the aftermath of the war and independence for the Philippines transformed Filipino Texas.

Filipinos in Military Towns and Cities

In the 1940s and 1950s, former Philippines Scouts assigned to Texas military bases served mostly in El Paso, San Antonio, and Killeen. While medics worked at San Antonio's Brooke Army Hospital, the largest group of former Scouts, including those associated with the U.S. Cavalry and World War II infantry, were largely stationed in El Paso's Fort Bliss. In 1962, Socorro Montague (born in 1926 in the Philippines) arrived in El Paso with her first husband (a former Philippines Scout and U.S. Army artillery soldier named Julio Alarilla) and their first three children. By that time, she recalled, El Paso's Filipino population had grown to between 100 and 200 families. In the 1960s and 1970s, almost all married couples consisted of Filipino military men and Filipino women. According to Montague, Filipino El Pasoans did not have the "gumption" to start an association, but in 1971, military wife Candice Apuan, who had seen Filipino military wives in other cities form organizations, founded the Filipino-American Association of El Paso. Military wives ran the organization, which facilitated social events. During the Vietnam War at least three Filipino El Pasoans died in combat, and some veterans of the war struggled with drug addiction.[22]

Filipino American military personnel continued to migrate to El Paso in the 1970s. Many Filipino American military families, including retirees, preferred El Paso for its low property prices. In 1980, the widowed and then re-married Montague opened a country and western nightclub called Saso's, which was connected to a Filipino-American restaurant, and these places became a community gathering place for Filipinos until 1996, when it closed. In 1988, Montague was elected president of the local Filipino association, and it began organizing native dance demonstrations at Texas and New Mexico military bases, as well as holding Miss Philippines pageants. With the arrival of large numbers of nurses in the 1980s, a Philippines Nurses Association was formed. In 2005, the association included hundreds of nurses and thirty doctors.[23]

San Antonio's Filipino community evolved in a manner similar to El Paso's. Along with six other former Philippines Scouts, Alfredo Quijano was assigned to San Antonio's Brooke Army Medical Center in

1949, where he was happy to work in personnel, as he wished to see no more combat. Quijano and other Filipinos from Brooke and Fort Hood settled in the Skyline Park neighborhood, where they formed a small Filipino community. In 1952, Alfredo's wife, Cristina, and their two children joined him in San Antonio, where the couple raised five children.

Many of the Filipino military men who were stationed at Texas military bases were Filipinos who joined the U.S. military not in the Philippines but in the United States. Alejandro Atienza San Luis, originally of Los Banos, Laguna in the Philippines, married Adela Sustaita of Nuevo Laredo, Mexico when he was 28 and she was about 15, and the couple had two daughters, including Virginia, who was born in the Fort Sam Houston Hospital in 1936. Alejandro was an Army man. "My father took us to the Philippines, after the 2nd World War, hoping to settle there," wrote Virginia, "Didn't happen. We stayed one year and returned 'home.' That was in 1949. I went to school in San Antonio, married and had 3 children." She remarried to Freddie Dizon in her sixties.[24]

Nemesio Domingo was drafted into the U.S. military during World War II, and after the war, he was stationed in Killeen, Texas, where, in 1952, he and his wife Adelina produced a son named Silme. In 1960, the family moved to Seattle, where Silme eventually became a labor activist with the International Longshoremen's and Warehouseman's Union. While fighting for workers' rights and a better union in 1981, Silme and another activist were gunned down and killed; Silme is remembered as a labor activist hero.[25]

In 1960, there were 348 Filipino Texans in El Paso County, 213 in Bexar County (San Antonio), 149 in Bell County (Killeen), 155 in Harris County (Houston), 83 in Nueces County (Corpus Christi), 80 in Galveston County, and 72 in Bee County (Beeville). The population of Killeen was about 0.5% Filipino, by far the highest among all Texas cities; the city's Filipino population was almost equally male and female. In Galveston, the number of Filipino females was two-and-a-half times the number of males, likely because of the Filipino nurses working in Galveston and Houston. In Corpus Christi the number of males equaled four times the females, as the majority of Filipinos there were U.S. navy men. Overall, the sex balance in Texas was not as severe, with 895 males and 728 females. The increase in the number of Filipino females was in part a result of Filipino military men marrying Filipina women while serving overseas, partly due to the wives of Filipino military men immigrating to Texas after their husbands had already immigrated, and partly due to the increasing number of Filipina nurses, who had begun to immigrate after 1948.[26]

On March 12, 1941, The Naval Air Station at Corpus Christi opened. Two other naval bases also opened that year in nearby Kingsville and Beeville. As the bases grew—the naval air station at Corpus Christi became the largest in the nation—the southern Texas coast became a major population center of Filipinos. Filipino nationals were actively recruited by the U.S. Navy, so a large number of Filipino nationals joined the U.S. Navy. In the early years, most of these men served as stewards, but because of a Navy policy change, many more Filipinos began serving as sailors in the 1970s.[27]

Roger Munoz, born in 1939 in the Philippines, began working for the U.S. Navy at the age of seventeen. In 1964, after three years of college and working for the Navy at Sangle Point for seven years, Munoz told the U.S. Navy he had only a high school education (because college-educated Filipinos were not accepted) and joined the U.S. Navy as a steward, working in the mess hall. He arrived in Corpus Christi in 1964, when the town's roads were unpaved and there were very few Filipinos, the first ones having arrived, Munoz estimated, around 1946. Munoz and thirty-five other Filipino navy men lived in Corpus Christi and often visited the home of a Mr. Monzon, who had married a Mexican American woman. Among those thirty-five men, ten married Mexican American women in Corpus Christi, and the rest married elsewhere.[28]

In 1978, Munoz met his future wife while deployed in the Philippines. In 1979, they began living in Corpus Christi, where an estimated one thousand Filipinos had organized themselves into an association. Most were active or retired Filipino American navy men and their families. Throughout the post-war decades, Corpus Christi, El Paso, and San Antonio attracted Filipino American military men because real property in those cities was inexpensive. For example, houses in Corpus Christi were less expensive than houses in the navy city of San Diego.[29]

In Corpus Christi, Filipino American families concentrated in the Flower Bluff neighborhood near the naval air station. Beginning in 1981, local hospitals began employing Filipina nurses, and their numbers increased tremendously over the years. Most of the Filipino immigrants in and around Corpus Christi in the 1990s and 2000s were Filipina nurses and their families. These nurses often married Filipino American military men, but as time passed nurses often immigrated with their husbands and children. Furthermore, more U.S.-born Filipino Texans were trained as nurses. After the U.S. Navy stopped recruiting Filipino nationals in 1992, the number of Filipino soldiers and sailors migrating to Texas military bases dropped off tremendously. Filipino nurses and doctors continued to grow in number, and their population surpassed that of Filipinos associated with the military even in naval cities like Corpus Christi.[30]

Nurses, Engineers, People Power and Beyond

In the 1950s and 1960s, increasing numbers of Filipino professionals—mostly nurses and doctors—settled in Texas. These immigrants tended to come from wealthier families than did the Filipino nationals who joined the U.S. military. One of the earliest Filipino doctors to immigrate to the United States was Dr. James Diamonon. Born in Manila in 1931 and having experienced a childhood he characterized as a "life of splendor," Diamonon survived Japanese occupation and graduated from medical school in the Philippines in 1956. He interned in New York City and took his residency in surgery in 1959 at the University of Texas M.D. Anderson Hospital and Tumor Institute in Houston. "My God, I'm in the Philippines," thought Diamonon when he first encountered the Houston climate. In the early 1960s, Diamonon knew very few Filipinos in Houston, and the ones he did know tended to leave Houston within two years, after finishing their medical training. Nevertheless, Dr. Diamonon did meet nurse Maria Nieves, who worked at UTMB-Galveston. The Filipino couple married in 1961.[31]

In 1948, the United States established the Exchange Visitor Program (EVP) to fill U.S. needs for professionals, including nurses. One of

Dr. Pura Santiago working in a lab in San Antonio's Nix Hospital in 1948. She was a visiting M.D. planning on returning to the Philippines.

Dr. James Diamonon, M.D., in his Houston office, 2004.

the earliest Filipino nurses in Texas was Francisca Primero, who was described as a "pretty 23-year-old nurse who survived Japanese occupation of her homeland." Hailing from Cavite, home of a U.S. military base, she began her postgraduate studies at Baylor University in September 1948. While most of the EVP nurses were required to return to the Philippines, some married American citizens and could remain in the U.S. EVP nurses worked for two years at a relatively low salary.[32]

The immigration reform of 1965, along with subsequent federal legislation from 1970 to 1990, made the immigration of Filipino nurses easier. In Texas, between 1970 and 1973, Filipino nurses, who were throughout the twentieth century predominantly female, held temporary nursing licenses until they passed Texas's licensing board examination. The number of Filipino nurses in Texas during this period increased from 60 to 1,752. Because of differences in nursing education in the Philippines, only 20% to 25% of Filipino nurses passed the board exams, and the state of Texas, spurred on by white-dominated nursing associations, refused in 1973 to grant temporary nursing licenses. In response, the Immigration and Naturalization Service stopped issuing H-1 Visas to foreign nurses seeking work in Texas. The Texas Hospital Association protested, saying the INS action would be "a catastrophic experience for Texas hospitals." The hospitals' lobbying efforts succeeded and the INS revoked its action.[33] As a result, the number of Filipino nurses training, working, and earning permanent residency and citizenship in Texas increased.

The most popular occupation among Texas's Filipino immigrants was nursing. By 1990, an estimated 2,000 Filipino nurses worked in the Houston area, and by that time, the pass rate on the state board exam had increased to 37%. By the early 2000s, the number of Filipino and Filipino American nurses working in the Houston area was estimated to be 4,000. It was a point of pride among Filipino Houstonians that without Filipino nurses, one of the largest medical communities in the United States could not continue to operate. Additionally, the number of Filipino and Filipino American physicians increased; in 2004, about fifty Filipino doctors belonged to the Harris County Medical Society. Hundreds of Filipino physicians belonged to the Texas Association of Philippines Physicians.[34]

In the 1970s, Dr. Diamonon proposed, and then headed, the first emergency medical *department* in the city of Houston, at St. Joseph's Hospital. In the early 1980s, Dr. Diamonon served as the hospital's Chief of Surgery. Meanwhile, Filipino nurses also advanced upward in hospital hierarchies. Lucy Pendon first began nursing in Texas in the mid-1960s and in 1975, she set up the Staff Development Department at Community Hospital of Brazosport. Pendon recruited other Filipino nurses, and some even slept in her home upon first arrival. In 1982, Pendon served as the president of the Texas Society for Hospital Educators. Other Filipino Texan nurses started their own health staffing businesses, further increasing the numbers of Filipino nurses.[35]

After the 1965 immigration reform, the Filipino Texan community of Houston grew faster than other Filipino Texan communities. Overall, Filipino Texans were concentrated in professional fields. In the 1990s and 2000s, about 78% of adult Filipino Houstonians had earned a college degree, more than any other Asian Houstonian ethnic group. In the Philippines, those of native Filipino descent (rather than, say, Chinese descent) tended to prefer professional work over running businesses. The same preference was evident in Texas. From the 1970s into the new millennium, a plurality of Filipino Houstonian women worked as nurses, and a major portion of Filipino Houstonian men worked as engineers. Other Filipino professionals worked as accountants, attorneys, and civil servants. During the oil boom years of the 1970s and early 1980s, Houston's abundance of jobs attracted thousands of Filipino engineers. Consecutive harsh winters in the late 1970s in the Midwest and Northeast also pushed Filipino Americans to this warm-climate city. Filipino Houstonian engineers worked for Exxon, Shell, Bechtel, Brown and Root, and other companies. Filipino Houstonian women, who comprised a solid majority of the Filipino population, worked in large numbers as nurses at the Texas Medical Center and other local hospitals.[36]

In the 1980s, a typical Filipino couple in Houston consisted of a male engineer and a female nurse. When the oil bust of the 1980s caused high unemployment among engineers in Houston, the pairing of engineers and nurses proved both useful and problematic for the couples. Because the demand for nurses remained strong, the wives retained their jobs, but the economic recessions cost many of the husbands their jobs. As a result, many Filipino American men stayed at home caring for the children while the wives worked. The conflicts resulting from this role reversal caused some Filipino couples to seek divorces, recalled Filipino Houstonian lawyer Lope Lindio. A community leader since the late 1970s, Lindio encouraged couples to save their marriages.[37]

In the Philippines, political and social organizing were major pre-occupations, according to Lope Lindio, and Filipino Texans similarly had a "compulsive sense of organizing." In the early years, community organizations were necessary simply to maintain a sense of community among the small numbers of Filipinos. In the late 1950s, Filipino Navy men stationed on the Texas coast gathered in places like Galveston or Hermann Park in Houston for picnics and Filipino food. A dozen or so Filipinos attended any one of these meetings, and they called themselves the Filipino Organization of Texas. As Filipino immigration increased, Filipinos started community organizations in every major Texas city. In 1969 or so, the San Antonio Filipino community formed Filipino Americans of San Antonio, which promoted their community and Filipino culture at San Antonio's annual Texas Folklife Festival. The money raised at the Festival was used for college scholarships for local Filipinos.[38]

James Diamonon was, in 1963, the president of an early Filipino Texan organization known as the Filipino Association of Texas. A related organization named the Filipino Association of Metropolitan Houston (FAMH) came into being in 1968, and Filemon Reyes was its first president. In the 1970s and 1980s, as Filipino immigration increased tremendously, organizations like the FAMH became the umbrella organizations for quickly-proliferating community, cultural, social, regional, alumni, and professional organizations. By the 1970s, Philippines nurses associations had formed in San Antonio, El Paso, and Houston. The variety among organizations was great; Filipino Catholics even formed groups dedicated to patron saints of the Philippines. At the height of organizing, about forty Filipino organizations existed in Houston alone. New organizations split off of old ones. For instance, the Filipino American Society of Texas (FAST) was an alternative to the FAMH; even in El Paso there formed two "umbrella" Filipino organizations. Organization members were sometimes exhausted by heated intra- and inter-organizational politics, but individuals were energized by winning organization elections. All members, of course, felt a degree of personal fulfillment when helping their local Filipino communities by organizing cultural events or helping those in need.[39]

By 2005, despite an increasing Filipino population, there were only about twenty-five Filipino Houstonian community organizations. As organizations disappeared, they were not replaced by new organizations. The younger generation of community leaders felt less need to form overlapping groups. "While before they were fighting over little things," said Lope Lindio, "now they have become more accommodating, not so passionate."[40]

Between 1972 and 1986, some Filipino immigrants left the Philippines out of fear of persecution under the Ferdinand Marcos government. Lope Lindio, who immigrated first to Illinois, was among them. Some of these Filipinos left their homes in the Philippines only to lose the rest of their wealth in the United States through failed business ventures. Others, however, succeeded economically. Local Filipino Texan communities were sometimes divided over the Marcos regime. Some supported Marcos because of political and business ties or because of region-related loyalties. For the most part, though, such differences were set aside, according to Lindio, who said, "We are Filipinos first."[41]

Much like early Korean Texans, Filipino Texans formed early communities around large medical districts, such as Houston's. In the 1970s, Filipino nurses lived near the Houston medical district in part because they either owned no cars or could not drive. As Filipinos saved more money, acculturated, and sought the best education for their children, Filipinos concentrated in other areas. In the 1980s, many Filipinos lived in the Houston suburb of Alief and Northwest Houston for their better schools. Filipinos also concentrated in the 1980s and 1990s in Southwest Houston, Fort Bend County, and the northern suburbs of Dallas in order to send their children to better schools and to live and work in Asian communities. By the 1990 Census, the Filipino Texan population had clearly shifted from San Antonio, El Paso, and military towns to Houston, Dallas, and their suburbs. The counties with the largest Filipino

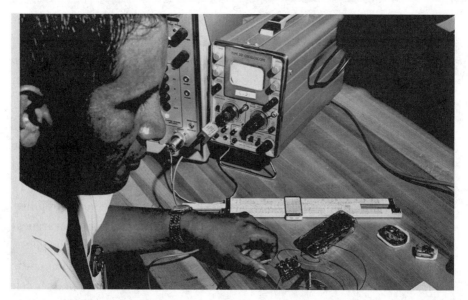

Dolfo Dizon was an early research scientist at NASA. This photo was likely taken in the early 1960s.

A young Filipino couple elected to represent the community at a fiesta organized by San Antonio's Filipino-American Association. In La Villita neighborhood, March 23, 1974.

populations were Harris (Houston), 11,697; Dallas, 4,711; Bexar (San Antonio), 3,208; Fort Bend, 2,861; Tarrant (Fort Worth), 1,674; El Paso, 1,164; Travis (Austin), 1,042; and Nueces (Corpus Christi), 1,019. Nevertheless, compared to other Asian ethnic groups, Filipinos were concentrated in places with military bases.[42]

The "People Power" revolution in the Philippines overthrew the Marcos government and brought a democratic form of government to the Philippines. The revolution inspired people worldwide and also raised awareness among Texans' of their own Filipino Texan community. In Dallas, publicized prayer services were held in honor of the Philippines' democratic transition. Having celebrated Filipino Cultural Awareness Masses for ten years, Filipino Catholics in San Antonio held in 1986 a special mass in thanksgiving for the Philippines' peaceful democratic transition. Then, after several more years of annual Filipino masses celebrating Santo Niño (the holy infant), a Filipino American parish was set up in the Archdiocese of San Antonio. In June 1998, the doors opened at the Santo Niño Catholic Church, the first Filipino American Catholic Church in Texas. It was the pride and product of many of Alfredo Quijano's generation in San Antonio, among others.[43]

The "People Power" revolution in the Philippines resulted in the nation's new president, Corazon Aquino, returning to the city of Dallas. Corazon Aquino had originally visited Dallas in 1980 when her husband, Benigno Aquino, a well-known dissident under the Marcos regime, was allowed out of prison to undergo heart surgery. Benigno Aquino preferred Dallas because of the presence of Filipino Dallasite, Dr. Rolando Solis, M.D., who diagnosed Aquino before he underwent heart surgery under the knife of a local surgeon. On a two-day visit to Dallas in 1989, President Aquino met with retailer J.C. Penney, a corporation that bought tremendous amounts of clothes manufactured in the Philippines. Aquino encouraged American companies to do more business with the Philippines.[44]

Increases in Filipino nurse immigrants, as well as births among Filipino Americans, brought about gender parity among Filipino Texans by 1980. In 1992, as a result of the end of the Cold War, the United States closed down its huge Subic Bay naval base in the Philippines, and

Filipino nationals were no longer allowed to join the U.S. Navy. Thus, a major source of Filipino male immigrants to Texas was cut off. Male immigrants from the Philippines thereafter tended to be the husbands of nurses.

Filipinos also began arriving to Texas to work as teachers. By 1992, several South Texas school districts had hired Filipino teachers to help fill vacancies in science classes and other hard-to-fill slots. By 1994, the Dallas Independent School District considered hiring Filipino teachers, who were being contracted through businesses like Multicultural Education Consultants. In the 1990s and early 2000s, Texas was a pioneer in hiring Filipino and other foreign teachers, as the nation struggled to deal with a shortage in teachers.[45]

Slightly less than 60,000 Filipinos lived in Texas in the year 2000, and a slight majority of them lived in the Houston and the Dallas-Fort Worth areas. Filipino Texans numbered over 20,000 in the combined Harris and Fort Bend Counties, where they were the fourth largest Asian ethnic group. In the four major "Asian" counties of Dallas-Fort Worth (Dallas, Tarrant, Collin, and Denton), Filipinos numbered nearly 12,700 and were the fifth largest Asian group. Because Filipino Texans were associated with health care, military installations, and education, they were more widely dispersed than other Asians. Still well-represented in military cities, it was estimated that three to four thousand Filipinos lived in Corpus Christi in 2001, making them by far the largest Asian ethnic group in the city. The 5,580 Filipinos in San Antonio also represented the largest Asian group there. In the military cities of El Paso and Killeen, Filipinos were the second-largest Asian ethnic group, behind the Koreans. In the twenty-one furthest south Texas counties, Filipinos constituted about 45% of all Asians. They were by far the largest Asian ethnic group in the predominantly-Hispanic cities of Corpus Christi, Brownsville, Harlingen, Edinburg, McAllen, and Uvalde.[46]

Filipino Texans, in their first hundred years, formed families mostly with Mexican Texans. The first full-blooded second-generation Filipino Texans were born after World War II. A shift from military service to professional work occurred after 1965, and the second generation, born after 1965, were also heavily concentrated in professional work.

While their parents sustained their Filipino identity through highly energized Filipino Texan organizations, second-generation Filipinos are a more diverse group. The interplay of integration and immigration will continue, even as the Filipino Texan identity evolves in a multicultural Texan society.

ENDNOTES

1 Mrs. Conrad S. Campnest, "Biography of the first Filipino in Texas," March 1979, available in "Filipinos" vertical File, Institute of Texan Cultures, San Antonio. Campnest was a great-granddaughter of Francisco Flores.

2 Campnest.

3 On quotes, see Campnest; Dizon, Carmel Babida, interview by Irwin Tang, July 23, 2005.

4 Campnest; Babida, interview.

5 Barbara M. Posadas *The Filipino Americans* (Westport, CT: Greenwood Press, 1999), 13; on Louisiana, see also Marina Espina, *Filipinos in Louisiana* (Laborde, 1988); *Handbook of Texas Online*, s.v. "New Philippines," *http://www.tsha.utexas.edu/handbook/online/articles/view/NN/usn1.html* (accessed Jan 5, 2005); *Handbook of Texas Online*, s.v. "Ladron De Guevara, Antonio," *http://www.tsha.utexas.edu/handbook/online/articles/view/LL/fla11.html* (accessed Jan 5, 2005).

6 "Filipinos brought to Texas," *Dallas Morning News*, Jul 25, 1902; "Little Brown Men," *Dallas Morning News*, Oct 15, 1904.

7 "Specimen from the Philippines," *Dallas Morning News*, May 5, 1901; Teodolfo Dizon, written account of his childhood, provided by son Freddie Dizon, San Antonio.

8 Dolfo Dizon, Freddie Dizon, Virginia San Luis Dizon, Carmel Babida Dizon, Mary Grace Villejo Rodriguez, interviews by Irwin Tang, San Antonio, July 23, 2005, hereafter known as "Group interview."

9 Group interview; U.S. Censuses of 1910, 1920, 1930, and 1960. I purposefully looked for evidence of Filipino farm workers, but found none except the tiny mention in this chapter; also, little evidence exists that there were many Filipino businesses.

10 Group interview.

11 Ibid.

12 Carmel Babida Dizon, interview.

13 Dolfo Dizon, interview.

14 "230 Register as Aliens at U.S. Building," *Dallas Morning News*, Aug 29, 1940;
    Harry C. Withers, "Keeping Step with Texas," *Dallas Morning News*, Mar 28, 1939.

15 "Filipino Leader Honored at Feast Of Dallas Group," *Dallas Morning News*, Dec 31,
    1933; "Filipinos Here Plan annual Tribute to Islands' National Hero," *Dallas Morn-
    ing News*, Dec 30, 1939.

16 *New York Times*, "Quezon Reaches Mexico," Apr 9, 1937; Institute of Texan Cul-
    tures photo collection, photos L-1550-WW through ZZ showing photos of Quezon
    in San Antonio, WW published in *San Antonio Light* on Apr 8.

17 "Filipinos Fear Being Mistaken For Japanese," *Dallas Morning News*, Dec 8, 1941;
    "Dallas Police Hold Three Natives of Enemy Countries," *Dallas Morning News*,
    Dec 23, 1941.

18 Alfredo Quijano, interview by Irwin Tang, San Antonio, Sep 16, 2004.

19 Ibid.

20 Ibid.

21 Dolfo Dizon, interview.

22 Colonel John Olson (retired), U.S. Army, phone interview by Irwin Tang, Oct 18,
    2005; Socorro Montague, interview by Irwin Tang, Oct 24, 2005; marriage pattern
    jibes with the relative male-female parity of Filipinos in military cities in the Cen-
    suses.

23 Montague, interview.

24 Virginia San Luis Dizon, to Irwin Tang, emails, Jul 24 and 25, 2005.

25 *http://www.bulosan.org/html/organizers.html* (accessed on Jun 5, 2005) and *www.
    historylink.org/output.CFM?file_ID=412* (accessed on Jun 5, 2005)

26 1960 U.S. Census, Vol. 45, pp. 64–124, 245–263; Roger Munoz, phone interview
    by Irwin Tang.; The War Brides Act of 1945 and The Information and Education
    Exchange Act of 1948 brought many Filipina war brides and nurses to the United
    States and Texas.

27 Quijano, interview; Freddie Dizon, interview.

28 Munoz, interview.

29 Ibid.

30 Ibid.

31 James Diamonon, interview by Irwin Tang, Houston, Dec 23, 2004.

32 "Filipino Nurse Arrives For Studies at Baylor," *Dallas Morning News*, Sep 17, 1948;
    Ben Ongoco, "Filipinos, Not New in Houston," unpublished article, 2003.

33 Catherine Ceniza Choy, *Empire of Care: Nursing and Migration in Filipino Ameri-
    can History* (Durham, N.C.: Duke University Press, 2003), 166–172.

34 Jo Ann Zuniga, "Hiring of nurses from Philippines sparks inquiry" *Houston
    Chronicle*, Nov 28, 1990; Ongoco; Diamonon, interview

35 Ongoco, "Filipinos, Not New in Houston."

36 Lope Lindio interview by Irwin Tang, October 1, 2005.; Stephen Klineberg, "Hous-
    ton's Economic and Demographic Transformations: Findings from the Expanded

2002 Survey of Houston's Ethnic Communities," Rice University, 2002.

37 Lindio, interview.

38 Lindio, interview; Munoz, interview; Quijano, interview.

39 Lindio, interview.

40 Ongoco, interview; Montague, interview; Diamonon, interview; Lindio, interview.

41 Lindio, interview.

42 Diamonon, interview; Lindio, interview.

43 John Sare, "Filipinos gather to give thanks," *Dallas Morning News*, Mar 3, 1986; Quijano, interview,

44 Catalina Camia, "Sweet Homecoming: Filipinos plan jubilant welcome for Aquino on her first trip back to Dallas as president," *Dallas Morning News*, Nov 10, 1989; Richard Alm, "Aquino's whirlwind visit ends," *Dallas Morning News*, Nov 12, 1989; Rita Rubin, "Doctor to help devise Aquino medical plan," *Dallas Morning News*, Feb 26, 1986.

45 Anna Macias, "Latinos worried by plan to hire Filipino teachers: Some fear DISD to count them as Hispanics," *Dallas Morning News*, Jun 2, 1994, p. 27A; Galutra Bahadur, "Schools face hurdles hiring from abroad," *Austin American-Statesman*, Jun 5, 2000, p. A1.

46 U.S. Census, 1980, 2000; Leanne Libby, "Vibrant Asian customs reel and rigadoon at masquerade," *Corpus Christi Caller-Times*, Feb 16, 2001.

★

CHAPTER EIGHT

THE INDIAN TEXANS

Irwin A. Tang, Sockalingam "Sam" Kannappan,
and Rakesh Amaram

Early Indian Texans

The first wave of Indian immigrants to America consisted mostly of Sikhs from India's Punjab province settling in the American West between 1900 and 1924. Some of these Sikh men settled in Texas after landing or living on the west coast and Latin America. Some of the Sikh men in Texas farmed cotton and most or all likely married Mexican or Mexican American women. According to the U.S. Census, there were two Indians in Texas in 1910 and four in 1920, two of them living in Dallas. By 1930, forty-nine Indians lived in Texas.[1]

Before 1946, some Indians living in Latin America crossed the Mexican border into Texas in violation of anti-Asian immigration laws. Some were arrested in places like El Paso and Fort Worth and deported.[2] The numbers were substantial enough such that the federal government hired Indian American farmer Frank Singh as a "confidential agent" to interpret for the U.S. border patrol in El Paso; Singh was shot to death by someone who was involved in the illegal "smuggling" of Asian immigrants into the United States.[3] One of the larger groups of Indians to attempt entry into Texas consisted of forty-four Indians who had been working on the Panama Canal; the U.S. government denied their entry in October 1912.[4] Another, or perhaps the same, group of forty-four Indians, likely Sikhs, dressed in traditional garb, arrived in Nuevo Laredo in January 1920 to apply for entry into Texas so that they might travel to California and work on the railroads and farms there. The *Dallas Morning News* called them "tall, dark-faced, strong, husky East Indians, and the chief was a turbaned Hindoo from the Punjab."[5] It is unclear what happened to this group, but some Indians from Latin America certainly succeeded in legally or illegally entering Texas from Mexico. For instance, S.S. Sainsi was born in the Punjab (his father a farmer and mother the daughter of a British military officer) and worked as a construction gang leader on the Panama Canal. He settled in Dallas before buying a home southeast of Irving in 1941, by which time, Sainsi had naturalized as an American citizen.[6] In addition to the Indian Texans living in Dallas, Indian philosophers, lecturers, dancers (including a "Hindu ballet"), and "Hindu" professional wrestlers also regularly visited the city during the period of 1920 to 1960.[7]

By the 1930s, Indians attended Texas universities. Lalchand H. Wadhwani transferred from John Tarleton College to Texas A&M College in 1935 and became known as "Frog," a nickname for mid-year transfers. Contracting a heart infection, Wadhwani struggled to live for months as "scores" of Texas A&M students (mostly white males in military training) volunteered for blood transfusions for "Frog." Two weeks after asking to be taken outside to watch the Texas A&M Aggie Band march, Wadhwani died. Graduate student D.H. Bhawani escorted Wadhwani's cremated remains back to their hometown of Hyderabad.[8]

The 1960 Census counted 103 Indians in Texas. From 1950 until the 1965 immigration reform, small numbers of Indians visited Houston to work, but very few stayed. Some of these Indians worked as engineers and researchers for Humble Oil and Shell Oil in Houston. Indian engineer M.A. Ganapathy, for instance, evaluated seismic equipment being developed by a Texas-based company. Like most others, Ganapathy returned to India just months later. The difficulty of being a vegetarian in meat-heavy Texas and the lack of an Indian Texan community contributed to the low number of Indians settling in Texas.

In 1956, Iqbal "Ike" Singh Sekhon arrived in Dallas as an SMU graduate student, and the turbaned young man immediately became a media darling, being featured regularly in the *Dallas Morning News* for the next several years. In 1956, according to Sekhon, there were five or six SMU students from India, and there was one Indian doctor at St. Paul University Hospital. Sekhon became a de facto spokesperson for India and Indians, making speeches (up to three to five a month) to local clubs, and telling the press soon after arrival that "the people of India hate communism" and are friendly to America. Sekhon introduced Dallasites to the Sikh religion, which, the newspaper reported, "prohibits cutting of the hair."[9] Sekhon, who majored in business administration, married SMU student Dolores Brooks, and the headline read, "Young Student from India Chooses Pretty Texas Bride." In July 1959, La Tunisia restaurant opened in Dallas, complete with waitresses wearing veils and dressed in Middle Eastern garb; Ike Sekhon, who, by religious tenet, wore a turban, was the manager of the restaurant. The restaurant owners sought an exotic atmosphere, and Mayor Earle Cabell and other local officials enjoyed meeting at La Tunisia, where they became quite familiar with Sekhon. In 1962, Sekhon and his daughter, Tunisia, helped open a much-anticipated "Far Eastern Fortnight" at the local Neiman-Marcus department store. Just days later, on October 20, 1962, the People's Republic of China attacked India and seized territory along the nation's border. In response, Sekhon organized in Dallas the India Committee against Chinese Aggression, and the concerns of local Indians were communicated to Mayor Cabell. The organization became the India Association of North Texas, and Sekhon served as president its first two years. This social and cultural group helped organize a 100th birthday celebration of Mohandas K. Gandhi in 1969.[10]

In contrast to Sekhon, Kumar Pallana arrived in Dallas as an entertainer in the 1960s. In 1966, Pallana introduced locals to yoga, and he later opened one of the state's first yoga centers. So unfamiliar with yoga were people that some believed that Pallana was part of a cult, and others confused yoga with yogurt. Kumar's son, Dipak, recalled that, in the 1960s, there were no divisions within the Indian community in Dallas in part because there were only a handful of Indian families in the area. In 1984, Dipak opened the Cosmic Cup café where Kumar met film direc-

Ike Sekhon (left) was a leader among Indian Texans. Ike was photographed here with his good friend, the musician Ravi Shankar, who is the father of the Asian Texan singer, Nora Jones. Circa 1960s.

A leader of the Indian Houstonian community, Sam Kannappan was also a pioneer in the field of engineering software. He examines a computer print out in this photo taken in the 1970s.

tor Wes Anderson. Kumar has since played supporting roles in various films, including *Bottle Rocket* and *The Terminal*.[11]

1970–1990: Growth and Diversification

The 1970 Census counted 294 Indians living in Texas. Mostly graduate students, they concentrated in college towns; the small city of Lubbock hosted forty foreign-born Indians, and Austin hosted twenty, all foreign-born. Houston was home to seventy-seven Indians, and Dallas to sixty-one Indians; Houston was home to only six U.S.-born Indians, and Dallas was home to twenty U.S.-born Indians, indicating that Dallas's Indian community was older. No Indians were counted in San Antonio, El Paso, Fort Worth, Beaumont, Corpus Christi, or Amarillo. Indians arriving after 1965 came from all over India, not just the Punjab.[12]

Sockalingam "Sam" Kannappan, a Tamil Indian, earned his master degree in engineering from University of Texas-Austin from 1968 to 1970. According to Kannappan, about sixty Indians studied at UT-Austin in 1968. Although civil rights and war protests were common in Austin, Kannappan remembered, Indian students were advised by friends not to participate because of their tenuous immigration status. After writing *The Serpent and the Rope,* one of India's most renowned writers, Raja Rao, was recruited to teach Indian philosophy at UT-Austin in 1966. "In the '60s and '70s, the search for values was very remarkable," Rao remembered. "I was really thinking America would be the greatest nation." Rao's two sons were both born in Austin, where he and his third wife, Susan, still reside.[13] Dr. E.C.G. Sudarshan joined the UT-Austin Physics Department faculty in 1969. His work in particle physics earned him a nomination for a Nobel Prize. During the 1960s and 1970s, most Indian graduate students in Texas studied engineering.

In the fifteen years after the 1965 immigration reform, thousands more Indian graduate students studied in Texas or moved there upon graduating from a U.S. university. Indian engineers and doctors sought jobs and settled mostly in Houston and Dallas. When Sam Kannappan moved to Houston in 1969, about 100 Indians lived around the University of Houston, most of them engineering graduate students and recent graduates of universities in Texas and elsewhere. These Indians, almost all of whom were men, lived in the Kings Apartments east of the university and in the Cougar Apartments on its west side. Around the city lived at least six other Indian families. The center of the Indian community and of Indian culture in Houston was the UH India Students Association. Indian Houstonians gathered at the university for major events such as the showing of Hindi films, the celebration of Diwali (a Hindu festival of lights), and shows featuring foreign Indian singers and dancers. Energy producer and military contractor Brown and Root and energy company Schlumberger were the major employers of Indian engineers in Houston. As early as the 1970s, some Indians in Texas eschewed professional work to open motels. The largely male communities of Indian Texans followed a general pattern—earning a graduate degree, especially in engineering, finding a job, returning to India to marry, largely through arranged marriages, and returning to the United States.

In the early 1970s, Indian organizations formed in Houston to facilitate both religious worship and to help Indian students and immigrants settle in Houston. In 1969, Indians in Clear Lake organized India Family Circle. In the early 1970s, Sam Kannappan, Dr. Venugopal Menon, Dr. P.R.J. Gangadaram, and Surat Moonat organized the UH India Student Association's Hospitality Committee to help visiting Indian heart patients being treated at the Texas Medical Center. Some heart patients died, and the committee organized Hindu last rites, a practice nearly unheard of in North America. In 1973, Dr. Sen Pathak, Dr. Kumar Kishen, and Dr. Narayan Hospeti established Houston's Hindu Worship Society to provide opportunities for Hindus to gather and worship. India Culture Center sought to promote Indian culture and local Indian unity. Raj Sayal united all Hindu organizations in Houston by forming the religious organization Hindus of Greater Houston, and in 1974, the Tamil cultural organization Barathi Kalai Manram was founded.

Indian Texan associations regularly helped new Indian immigrants. Dictator Idi Amin, in 1972, purged Uganda of 50,000 Indians, and 1,000 were admitted to the United States. With little money and no references, the Indian refugees in Houston were unable to lease housing. Led by Dr. Bhamy Shenoy, president of the UH India Association, local Indians collected money and acted as sponsors for the refugees to secure housing.

The Meenakshi Temple in Pearland, Texas. This Hindu temple was one of the first in the U.S. to be built according to traditional Hindu specifications.

The Thottam family at the Catholic communion ceremony of Prabha Thottam (in white). Many Indian nurses and their families were of the Christian faith.

Most Indian Houstonians were Hindu, and in the early years they worshipped in the homes of fellow Hindus. In 1975, the Hindu Worship Society established the first Hindu temple in Houston. After co-founding an engineering software company and pioneering engineering software on mainframe computers, Sam Kannappan turned his attention to spiritual and community matters, helping to establish the South's first major Hindu temple. In October 1977, a committee of thirty Indian Houstonians, under the leadership of Professor K.R. Thiagarajan, decided to construct a temple to the Goddess Meenakshi. This temple would be only the third traditional Hindu temple built in the United States; the others were built in New York City and Pittsburgh in the early 1970s. Subba Rao Kodali, a prominent local engineer, asked that a separate sanctum in the temple be built for Lord Balaji, and the agreement to do so solidified the support of the Telugu members. With approval from religious leaders in India, the group decided to install Vishnu and Shiva deities in the same temple, a rarity in India. Thirteen artisans from India constructed one part of the temple according to religious scripture while local labor worked on other parts of the temple; the two groups met in the middle. On June 27, 1982, the Meenakshi Temple was officially opened in Pearland, Texas, southeast of Houston. The rural location was chosen to avoid upsetting Houstonians opposed to the temple's presence. Rather underutilized in its early years, the large temple became a gathering place and a symbol of pride for Houston's Indian Hindu community. Occupying five acres of land in 1978, the temple grounds occupied almost twenty acres in 2005, and as many as 5,000 Indian Houstonians gathered at events there.[14]

In the early 1970s, Dallas's Indian community clustered into several smaller communities centered around Southern Methodist University, UT-Dallas, electronics companies like Texas Instruments, or hospitals and medical schools. As Indians increased in number and opened more businesses, the Indian community spread out and connected. By 1975, there were approximately 300 Indian families living in Dallas, Fort Worth, Richardson, and other suburbs. Speaking to the *Dallas Morning News*, Kirit Patel, an engineer working for consulting engineering firm Chenault, Brady & Freeman, said, "Ninety percent of us will be staying," referring to Indian students and professionals in Texas seeking legal residency.[15]

As the number of Indian Dallasites grew, so did their cultural influence and the number of non-Indians interested in Indian culture. By 1977, the *Dallas Morning News* counted six Yoga centers, which served in some ways as cultural centers. That same year, the *News* also reported on the city's religious "cults" and included followers of local Sikh Yogis, Tibet's Dalai Lama, the Bahai faith, Hare Krishna, and practitioners of transcendental meditation. Eastern religions had gained such popularity that the Hare Krishnas opened in East Dallas the western hemisphere's only Hare Krishna school, serving one hundred children. In June 1975, the Texas legislature passed a bill that allowed the Texas Welfare Department to inspect the school, which in 1976 moved to India.[16]

The number of Indian Texans increased 74-fold from 294 in 1970 to 22,231 in 1980. About half of that population (11,291) lived in the Houston area, and about one-quarter (5,006) lived in the Dallas-Fort Worth area. The immigration of single women, wives, and children, and the birth of Indian children in Texas had brought the male-female ratio closer to equal; the Indian populations in Harris and Dallas counties reached 44% and 48% female, respectively. Only around major universities was the gender imbalance severe; in Travis County (Austin), Indian males outnumbered females 504 to 192.[17]

With the sudden growth of the South Asian community, Indians consciously and coincidentally created sub-communities within larger local Indian communities. Indian Texans divided themselves in the same ways they were divided in India: by religion, language group, geography, and occupation. For instance, in 1973 Sikh Houstonians decided that they could not worship at the Indian Culture Center, a building where people smoked, drank, and kept their shoes on, all of which were inappropriate in a Sikh temple. Led in part by Jasbir Singh Sethi, a group of Sikh Indian Houstonians founded the American South's first gurdwara (Sikh temple) on two acres of land in Northeast Houston. With their own hands, they built the Sikh Center of the Gulf Coast Area, the first major non-Judeo-Christian building of worship in Houston and a center of culture, worship, and Sikh rituals for Sikhs throughout the South.[18]

Similarly, Malayali Indians in Houston tended to cluster together. Tracy Thottam recalled how her neighborhood in Missouri City in the

1980s was home to a large number of Malayalam-speaking Christian and Catholic families, almost all of which included a mother who worked as a nurse. The Malayali Houstonians tended to concentrate in the Houston suburbs of Missouri City, Stafford, and Bellaire, and the fathers of these families tended to be non-professional workers who followed their wives to the United States. Many of these nurses worked first in northeastern states in the 1970s and 1980s before moving to Texas in part for the climate, which resembled southern India's. Like the Filipino Texan nurses, some Indian nurses struggled with gender role issues; they worked full-time and were expected to satisfy traditional female roles at home. Like the Christian Malayali Indians, other Indians also concentrated geographically (in Sugar Land, for instance), because of class, occupation, language, and religious commonalities.[19]

Indian Texan Christians and Catholics in the 1970s tended to worship with non-Indians, but in the 1980s, as the population increased, they began borrowing space from churches, such as Grace Bible Church in northern Dallas, for Indian worship services. Congregations began, too, to organize according to the Hindi, Malayalam, and Tamil languages, and in the 1990s and 2000s some congregations, especially the Malayali groups, began buying their own church buildings. In 2005, there were about twenty Indian Christian congregations in the Dallas area.[20]

Similarly, Indian Dallasite activist Mike Ghouse recalled how the Muslim Indians of Dallas-Fort Worth lived throughout the area, but that they tended to work in downtown Dallas in managerial positions or in businesses. Thus, local Indian Muslims decided in 1974 to build their first mosque in Grand Prairie, a suburb near downtown where land was relatively inexpensive. Many Indian Texan Muslims have worshipped throughout the decades with the general local Muslim population—including Pakistanis, Bangladeshis, Arabs, and Persians. The Indian Muslim population, which in 2007 made up about 2% of the Indian Texan population, in later decades tended to work as computer scientists and engineers, and concentrated in certain suburbs, such as Richardson. As the Indian Texan population grew in major urban areas, Hindu, Muslim, Sikh, Christian, Jain, and Buddhist Indian communities grew more distinctive from each other. According to Ghouse, the various sub-communities were united during "national holiday" events organized by local Indian Associations, but regional, religious, or language-based organizations were often larger than the Indian Associations.[21]

The oil boom of the 1970s had brought thousands of Indians to the Houston area to work as engineers, doctors, and small businesspeople. The oil bust, beginning in 1982, sent Houston into a deep economic recession. Because a large portion of the Indian community worked as engineers for oil and energy companies, Indian Houstonians lost a disproportionate number of jobs. Sam Kannappan remembered that it seemed that a quarter of the Indian Houstonian community moved away from Houston in the early and mid-1980s before economic recovery and increased immigration from India sent the population figures upward again. Unemployed Indian Houstonians migrated to cities throughout the nation, including Dallas.

In June 1984, Indian President Indira Gandhi ordered a military take-over of the Sikhs' holiest temple, the Golden Temple, which was being occupied by Sikh militants. Many Sikhs all over the world, including many in Texas, were outraged. On October 31, 1984, Indira Gandhi was assassinated by two of her Sikh bodyguards. Indians worldwide were outraged, including many in Texas, especially Hindus recently arrived from India. Houston was home to large populations of both Hindu Indians and Sikh Indians, with 30,000 to 40,000 total Indians and 1,200 to 2,000 Sikh Indians among them. Tensions between Sikhs and Hindus in Houston were increased by the public statements of some local leaders. Sikh Houstonian Hardam Singh Azad helped form the Sikh Association of America in response to the conflict. In the months after the assassination of Indira Gandhi, Azad became one of the most widely quoted Sikh Americans. Speaking before a group of 2,000 Sikhs in Washington D.C. in January 1985, Azad spoke out against post-assassination mob violence and continued discrimination against Sikhs in India.[22]

Houston suddenly became a focal point for South Asians worldwide when new Indian president Rajiv Gandhi (Indira's son) announced that he would visit only two U.S. cities—Washington, D.C. and Houston—on his June 1985 trip. In mid-May, the FBI announced the arrest of Sikhs planning to assassinate Rajiv Gandhi during his Houston visit and an Indian government official visiting New Orleans; Azad publicly condemned the assassination plot. On June 6, about a week before Gandhi's visit, 200 Sikhs marched peacefully in downtown Houston in commemoration of the attack on the Golden Temple. One sign read, "The Gandhis stain India with blood of Sikh children." With security tight on June 15, President Rajiv Gandhi visited the Johnson Space Center and then spoke with Houston business leaders about Houston's high technology industries; these high-tech discussions were the official purpose of his visit. Upon arrival at the Albert Thomas Convention Center, he avoided 200 Sikh protestors, led in part by Jasbir Singh Sethi, shouting chants against Gandhi and Indian government policies that, according to Sethi, were acts of "genocide" against the Sikhs. A group of fifty pro-Gandhi demonstrators, organized by Houston's Hindu Worship Society, protested Sikh "terrorism" just two blocks from the Sikh protestors. Inside the convention center, Gandhi spoke to about 2,000 Indians, praising them for their hard work in the United States and encouraging engineers, doctors, and others to return to India.[23] Just a week after Gandhi left Houston, the city's Indian population was again in turmoil as Sikh terrorists were suspected in the bombing of an Air India flight from Canada to Great Britain, killing all 329 mostly-Indian Canadian passengers.

The events of 1984 and 1985 shook up the entire Indian community. Tensions between Hindus and Sikhs continued for years, and by 2005, many Sikh Houstonians still refused to attend Indian independence and Republic Day celebrations. Nevertheless, according to Sam Kannappan, events like blood drives organized by the Indo-American Chamber of Commerce brought the communities together. The Sikh community of Houston, which lived largely in the area around the Sikh Center of the Gulf Area, shrank as a result of both the controversy and the oil bust.[24]

Contrary to their image in the media, not all Sikhs agreed on Indian politics. Ike Singh Sekhon said in 1987 that the Sikh-Hindu conflict "has led to personality clashes among Sikhs over the stand to be taken on the violent Punjab crisis, the performance of religious ceremonies, and the attitude to be adopted toward the Indian government." About 40% of the congregation at Dallas's Sikh Temple of North Texas split off to form in 1985 the new Singh Sabha Temple. Similarly a group splintered from the

Sikh Center in Houston to form the Gurdwara Sahib of Breen. By 2005, about 1,000 Sikh families lived in Houston, most of them within seven miles of the Sikh Center; their proportion of the total Indian Houstonian population having dropped greatly.[25]

In 1984 the primary Dallas-Fort Worth Hindu organization, the Hindu Temple Society, purchased 7.5 acres of land in nearby Parker, Texas (east of Plano) to build a 7,500 square-foot traditional Hindu temple. Like Sri Meenakshi, this temple was to be located in a rural area, but many Parker residents objected to the Hindu temple because its architecture differed from that of the local buildings and because the Hindu religion was not a Christian religion. "I believe in the God of the Bible, so in essence, I (am) against it," said the Rev. Rick Fowlkes, pastor of the local North Ridge Baptist Church, after a November 11, 1986 town meeting. The Hindu Temple Society sought advice from the Dallas Anti-Defamation League, which helped negotiate a settlement with the city of Parker. Faced with opposition that some considered bigoted, the Hindu Temple Society decided to sell the Parker land to the city of Parker and a neighboring property owner for $8,000 less than what they paid for it. The organization in June 1988 purchased much more expensive land in the more Asian and the more urban Irving, Texas, which welcomed the temple. On April 28, 1991, the temple, named Ekta Mandir, was inaugurated, and the temple's first deity, Maha Lakshmi, was installed during a four-day ceremony spanning May 30 to June 2, 1991, to be followed by the installation of several other deities in the following months.[26]

Thousands of Indians in Texas sponsored their relatives to immigrate to the state in the 1980s. A great portion of these immigrants opened and ran businesses. Joining these Indians in opening businesses were some of those laid off during the oil bust. Indian Texans formed businesses serving both "ethnic" and mainstream markets. Indians in Texas opened mostly motels, convenience stores, gas stations, retail stores, Indian restaurants, and Indian grocery stores. Some Indians started engineering firms, and especially in the 1990s and 2000s, Indian Texans started high-tech computer and telecommunications businesses. In the early 1980s, many Indian Houstonian restaurants, jewelry stores, and other businesses moved from inside the 610 Loop to Hillcroft at

Highway 59 to serve the large Indian population in Southwest Houston. In the northern Dallas suburb of Richardson, Indian businesses tended to locate east of the expressway and Chinese businesses located west of it.[27] Large numbers of both Asians and Indians lived in the D-FW suburbs of Richardson, Plano, Irving, and Garland.

A major portion of Indian immigrant entrepreneurs ran motels. By 1984, nearly 14% of all non-chain motels in Texas were owned by families surnamed "Patel." Indians named "Patel" tended to come from India's Gujarat province and tended to run motels and other businesses. Ron Chandler, then-director of the Dallas office of the Immigration and Naturalization Service, explained in 1984 that a 10% down payment on a motel met Immigration and Naturalization requirements for permanent residence status, so "ten thousand dollars entitled one for permanent residence status and the Patels would buy and then sell [a motel] to one of their relatives."[28] Legal residency through such means was no longer possible by the late 1980s, but nevertheless, Indians purchased more and more Dallas motels.

Some Indian motel owners operated "hourly" motels. By 1987, the city of Dallas began cracking down on prostitution that had occurred at these motels for decades; the practice had begun long before most of the Indians had bought their motels. The city of Dallas sued some of the motels, and news articles such as one headlined, "Indian Entrepreneurs: Immigrant Patels cashing in on Dallas' sexually oriented motels" brought bad publicity to all Indian-owned motels, whether they sought illicit patronage or not. Some considered the media and legal attention racist, as Indian entrepreneurs seemed to be singled out. Many Indian immigrant families had little choice but to work in such motels, sometimes for little or no money, in exchange for the opportunity to establish themselves in the United States. By 1994, families named Patel owned about 80% of the 90 small motels in Dallas, and some Indian motel owners sued the city over "unfair" laws that singled them out. As many Patels expanded their motel businesses, they began to buy brand-name lodging such as Ramada Inn. By 1996, Indian Americans owned 46% of American economy hotels and 26% of the total lodging businesses. While many Patels started off working hard for little money in crime-ridden neighborhoods, some became wealthier than Indian doctors. Ironically, the crackdown on sex-related motels in Dallas's Harry Hines district helped Korean and Indian-owned businesses rehabilitate the area, which became the thriving Asia Trade District of Dallas.[29]

In the early 1970s, the Vietnam War caused a major shortage of medical doctors in Texas, a growing state with a large rural population. The federal government offered financial and citizenship incentives to encourage Indian doctors to work in America. Between 1974 and 1985, the number of medical doctors in Texas almost doubled, from 13,956 to 26,304, and Indian doctors were among the new doctors. Dr. Vijay N. Koli, M.D., educated in India, was doing postdoctoral training in London in 1978 when he decided to seek employment in Texas. Passing through tiny Goldplate, Texas, he met an elderly "tall Texas doctor" who told Koli that the town needed him. Dr. Koli practiced in Goldplate for four years before he and his wife moved to San Antonio where, in 2000, he became the first foreign-born president of the local medical society. In 2005, he was elected as the president of the American Association of Physicians of Indian Origin. According to Koli, Texas's "John Wayne" image discouraged Indian doctors from coming to the state in the early years, but during the oil boom of the 1970s, Indian doctors migrated at a faster pace. Indian-trained and other foreign doctors disproportionately chose to work in underserved rural Texas in order to earn their legal residency; they often preferred the rural areas where they were more appreciated and where they could avoid "neck-and-neck competition" and its resulting racial discrimination. In 2005, over 2,000 of Texas's 43,000 doctors were Indians born in the United States, India, or elsewhere.[30]

The High-Tech 1990s and the New Millenium

According to the 1990 Census, 9,733 Indians lived in Dallas County, 4,245 lived in Tarrant County, 1,529 lived in Denton County, and 1,309 lived in Collin County, the total of the four counties of the Dallas-Fort Worth metroplex being 16,816 Indians. In the same year, 20,214 Indians lived in Harris County (Houston), and 3,983 in Fort Bend County (southwest of Houston).

In the 1990s, the number of high technology, telecommunications, computer, internet, and energy companies and research centers in Texas increased tremendously, as did the number of college-educated Indian immigrants. Most Indian high-tech workers arrived to Texas with H-1B visas, and a large portion of them were computer software workers. Paul Pandian, a Christian Indian Dallasite, first came to Dallas in 1975 as an employee of Rockwell International's electronics headquarters. In 1985, Pandian started a company which supplied employees for large telecommunications companies like Alcatel, Motorola, and Lucent. By 1995, the company established a base of operations in Bangalore, India and by 2005, the company outsourced labor to 1,000 people, most of them being workers in India and about 10% of them being workers in Dallas. Paul Pandian's wife, Geetha, is a physician who joined the faculty of the Southwestern Medical School.[31]

The 2000 Census counted about fifty thousand Indian Texans living in each of the areas of Houston and Dallas-Fort Worth. Additionally the Census counted 12,990 Indian Texans in Fort Bend County. As the hi-tech industries of Texas boomed, Indians became the largest Asian ethnic group in the Austin-Round Rock area, where their population more than tripled over ten years to 10,680 in the 2000 Census. Indians were also the largest Asian ethnic group in Dallas, Lubbock, Denton, and Midland counties, among others. Indian community leaders say that the Census undercounts Indians. There were likely more than 100,000 Indians living in the Houston area in 2005, and perhaps 70,000 or more in the Dallas-Fort Worth area.[32] But Indian Texans are likely *less* undercounted than most other Asian ethnic groups in Texas because of its large proportion of professionals with legal immigration statuses. Since 1965, Indians' geographic pattern of settlement in Texas has largely matched that of Chinese immigrants in part because of both groups' associations with engineering work, high technology, and universities.

In 2001, Indian Houstonian leaders planned a massive Republic Day celebration to mark both the fiftieth anniversary of the forming of the Indian republic and the arrival of the new millennium. As India celebrated Republic Day on January 26, 2001, an earthquake struck the province of Gujarat, killing nearly 20,000 people. Indian Houstonian leaders were not sure whether to go ahead with their Millennial Festival, as they had coined that year's Republic Day celebration. Indian Houstonian leaders, Sam Kannappan among them, decided to turn the celebration into a fundraising effort for the Gujarat earthquake victims. Indian Houstonians hailed from Gujarat more than any other Indian province, and 25,000 Indian Houstonians marched in the parade, which ended in the George Brown Convention Center. To show their support for victims of the earthquake, many of Houston's elected officials attended the Millennial Festival. Impressed by the huge turnout, the politicians changed their view of Indian Houstonian political power. Previous to the Millennial Festival, Houston politicians tended to "ignore" Indian leaders when they invited the politicians to events, but after the Millennial Festival, the same politicians began listening to Indian leaders and attending local Indian events. The Indian Houstonian community "adopted" the Gujarat village of Krishnanagar, rebuilding 200 homes there; Indian Houstonians also flew to Washington, D.C. to personally lobby U.S. Congressmen to increase U.S. aid for Gujarat earthquake victims, which the government subsequently did.[33]

The terrorist attacks of September 11, 2001 horrified the entire South Asian American population of Texas. Among the Indian Texans, Muslims and Sikhs were disproportionately affected by the post-September 11 backlash. Muslims Indians were associated with local mosques, some of which were vandalized, and Sikh Indians were associated with the terrorists because Sikhs wore turbans and lengthy beards. The post-September 11 backlash did, however, provide an opportunity for Indian Texans to show solidarity with Pakistani Texans. Indian leaders in Houston worked with Pakistani leaders and city officials to prevent and address post-September 11 anti-Asian violence, harassment, and discrimination. Indian and Pakistani Houstonians met together in both the Pakistani Houstonian Royal Hall and the Indian Houstonian Gandhi Center.[34]

Watching a streak of smoke in the sky, many Texans witnessed to their horror the death of astronaut Kalpana Chawla and several others when the Space Shuttle Columbia disintegrated on its return trip to Earth on February 1, 2003. Chawla was the first American of South Asian descent to travel in space, and she was the second person of Indian descent to do so. On her first space shuttle mission in 1997, Chawla operated the shuttle's robotic arm, and on her second and last mission, she conducted science experiments. Born in Karnal, India, Chawla earned a master's degree in aerospace engineering from the University of Texas and a doctorate degree from the University of Colorado. She began astronaut training in Houston in 1994, where she lived until her death. While relatively unknown among the Indian Houstonian community during her life, the community mourned her death and embraced her as a symbol of pride.[35]

Indians in Midland-Odessa

by Rakesh Amaram

In 1970, there were virtually no Indians in Midland-Odessa. By the 1980s, there were only ten to fifteen Indian families. In 1990, there were 228 Indians in the Midland-Odessa area. By 2000, the Indian population had more than doubled to 532 in a regional population of 200,000. The majority of the Indians migrating to Texas settled in Houston and Dallas. But competition among professionals in the metropolitan areas was fierce, and many Indians, especially those in the medical field, looked elsewhere for employment. The development of Midland-Odessa as a center for petrochemical production and distribution resulted in a quickly growing economy and a dramatic increase in opportunities for medical professionals and other skilled workers. Mahendra Thakker, a chemical engineer who moved to Odessa in 1972, explained that the few doctors in the area were at their maximum capacity and there was a lack of medical specialists. There were only a few Indian couples in West Texas at the time. One by one, other Indian families began moving to the area, most of them entering the medical profession or technical industries. Dr. Jayaram Naidu, one of the first Indian doctors to move to Odessa, settled there to avoid the fierce competition in major cities as well as to capitalize on the tremendous opportunities present for doctors in the region. According to Naidu, in Odessa there were "no limits to success."[36]

Dr. Naidu felt that, although the public was very accepting of Indians moving into Midland-Odessa, significant resistance came from

Astronaut Kalpana Chawla was the first American of South Asian descent to travel in space. This photo was taken in 2002, one year before her tragic death.

Mike Ghouse has been a leader within the Indian American community in Dallas-Fort Worth.

local physicians who initially saw the Indian doctors as threats to their practices, despite a severe need for doctors in the area. The local Indian physicians were initially unable to receive privileges to practice at the hospital. Dr. Naidu said that over time, however, the resistance from the other physicians faded. Dr. Thakker said that he too felt accepted most of the time, but when promoted to manager he lost an employee who refused to work under an Indian.[37]

Life for Indians in West Texas and other smaller Texas communities differed greatly from life in Dallas and Houston. The "cliques" of Indian province and language that are evident in the larger urban areas formed less rapidly in smaller cities, creating a much more unified population. Their small numbers also fostered close relationships with other South Asians who had similar cultures. The sometimes-hostile relationships seen between the nations of Pakistan, Bangladesh, and India never carried over to the people of West Texas. Krishna Khandelwal states that in the beginning, most Indians in the area were unified in one group.[38] The pattern of separating into groups based on language, province, and religion that occurred in larger Indian Texan communities during the 1960s through the 1980s only began to occur in Midland-Odessa around the time of the new millennium.

Maintenance of culture in small Indian Texan communities required a great deal of effort. Dr. Thakker lamented that, for a while, the only Indian influences on his children came from him and his wife. Starting around the late 1970s, local Indians began holding Hindu prayers, called pooja, at individual households every other week. These meetings were important for preserving Indian culture but also served as vital social gatherings. As the number of local Hindus increased, many considered gathering for worship at an old, unused Christian church. Several local Indians then received anonymous threats against using the church, and the Indians decided to seek a more non-confrontational solution, one that would not cause any noticeable change in the community. In 1987 a house was purchased in Midland, and as of 2004 it still served as the main gathering place for Hindu Indians of Midland-Odessa.[39]

As the Indian population grew, the community began to flourish, creating a magnitude of community and culture found previously only in big cities in East Texas. Indians of all professions began moving to Midland-Odessa. According to Thakker, a new "wave" of business-based Indians came to the area, purchasing many of the hotels in Midland and Odessa. The highlight of the year for many Indians is the Diwali festival, in which local children and adults perform music and dances and local people experience Indian culture. Diwali celebrations began as small gatherings at Texas Tech University in Lubbock but have since become important events in the region. A classical Indian vocalist and a tabla player from Houston began in the mid-1990s to conduct summer camps, and by 2004, Indian movies were shown once or twice a year in local theaters. Other cultural activities have included classical dance lessons, a sari exhibit at a local art museum, and visiting Indian musicians and dancers. These events are a testament to the Indians of Midland-Odessa and their commitment to culture and community.[40]

The American-born Indian Texans

Rahul Mahajan's parents immigrated as physics graduate students to the United States in 1968, and in 1978, when Rahul's father, Swadesh, was hired as a physics professor at UT-Austin, the family moved from Princeton, New Jersey to Austin, Texas:

> It was a big shock in terms of the racial attitudes and the way I was treated . . . when I came [to Austin]. I was in the fourth grade. Early on, I was introduced to the class, and the teacher said I was an Indian or something. So one of the kids in the class said, "What was his Dad's name? Chief Stinking Blanket?" . . . If there was bullying on the playground, basically the teachers' attitude was "I don't want to hear about it. I don't want to do anything about it. You deal with it among yourselves."[41]

Asian Texan children were bullied throughout the state, and unfortunately, Rahul's teacher's attitude was not uncommon. Rahul Mahajan believed that Asian Texans experienced "less contempt and more exclusion," than African Americans and Hispanics.

Indian Texan youth were less likely than many youth from other Asian ethnic groups to join gangs or commit crimes in part because, on average, Indian Texans were wealthier, lived in safer neighborhoods, and were better-educated. Additionally, conservative Indian parents "repressed" their children, but they did so, according to Mahajan, "gently." Living in a diverse Texas society with liberal sexual practices, Indian Texan children often struggled with "stifling" parents who encouraged conservative courting practices and marriage with Indians of the same language-group and religion. In the aftermath of the terror attacks of September 11, 2001, Rahul Mahajan become active in anti-war activities. Although Mahajan was a Hindu Indian, people sometimes felt threatened by his opinions because they mistook him for a Muslim Arab. Nevertheless, in 2002 Mahajan won the Green Party's nomination for Texas governor, making him the first Asian to ever make the ballot for that office.[42]

Despite their relative average wealth, many Indian Texans have struggled with racism, culture clash, and politics both within the diverse Indian Texan population and with other racial groups in Texas. Second-generation Indian Texans, although largely concentrated in professional work, have crossed into new territories—both occupational and cultural.

ENDNOTES

1 Karen Leonard, "California's Punjabi Mexican Americans," *The World & I*, vol. 4(5), May 1989, pp. 612–623.

2 See for instance "Foreigners to be Deported," *Dallas Morning News* Dec 15, 1912.

3 "El Paso Hindu's Death Blamed on Smugglers," *Dallas Morning News*, Sep 25, 1933.

4 "Hindus Are Kept Out," *Dallas Morning News*, Oct 20, 1912.

5 Frank Carpenter, "2000-Mile Strip on Mexican Border Policed by Soldiers," *Dallas Morning News*, Feb 2, 1913.

6 "Native of British India Buys Home Near Irving," *Dallas Morning News*, May 13, 1941.

7 Various articles, search for "Hindu" in *Dallas Morning News* Historical Archive, 1920–1950.

8 Associated Press, "Hindu at A.&M., Who Called Himself Frog, Loses Life Battle," *Dallas Morning News*, Jun 10, 1939.

9 Iqbal Sekhon, phone interview by Irwin Tang, Oct 13, 2005; "Sikh Says Marxism Unpopular," *Dallas Morning News*, Jun 27, 1956; "Guest from Bombay," photo caption, *Dallas Morning News*, Apr 27, 1958.

10 Iqbal Sekhon, "La Tunisia C/O Dallas," photo and caption, *Dallas Morning News*, Jul 2, 1959; "La Tunisia: Trio Leases Swank New Restaurant," *Dallas Morning News*, Aug 12, 1959; "Fortnight: Far East Curtain Up," *Dallas Morning News*, Oct 16, 1962. "Indian Celebration," photo and caption, *Dallas Morning News*, Jan 17, 1969.

11 Dipak Pallana, phone interview by I. Tang, Feb 15, 2007.

12 1970 U.S. Census.

13 Anne Morris, "A Rao retrospective: India prepares to honor one of its greatest writers, who lives quietly in Austin," *Austin American-Statesman*, Mar 23, 1997.

14 Sam Kannappan, interview by Irwin Tang, Houston, Jul 30, 2005; Prakash M. Swami, *Experiences of an Immigrant—Sam Kannappan* (Houston: Sam Kannappan and Family, 2003.)

15 Paul Pandian, phone interview by Irwin Tang, Aug 15, 2005; Doug Domeier, "Indian Family: Tea, Mexican Food Spice Life in U.S.A.," *Dallas Morning News*, Nov 7, 1974.

16 Kent Biffle, "Sikh and ye shall find yoges living in Dallas," *Dallas Morning News*, March 14, 1977; "Temple for sale . . . perhaps," *Dallas Morning News*, Nov 19, 1977; Aziz Shihab, "Religious cults—'the times they are a-changin,'" *Dallas Morning News*, Nov 27, 1977.

17 U.S. Censuses of 1930, 1960, 1970, 1980; 1980 U.S. Census, Volume 45, Tables 15 and 30 (SMSA) and Table 50.

18 Jasbir Singh Sethi, telephone interview by Irwin Tang, Sep 10, 2005.

19 Tracy Thottam, interview by Irwin Tang, Feb 15, 2007, Austin.

20 Pandian, interview.

21 Mike Ghouse, phone interview by Irwin Tang, Feb 12, 2007, DFW.

22 Population estimates from "Gandhi visit seen as boost to city," *Houston Chronicle*, Jun 15, 1985 and Bruce Nichols, "Security Tight for Gandhi: Houston Sikhs planning protest," *Dallas Morning News*, Jun 15, 1985; on Azad, see "Sikh warns of 'ticking bomb,'" *Houston Chronicle*, Jan 27, 1985, p. A7.

23 Eric Hanson and Steve Friedman, "Sikhs here are readying to commemorate assault," *Houston Chronicle*, Jun 7, 1985; Bruce Nichols, "Gandhi tours space center, meets Indians in Houston," *Dallas Morning News*, Jun 16, 1985, 43A.

24 Sethi, interview. Steve Maynard, "Sikhs urged to seek U.S. support," *Houston Chronicle*, Jul 21, 1986.

25 Ravi Sidhu, "A FAITH DIVIDED U.S. Sikhs differ in response to India's Punjab conflict," *Dallas Morning News*, Oct 10, 1987, 1A; Sethi, interview.

26 Judy Howard, "Parker Residents Disagree on Permit for Hindu Temple," *Dallas Morning News*, Nov 12, 1986; Louis Moore, "HINDU HOME Faith to build its first area temple in Irving," *Dallas Morning News*, Jul 1, 1988, 21A; *http://www.dfwhindutemple.org/about_temple.htm*, official temple website, retrieved Aug 22, 2005.

27 Pamela Yip, "Ethnic enclaves form the foundation for commerce," *Houston Chronicle*, Mar 21, 1993; Pandian, interview.

28 Scott McCartney, "The name Patel swamps Texas hotel-motel scene," *Dallas Morning News*, Mar 25, 1984.

29 Some of the motels sued by the city of Dallas in 1988 were in the Harry Hines District where the new Koreatown was established in the 1990s. See, among others, George Rodriguez, "Indian Entrepreneurs: Immigrant Patels cashing in on Dallas' sexually oriented motels," *Dallas Morning News*, Jun 14, 1987, 1A; Al Brumley, "Dallas sues 5 motels accused of allowing prostitution," *Dallas Morning News*, Aug 27, 1988, 34A; Sylvia Martinez and Anne Bellie Gesalman, "City, neighbors fight small motels: They say industry breeds crime; owners say rules unfair, claim bias," *Dallas Morning News*, July 31, 1994, 37A; Edwin McDowell, "Finding a way into inns' mainstream/Indian Americans succeed at hotels," *Houston Chronicle*, Mar 31, 1996, p. 2.

30 Vijay N. Koli of San Antonio, phone interview by Irwin Tang, Sep 19, 2005.

31 Pandian, interview

32 See Census 2000; also estimates according to Kannappan and Pandian.

33 Kannappan, interview.

34 Ibid.

35 NASA, "Biographical Data," *http://www.jsc.nasa.gov/Bios/htmlbios/chawla.html*, as retrieved on May 25, 2005; also Kannappan, interview.

36 On 1970 population, see Sireesha Amaram, interview by Rocko Amaram, Odessa, TX, Jul 27, 2004; on the rest, see Mahendra Thakker, interview by Rocko Amaram, Odessa, TX, Jun 29, 2004; Jayaram Naidu, interview by Rocko Amaram, Odessa, TX, Jul 9, 2004.

37 Naidu and Thakker interviews.

38 Krishna Khandelwal, interview by Rocko Amaram, Midland, TX, Jul 16, 2004.

39 Thakker, interview; on pooja, Khandelwal, interview; on opposition, Naidu, interview; on new location, Khandelwal, interview

40 Thakker, interview; on Diwali, culture, Amaram, interview.

41 Rahul Mahajan, interview Irwin Tang, Austin, Oct 27, 2005.

42 Ibid.

★

CHAPTER NINE

THE KOREAN TEXANS

Irwin A. Tang, Lucy Lee, and Michelle Cho

Korean Texans from Latin America

Little is known about the Korean Americans who lived in Texas before the Korean War. The U.S. Census, which reliably undercounts Asian Americans, counted four Koreans in Texas in 1920 and seventeen in 1930, seven of whom lived in Dallas.[1] The earliest Korean Texans came from four places: Mexico, Korea, Hawaii, and the West Coast. In 1905, one thousand thirty-three Korean men, women, and children were tricked into working on henequen plantations and factories in the Yucatan province of southern Mexico.[2] "Our parents did not know it," said Rosa Sunoo, nine years old at the time. "We thought we were going to Hawaii, but the Japanese had sold us to Mexico as slaves."[3] Working twelve hours a day, being continually flogged during the workday by their "employers," and prevented from leaving the plantations, the Korean workers and their children were essentially slave laborers, except that they *ostensibly* earned between twelve and thirty-five cents a day, sometimes paid in-kind. They lived in huts, suffered from heat and snakes, and often attempted escape. During this time, the Korean National Association also established a

Korean military academy in Mexico named Soong-mu Academy, which trained 118 Korean cadets for a war of independence against Japan. In 1910, the extremely violent Mexican Revolution began, and some Korean cadets apparently participated, on the side of the revolutionaries. In 1909, the 1,033 Korean workers completed their work contracts and were freed. While 288 of the Korean workers left for Cuba, many certainly attempted entry into the United States at El Paso, Texas.[4]

Rosa Sunoo grew up speaking Korean, Spanish, and an indigenous language of Mexico. She was sixteen when a Korean American minister arranged a meeting between her and a Korean American named Mr. Yoon. "[Mr. Yoon] didn't want to, but my father just begged him to take me to America." In El Paso, Texas, Mr. Yoon married Rosa, and the couple adopted Rosa's sister Maria, so that the sisters could remain in the United States. The family then moved to Los Angeles.[5]

In the aftermath of the Korean War (1950–1953) and during the Latin American economic boom of the 1970s, Koreans immigrated to Paraguay, Brazil, and Argentina. They learned to speak Spanish and Portuguese as they opened stores and sold Korean-made clothes and consumer products. From there, a favorite city to relocate to was El Paso, Texas. Beginning in 1980, Koreans from Los Angeles, New York City, and South American cities like Asunción, Paraguay began opening stores in downtown El Paso, in and around what used to be its Chinatown. Selling to both El Pasoans and dealing wholesale to retailers in Mexico's Chihuahua province, some spoke fluent Spanish to their customers and all spoke Korean to their suppliers. By 1991, Korean families from South America and other U.S. cities had begun transforming the southern border by settling and opening stores in border towns like Calexico, California; Nogales, Arizona; and Texas cities like Del Rio, Laredo, Brownsville, and Eagle Pass. In contrast to their impressions of other U.S. cities, some Koreans preferred the primarily Hispanic border cities for their friendly atmosphere and because a lack of English language skills was better accepted. The 1994 devaluation of the Mexican peso sent some Koreans away from the border, but more came to replace them. By 1996, a third of El Paso's 300 downtown businesses were run by Koreans. The 2000 Census counted 2,226 Koreans living in border counties, about 5%

of the Korean Texan population. The thriving Korean community then constituted the largest Asian ethnic group in El Paso.[6]

Korean Texans and the U.S. Military

With the end of the Korean War, the United States established large, permanent military bases in South Korea to guard against a North Korean invasion. Also after the Korean War, Fort Hood near Killeen, Texas grew into one of the largest military bases in the world, and over the decades, tens of thousands of American soldiers stationed in South Korea left from or returned to Fort Hood. Since the end of the Korean War, thousands of Korean women have met American military men in Korea, married them, and returned with them to Texas military bases, especially Fort Hood, El Paso's Fort Bliss, and San Antonio's Fort Sam Houston.

For the entire state of Texas, the 1960 census counted 473 Koreans, approximately equal in males and females, 204 of them having been born in the United States. A large portion of Korean Texans lived in the military-oriented cities of El Paso (ninety-eight Koreans) and San Antonio (sixty Koreans). Only fifty-five Koreans lived in Houston and Dallas. The 1970 Census counted 2,102 Koreans in Texas. The two largest Texas cities—Dallas (177 Koreans) and Houston (139 Koreans)—were home to only about 15% of the total Korean population. The two militarily-oriented cities of El Paso (238) and San Antonio (207) were home to over 21% of the total. The balance—about 64 percent—lived in other cities. Many Koreans lived in Killeen, where Fort Hood soldiers had returned from Korea with military wives. According to the 1970 U.S. Census, 674 (or 73%) of the 926 "second-generation" Korean Americans in Texas had white parentage. Similarly, the figures for Japanese Texans and Filipino Texans were 74% and 65%, respectively. However, for Chinese Texans, a group less associated with U.S. military bases, the figure was 30%. Certainly, U.S. military activity was not the only factor, but a major factor. Many, if not most, of the white parentage represented in the Korean statistics were U.S. military men. As more Korean "war brides" and nurses arrived after 1965, they produced in Texas a two-to-one ratio of Korean females to Korean males in the 1980 Census. By 1990, as more Korean university students, families, small business owners and professionals immigrated to Texas, that ratio fell to three-to-two.[7]

While there were many successful marriages between U.S. military men and the women they met in Korea, a high portion of these marriages ended in divorce, in part because of cultural conflicts, communication issues, and the circumstances under which the couple married. Dallasites learned of these issues in 1959 when a policeman rescued a Korean "war bride" and her two children from starvation in their Fort Worth home. The "war bride" had been abandoned by her husband, a non-Korean. He said to a newspaper, "She doesn't understand this country. She doesn't understand anything." He suggested she be "sent back" to Korea, but he wanted to keep the children.[8]

When Koreans first arrived in Killeen in the 1950s and early 1960s, the largest Asian groups were the Japanese and Filipinos. Among the Japanese in 1960, females outnumbered males, 154 to 66, indicating that most of the adult Japanese were military wives. The Filipinos had near gender equality at 54 males and 59 females. The population of military wives grew rapidly, and when Korean Lisa Humphries (wed to a white American soldier) first arrived in Killeen in 1969, she estimated that about 600 Koreans were already living there, the vast majority of them military wives. Humphries balked at the hot weather and the small town culture, so she lived in other cities before returning to Killeen in 1972 to find that there were then more than 1000 Koreans. In those early years, the Korean wives were largely isolated by language and cultural barriers. Humphries recalled that wives would get together to play cards, but because there was little else to do, they started petty arguments. To help the wives with their cultural and marital issues, Humphries in 1974 organized the Korean Wives Association, and she has been a major advocate for the Korean community ever since.[9]

When Bok Chu An arrived in Killeen with his wife in 1972, there were only four other non-military families. These families were each headed by a Korean man and a Korean woman. An's wife's sister had married an American soldier and, like most Korean military wives, she sponsored some or all of her immediate blood relatives for immigration to the United States. The five all-Korean families met for dinner despite

Pong Brown, at the age of 18, met her first husband when he was a soldier stationed in Korea. Married again, she runs two cleaners in Killeen.

The Shinns are one of many Korean Texan families who own doughnut shops. They operate Donut 7 in Austin, Texas.

the lack of kimchi. Bok Chu An worked construction jobs for $1.60 per hour and saved money. Nineteen months after arriving to Killeen, his family bought a house. In the 1970s, the number of siblings and parents that Korean military wives sponsored for immigration to Texas accelerated; that number then hit a plateau during the 1980s. Many such relatives stabilized their lives in military cities like Killeen, El Paso, and San Antonio before moving to Dallas or Houston; a large number of these immigrants opened businesses.[10]

Many Korean Killeenites worked at home, sewing clothes for major clothing manufacturers. Dallas-based clothes companies drove truckloads of cloth to Asian Killeen homes. The largest concentration of Vietnamese, Korean, and other Asian home sewing workers lived in Dallas-Fort Worth, where home sewing workers in the early 1990s numbered between 20,000 and 80,000. Through sewing work, Asian women who spoke little English could earn enough to help their family purchase a home or a second car. After some Killeen residents complained about the home sewing operations, Lisa Humphries pointed out to the city government that the income to local workers from just one sewing contractor boosted the local economy by a million dollars each month. Beginning in 1992, the federal Department of Labor cracked down on Texas clothing manufacturers for paying home sewing workers less than minimum wage and no overtime, and for employing children. After passage of the North American Free Trade Agreement, companies found even lower-waged labor in Mexico. Home sewing was eliminated in Texas.[11]

In the early 1970s, downtown Killeen was a deteriorating area where prostitutes solicited soldiers. "I would lock my car doors and drive fast through downtown," recalled Lisa Humphries. Korean military wives and other Korean immigrants, often with money saved from sewing, opened up dry cleaners, barber shops, alteration shops, groceries, gas stations, and herbal apothecaries in the low-rent buildings downtown, as well as throughout the entire city. Korean businesses helped revitalize and clean up downtown Killeen, and, by 2004, dozens of Korean-owned businesses gave the area the feel of a Koreatown. Despite a mid-1990s political effort to allow only English language business signs in Killeen, Korean businesses were well-patronized by non-Koreans.[12]

In addition to a high divorce rate, Korean military wives often struggled to overcome language barriers, their lack of education, and cultural differences. They often suffered from culture shock and home-sickness. Many felt isolated, even from their English-speaking children. Their husbands often worked and fought abroad for long periods.

Korean military wives were sometimes lured or tricked into prosti-tution by both Koreans and non-Koreans. Some of these prostitutes had purposefully entered into fake marriages with American soldiers. In the mid-1980s, police in various Texas localities carried out well-publicized and successful crackdowns on Korean prostitution.[13]

Troubled Korean wives often sought solace and advice from Korean Christian churches, which were already social and cultural centers for the Korean communities. Reverend James (Young) Moon was first in-spired to move from New York to Killeen because he felt a deep pathos for Korean military wives, according to his wife, Ai Moon. "Sometimes, he listens to the wives' struggles for eleven hours straight."[14]

In the early 1970s, Killeen's Korean Society was founded, and so was the city's first Korean church—Korean Memorial Baptist Church. Soon after, Pastor Paul Kim founded the city's only Korean Method-ist Church. By 2004, there were thirty-five Korean churches in Killeen. Some congregations numbered in the hundreds, while others only twen-ty. Sermons were given in both English and Korean. Sometimes the Ko-rean wife attended the Korean language sermon while her husband and children attended the English sermon.[15]

"They came with empty hands" recalled Humphries, and they re-vitalized Killeen. With 7,000 Koreans and a few thousand other Asians living in Killeen in 2004, Asian Americans made up over ten percent of the total Killeen population. Since 1960, Killeen has been, by proportion of total population, one of the most Asian cities in Texas and one of the most Korean cities in the nation. With the majority of Korean immi-grants in Killeen being military wives, and almost all of their children being biracial, the Korean population in Killeen was unusual among Ko-rean American communities.[16]

Korean Adoptees

Texans began adopting Korean orphans as soon as the war ended in 1953; in that year, a fifteen year-old Korean houseboy working for a U.S. military man was adopted (after the man's death) by the man's parents, who lived in Dallas. Large numbers of children were adopted by Dallasites beginning in 1961, and the children became highly-photographed darlings of the local newspaper. Adoptive parents of Korean orphans began meeting in the Dallas area in 1961 and celebrated a ten-year anniversary in 1971. One Korean Texan who was adopted in the 1980s remembered how the Korean orphanage in which she lived organized events with the U.S. military. At barbecues and other events, orphanage girls met potential adoptive parents. Adopted by a high-ranking American officer whose family "lived like robots, with maids, and everything done for them," she cried until she was brought back to the orphanage. A U.S. military contract worker later adopted her.[17]

Korean Dallas-Fort Worth and Korean Houston

Many of the early Koreans in Dallas were university students. As early as 1930, for instance, SMU theology student Young Bin Im gave a speech at First Methodist Church.[18] In 1948, as new federal legislation allowed for foreign nursing students, Korean women began studying nursing in Texas. One of the first was Mrs. Yang In-Ai, who arrived at Baylor University in 1948.[19] After the 1965 immigration reform allowed for large numbers of nurses to immigrate, the number of Korean Texans increased greatly. Son Geeja was the first Korean nurse to settle permanently in Dallas, and a second nurse, Man Ja Chae-Lee, arrived in 1966. Both worked at Parkland Hospital and were joined by a third nurse, Hung Ok Lim, in 1967; she had been the Vice-President of Severance Hospital in Seoul, Korea. By 1970, about thirty-five nurses had immigrated to Dallas to work at Parkland Hospital in Dallas's Oaklawn neighborhood. In Korea, many of them had been high-ranking nurses who had graduated from well-regarded nursing programs. Being a nurse in the United States represented a great professional opportunity as well as a chance to immigrate to this nation. The nurses' families usually joined them about a year after they arrived in Texas. In the early years, the nurses usually worked the night shift due to language difficulties, and, on Sundays, Reverend "Peter" Suk Bouk picked them up from their dormitories and drove them to the Korean Church of Dallas. In addition to nurses, the congregation also included several students from local universities.[20]

In 1968, nurse Ho Un Ok helped to found Dallas's Korean Nurses Association, one of the nation's first Korean nurses associations. She served as its first president. Besides coordinating social activities, the association helped the Korean community of Dallas with their health issues. The community at large grew, and in 1969 about 100 Koreans attended the first meeting of the Korean American Society. By 1970, the Parkland-centered community patronized its own Korean grocery store, named Go Pa Ho. The Korean community consisted mainly of nurses; engineers and doctors who had obtained contract work in Dallas; a handful of exchange students; and family members.[21]

As in other Texas cities and towns, Korean Christian and Catholic Churches became centers of community organization. Korean churches taught the English language to immigrants and the Korean language to their children. Churches housed the elderly, organized soccer and social events, allowed Korean merchants to make connections, sent Korean missionaries on service and proselytizing missions around the globe, and organized support groups. The congregation of the Korean Church of Dallas began meeting in 1966. By 1975, Dallas's Korean community numbered around 1,200, and Korean denominational churches began forming—some "branching off" from extant Korean churches. The first church to branch off from the Korean Church of Dallas was a Korean Baptist congregation established and supported by Gaston Avenue Baptist Church. Such splits in congregations were not without church politics and interpersonal conflicts. By 1977, there were ten Korean churches in the Dallas area. In 1977, St. Andrew's Korean Catholic Church was formed in downtown Dallas by Im Chun Goon, who had moved there from Houston. New Korean churches "branched off" with relative frequency. Korean Dallasite John Chu remembered how his childhood church "branched off" five times, frustrating his mother so much that they quit attending church for some time.[22]

Members of a Korean church in Dallas act out a Christmas play. The church has been the center of many Korean Texan communities.

Savannah Choi chose a non-traditional field. She worked as a fashion model for catalogues and advertisements in the 1990s.

In the 1970s, John Chu's family started in Dallas a company that contracted sewing work to local Korean immigrants. The Chu family themselves had risen from poverty. In Korea, the family had lived in a garage, and John's parents sold their wedding rings to survive. "I remember the milk man would deliver milk everyday, and my older sisters wouldn't get any because I was the only son," remembered Chu, born in 1969. When the family immigrated to the United States, they seized the opportunity to prosper. The parents worked until two or three in the morning each day. "They had to get things done," said Chu, citing what could be a common theme among Korean Texans. Regarding the home sewing workers, Chu said:

> They lived in very bad apartments. Half their rooms were filled with clothes for sewing. They had to use a room separately for sewing. There was a lot of dust. I saw that and I thought it must be hard for them.[23]

By 1970, there were about 200 Koreans living in Houston, many of whom were Korean military wives. Korean Texans ran a cluster of businesses along Telephone Road in southeast Houston, and some Korean families lived in that area. In the early 1970s, many Korean Houstonians were university students who met to socialize and worship. In 1970, students formed one of Houston's early Korean churches, Korean Ethnic Church. For three years, the students held only bible studies. As the congregation grew, they rented a building from the Second Baptist Church and hired a seminary student as their pastor. By 1978, the congregation had grown to 250, and the congregation worked each night to convert a grocery store into their new church. One minister described this time in nostalgic terms:

> We built this church with our own hands . . . with cardboard, nails and hammers. We came after work and stayed here until two or three in the morning. Then, we went back home and slept a couple of hours and went to work . . . At that time, a simple thing like putting the lights on the ceiling made us so happy.[24]

By 1980, a major portion of the Korean immigrants in Houston and Dallas were professionals—nurses, doctors, engineers, and computer programmers. Most immigrants, however, owned businesses or worked in Korean-owned businesses. The oil boom of the 1970s and early 1980s produced strong economic growth and abundant job opportunities. In Houston, immigrants who spoke little English could obtain good jobs. Office building space in Houston doubled between 1975 and 1982, and Korean businesses dominated the cleaning business. Thousands of Koreans throughout Texas worked as janitors and office cleaners. Floor sweepers in Houston started at $8 an hour. One cleaning service grew to one thousand employees by the 1990s.[25]

With the oil boom expanding the Houston economy, the population of Korean Houstonians grew by the early 1980s to 30,000—many of the new residents coming from Dallas. In the 1970s, as Chinese Texans sold their small groceries, Korean immigrants began opening small groceries, convenience stores, gas stations, and other retail stores, especially in lower-income African American and Hispanic neighborhoods, where opening a business required less money. Many Korean businesses, including clothes and wig stores, catered specifically to African Americans and Hispanics. In all neighborhoods, opportunities for Korean entrepreneurs increased steadily as the Texas economy and population grew. Many Korean merchants started out by running "road sales," or street vendor stands next to supermarkets or at flea markets. Many of these operations grew into larger retail outlets. Korean Texan merchants used connections with Korean-owned manufacturers and distributors to supply their stores. While some businesses made little money per hour, Koreans made the most of their situations by working long hours and making the workplace a living space for their families.[26]

With the oil bust of the mid-1980s, office vacancies in Houston skyrocketed and, with it, unemployment among Korean Houstonians. Korean office cleaning services replaced many of their Korean workers with Hispanic workers, and those Koreans who continued as laborers suffered wage cuts. The economic crisis caused a mass migration of Korean Houstonians to Dallas, Atlanta, New York, and California, reducing the population to less than 20,000. Rather than work for lower wages or go unemployed, many of the remaining Korean Texans started small businesses. Entrepreneurship blossomed, and by 1993, about 31% of Korean immigrants in Houston were self-employed.[27]

In 1985, with an estimated population of 20,000 Koreans, Houston was home to thirty-four Korean churches, most of them Southern Baptist. While other Korean congregations in 1985 met at predominantly white churches, the only Korean Southern Baptist church with its own building was the Seoul Baptist Church. Its pastor, Reverend Soon Il Kim, explained in a 1985 article that Koreans have more churches than any other ethnic group and that "the non-Christian Korean who lives here is very solitary and lonely."[28]

Austin's Korean community grew more slowly than Dallas's and Houston's, and in the 1970s and 1980s it was still largely associated with the Korean student community at UT-Austin. In the 1990s and 2000s, the Korean Austinite population grew faster than the student population in part because of increases in tuition and in part because of the growth in the number of Korean business-owners. The growth of high-technology companies in Austin attracted Korean engineers and computer scientists. A major component of Austin's high-tech landscape was Samsung Austin Semiconductor, a division of the Korean corporation, Samsung Electronics (worth $60 billion in 2007). Built in 1998, Samsung's $1.3 billion Austin plant was its only semiconductor manufacturing plant outside of the United States.[29]

As much as any Asian ethnic group in Texas between 1970 and 2005, Korean Texans owned and ran businesses. Because many came to the United States with little money and could not secure a bank loan, many Koreans borrowed from family or through informal mutual loan groups known as *gyes*. Some saved money by sewing or cleaning. Racial discrimination, language barriers, professional licensing issues, lack of employment opportunities, and cultural differences motivated Korean professionals to run businesses unrelated to their professions rather than pursue professional work. For the same reasons, Koreans sought to be self-employed rather than work for others. Ken Shinn, born in Yang Pyung, Korea, earned a graduate degree in forestry in 1973 from Stephen F. Austin University. He ran a small business in Mississippi before moving in 1983 to Austin, Texas, where he opened a doughnut shop. Shinn decided to move his family to Texas because of Mississippi's more palpable racism, its conservative atmosphere, and its poorer economy.[30]

Of the estimated 700 donut shops in the D-FW area, 500 or more are run by Korean Americans, and another large portion are run by Cambodians. These family-owned operations make their donuts the old-fashioned way—with rolling pins and manual donut cutters. David Cho was a successful architectural engineer in Korea when he and his wife decided that he should attend graduate school in Texas. When plans went awry, the couple "didn't want to go back to Korea with empty hands," according to daughter Michelle. Arriving in the Dallas area in the early 1980s, David Cho worked as a janitor and then operated a series of donut shops and a restaurant before settling on the wholesale business in 2004. Michelle, born in 1982, remembered how she would wake up as a child at 3 a.m. to go with her mother to the donut shop, where Michelle slept in a back room (built by her father) until she went to school. She recalled a price war with a Cambodian-owned donut shop in which the competition won, but the Cho family regained their customers because of her father's deliciously "fluffy" donuts. Nevertheless, Michelle said, "when my father talks about buildings, I can tell he misses architectural engineering. It's sad."[31]

The combination of long hours and over-qualification was sometimes frustrating, as expressed in an interview excerpt in Victoria Kwon's 1997 monograph on Korean Houstonians:

> Who would want to work like this? Everyday, I have to work in my shop for at least 11 hours without any breaks. No vacations, no holidays, no weekends. Hustling with customers all the time. If I could have a decent job with fair pay, I would take that over this any day. Sitting in a cool, clean office with the respect I deserve would be all I want. But would I get that? No. There is no such job for me. I can't speak English as well as they do, I don't laugh at the same joke they do. I am an outsider, so I can't get the same treatment. That is why I am here. At least there is money in this.[32]

In addition to these frustrations, Korean store owners dealt with cultural differences between themselves and their customers. While most relations were friendly, Korean store owners complained, for instance, that shop lifters, even when caught, showed no shame. Finally, while Korean Texans helped each other start businesses in the same areas (such as doughnut shops), competing so closely with other Koreans also caused friction between business owners. Intense competition may have contributed to the development of Korean gangs, hired to intimidate competing businesses. In the 1980s, many Korean homes were broken into and raided when the owners were believed to be away on business. One Korean elder recalls coming home to find not only his valuables gone, but also his rice and "kimchi" half eaten. Korean gangs were common until they died down in the 1990s. While the original members of the gangs likely moved away from Dallas, new and smaller "gangs" still exist. But most of these are simply groups of friends who gain the reputation of being a gang due to their inseparable nature.

Asian American store owners, highly exposed to the public, were killed at a high rate as a result of armed robberies and other crimes. Criminals came in all colors, but Koreans sometimes suspected that their race was an issue. San Antonio and its Asian American community were rattled when, from 1999 to 2002, seven Asian store owners and Asian workers were murdered and one was sexually assaulted in a string of four attacks. In response, the San Antonio Asian community established a committee to seek improved police protection and preventative measures. It resembled the Dallas Korean Crime Commission established in 1999 to deal with crime committed by both Koreans and non-Koreans alike.[33]

What may be termed the anti-Korean store movement began in New York City in the late 1980s. Leaders such as Rev. Al Sharpton led boycotts against Korean store owners considered disrespectful of the African American community. The movement spread to Los Angeles, where Ice Cube recorded a violently anti-Korean song, and hate crimes against Koreans increased. In 1991, a Korean merchant in Los Angeles shot and killed an African American teenaged girl—Latasha Harlins—after a shoplifting incident and a scuffle. In 1992, during the Los Angeles Riots, thousands of Korean stores were looted and burned. As far away as Texas A&M University, some African American student leaders stated after the riots that Asian American businesses should leave black neighborhoods. Horrified Korean Texans watched on television Los Angeles's Koreatown burning, and over a decade later, Ken Shinn still referred to the Los Angeles Riots as the "Korean Riots." Korean Dallasites feared the same fate as that of Korean Los Angelinos and decided to change some behaviors considered particular to Korean culture. Rather than avoiding eye contact with customers, store owners looked in patrons' eyes. Rather than avoiding conversation, they chatted with customers.

For four years leading up to the April 1992 LA Riots, Dallas's Korean Chamber of Commerce and the city's Black Chamber of Commerce had been working together to improve relations through activities and scholarships in the African American community. The chambers' worst fears were sparked when shots were fired and massive looting broke out at a Korean-owned flea market less than three months after the LA Riots. But Korean and African American vendors agreed afterwards that the riots were not race-related. In December 1992, Korean and African American religious leaders in Dallas met to improve understanding and racial harmony.[34]

The specter of slain teen Latasha Harlins suddenly rose in the city of Fort Worth in September 1994 when local Korean convenience store owner Jason Noh shot and killed African American Darrell Bivins over a shoplifting conflict. Immediately after the murder, Reverend Michael Bell, chairman of the Tarrant County Clergy for Inter-Ethnic Peace and Justice, led several days of protest in front of Noh's closed business, demanding that the store close permanently. Anger spread and some urged the City Council to close down many of the Asian-owned convenience stores in the crime-ridden Stop Six neighborhood, where the shooting occurred. African Americans complained that Asian American store owners sold alcohol to minors, showed disrespect to blacks, and wore pistols on their hips. The Korean Americans condemned Noh's violence, but countered that convenience store owners are often shot by guns and that "shameless" shoplifters enraged store owners.[35]

Fearing riots, local Koreans contacted Dr. Chai Ho Ahn, M.D., who called his daughter, Dr. Suzanne Ahn, M.D. Suzanne, a civil rights activist. She called her friend, U.S. Congresswoman Eddie Bernice Johnson, a

Democrat representing a Dallas-Fort Worth district. Ahn and Johnson's friendship proved valuable. Rep. Johnson asked Rev. Bell to restore calm among local African Americans. Reverend Bell and the Korean American Association (KAA) of Fort Worth then negotiated an agreement. Korean store owners vowed to stop alcohol consumption in front of their stores, establish a committee to resolve future grievances, and cease the selling of certain gang-symbolizing products. The Korean American Association also donated $2300 towards local scholarships for African Americans and committed to hiring African American workers. "We, Korean Americans, have been dormant politically and socially in this region, but we think now is the time for change," said the Fort Worth KAA President Dr. S. Gerald Koh, "It is time to step forward with renewed direction and enthusiasm into the mainstream of America."[36]

Neighborhoods, Business Districts, Politics, Charity and Beyond

Korean Texans have established several distinctively Korean business districts in Texas. The first major districts were in Killeen, the Spring Branch neighborhood in Houston, and Irving, Texas. School district and racial concerns both influenced where Koreans chose to live. In the 1970s, Koreans began moving to Spring Branch in northwest Houston to send their children to the independent school district's quality schools. They opened up sandwich shops and shoe repair services before opening grocery stores. Professionals also moved into the area, in part to work for businesses and serve the community. In the late 1970s and early 1980s, a Korean commercial center developed. By 1997, one hundred twenty Korean businesses catering largely to other Koreans were located in the area circumscribed by Long Point, Hammerly, Gessner, and Bingle streets.[37] By 1998, an estimated 15,000 to 20,000 of the 40,000 Korean Americans in Houston lived in Spring Branch, and Korean residents, with the political support of City Councilperson Martha Wong and Mayor Lee Brown, put forth money for Korean-language street signs at ten intersections along Long Point Road. As in the "Bellaire" Asian business district in Southwest Houston, where Chinese-language signs had been added to street corners, the Korean-language signs would have supplemented existing English language signs. Hundreds of non-Korean residents signed a petition against the street signs and the area's city council member, Bruce Tatro, also opposed the idea. The Koreans withdrew their proposal, but the conflict remained a divisive campaign issue three years later.[38]

In 1981, Ran Lee opened the first Korean store—Oriental Food & Gift Shop—on Belt Line Road in Irving, Texas. In 1985, Korean Dallasite Keith Chung moved his company, Electronic Manufacturing Support System, from Oak Cliff to Irving, and he helped develop Korean businesses there because, as he admitted, "If we had tried to build Koreatown in Dallas, there would have been outrage because people have been established there a long time. Irving does not have the intensity of roots." By 1986, there were almost fifty Korean-owned stores in a half-mile stretch of Belt Line Road. In those years, about 10,000 of the 30,000 Koreans in Dallas-Fort Worth lived and worked in Irving. But as Koreans felt greater acceptance throughout Dallas-Fort Worth, and as they chased market opportunities, they left Irving for other suburbs and cities.[39]

By 1991, thirty percent of the Korean population of Irving and forty percent of the Irving Koreatown businesses had left, some for a developing Korean business district centered around the intersection of Harry Hines and Royal Lane in northwest Dallas. In the 1980s, the Harry Hines area was a red-light district where street prostitutes openly solicited customers. Although Koreans from New York and California moved to Texas in part to avoid crime, mere vice could not prevent Korean entrepreneurs from snatching up low rent buildings in a more central location. As the lights of commerce shined, many of the prostitutes left. In the mid-1980s, the Shinchon Supermarket opened, and in later years, Koreans took over the small shops along Shoppers Alley, a small shopping center consisting of a driveway lined on each side with small businesses. In the 1990s, more shopping centers were added, and not just for Koreans. Dr. David Kim opened an entire shopping center dedicated to the surrounding Hispanic neighborhood called Plaza Latina. Steve Son began his jewelry business by peddling jewelry out of his briefcase, "even in restrooms and restaurants," he recalled, "I'd talk to them." In the early years of New World Jewelry, he sold thick gold necklaces made popular by rap artists, but he later specialized in custom-made jewelry. David Moon's wildly successful Sam Moon "wholesale" merchandise store, which sells goods to retail customers at slightly above the wholesale price, attracted all ethnic groups and expanded into other neighborhoods.[40]

While recent immigrants and illegal immigrants lived in apartment complexes near their workplaces in Koreatowns, established Koreans sought to live in suburbs with good school districts and Korean communities. While Dallas suburbs Garland and Irving were popular early, Koreans in the 1990s established communities in Plano, Carrollton, Coppell, and Lewisville. By residing in the same school districts, Korean Texans maintained culture and community. In 2005, the Korean Texan population was estimated at 120,000, with at least 50,000 Koreans living in the Dallas-Fort Worth area.[41]

Korean Texans lived and worked at a frenetic pace. They quickly changed businesses and occupations, moved across cities or state, migrated to new school districts, and started new churches. The rapid movement allowed Korean Texans to flow with market forces and keep their children in the best schools. Their flexibility and hard work paid off, as many Koreans went from being sewing workers to owning more than one business, while others came to Texas with savings and built their wealth from there. One driving force for the Korean Texan immigrants was an overriding pride, which many of their children inherited. Many Korean Texans refused to accept failure and its accompanying shame, even if it meant years of struggle. Young Koreans even fashioned the words "Korean Pride" on their clothing and notebooks.

With success came attempts at repaying obligations to family, friends, and communities who made their success possible. One of the earliest Korean immigrants to Dallas, Dr. Wonmo Dong helped to found in 1969 the Korean Society of Dallas. While he was an active member of the Dallas Korean community, Dr. Dong worked to democratize South Korea. In 1973, Dr. Dong and South Korean dissident Kim Dae Jung founded the largest Korean pro-democracy organization in the United States—Korean Congress for Democracy and Reunification (KCDR).

The organization worked to bring democracy to Korea, which was ruled by a military dictatorship. In 1973, Kim Dae Jung was kidnapped by the Korean Central Intelligence Agency. As president of the KCDR, Dong helped secure Kim's release in 1983, and Kim Dae Jung was later elected president of a democratic South Korea. Dr. Dong was a professor of political science at Southern Methodist University from 1968 to 2000, serving as the Director of the Asian Studies Program from 1979 to 1998.[42]

President Kim began normalizing relations with North Korea, which allowed Korean American charities to funnel food and supplies to the impoverished people of North Korea. One of the more successful altruists was Paul Shinn of Houston, Texas. Through his church, Korean Central Presbyterian, Shinn began Christian missions to China, and then to Najin, North Korea. Even as the Christian aid group World Concern withdrew for the sake of safety, Shinn's organization, Manna Mission, arrived in Najin in 1997 with eighty tons of flour. By 1999 a huge oven shipped from Houston began baking 7,000 loaves of bread each day for school children. An electricity generator was bought for the bakery, and a medical clinic was also opened. Manna Mission was funded by eighteen churches, as well as Shinn's family. Arriving in Houston in 1976, the Shinn family of five lived with other Korean families in small apartments in Spring Branch. Upon saving enough money, the family opened a wig shop, which eventually grew to a chain of five wig shops, serving communities as varied as African Americans to chemotherapy patients. After his wife nearly died of an asthma attack in the early 1990s, Paul Shinn sold four of the five wig shops and, unbeknownst to his family, went into debt to fund Manna Mission. He died at 66 in the year 2004. "Most people take out a second mortgage to remodel their kitchen," said son George, "My dad did it for charity."[43]

Dr. Chai Ho Ahn immigrated to New York City in 1954 to work as a tuberculosis specialist. At the age of 36, he lived on a hundred dollars a month and sent as much back home as possible. South Korea was extremely poor, and Ahn's wife and four children lived in a six-foot square room without heat. Through a complicated process that involved a $10,000 bribe to the Korean government and negotiations between Korean American Foundation president Howard Rusk and Korean Presi-

Wendy Gramm and Senator Phil Gramm pose with a photograph of Wendy's grandmother at a special reception for them at the Institute of Texan Cultures, San Antonio.

Dr. and Mrs. Chai Ho Ahn pose before the family portrait in their home in 2007.

dent Syngman Rhee, Dr. Ahn's wife and children were allowed to leave Korea and join Dr. Ahn in Arkansas in 1959. They then moved to Tyler, Texas, where Dr. Ahn conducted research on tuberculosis. Having suffered through the disease himself, he had had his right lung removed in order to remain in the United States. While working in Tyler, he supported his parents and his brother's family in Korea, but he felt obligated to the entire village, which had scraped together $143 to support his college education.

> I was fifteen when I first wanted to do something for the village people, and this desire became even stronger just before the surgery to remove my right lung in 1955. At that time I begged God to bring me through successfully so that I could repay my old debt to the Kamchun villagers . . .[44]

In the summer of 1968, he began a series of fourteen medical missions over a period of twenty-eight years to rural Korea. On the first trip, he brought $100,000 in medical supplies and began a program of vaccinations, treatment, and surgery.[45]

Following in Dr. Ahn's footsteps, daughter Suzanne Ahn earned her M.D. and practiced as a neurologist in Dallas. During Ann Richards's term as governor (1990–1994), she appointed the relatively youthful Dr. Suzanne Ahn to the Air Quality Control Board and to the Texas State Board of Medical Examiners. Ahn advised Governor Richards to appoint Chinese Houstonian Bob Gee to head the Public Utilities Commission, which she did.

Because the Democratic Party was being criticized for receiving illegal donations from foreign Asian contributors, Dr. Suzanne Ahn was questioned by the FBI. She went on TV news show *Nightline* to criticize the FBI tactics. "When white men violate campaign finance rules," she said, "they pay a fine and nobody gets hurt. There is no maligning of the entire race. I think there is an incredible double standard here." Later, when nightclubs around SMU refused to allow Asian Americans into their businesses, she organized protests; the nightclubs eventually went out of business. In 1995, Suzanne Ahn flew to Washington, D.C. to lobby senators to vote for a bill supporting the civil rights of mistreated Filipino American cannery workers in Alaska.[46]

In spring of 2002, Suzanne Ahn, a non-smoker and an advocate for cleaner air, was diagnosed with inoperable lung cancer. Before her death, she donated $100,000 to the Asian American Journalists Association to encourage writers to focus on Asian American justice issues. "I think racism is a poison," she said not long before her passing. "It really can take away someone's self-esteem . . . We have to constantly strive and teach our children how to deal with [racism], as well as to instill the love and confidence in them so they can meet the challenges."[47]

ENDNOTES

1 *Dallas Morning News*, Aug 9, 1931.

2 Pong Hyon Paek, *The Koreans in Mexico* (UT-Austin Master Thesis, 1968), 28, 32, 34, 44, 52; Warren Kim, *Koreans in America* (Seoul, Korea: Po Chin Chai Printing Co. Ltd., 1971), 14–21.

3 "Korean Immigrants in America, Chapter Six: The Marriage by Matchmakers," *Minjok-Tongshin English Edition*, retrieved on Oct 19, 2005 at *http://66.28.44.150/article/index.php3?type=special&code=589.*

4 On military academy and participation in revolution, see Bong-youn Choy, *Koreans in America* (Chicago: Nelson-Hall, 1979), 151–152; Paek, 28, 32, 34, 44, 52; Kim, 14–21; the number of Korean workers may have numbered up to 3,000, according to John Kenneth Turner, *Barbarous Mexico* (Austin: University of Texas Press, 1969), 8.

5 "Korean Immigrants..."

6 Carlos Hamann, "Koreans flourish on border: Greater opportunity, acceptance found there," *Dallas Morning News*, Oct 20, 1996; Paul Salopek, "Korean business booming in downtown El Paso," *Houston Chronicle*, Apr 21, 1991; also Irwin Tang's conversations with Korean students at UT-Austin; U.S. Census, 2000.

7 1960 U.S. Census, Volume 45, page 680; 1970, 1980, 1990 U.S. Censuses; see 1970 Census, Vol. 45, table 141, p. 1285; also conversations with Lisa Humphries and Neggie Loudermilk, see below and Ch. 11.

8   "Policemen Help War Bride, Tots," *Dallas Morning News,* Dec 12, 1959; "Mate Tells War Bride To Go Back," *Dallas Morning News*, Dec 22, 1959.

9   Census 1960, Volume 45, p. 120; Vol 45, p. 680–686; Lisa Humphries, interview by Irwin Tang and Lucy Lee, Killeen, Texas, June 2004.

10 Bok Chu An, interview by Irwin Tang, Aug 17, 2004.

11 Lisa Humphries, interview; Andrea Gerlin, "Spread of Illegal Home Sewing is Fueled by Immigrants," *Wall Street Journal*, Mar 15, 1994; Jason Johnson, "Garment workers fear labor law crackdown," *Dallas Morning News*, May 21, 1992; Mark Smith, "HOME-SEWN TROUBLE/Unregulated work unravels labor law," *Houston Chronicle*, Aug 7, 1994.

12 Humphries, interview by Lee and Tang.

13 "Prostitutes Recruiting Koreans, Police Say," *Dallas Morning News*, Feb 18, 1985; "Base town becomes recruitment center," *Houston Chronicle*, Dec 25, 1986; Sharon Cohen, "Import business trades on women/Growing Korean prostitution network in U.S. moves into suburbs," *Houston Chronicle*, Dec 25, 1986; Joel Williams, "Massage parlor crackdown chases businesses to Valley," *Dallas Morning News*, Apr 29, 1990.

14 Ai Moon, interview by Irwin Tang and Lucy Lee, Killeen, June 2004.

15 Humphries, interview by Lee and Tang.

16 Estimate of 7,000 by Lisa Humphries; see also Census data.

17 "Happy Korean Lad Remembers Home," *Dallas Morning News,* Sep 5, 1953; on adoptees, see *Dallas Morning News*, June 21, 1956 and June 20, 1971; on quotes, interviewee name withheld, interview by Irwin Tang.

18 "Korean to give talk at Methodist church," *Dallas Morning News*, Feb 24, 1930.

19 "Korea Nurse Plans Study at Baylor," *Dallas Morning News*, May 4, 1948.

20 Lucy Lee to Irwin Tang, email, Aug 19, 2004, based on interviews with Korean Dallasite nurses.

21 Ho Soon M. Cho, interview by Lucy Lee, 2004.

22 Frank Taggart, "Churches split Koreans: Local community divided by rift," *Dallas Times Herald*, Oct 18, 1975; Bill Kenyon, "Churches extend efforts to Asians," *Dallas Morning News*, May 21, 1977; John Chu, interview by Lucy Lee, 2004; also Lucy Lee to Irwin Tang, email, Aug 19, 2004, based on various interviews.

23 Chu, interview.

24 Victoria Kwon, *Entrepreneurship and Religion: Korean Immigrants in Houston, Texas* (New York: Garland Publishing, 1997), 86–87.

25 Ibid., pp. 67, 62.

26 See Kwon.

27 Kwon, pp. 62–64, p. 54.

28 Steve Maynard, "Seoul Baptist Church: Koreans in Houston embrace Christianity," *Houston Chronicle*, Nov 30, 1985.

29 Ken Shinn, interview by Irwin Tang, Oct 19, 2005; *http://www.samsung.com/ AboutSAMSUNG/ELECTRONICSUSA/CompanyProfile/SamsungAustinSemicon-*

ductor/index.htm, Samsung's official site, accessed March 28, 2007.

30 Shinn, interview.

31 Michelle Cho, conversation with Irwin Tang, 2004.

32 Kwon, 65.

33 See MacCormack, "A compelling year in S.A.," *San Antonio Express-News*, Dec 29, 2002, among other articles in that paper; Dave Michaels, "Crimes against Koreans target of commission," *Dallas Morning News*, Jul 28, 1999.

34 Jason Johnson, "Easing the Tension: Dallas blacks, Korean retailers learn from melee," *Dallas Morning News*, Jul 8, 1992; Judith Lynn Howard, "Blacks, Koreans show unity Dallas leaders pledge to improve relations," *Dallas Morning News*, Dec 15, 1992.

35 Selwyn Crawford, "Black Clergy, others picket store where man was killed by owner," *Dallas Morning News*, Sep 20, 1994; Crawford and Anna Macias, "Black FW residents urge store closings," *Dallas Morning News*, Sep 21, 1994; "Shooting victim's relatives want assailant's store closed," *Austin American-Statesman*, Sep 22, 1994; *Dallas Morning News* editorial, "Store Shooting: Controversy shows need for racial dialogue," Sep 22, 1994; Crawford and J. Lynn Lunsford, "Cultural chasm: Blacks and Asians in FW at odds over treatment at stores," *Dallas Morning News*, Sep 27, 1994.

36 Chai Ho Ahn, interview by Lucy Lee, 2004; Gracie Bonds Staples, "Racial tensions addressed," *Fort Worth Star-Telegram*, Nov 29, 1994; Selwyn Crawford, "FW Koreans, blacks reach deal," *Dallas Morning News*, Nov 30, 1994.

37 Kwon, 68.

38 Eric Berger, "Spring Branch residents oppose plan for putting up Korean signs," *Houston Chronicle*, Jul 31, 1998; Berger, "Korean sign effort dropped," *Houston Chronicle*, Aug 4, 1998; Berger, "Korean civic leaders blast councilmember over sign flap," *Houston Chronicle*, Aug 5, 1998; Kathryn Wolfe, "Spring Branch politics fuel Korean sign debate," *Houston Chronicle*, Jul 22, 2001.

39 Stacey Freedenthal, "Koreatown: Once-booming area catering to Asians falls on hard times," *Dallas Morning News*, Sep 29, 1991; Julie Wright, "Koreans feel at home in Irving shops," *Dallas Morning News*, Feb 1, 1987.

40 John Kirkpatrick, "A Wholesale Restoration: Asian American businesses renew languishing district," *Dallas Morning News*, May 11, 1999; Esther Wu, "For Korean-Americans, success builds from homeland to U.S.," *Dallas Morning News*, Jun 2, 2005.

41 Ibid.

42 "SMU Professor recognized as a pioneer of South Korean Democracy Movement," *SMU News*, Apr 27, 2000.

43 Edward Hegstrom, "A Labor of Loaves: S. Korean native aids N. Korean kids," *Houston Chronicle*, Jun 17, 2000; Edward Hegstrom, "Promise fed N. Korean kids," *Houston Chronicle*, Mar 22, 2004.

44 Chai Ho Ahn, *The Life of a Korean Doctor: The Autobiography of Chai Ho Ahn*

(Seoul: The Institute of Korean Studies, 1997).

45 Ibid.

46 Sam Chu Lin, "Proud to be Korean American," *AsianWeek*, Jan 10, 2003. Joe Simnacher, "Doctor fought for many causes," *Dallas Morning News*, Jun 23, 2003; Lance LaPine and Sharon Lapine, "Remembering Suzanne: Dr. Suzanne Ahn Hays, 1952–2003," *AsianBeat: Dallas/Fort Worth Asian Monthly News*, Sep 2003.

47 On quote, *Koream Journal* interview at koreamjournal.com, 2003, *http://www. koreamjournal.com/search_detail.asp?id=552* accessed on Feb 29, 2004.

CHAPTER TEN

★

THE CHINESE TEXANS, 1945–2005

Irwin A. Tang and Rebecca Teng

Segregation, Migration and the Chinese Texan Struggle for Civil Rights

It is unclear when Chinese Texans began to vote. In 1874, during Reconstruction, 150 Chinese in Robertson County registered to vote. But by the 1896 elections, white men with guns stood before the Robertson County election booths, enforcing Texas's "white primary" system, in which only whites were allowed to vote in extremely important Democratic Party primaries. Chinese Texans born in the 1930s remember their parents voting in Houston and San Antonio elections and primaries. Among these voters was Edward K.T. Chen, a former diplomat for China who always voted and participated in Democratic Party primaries. In the 1936 election, about fifty Chinese El Pasoans voted. In the 1960s and 1970s, according to Sonny Lew, Chinese San Antonians voted in presidential elections, and they tended to vote for the Democratic Party, which actively sought their support.[1]

Not long after their arrival in 1870, Chinese Texans owned farmland and many urban properties on which they ran their businesses. But in 1937, Texas State Senator Franklin Spears of San Antonio introduced in the Texas Senate a bill that would amend the 1921 Alien Land Law (see Chapter 4) to prohibit all aliens ineligible for citizenship from owning land within cities and towns. The bill was aimed at preventing Chinese from owning grocery stores and would have applied to all Asians. Led by A.L. Becker, the founder of the Handy Andy grocery stores, the San Antonio Retail Merchants' Association lobbied for the amendment. The Texas cotton industry lobbied against it, fearing a boycott by major cotton importers, Japan and China. Becker testified at a March 9 hearing that there were 110 Chinese-owned groceries in San Antonio and that the Chinese were secretive, rarely seen in public, and so frugal that it constituted unfair competition.[2]

Rose Wu (maiden name "Don") of San Antonio testified that the bill was unjust and that Becker had exaggerated the numbers of Chinese stores. "You say there are tong killings," she added, "Tongs are not gangsters. Americans are murdered everyday. The Chinese have their own laws and settle their own affairs without bothering the American courts. Play straight and we will play straight with you." She said that the Chinese do not utilize welfare benefits. Rose Wu, whose father and grandfather were both American citizens, had graduated from Wellesley, but she reminded the state legislators, "I do not forget my blood." Edward K.T. Chen, the Assistant Chinese Consul of Houston, called the bill open discrimination against the Chinese and Japanese, and Delphine Tafolla Swain of the League of United Latin-American Citizens of San Antonio also testified against the bill. The American-Chinese Citizen League of San Antonio published a pamphlet: "Some Facts You Ought to Know: Should Texas Eliminate the Orientals?" The bill died in committee.[3]

Before the 1960s, housing discrimination segregated Chinese Texans' to living and operating stores mostly in African American and Hispanic neighborhoods. Martha Wong (maiden name Jee), born in 1939, remembered that during her childhood, most of the Chinese in Houston lived in black neighborhoods; her family lived in the rear of their store because they were not allowed to rent in the surrounding white neighborhood. When Mitchel Wong's parents, living in San Antonio, prepared in 1937 to purchase property to establish a grocery store in Corpus Christi, the "city fathers" wrote them a letter informing them that they were not welcome there. The family set up shop in Austin instead and eventually ran four grocery stores in mostly black and Hispanic east Austin; Mitchel eventually opened a highly successful Austin optometry practice.[4] Housing segregation likely shaped Chinese migrations to Texas; for instance, Chinese from other Southern states likely felt comfortable moving from one black neighborhood to another, say, in Houston.

Although some Chinese Texan men flouted white racists by marrying white women, these couples risked being prosecuted under Texas anti-miscegenation laws. It is unclear when Chinese Texan children were allowed to attend white schools, but clearly Texas integrated Chinese school children long before Mississippi did. On the first day of school in Mississippi in 1927, nine year-old Martha Lum, because she was Chinese, was kicked out of the white school that her father, Gong Lum, had placed her in. A grocer, Gong Lum sued Mississippi and in the first Supreme Court case to challenge school segregation, Mississippi's right to segregate schoolchildren was affirmed. Gong Lum, wife Kate, daughters Martha and Berda, and son Briscoe, moved first to Arkansas and then, in the 1940s, to Houston, where his children attended white schools. In Martha Wong's case, her parents moved the family to Mississippi and then back to Houston so that Martha and her older sister could go to white schools. In addition to its less severe segregation, Houston's economic growth from the 1930s to the 1970s spurred Chinese to move there from Southern states, resulting in most of Houston's Chinese population growth during that period.[5]

In the late 1930s Texas-born Chinese began attending Texas A&M University. The sons of Japanese Texan farmers had begun attending Texas universities in the 1920s, and Chinese Texan Inez Lung Lee received both undergraduate and graduate degrees from UT-Austin that same decade. However, consistent Chinese Texan college attendance seemed to coincide with the onset of World War II. In 1939, Edward King Tong Chen became the first Chinese American graduate of the University of Houston. Charles Chan (Chen's brother) and Jane Eng were Rice University's first Chinese American students. Chan graduated in 1941 with a degree in architecture, and Jane Eng left school to marry Albert Gee. In 1948, one year before the Chinese Communist Revolution, Dr. Paul Fan joined the geology faculty at the University of Houston and his wife, Dr. Joyce Fan, joined as a chemistry professor; in 1963, she was hired as the chairperson of Houston Baptist College's chemistry department.[6]

Before the 1970s, Chinese Texans' college degrees were often worthless. Racially discriminatory employers shut out Chinese Texan engineers, accountants, teachers, and others from their chosen professions, forcing Chinese Texan engineers to wait tables at Chinese restaurants. Martha Wong recalled how her sister earned an accounting degree but went unemployed because she was Asian; the Spring Branch school district denied Martha Wong a teaching job because of her race, but Wong, with an education degree from UT-Austin, took a job with the Houston school district, which already employed two other Chinese Americans. In the 1950s and 1960s, the Houston branch of the Chinese-American Citizens Alliance lobbied Texas universities to abolish their "unwritten rule" of shutting out Chinese American law school, medical school, and dental school applicants. Among other campaigns, the organization's members returned their Exxon credit cards to protest the oil company's shutting out of Chinese job applicants. The campaign succeeded in allowing a Chinese female accountant to work at Exxon and in changing company policy.[7]

Before the 1960s, all Houston restaurants were segregated, meaning, in this case, that African Americans could not eat at white restaurants; other cities' restaurants were segregated in some form or fashion, as well. Social rules for the Chinese varied, but they were generally treated less harshly than black Texans. Conforming to social rules, Chinese-owned restaurants were also segregated. In the 1940s and 1950s, Ben Mar of El Paso ran "a restaurant for white people and a restaurant for everyone else." Mar defied segregation at his Chung King restaurant, which was meant for whites, by serving nonwhites who would "stand in the back of the restaurant in the afternoons if they were hungry."[8]

When Chinese Houstonian Albert Gee was elected president of the Houston Restaurant Association for 1962-63, he used his position of power to spearhead a campaign to desegregate Houston restaurants. Speaking to white and Chinese restaurant owners even before the 1964

Civil Rights Act, he encouraged them to serve African Americans. While many Texas schools, universities, and restaurants refused to desegregate, Albert Gee "convinced members of the Association to comply with the law," accelerating the equal treatment of African Americans in the city with the South's largest black population. "We had experienced a lot of prejudice in the early days, and we didn't like it," wife Jane Eng Gee said, "So if we didn't like it, others shouldn't suffer through it."[9]

Albert Gee was born in 1920 in Detroit, Michigan. After the death of his father, his mother took the family of four back to the home village in Hoi Ping County of Guangdong Province. Albert Gee moved to Houston in 1936 to work in the restaurant business with his uncle, Harry Gee, Sr. In 1946, Albert Gee opened a pagoda-styled restaurant on Main Street called "Ding How," which introduced Houston to authentic Cantonese food. He later introduced Chinese take-out. By the 1950s, Houston papers referred to Gee as the unofficial "Mayor" of the Houston Chinese community, and Albert and Jane became media darlings; photos of them at social events, such as the Miss Chinatown pageants sponsored by the Chinese American Citizens Alliance, were regularly featured in local papers. By raising money for local charities and acting as a community liaison and representative, Albert Gee nurtured good relationships between the Chinese and other racial communities. A national ethnic and civil rights leader, Albert Gee served twice (1971-1975) as president of the national Chinese American Citizens Alliance.[10]

Retail Life

The early history of Chinese Houstonians was similar to that of Chinese Dallasites and Galvestonians. The Census recorded eight Chinese in Houston in 1880; they were mostly male and launderers. One man, Wah Yuan, was married to a (white or Hispanic) woman named Anna, and the couple had a son named Lincoln, apparently the first Chinese born in Houston. The first Chinese woman in Houston was Ah Gan, the newly-wed bride of Sam Lee; she arrived in 1886. From 1880 to 1896, the number of Chinese laundries grew from five to nineteen, and by 1910, there were only three; the Chinese population of Houston plummeted from forty-three in 1900 to eleven in 1910; in Dallas the number dropped from sixty-three in 1890 to twenty-four in 1900; and in Galveston from sixty-eight in 1900 to sixteen in 1930. Chinese Exclusion certainly contributed to the drops in population. The establishment of the steam laundry forced Chinese to diversify economically. Chinese-owned restaurants grew in number beginning in the 1890s, and the first Chinese grocery store in Houston was listed in 1900.[11]

The Chinese Houstonian community began growing rapidly in the 1930s and continued to grow through 2005 to become one of the largest, most politically powerful Chinese communities in the nation. Between 1930 and 1950, the Chinese Houstonian population grew twenty-fold from 31 to 620, nearly equaling the Chinese San Antonioan population of 656, which had only doubled in the same period. In earlier decades, Chinese immigrants tended to come from Mexico and settled in El Paso and San Antonio; between 1930 and 1965, many Chinese came from other Southern states such as Mississippi, Arkansas, and Louisiana, and they settled largely in Houston. Whereas the Chinese Consul general often visited El Paso at the turn of the 20th century, in 1933, the regional Chinese Consular office moved from Galveston, where it had been for one year, to Houston, to facilitate the purchase of U.S. cotton by the Republic of China. The center of Chinese political power also shifted from San Antonio to Houston, starting in November 1954, when Edward K.T. Chen and Albert Gee established a very active branch of the Chinese-American Citizens Alliance (CACA) in Houston. By 1960, the city's Chinese population was 1,874, twice that of San Antonio's.[12]

Most Chinese Texans in the middle four decades of the twentieth century owned or worked in small and medium-sized family grocery stores and restaurants. The growing Texas population offered opportunities for Chinese to open stores in neighborhoods that had not yet been saturated by other Chinese-owned stores and restaurants, such as had occurred in California. Because Chinese stores were dispersed throughout Texas cities, Chinese residences were, too; thus, *new* Chinatowns, in general, did not form in the 20th century until after the 1965 immigration reform. Chinese tended to live in converted bedrooms and homes in the same buildings as their stores. Living quarters were behind, above,

Albert Gee helped end racial segregation in Houston restaurants. This photo of the Houston Restaurant Association officers was taken when Gee was Vice-President of the group.

Mothers and children at Houston's Chinese Baptist Church, circa 1950s. They pose before the American and Republic of China flags.

or below the stores and were often cramped and lacking in amenities. For the first five years of Martha Wong's life, her family, which grew to six in number, lived in their Houston grocery store's storage room. Running one of the few Chinese grocery stores in Houston located in a white neighborhood, they were expected to speak English to each other in public. The practice helped Martha win high school speech tournaments, and later, public office.[13]

After serving in World War II as a sharpshooter and a cook at an army base in Tacoma, Washington, Francis Bing Chun Wong moved to San Antonio. Hearing about the "wide open market" for small businesses in San Antonio, some of his Chinese male veteran friends followed him there. "When one comes, more come," noted his daughter, Sophie Wong Lim, born in 1951 in San Antonio. When Chinese with, say, the name "Wong," came to San Antonio or Houston, they attracted other Chinese named "Wong." New arrivals learned from established same-name residents, received aid from them, socialized with them, and eventually opened up their own businesses. Sophie remembered that during her childhood, "I ran around with the Wong bunch."[14] In many ways, these Chinese lived typical Texan lives. Sophie Wong Lim's family lived in two bedrooms and a living room behind their store. She and her age cohort did their homework in the store, while their parents worked. Her parents cooked dinner in the store kitchen. At night, after the stores closed, grocery owners bowled.

Same-name, or clan-based, migrations resulted in Texas cities being home to disproportionately large numbers of certain clans. As late as 1976, about twenty percent of the Houston Chinese community was named Wong (or Wang), Gee (or Jee), or Lee (or Li). Associating by name was complicated by the fact that "not all of the Lees were Lees," remembered Dr. Ed Chen (the junior). About thirty or forty percent of the immigrants to Houston during the early decades of its mid-century growth were "paper" sons and daughters. Ed's mother, Janey Eng, carried immigration papers bought for her by her father in China, and she memorized "coaching papers" to fool officials.[15]

The Chinese grocery store became a cornerstone of urban minority neighborhoods throughout Texas. These Mom-and-Pop neighborhood grocery stores cut fresh steaks off of slaughtered cows, scaled and sold fresh fish, and offered fresh produce. The Chinese store was a hang-out place, too. Tim Eng remembered how the all-black patrons, especially the older men, used to sit around the store and joke and tell stories with his father, Bing Eng, whom they always called "Joe." Typical of Chinese Texans of that time, Bing Eng was a kind and responsible community member, but also "a tough guy." Like the other Chinese stores of Houston, Eng offered interest-free credit for customers needing goods before their next paycheck. One elderly African American man always asked "Joe" to "put it on my credit," but never paid the tab. Eng never asked for the money because he felt compassion for this old man who had lost a great deal during World War II, just like Eng had. On the other hand, when Bing Eng's brother was injured in a store robbery, Eng grabbed his shotgun and chased the robber around the neighborhood.[16]

Those who owned and ran grocery stores in San Antonio tended to be second-generation Americans, while those who ran restaurants tended to be first-generation immigrants. In Houston, first-generation Chinese Americans were well-represented in both areas. Many Chinese immigrants worked as store and restaurant employees, but San Antonio grocery stores hired large numbers of African Americans and Hispanics, believing that Chinese employees might open their own competing store.[17]

The stability of the store culture, with its tightly-knit two-parent families (as opposed to families separated by the Pacific Ocean), produced Chinese American second- and third-generation children who were educated in the United States and who sought to work in professional fields. As a result many Chinese San Antonioans and El Pasoans in the 1960s sought employment in booming Houston or attended college in other cities. The Chinese became more Americanized, and the languages of Toishanese and Spanish lost ground to English, Mandarin, and Cantonese, the primary languages of the post-1965 immigrants. Adding to the geographical shift was the fact that Chinese immigration after 1965 tended toward quickly growing areas like Houston and Dallas. From 1960 to 1970, the San Antonio and El Paso populations grew incrementally, while the Chinese Houstonian population doubled to 3,677; Chinese Dallasites tripled to 711; and Chinese Austinites more than tripled to 332.[18]

By 1975, with their children flocking into professional work, Chinese Texans sold their stores to recently-immigrated South Asians, Southeast Asians, and Koreans. "Now it's the Vietnamese and Pakistanis getting killed," commented Bobby Moon, who was born in Mississippi and whose family ran a grocery in Houston; Moon knew several Chinese American grocers killed by armed robbers.[19] By 1975, Chinese Texan groceries had evolved greatly. They had moved from downtowns to minority neighborhoods and then into white neighborhoods; quit growing their own vegetables and butchering their own meat; started buying foods from major distributors; and felt the squeeze of chain supermarkets, convenience stores, freeways, and car culture on their local markets.

With small groceries closing, the number of Chinese restaurants grew tremendously. Since the opening of Albert Gee's Ding How Restaurant in the 1950s, Houston has become the Chinese food capital of the South. Houston is home to the largest number and many of the best Chinese restaurants in the region. Scrumptious Chinese food in Texas is made affordable by the employment of thousands of Chinese and Mexican immigrants at low wages. These immigrants tend to be of lower education, unless they are Chinese graduate students. And their immigration statuses tend to be more questionable. The restaurant owners, typically immigrants themselves, often work long hours for low returns. Anna Lin was born in Taiwan in 1971 to parents who had escaped Communist China during the revolution. After running a gas station in Florida for two years, the family moved to the Houston suburb of Spring in 1985 because of its good schools. They ran a sandwich shop in an office building. But when offices became vacant, they closed the shop and opened a barbecue restaurant in Houston. Mr. Lin stood for hours each day over a mesquite smoke pit cooking meat, and both parents developed arthritis from the repetitive motion of chopping meat. Living cheaply, the parents put Anna through law school and son Brian through medical school. "I feel guilt-ridden," said Anna. "Everything they've done, they've done for me and my brother."[20]

McCarthyism, International Politics, and Gangs

In the decade after the Chinese Communist Party took over China in 1949, the federal government investigated Chinese Americans for their communist sympathies. Dr. Edward Chen (the junior) recalled events in 1953, as peace was being negotiated in the Korean War:

> My father [E.K.T. Chen] was a doctoral student at the University of Texas. One weekend he came home [to Houston] and told my mother that the FBI had been by to see him. They did not suspect his loyalty to the United States because of his past employment with the Consulate of the Republic of China and his work at the University of Houston. However, they wanted him to help in their investigation of other students. He did help them and the FBI was able to identify those who supported the Communist government.[21]

E.K.T. Chen later translated Chinese documents for the FBI in both Houston and New York City. While working for the FBI, Chen warned Chinese American leaders in San Francisco of a government crackdown. When, in February 1956, the FBI allowed only twenty-four hours for twenty-six forewarned Chinese American organizations in San Francisco to turn over all of their records, they shot back with a resolute defense of their rights published in a pamphlet entitled "Statement of Principle."

Anti-Communist "McCarthyism" of the early 1950s accelerated the disintegration of the Chinese El Pasoan community, according to Maria (Mae) de Los Angeles Mar Skates:

> McCarthy came in, and everybody was accusing everybody of being a Communist. And I think in a way that set a wave of shock through most of the Chinese population here, because they felt that it was just a matter of time before they would come after them.[22]

Chinese American writer Henry Liu, a critic of the Nationalist Party in power in Taiwan, was murdered on October 15, 1984 in Daly City, California by three members of an international Taiwan-based criminal organization known as the United Bamboo. Two FBI agents infiltrated the Houston branch of United Bamboo by swearing allegiance and drinking a mixture of blood and wine. Federal prosecutors then convicted Houstonian Chen Chih-Yi of helping to organize the killing of Liu and the escape of the killers through Houston. Chen, a Houston resident since 1970 and an ex-produce businessman, was regarded as the head of finance for the U.S. branch of United Bamboo.[23]

On June 3 and 4, 1989, the Communist government of the People's Republic of China quashed that nation's democracy movement by killing thousands of student and worker activists in Beijing's Tiananmen Square. The Chinese Texan community was shocked, saddened, and enraged. From April through December 1989, thousands of Chinese university students and Chinese Americans participated in pro-democracy demonstrations in Lubbock, College Station, Austin, Denton, Dallas, and Houston. With their fists raised, students mourned and protested the deaths of democracy activists. Some called for the overthrow of the Communist government. In 1989, Xun Ge was a physics doctoral student at Texas A&M University, but outside of class he coordinated underground Chinese democracy activists around the globe. In December 1990, he interrupted his studies to fly to Beijing to personally confront the government about its detainment of pro-democracy movement leader Juntao Wang. In 1994, the Communist government exiled Wang to the United States.[24]

After the Tiananmen Square Massacre, a U.S. law passed allowing Chinese at risk of persecution to remain in the United States. G.F. Zhou, whose father had been killed by Communist supporters in China, decided to stay in Texas, leaving his wife and daughter in China. Already elderly, Zhou struggled to survive in Texas, living, as he called it, "not a glorious life." In contrast, Chinese ballet dancer Li Cunxin was in 1981 on a cultural exchange program in Houston when he married his lover and fellow dancer, Elizabeth Mackey. Then, when Li attempted to defect from China, Houston's Chinese Consular office held him against his will and interrogated him for twenty-one hours as FBI agents surrounded the building. "No, I won't go back," Li told the Communist officials. "Do whatever you like with me." The Chinese government let Li defect, and Li Cunxin became the principal dancer for both the Houston Ballet and the Australian Ballet.[25]

The New Immigrants, the Students, and the Professors

During the McCarthyism era of the 1950s, strained relations between the U.S. and the People's Republic of China (PRC) resulted in the cessation of students from that nation attending U.S. universities; students from the PRC did not resume attendance until the 1980s, after President Carter had recognized that nation. Thus, most Chinese university students from the 1950s to 1980 came from Taiwan and Hong Kong. Chinese immigrated to Texas mostly by attending graduate school in the state, through family reunification, or by obtaining work as a technical worker (such as a computer programmer) after graduate school or through an H1-B Visa.

The first Chinese foreign student may have been H.Y. Moh, (Mu Xiang-yue), who earned a master's degree from Texas A&M University in 1913-14 and returned to Shanghai to become one of China's leading cotton manufacturers.[26] By 1952, there were seventy-four Chinese international students in Texas, and by 1974, there were well over 1,000 Chinese students. In the late 1960s and early 1970s, most Texas college towns gained "instant" Chinese communities. The number of Chinese students at Texas A&M University increased from about thirty in 1967 to over 200 in 1972. Dr. Yi-Noo Tang, born in 1938 in Hunan, China, lived and studied in Hong Kong before earning a Ph.D. in chemistry at the University of Kansas. In 1967, Texas A&M University hired Tang, who became the university's second Chinese professor. Teaching chemistry for thirty years at Texas A&M, he won two teaching awards. Yi-Noo and Eugenia Tang (maiden name Ying) remembered the early years:

> In general, southern hospitality applied . . . Many Texans went out of their way to be nice and helpful. Others took the gesture of pretending you were not there. There was discrimination. Once I was refused service at the University post office . . . For the first six or seven years, a certain Biology professor wrote to the *Eagle* editorial page to scold the Asians in America, telling us to "take your sperm and get out of this land."[27]

Both Yi-Noo Tang and his son, Irwin Tang, organized against local Ku Klux Klan activities in the late 1980s and early 1990s, resulting in retaliation. Despite racism, Chinese college town communities thrived, with cultural activities organized by university Chinese Students Associations, Taiwanese Students Associations, and Hong Kong Students Associations. At Texas A&M University, the latter two split off from the CSA in the 1970s, dividing the students by national and political affiliations. A major Chinese student community lived north of the university, making the area distinctly Asian.[28]

Over the years, Texas universities educated thousands of Chinese and Chinese Americans who bolstered economic and cultural sectors in the U.S. and Asia. Hong Kong director Tsui Hark (born in Vietnam), a UT-Austin film school graduate, achieved world fame for his action films. Taiwan-born engineer Wen Ho Lee, a Texas A&M University graduate, was a research scientist at Los Alamos National Laboratory before being falsely charged of spying for China. Paul Chu, born in China, a transplant to Taiwan, and a professor at the University of Houston, was considered for the 1987 Nobel Prize for his development of superconductivity at relatively warm temperatures.[29]

Houston Chinatowns

Houston's earliest "Chinatown" was not so much a commercial Chinatown as it was a number of important Chinese organizations which clustered around the On Leong Merchants' Association, established in September 1944. The Chinese Baptist Church was founded in 1953, and the CACA was founded in 1954. The nearby Chinese Consulate and the Kuomintang (Chinese Nationalist Party) organization were especially important in the mid-century period. As in most Chinatowns, merchant organizations and family associations were at the center of Houston's Chinatown. By 1979, when the Engs of Houston formed a local family association, there were about a dozen such associations. But by then, another Chinatown had already been established.[30]

By the late 1970s, the Chinese Houstonian community consisted largely of professionals and restaurant owners and workers. With the oil boom, Chinese and Chinese American engineers and other professionals flocked to Houston to work for companies such as Brown & Root, Texaco, and Exxon. Thomas Hung (born in Taiwan) was typical of Chinese graduate students of this time. After graduating from UT-Austin in 1974, Hung moved to Houston to work as an engineer for Brown & Root. He settled in southwest Houston, where many Chinese found inexpensive housing.[31]

By the mid-1970s, a newer Chinatown developed around east downtown Houston, along Chartres Street, where the On Leong and other Chinese associations had relocated. In 1975, Houston developer Lang Yee "Bo-Bo" Woo, seeking to expand this Chinatown, opened the first Chinese theatre on land purchased from the On Leong Merchants Association. With the success of the movie theatre, which often showed kung fu films, Woo attempted to attract Chinese American capital from New York and San Francisco; by 1982, a Chinatown shopping center had opened, and both Hong Kong and Vietnamese American money had been invested in three blocks of grocery stores, restaurants, and a bakery. But limited parking, high property prices, and area murders in the early 1980s discouraged Chinese from living in this Chinatown, which became associated with Chinese gambling parlors and Vietnamese gangs. The new Chinese Houstonians sought safe, affordable suburban neighborhoods with good schools; professionals would eat at the downtown Chinatown and sleep in the suburbs. Many Chinese professionals' families lived in the western suburb of Alief to send their children to Alief-Elsik and Hastings high schools. The majority of Chinese professionals worked for energy, industrial and high-tech companies, as well as universities and NASA.[32]

Ling-Chieh "Louis" Kung was the founder in 1961 of Houston-based Westland Oil Corporation. Kung, a nephew of Madame Chiang Kai-shek and a descendant of Confucius, married actress Debra Paget, and constructed a four-story home/office building whose underground compound delved seventy feet deep into the soil of Montgomery County. Louis and Debra raised their children in this building, which doubled as a nuclear war shelter able to support 1,500 people for ninety days.[33]

When low oil prices resulted in the "oil bust" of 1982 to 1987, many Chinese Houstonian engineers and professionals were laid off. Debbie Chen (born in 1970 in South Dakota), remembers moving to Alief in 1983, just after the layoffs began. "Chinese families were practically giving away their houses because they couldn't afford their mortgages anymore." Professionals resorted to bagging groceries or opening small service businesses. Others moved to California. As the economy recovered, Chinese immigrants continued to immigrate to west and southwest Houston, including the suburban town of Bellaire. Bellaire was an all-white community when Albert Gee and wife Jane attempted to buy property there in 1951. "Some neighbors objected, and the owners of the property wouldn't sell us the lot," remembered Jane. "We had to get around it, which we did." The Gees became the second Chinese family in Bellaire. Dave Leo Wingshee was born and raised in Bellaire, living there from 1961 to 1969. He recalls a small, tightly-knit Chinese community that socialized with other Chinese through the Chinese Baptist Church located in downtown Houston.[34] In later decades, Chinese Houstonians sought to enroll their children in the Ivy-League feeder school, Bellaire High School, which, in the 1980s, was the only Houston school offering Chinese language classes.

Because of the oil bust, some Houston suburbs became "eyesores" of failed businesses and vacant lots. In the 1980s and 1990s, Chinese and Asians revitalized southwest Houston in boomtown fashion. In 1983, Hong Kong-born T.D. Wong (who had developed a Chinese shopping center in Monterrey Park, California), his nephew Kenneth Li, and Houston developer Chun Yao opened the doors to the DiHo Plaza, a Chinese shopping center located on Bellaire Boulevard between Alief and Bellaire. Anchored by the DiHo Market, a Chinese supermarket, the plaza more than doubled in size in just a year. Businesses like World Book Store, Sun Sing Movie Theatre, Golden Palace Restaurant, and the Vietnamese Givral Sandwich Shop proliferated. Early on, many Southeast Asian businesses, including those owned by Vietnamese of Chinese descent, opened in the multiethnic neighborhood. Chinese from all over the state visited the Bellaire Chinatown for meals and groceries. With thousands of Chinese arriving each year, the Houston area became home to the largest population of Chinese Americans in the South. Chinese residents spearheaded the movement of large numbers of Asians into mostly-white suburbs such as Sugar Land, Stafford, Missouri City, Katy,

Spring, the Woodlands, and Clearlake. By 2005, at least 100,000 people of Chinese descent lived in the Houston area.[35]

The rapid growth of the Chinese Houstonian population paralleled the rapid growth of Chinese immigration in the 1980s and 1990s. The Bellaire Chinese business district was born just as immigration from the People's Republic of China recommenced. While some community organizations developed along ethnic, national, and language lines, others did not. Founded in 1979 to serve Chinese Houstonians, the Chinese Community Center expanded as the Asian community grew, and it is now a United Way agency serving all Asian Americans. In 1992, the Taiwanese Community Center opened its doors in Southwest Houston, and in the 1990s, mainland Chinese immigrants also established organizations.

The Chinese Experience in Dallas

by Rebecca Teng

Before World War II, the largely male Chinese community of Dallas led often difficult lives. William Wu recalls his grandfather and great-grandfather's experiences in Dallas: "Besides working, the Chinese did not have any other activities; they pretty much kept to themselves.... They were not able to integrate." Buck Jung, whose father arrived in 1931, noted that the early Chinese community consisted mostly of bachelors, who lived across the street from their 24-hour restaurants. Chinese Exclusion, the lack of Chinese women, and Dallas's inland location limited Chinese immigration to the city.[36]

After the 1943 repeal of the Chinese Exclusion Act, more students and merchants came to Dallas for educational or professional opportunities. Chinese with different backgrounds and speaking both Mandarin and Cantonese bonded out of necessity. In 1948, Dr. H.C. and Catherine Teng, like others, came to Dallas from Shanghai for advanced training. That same year, Buck and Helen Jung came to Dallas to join Buck's father, a merchant. When Helen Jung gave birth, Dr. Teng attended to her, and because they spoke different dialects, they communicated through written

Chinese. As more professionals with slightly more leisure time migrated to Dallas, they formed a Sunday School at the First Baptist Church of Dallas in 1953. There, the Dallas-born children could socialize, and they did so in English. An address book of the Chinese in Dallas from 1958 listed 162 individuals. Thirty-four of the seventy family listings were college students, health care professionals, or engineering professionals.[37]

Chinese students in the 1950s and early 1960s attended Dallas Theological Seminary, Texas Women's University, the University of North Texas, and the University of Texas-Southwestern Medical School. New options for inexpensive education opened: the Dallas County Junior College District in 1965 and the University of Texas at Dallas in 1969. Edward Lee, one of the 1968 founders of Dallas's first free-standing Chinese church, Dallas Chinese Bible Church, noted that the initial church population consisted of approximately 75% students and 25% families and professionals.[38]

Many of the engineers who had graduated from local universities, along with Chinese professionals from throughout the nation, were hired by the growing Dallas engineering, defense, and semiconductor firms such as Chance-Voight, General Dynamics, and Texas Instruments. Morris Chang (born in Ningpo, China in 1931) began as an engineering manager at Texas Instruments in 1958, and by the time he left in 1984, he was the vice-president in charge of the company's worldwide semiconductor business. By founding Taiwan Semiconductor in 1987, Chang launched Taiwan to the forefront of the computer chip industry and high technology in general.

The opening of Dallas-Fort Worth Airport and the Dallas Market Center's addition of the World Trade Center in 1974, followed by telecom industry deregulation in the early 1980s, made Dallas more attractive for Chinese immigrants. Richardson earned the name "Telecom Corridor" after capturing telecom companies such as Nortel Networks and Alcatel, creating a major pull for immigration. During the high-tech heyday of the 1990s, the Dallas area's renowned Telecom Corridor and high-tech emphasis drew many Chinese engineers and computer programmers to the city, attracting them with jobs and nearby excellent school districts for their children. However, the high-tech crash in 2001 caused many

Speaking passionately at a rally at the State Capitol, Houston City Council member Gordon Quan grew up in a typical Chinese Houstonian household of the mid-20th century. His parents ran a grocery.

Dr. Morris Chang was one of the most successful of Dallas's early Asian American high-tech community. He left Texas Instruments to start Taiwan Semiconductor.

layoffs of high-tech employees in Dallas and Austin and prevented many students and professionals from earning permanent resident status.[39]

By 1963, of the 200 or so Chinese in Dallas, only about ten or twelve were women. In addition to the gender imbalance, according to Edward Lee, who came to Dallas as a Hong Kong high school graduate in 1962 to enroll in SMU's Engineering Co-op program, loneliness and a lack of good Chinese food or services stymied growth in the Chinese community. Indeed, there were not even any Chinese organizations in the city. With the post-1965 immigration and growth in professional employment opportunities, the population of Chinese grew rapidly. In 1973, the Texas Chinese Association, the first secular Chinese community organization in Dallas, released the Greater Dallas-Ft. Worth Chinese Directory, listing four Chinese church groups, 592 directory listings of individuals or families, approximately 285 students (some doubly listed as students and residents), and 24 restaurants. By 1979, an estimated 5,000 Chinese and 11,000 Southeast Asians lived in Dallas. The Chinese were largely dispersed throughout Dallas-Fort Worth, but by 1983, when an estimated 20,000 Chinese lived in the Dallas area, about 5,000 resided in the suburb of Richardson, where a small Asian commercial district developed. Chinese continued settling in the suburbs; between 1990 and 2000 the Chinese population in Collin County (Plano) surged from 3,116 to 12,788, a 310% increase.[40] Of course, increasing Chinese populations created a "snowball effect" of more Chinese arriving to start businesses to serve growing Chinese populations.

As the Chinese community grew in the 1980s, so did its organizations and their services. In 1980 and 1981 respectively, concerned citizens such as Robert Hsueh, an immigration lawyer, founded the Chinese Lion's Club and the Chinese Chamber of Commerce. In 1983, the newspaper war began between two daily and four weekly Chinese-language newspapers, struggling over an expanding market. In 1984 and 1986, after leaders recognized the need for alliances and local influence, they helped found the Asian American Voter's Coalition and the Greater Dallas Asian American Chamber of Commerce.[41]

And Chinese American influence did increase, as voters elected Stanley Joe as Garland councilman, Harry Joe as Mayor Pro Temp of

Irving, and most recently, Joe Chow as Addison mayor. As a columnist for the *Dallas Morning News*, Esther Wu has for decades been the voice of local Asian Americans. The 2000 Census counted only 33,206 Chinese in the Dallas, Tarrant, Denton, and Collin Counties; the true figure is certainly over 50,000.

Conclusion

In the sixty years spanning 1945 to 2005, Chinese Texan communities underwent a great transformation. In the early years of this period, Chinese Texan communities primarily consisted of families running small businesses (mostly groceries). The communities were organized by family associations, merchants associations, tongs, and churches. Immigration reform, the Civil Rights Movement, and international politics helped shape new Chinese Texan communities made up largely of professionals and restaurant owners and workers. The professionals were diverse. They included immigrants graduating from U.S. universities, as well as second- and third-generation Chinese Americans. They concentrated in engineering, computers, and hard sciences, but expanded their proportions in medicine, business, law, service and other fields. In this new era, the owners and workers at restaurants and other small retail businesses tended to be immigrants. Political power shifted. Family associations, merchants associations, and self-policing tongs gave way to official police authority, local and state government, community organizations, churches, and student organizations. Despite the radical changes and the seemingly deep divisions within Chinese Texan communities, Chinese Texans remained united by a set of similar struggles. They fought against racism, segregation, and discrimination. And they worked hard to secure economic security and quality education for themselves and their children.

ENDNOTES

1   Alwyn Barr, *Reconstruction to Reform: Texas Politics, 1876-1906* (Dallas: Southern Methodist University Press, 1971), 199-200; Edward C.M. Chen, interview by Irwin Tang, Houston, Texas, February 1, 2004; Nancy Farrar, *The Chinese in El Paso* (El Paso: Texas Western Press, 1972), 37.

2   Farrar, 10; William Thornton, "Chinese Woman Protest Bill to Ban Their Race: Measure to Keep Alien from Owning Property is Given Hearing," *Dallas Morning News*, Mar 10, 1937; Associated Press, "Alien Property to be Studied," *San Antonio Express*, Mar 10, 1937.

3   Thornton; Associated Press; pamphlet available at Center for American History, UT-Austin, "Chinese" vertical file; Chen, interview.

4   Martha Wong, interview by Stephen Wong, 2004; also *claycrenshaw.com/Wong/bio. html*, accessed Dec 19, 2005; Mitchel Wong, interview by Irwin Tang, Austin, Texas, May 26, 2004.

5   Edward Chen, "Into the Future – Together: Two Lunar Centuries of Progress, 1877-1997: Houstonians of Asian Heritage," unpublished manuscript based on personal knowledge and research; Martha Wong, interview; Chen, interview; Tom Mulvany, "Chinese in Houston: A common bond of getting ahead," *Houston Business Journal*, Jul 29, 1974.

6   Mulvany.

7   Martha Wong, interview; Chen, interview.

8   Maria de los Angeles Mar Skates, interview by Anna L. Fahy, Dec 1997 and Nov 24, 1998.

9   Jane Eng Gee (of Houston), phone interviews by Irwin Tang, Jun 8, 2004.

10 See photo archives at Houston Public Library Center for Texas History; Jane Gee, interviews.

11 Edward C.M. Chen and Fred R. von der Mehden, "Chinese," chapter from *The Ethnic Groups of Houston, New Series, No. 3* (Houston: Rice University Studies, 1984); Edward Chen, "Into the Future"; *Houston Chronicle*, "The Chinese are Leaving," Apr 28, 1902.

12 Chen, interview.

13 Sophie Lim (of San Antonio), phone interview by Irwin Tang, Jun 7, 2004; Tim Eng (of Houston), phone interview by Irwin Tang, May 10, 2004; Kong Woo, interview by Yvonne Lim and Irwin Tang, San Antonio, 2004; Martha Jee Wong, interview.

14 Lim, interview.

15 *Houston Chinese Directory, 1976-1977*, published by Southwest Chinese Publishing, Inc., Houston, 1976; Chen, interview.

16 Eng, interview.

17 Lim, interview; Eng, interview.

18 Lim, interview; Eng, interview; Edward J.M. Rhoads, "The Chinese in Texas," *The Southwestern Historical Quarterly* 81 (July 1977).

19 Bobby Moon, phone interview by Irwin Tang, Nov 15, 2003.

20 Sonny Lew, phone interview by Irwin Tang, Jun 11, 2004; Anna Lin, interview by Irwin Tang, Austin, Mar 27, 2004.

21 Edward Chen, "The Gold Mountain on the Gulf: The History of Houston's Chinese," *U.S. Asia News*, Dec 25, 1987.

22 Ibid; Mar Skates, interview.

23 Stephen Johnson, "Street Gang Past catches up with Asian immigrant," *Houston Chronicle*, Sep 23, 1985; "9 members of 'United Bamboo' convicted of racketeering charges," *Houston Chronicle*, Dec 18, 1986.

24 Edward Vela, "Local Chinese back Beijing protests," *Dallas Morning News*, May 22, 1989; Norma Adams Wade, "Area Chinese plan support group," *Dallas Morning News*, Jun 5, 1989; Michael Browning, "Fair trial sought for dissident," *Dallas Morning News*, Dec 18, 1990. Conversations with Xun Ge, by Irwin Tang, 1989-1990; *http://www.humanrightswatch.org/campaigns/china/scholars/t15/wangjuntao.htm*; label websites with topics *http://www.ifcss.net/people.htm*.

25 G.F. Zhou, interview by Irwin Tang, December 2004; Cunxin Li, *Mao's Last Dancer*, (New York: G.P. Putnam's Sons, 2003), 338.

26 Rhoads, 29-30.

27 Yi-Noo Tang, written statement to Irwin Tang, 2004.

28 Yi-Noo Tang, conversations with Irwin Tang, 2004.

29 Dick Stanley, "Controversy over Nobel hot," *Austin American-Statesman*, Oct 16, 1987.

30 *Houston Press Chronicle* Oct 24, 1944; Janet Sanders, "For these Houstonians, if you have the name, you're family," *Houston Chronicle*, Apr 15, 1979; Mary Carter, "Orientals Maintain Club Here: Woman Scribe Finds Chinese Colony of Interest," *Houston Post*, Sep 15, 1946.

31 Thomas Hung, interview by son Stephen, 2003.

32 *Houston Chronicle*, Oct 14, 1974; *Houston Chronicle*, Mar 14, 1982; *Houston Chronicle*, Mar 14, 1982, Jan 7, 1982, and May 15, 1983.

33 Jennifer Dawson, "Bizarre Bomb Shelter becoming data center," *Houston Business Journal*, May 9, 2003.

34 Debbie Chen, interview by Irwin Tang, 2004; Gee, interview; Dave Leo Wingshee, phone interview by Irwin Tang, 2003.

35 "Eyesore" quote from Elionne L.W. Beldon, *Claiming Chinese Identity: Reconceptualizing Culture, History, Politics*, (New York: Garland Publishing, Inc., 1997) 14; *Houston Chronicle*, Aug 11, 2002; *Houston Post* Sep 30, 1984.

36 William Wu, interview by Rebecca Teng, Richardson, Texas, Jan 14, 2004; Buck Jung, interview by Rebecca Teng, Dallas, Texas, Jun 7, 2003.

37 On birth and arrival of Teng family, see Dr. H.C. Teng, interview by Rebecca Teng, Dallas, Texas, Jun 3, 2003; on church, see Jung, interview; *Address Book of Chinese in Dallas, Texas, 1958*, compiled by Catherine Teng, 1958.

38 On university openings, see Payne, *Dynamic Dallas: An Illustrated History* (Carlsbad, Heritage Media Corps, 2002), 221; Edward Lee, interview by Rebecca Teng,

Dallas, Texas, Jun 17, 2003.

39 Payne; David Way, interview by Rebecca Teng, Garland, Dallas, Jun 16, 2003; Francis Choy, interview by Rebecca Teng, Plano, Texas, Jun 25, 2003; Edward and Michael Chiang, interview by Rebecca Teng, Dallas, Texas, Jun 16, 2003.

40 Edward Lee, interview; Paul Chan and Lawrence Tai, coordinators, *Greater Dallas-Ft. Worth Chinese Directory 1973*, 1973; on population in 1979, see Maggie Kennedy, "Enjoy the New Year, Chinese style, that is," *Dallas Times Herald*, Jan 26, 1979; Cope Meyers, "Papers fight for growing market" *Dallas Times Herald*, Nov 22, 1983, 10A.

41 Robert Hsueh, interview by Rebecca Teng, Richardson, Dallas, Jun 25, 2003.

★

CHAPTER ELEVEN

Japanese Texans after World War II

Naoko Kato

B efore World War II, the Japanese in Texas were mostly in rural areas, with the highest concentrations in Harris, Bexar, Cameron, Hidalgo, and El Paso counties. Pre-war Japanese Texans mainly made a living out of farming rice, vegetables, and sugar cane. Although these families continue to constitute communities of Japanese throughout Texas, the Japanese population shifted from rural to urban after World War II. The Japanese population in Texas increased from 458 in 1940 to 957 in 1950; 4,052 in 1960; 6,537 in 1970; 10,502 in 1980; and 15,172 in 1990, with two-thirds of the population in 1990 living in the Houston, San Antonio, and Dallas-Fort Worth metropolitan areas. There is a particularly significant increase between 1950 and 1960, which is largely due to the Japanese war brides that came to Texas after the War. As Japan became economically successful in the 1970s and 1980s, business-related Japanese arrived in Texas, settling in the metropolitan areas.[1]

The Taniguchi Family

Just as anti-Japanese sentiment motivated Japanese Californians to re-settle in Texas in the pre-war years, Japanese Americans returning to

California from World War II internment camps were faced with hostility and made their way to Texas, where there were fewer Japanese. The story of the Taniguchi family represents three generations of prominent Texas architects as well as Japanese American migrations from California to Texas and from rural Texas to urban Texas. Isamu Taniguchi, a first-generation Japanese American (or "issei"), was a Brentwood, California farmer and leader among the Japanese American community. Like other Japanese American leaders, Isamu was arrested by the FBI immediately after Pearl Harbor. He was interned at Crystal City, Texas. During his four-year confinement in the camp, he heard about the Rio Grande Valley's rich agriculture and inexpensive labor. Shortly after the War, Isamu returned to California, only to find that his farm had been looted and pillaged. In 1946, Isamu and wife Sadayo moved to San Benito in the Rio Grande Valley to escape anti-Japanese hostility and to re-establish their farming business. The couple's son, Alan Yamato Taniguchi, was earning a degree in architecture at the University of California, Berkeley when the War broke out, and he was interned. After the War, he finished his degree and married Lesley Etsuko Honnami. They moved to Harlingen, Texas in 1950 to join his parents. Alan spent the first two years building a house for his father, and then built his own house in Harlingen. Alan set up his own architectural practice in Harlingen, and designed California-styled residences that looked very modern and different from other houses in the Valley. The American Institute of Architects and Texas Society of Architects recognized many of his projects for design excellence.[2]

Alan's son, Evan Taniguchi, was born in 1952 in Harlingen, where he lived with his brother Keith, parents, grandparents, and other extended family. The grandparents spoke Japanese at home, and Evan attended Japanese language schools every Saturday morning where he played with other Japanese boys in the Valley. Evan and Keith were the only Asians in their elementary school in the Valley, along with their friend, Ted Otsuki. Growing up, Evan thought of himself as an Anglo-Saxon, but he now identifies himself as a Texas-born Japanese (rather than an American-born Japanese).[3]

In 1961, UT-Austin's School of Architecture hired Alan as a professor. He commuted for several years, after which the whole family moved to Austin. Besides the Taniguchis, Kaoru and Kei Dyo, who moved his pediatrics practice to Austin, left the Valley around the same time as the Taniguchis. By 1960, only a quarter of the Japanese in Texas lived in rural areas, as Japanese seeking professional work migrated to the cities. In Austin, the politically liberal Taniguchis became mainstays in public service. In addition to volunteering for the underprivileged and people with HIV, Evan's mother Lesley campaigned for John F. Kennedy and Texas Senator Ralph Yarborough. Alan chaired the zoning committee of the Austin Planning Commission, Austin Revitalization Task Force, and state committees for the humanities. He was also a trustee for Austin's traditionally African American Huston-Tillotson College, for which his son Evan continues as vice-chair of the Board. While serving as Dean of the School of Architecture, Alan increased recruitment of minorities and relaxed the curriculum to encourage students to explore their individual design strengths. Alan led his students in protest against the removal of trees along Waller Creek for expansion of the football stadium. Architecture students chained themselves to the trees while Alan stood before the bulldozers.[4]

Designed to symbolize friendship between Americans and Japanese, Japanese gardens were built in Houston, San Antonio, Fredericksburg, Austin, and Fort Worth. In 1969, Isamu Taniguchi built the Japanese garden in Austin's Zilker Park to thank the city for the opportunities it provided for his family. Isamu also created a memorial at the Crystal City Internment Camp. Evan Taniguchi continues to incorporate Japanese concepts of simplicity, elegance, and balance with the natural world into his residential designs. Evan has been running Alan Y. Taniguchi Architects & Associates since Alan passed away in 1998, and their projects have included the Palmer Events Center in Austin.[5]

"War Brides"

Japanese "war brides" married American military men during the decades of U.S. military occupation and military stationing in Japan after World War II. Texas, having a high concentration of military bases, was one of the major destinations for these women. Between the 1950 and

1960 Censuses, the proportion of Japanese Texans who were women in-creased from under 47% to 63%. The immigration of Japanese military brides in the 1950s was the major factor in the quadrupling of the Japanese Texan population, changing the nature and the face of Japanese Texas. Because Japanese war brides continued to make up a major portion of Japanese migration to Texas, females, as late as 1990, made up over 66% of the Japanese Texan population. Military brides tended to immigrate first to cities with large military bases such as San Antonio, Killeen, and El Paso, but they also settled in large numbers in Houston and Dallas-Fort Worth. Most of the Japanese war brides that immigrated to Texas in the early decades had suffered some form of social dislocation in Japan during World War II and its resulting economic upheaval—leading them to work on American military bases in Japan, where they met their future husbands.[6]

War brides in Texas began arriving in significant numbers around the end of the U.S. occupation of Japan in 1952. Some were fortunate to have loyal husbands, but in many cases, once they arrived in Texas, the husbands left them, leaving the brides and their children to survive alone. A glimpse into the lives of Japanese war brides in Texas was offered by a Japanese documentary filmed in 1975; the film centered around a Japanese restaurant in Dallas owned by a war bride. The restaurant attracted newcomers such as Japanese business people temporarily working in Dallas, as well as Texans that used to work in Japan, but most importantly, it served as a gathering place for war brides. The women interviewed showed nostalgia for Japan. Etsuko Hotta said she did not obtain American citizenship despite living in Texas for 23 years because she feared losing her Japanese citizenship. She imported Japanese products from California and Japan to use in her restaurant and commented that the longer she lived in the U.S., the more she longed for Japanese food, despite its extra expense. Her dream was to save enough money to build a small house in her hometown in Japan and open an embroidery shop there. She said that not a day had gone by without her remembering Japan, and that she had always felt nostalgic.[7]

Some women said they were aware that, with so few Japanese in Texas, they represented all Japanese or Japanese Americans, and this awareness influenced their behavior. Their social isolation as war brides compounded this feeling. Asako Cazby brought up over 200 children in foster care as well as her own three children after her husband disappeared shortly after their arrival in Texas. She worked from morning to night, because she believed that if she showed how hard she worked, others would associate her diligence with Japanese, creating a positive image of Japan.[8]

In 2004, only thirty women remained active members of the Japanese Wives Club in Killeen. Negishi "Neggie" Loudermilk, the president of the Club, was born in 1929, and raised in Tokyo. As a teenager, she was almost killed by a U.S. bomb during World War II. After the war, she attended Miji University while working as a telephone operator at the former Kaijo Hotel, which served as a hotel for American female civil servants working for the American occupation forces. At this job, she met Army Sergeant John Loudermilk (1932–2002), born in Hico, Texas. After Neggie and John married in Japan in 1954, Neggie's father disowned her. In addition to her affection for Loudermilk, Neggie admitted, "I was curious of what America is." When she arrived in Hico in 1957, the townsfolk were curious about her, "I went to the grocery store and people stopped and looked at me." In the early- to mid-1960s, John and Neggie moved to Copperas Cove, near Fort Hood. At this time, about 200 Japanese military wives lived in the Fort Hood-Killeen area. In the mid-1960s, John, like many of the war bride's husbands, served in the Vietnam War. Some of these men died in combat.[9]

Japanese war brides sought community, friendship, and solace by gathering at each others' homes. Especially during times of war, they needed each others' company. Japanese military wives cooked for each other, improvising with local ingredients to make something "close to the taste of home." By 1965, the wives began purchasing some ingredients from a Killeen grocery store opened by a Japanese woman and her military husband. Some of the Japanese women formed the Japanese Ladies Club for socializing and support. They taught origami and Japanese calligraphy to children, and donated money for several years to Central College. In the early decades, the Japanese, Korean, and Vietnamese war brides and military wives formed separate ethnic communities. Although the Japanese wives comprised the largest of the military wife communities in the 1950s, these Japanese communities did not grow as large as the Korean military communities because the Japanese wives rarely sponsored their parents and siblings to join them in the United States. The Japanese economy prospered earlier than other Asian economies, so family members tended to remain in Japan.[10]

While many Japanese women waited tables or altered and sold clothes, others ran restaurants or worked as bookkeepers and teachers. When Neggie began working as a real estate agent in the late 1960s, she was the first Asian professional in the private sector in the Killeen area. Neggie and her father eventually made amends before his death.[11]

Old Texans and New Immigrants

In March 2004 in Webster, Texas, many of the older Japanese Texan families celebrated the 100th anniversary of the arrival of Seito Saibara to Texas. The Saibara, Kishi, Hada and other families reminisced about their family histories and why their ancestors came to Texas. Diane Tanamachi said that, before Texas's 1921 alien land law, it was easier for Japanese to buy land in Texas than in California. At the reunion, all of the youngest generations of Japanese Texans were of mixed blood, their ascendants having married whites or Hispanics.

Four months later, Japanese Texans celebrated again, with cheers and tears. For fifteen years, Sandra Tanamachi (daughter of Jerry Tanamachi) had led a campaign to change the name of "Jap Road" in Jefferson County. "Jap" is considered an offensive racial epithet. The road had been named in reference to Yoshio Mayumi, a former Japanese banker who bought 1,734 acres of nearby land to farm rice in 1905. Warmly remembered for building a community hall and driving local people in his car to a nearby town's hospital, Mayumi returned to Japan after passage of Texas's alien land law. On July 19, 2004, the Jefferson County Commissioners organized a special town meeting on the "Jap Road" issue. White and Japanese American World War II veterans, national Japanese American leaders, Jewish and African American representatives, and Japanese Texans sat on one side of the room, and those who wished to keep the "Jap Road" name (all of whom were white) sat on the other side of the meeting hall. After many on each side stated their opinions, the commissioners voted 4–1 in favor of changing the road name, which was renamed "Boondocks Road." A "Jap Lane" in Harris County was subsequently renamed.[12]

As a result of growing U.S.-Japan economic relations, many Japanese business people began immigrating to the United States and Texas in the early 1970s. Many or most of these Japanese were only temporarily stationed in the U.S. and returned to Japan in three to five years. Because of this, they had their own organizations separate from other Japanese Texans, and their children often attended Japanese supplementary schools that taught curriculum approved by Japan's Ministry of Education. These schools could be found in El Paso, Houston, Dallas, San Antonio, and Austin. These Japanese revitalized and helped sustain Japanese culture in Japanese Texan communities that had become highly acculturated to American ways of life. The 2000 Census counted 28,060 Japanese residing in Texas (including over 10,000 multi-racial Japanese). The Japanese Texan community today consists of Japanese families who live here because of their employment by Japanese corporations, Japanese "war brides" and their descendants, and Japanese American families that have lived in Texas for over a century.

A tearful Sandra Tanamachi embraces her son after her decade-long campaign to change the name of "Jap Road" succeeded.

ENDNOTES

1 Thomas Walls, *The Japanese Texans* (San Antonio: Institute of Texan Cultures, 1987), 205, 224.

2 Evan Taniguchi, interview by Naoko Kato, Austin, June 8, 2004.

3 Ibid.

4 University of Texas at Austin School of Architecture, *History of the School*. Retrieved October 8, 2004 from *http://www.ar.utexas.edu/History/Taniguchi*; also Taniguchi, interview.

5 Taniguchi, interview.

6 Evelyn Nakano Glenn, *Issei, Nisei, War Bride: Three Generations of Japanese American Women in Domestic Service* (Philadelphia: Temple University Press, 1986), 59; U.S. Census 1990.

7 Japan Broadcasting Corporation. 1975. *Texas Ohamaya: War Brides' Thirty Years*. Produced and directed by Ken Sakurai. 100 min. Videocassette.

8 Ibid.

9 Neggie Loudermilk, interview by Irwin Tang, Killeen, Texas, Aug 17, 2004.

10 Ibid.

11 Ibid.

12 Irwin Tang, "Japanese Americans in the Lone Star," *AsianWeek*, Apr 23, 2004; Irwin Tang, "The Road No Longer Taken: 'Jap Road' to be Renamed," *AsianWeek*, Jul 30, 2004.

★

CHAPTER TWELVE

THE VIETNAMESE TEXANS

Thao L. Ha

First Wave Leaders

April 30, 1975. A falling bomb blew apart a C-130 airplane, and Quang Phat draped his body over his wife, Lan, and their eighteen-month old daughter, Trang, to protect them from flying shrapnel. The explosions stopped, and Quang led a group of people to the burning airplane; he explained that the North Vietnamese would not bomb the same plane twice. They waited near the burning plane as a series of thunderous blasts eradicated another twenty planes. Silence fell, and after an examination of the skies, Quang led the group to one of the few planes left standing. Boarding the plane, there was sadness in their hearts. But they knew that leaving home was the only way to stay alive. Quang piloted the cargo plane off the crumbling runway. They flew to an island off the Gulf of Tonkin where U.S. troops escorted them to a refugee camp in the Philippines. From there they went to Guam, and then to Eglin Air Force Base in Florida. A San Antonio, Texas family eventually sponsored the Phat family. The escape of the Phat family was as dramatic as any of the thousands of Vietnamese war refugees and political refugees who escaped Vietnam during the first decade of Communist rule. The danger and daring of their escapes and the trauma of re-establishing themselves in a foreign nation came to represent both their collective struggles and their collective character.

Over 20,000 Vietnamese left Vietnam in 1975, and the United States accepted the majority of theses immigrants. During the following two years, another 20,000 Vietnamese fled Vietnam to avoid Communist persecution and deteriorating conditions. These early refugees were generally better-educated, wealthier, and spoke better English than the subsequent refugees. Fifty percent of the heads of households of this "first wave" had attended secondary school, and more than 25% were college and university graduates.[1] Many of the immigrants from the first wave had ties with the U.S. government, the U.S. military, and U.S. companies.

In March 1978, the Vietnamese government began to close down all private retail businesses and take away property, homes, and land. The use of torture, forced labor, and high taxes resulted in a state of lawlessness and extreme poverty. The government especially persecuted ethnic Chinese Vietnamese. Over a million refugees left Vietnam by boat between 1978 and 1980. Hundreds of thousands likely died attempting to sail to Malaysia and other nations. They were killed or raped by Thai pirates, and they died by disease and harsh weather. Those who survived often did so by committing some form of violence. Survivors languished in Malaysian and Thai refugee camps often for months or years. In order to accommodate the flood of "boat people," as this second wave of Vietnamese refugees came to be known, the U.S. government began to admit refugees in March 1977 under seventh preference visas which apply to people escaping communism.[2]

The Expedition to Texas

Camp Pendleton in Southern California, Fort Chaffee in Arkansas, Eglin Air Base in Florida, and Fort Indiantown Gap, Pennsylvania processed hundreds of thousands of Vietnamese refugees. Between 1975 and 1976, Fort Chaffee, Arkansas received upwards of 50,809 Indochinese refugees. The government contracted with schools like Westark College to provide educational opportunities, including culture and life skills classes, for the refugees. Families in Texas sponsored thousands of these early Vietnamese refugees living at Fort Chaffee; they were only the first of multiple waves to come. Major cities like Houston and Dallas received thousands of families, while cities like San Antonio and Austin received several hundred. Smaller communities received very few refugees directly from the U.S. resettlement camps.

In addition to those sponsored by Texas families, Vietnamese refugees migrated to Texas after their initial resettlement for the warmer weather and the more numerous work opportunities. There were fewer than a hundred Vietnamese in Texas in 1970. The 1980 census counted nearly 30,000 Vietnamese in Texas including over 13,000 in Houston's Harris County; the actual numbers of Vietnamese in Texas were much higher than the census figures, as many Vietnamese did not respond to the Census. Within a few years, the Vietnamese had grown from a tiny community into Houston's largest Asian ethnic group. Because of Houston's ample blue-collar employment opportunities, its location near the Gulf coast and that area's seafood industries, and its warm climate, it became a favorite destination for Vietnamese immigrants. A fifty-year-old machinist recalled his early years in Houston:

> My wife and I came to Houston from Tennessee because we heard from friends that there was a lot of jobs here. When we came in 1980, my friend got me a job to run a machine at Triangle. I worked there for over ten years. It was a good way to make money with no American education. My brother came here in 1985 from Kansas to be a shrimper. Now he has a boat and makes good money with no school, either.[3]

Houston's Vietnamese community first organized itself in 1977. The earliest organizers were first-generation professionals who wished to see Houston's Vietnamese community come together to recreate a sense of home for the displaced refugees, to create networks of people and associations, and to help arriving Vietnamese refugees. Vietnamese in other major Texas cities followed Houston's example. In 1980, the Census counted 5,512 Vietnamese in the Dallas-Fort Worth area. The population was much smaller and more spread out than the Houston

Vietnamese, but the D-FW community had been growing quickly. By 1979, Dallasite Hoang Tran's grandparents were shopping at Vietnamese food markets and eating at Vietnamese restaurants near Dallas' downtown. In 1982, the Vietnamese American Community of Greater Dallas was formed and led by Dr. Dap Pham. The organization was established as a centerpiece for networking and helping with community issues. The cities of San Antonio (with 866 Vietnamese in 1980) and Austin (818 Vietnamese in 1980) also founded Vietnamese associations in the early 1980s. Most of these organizations were formed by doctors, attorneys, and other Vietnamese Texan professionals.[4]

While thousands of Texans helped to resettle Vietnamese refugees through sponsorship and church-related resettlement programs, many other Texans clearly did not welcome the Vietnamese newcomers. Letters to Texas congressmen from constituents were more than ten to one against accepting the refugees. Regardless, Vietnamese continued to come. Contributing to this attraction was its proximity to the Arkansas resettlement camp and the presence of stable and organized Vietnamese Texan communities. The Vietnamese in Texas sought work wherever they could find it, making employment a top priority. Oftentimes, their jobs contradicted their skills, and many Vietnamese who held professional jobs in Vietnam took on menial jobs in Texas. According to Rutledge, "between 1975 and 1977, fewer than five percent of [Vietnamese] heads of households were unemployed after 27 months in Houston, Texas." According to another scholar, Texas's employment opportunities and its meager social welfare benefits attracted to the state Vietnamese refugees who sought employment and discouraged migration by those who needed government aid.[5]

Community over Texas's Troubled Waters

The immigration of Vietnamese refugees to the Texas coast radically transformed its cities and towns. Before 1975, there was probably not a single Vietnamese American living on the Texas coast. After the initial migration of Vietnamese refugee families to the Texas coast in 1979, Texas shrimping and crabbing cities and towns were home to, by proportion of total population, more Vietnamese than anywhere else in Texas. According to the 1980 Census, the population of Kemah was over 7% Vietnamese; Palacios and Seadrift were both over 5% Vietnamese. Port Arthur was over 2% Vietnamese. Other Vietnamese communities established themselves in Rockport, Beaumont, Anahuac, Galveston, and Port Aransas. News traveled quickly throughout the U.S. that Vietnamese could shrimp and otherwise work in the seafood industry on the Gulf Coast, and thousands of refugees who were desperately seeking work with no formal education migrated to Texas and other Gulf Coast states. Because of their initial poverty, Vietnamese families working as shrimpers, crabbers, seafood processing workers, boat repairmen, and small business operators often lived in mostly-Vietnamese trailer parks, as opposed to the housing projects, apartments, and homes of the Vietnamese in major Texas cities. The demographic profile of the Texas coastal Vietnamese differed substantially from the Vietnamese who settled in the major Texas cities. While many of the city Vietnamese had been professionals and businesspeople, many of these Vietnamese refugees originated from the Vietnamese coastal area of Phuoc Tinh, where many had worked as shrimpers and fishermen.

Networks of Vietnamese fishermen, their families, and friends pooled their savings in rotating credit systems. The money was used to buy boats and equipment. Entire extended families worked a single rickety boat until they saved enough money to buy a better boat, then two boats, and so on, until nuclear families could support themselves. Local white fishermen persuaded many of the local bait shops to refuse service and sales to the Vietnamese shrimpers. They were sold boats at unreasonable prices, and white shrimpers were even successful in lobbying the state legislature for restrictions on new shrimp boat licenses. Vietnamese shrimpers who had difficulty selling to white wholesalers sometimes sold their shrimp directly to consumers. The segregation of the seafood economy may have actually encouraged the Vietnamese to achieve vertical integration in the Gulf seafood economy, as Vietnamese entrepreneurs opened their own wholesale businesses, boat docks, boat repair shops, and seafood restaurants.[6]

In the late 1970s and early 1980s, tensions between white shrimpers and Vietnamese shrimpers were high. Many whites in the area alleged

Khang T. Bui, his wife by his side, explained in 2003 at his Port Arthur dock office how the Vietnamese Texans fought back—sometimes with guns—against the Ku Klux Klan.

Vietnamese Texan shrimpers on their shrimping vessel in Port Arthur, 2003. As the Vietnamese prospered, they bought larger boats.

that the Vietnamese were being subsidized by welfare grants and other funds from the government. Others disliked the Vietnamese fishermen's work practices, such as following their competitors' boats to a catch, and unloading their boats across other boats' decks. White fisherman laid out traps in trap areas reserved according to informal rules; the Vietnamese fisherman, not knowing this, laid traps too close to the whites', according to the latter. Angry white fishermen destroyed fishing equipment belonging to the Vietnamese, who then felt insulted and angry. According to some Vietnamese shrimpers, the real reason for interracial tensions was that Vietnamese shrimpers worked harder and thus caught more shrimp than the whites. Chanh Nguyen, a Vietnamese Texan fisherman during that period, stated:

> I think they jealous of the lots shrimp and crab we catch. I say we stay out sea more far and for longer time. We work harder than the American people do. They hate us because we get all the fish and so they want to mess up our nets so we can't catch anymore.[7]

Tensions came to a boil on August 3, 1979, as Seadrift crabber Sau Van Nguyen attempted to pull a new boat from the water. A local white crabber, Billy Joe Aplin, showed up and stood on Nguyen's hand, pinning it to the trailer hitch. Aplin told Sau, "If you Vietnamese don't move out of Seadrift, we're going to cut your throats." Aplin, who had a reputation for harassing Vietnamese fishermen (and who claimed to have been harassed by Vietnamese fishermen) then cut the shirtless Sau twice across the chest. Sau and his brother left and returned to the dock with a gun. When Aplin began hitting Sau, he shot Aplin, killing him. Later, in Port Arthur, Sau sought out a policeman and said, "I am a murderer. I killed a man."[8]

In the aftermath of the Aplin killing, angry whites set four Vietnamese shrimp boats aflame and firebombed a Vietnamese trailer home. Billy Joe's brother, Daniel Aplin, called Seadrift a "powderkeg." The town imposed a 9 p.m. curfew, and almost all of the 100 Vietnamese living in Seadrift (twenty-three of twenty-five families) fled to Houston, Louisiana, and other places. For lack of workers, the local crab-packing plant closed its doors. Another of Aplin's brothers, B.T. Aplin, turned in to the police three whites planning on using explosives against the Vietnamese.[9]

A communications specialist from the Department of Justice arrived in Seadrift and determined that one of the biggest problems on the coast was the lack of a Vietnamese language interpreter, which the Catholic Church then quickly provided. The Catholic Church eventually assigned a priest and a layman to live in Seadrift and mediate between whites and Vietnamese. Throughout the early struggles of the Gulf Coast Vietnamese Americans it was these two entities—the federal government and the Catholic Church—that most eased Vietnamese integration into local communities.[10]

On November 2, 1979, Sau Van Nguyen and his brother were acquitted of murder and accomplice charges, respectively, and they were taken elsewhere in the nation. Less than three weeks later, the Seadrift City Council met to discuss the Ku Klux Klan's plan to come to the small town. Six hundred people, or about half of the entire Seadrift population, attended the meeting, and many cheered when one man said the town should oppose the KKK. The City Council unanimously passed a resolution against the Klan's entry.[11] In an effort at reconciliation, the Vietnamese fishermen publicly apologized for Aplin's murder, and meetings were set up to teach the Vietnamese about informal fishing rules.

Over a year passed after Nguyen's acquittal before the KKK and their local supporters began terrorizing locals along the Texas coast. In January 1981, Eugene Fisher of the Kemah-Seabrook area met with the Grand Dragon of the Texas KKK to discuss white fishermen's complaints that the Vietnamese were "over-fishing" and depleting shrimp populations. In addition to intimidating the Vietnamese and those who did business with them, the KKK, led by Louis Beam, organized a February 14, 1981 KKK rally in all-white Santa Fe, Texas. The rally featured thirteen men in military fatigues, and women and children in KKK hoods. Beam said that the KKK would allow the government ninety days to "rectify the situation" or the Klan would "take laws into our own hands." Along with mentioning Klan "military camps," Beam demonstrated how to burn a Vietnamese shrimp boat. On March 15, 1981, the Klan steered a boat through the Kemah-Seabrook waters while firing a cannon mounted on the boat and burning the effigy of a Vietnamese American shrimper. Mai Do recalled the scene: "When the boat came towards our dock, I was so scared because a man pointed a gun at our door. I did not want my husband to shrimp that season because he would probably be killed." Many local Vietnamese were clearly terrified.[12]

Some Vietnamese simply moved away from trouble. Nancy Truong remembered that her family moved away from one coastal city because a cross had been burned on their lawn. They eventually settled in Galveston.[13] Other Vietnamese retaliated against violence and vandalism with their own acts of intimidation and self-defense. Khang T. Bui, a shrimp boat repair shop owner and dock owner in Port Arthur, recalled times when Vietnamese defended themselves with guns. In Palacios, for instance, armed Klansmen intimidated the Vietnamese community by surrounding a Vietnamese trailer park. "After that," said Bui, "we defend. We got guns inside [the trailers]. Defend. That's it. And they know it. They cannot mess with Vietnamese, so they disappear."[14] The Vietnamese immigrants had survived the Vietnam War and were not averse to, say, paying an intimidating visit to the home of a KKK supporter.

The Vietnamese also sought legal help. Morris Dees, a civil rights attorney for the Southern Poverty Law Center, which had been monitoring KKK activities, on April 16, 1981, filed a lawsuit on behalf of the Vietnamese fishermen against Louis Beam and the KKK. Filed in the Southern District of Texas, the civil suit sought to stop the Klan's harassment of Vietnamese in Galveston Bay by showing that the KKK had violated the Vietnamese fishermen's civil rights. One day before shrimping season began, the judge in the case ordered an injunction prohibiting any KKK members or its associates from interfering with Vietnamese fishermen at work. When shrimping season started the next day, U.S. marshals were assigned to protect the Vietnamese fishermen, who worked through the season without any further incident. The judge found that the Klan had violated the Vietnamese fishermen's rights by acting "intentionally to impede and prevent the plaintiffs from pursuing their lawful occupation."[15]

In 1980 the median age of Vietnamese Texans in large cities was nearly 30 while the median age of Vietnamese in Port Arthur was 15.0 years of age. In Beaumont it was 17.3 years, and in Galveston-Texas City it was 18.2.[16] The younger median age reflected larger numbers of children and perhaps more recent immigration. Some Vietnamese began as boat hands and then advanced to other jobs; some moved from the coast to large cities like Houston after establishing themselves. Some used money saved from shrimping to open restaurants and other land-based businesses.

Dat Nguyen was raised in Rockport, Texas amidst the Vietnamese community's conflicts with the KKK. He remembered that in the first grade, "My Mom and Dad used to tell me when I went to school 'hang out with your cousin, hang out with your family members' because we couldn't trust anybody." In those years, his family shrimped for a living, and he sometimes tired of it, especially in the summers: "All my friends were hanging out and here I am, 4 a.m., my brother's waking me up [to go shrimping] . . . I would be mad, I was so frustrated." Dat's teen years were marked with troubles. He and his friends stole car stereos, and he sometimes carried a gun. Dat, however, was a gifted athlete, and he fell in love with football, which kept him out of trouble.[17] As a middle line-backer for Texas A&M's football team, Dat Nguyen won awards for being the best college defensive player in the nation. In 1999, Dat Nguyen began playing professional football for the Dallas Cowboys, and by 2005, he had led the team in tackles for two seasons. Nguyen married his college sweetheart, Becky Foster, and their daughter Aubrey Mai was born in June 2004.

With the Klan conflict behind them, the Vietnamese shrimpers prospered in the 1980s and 1990s. They moved from their mobile homes to modest and large homes in residential suburbs. Eventually, the Vietnamese dominated the shrimping industry along the Texas Coast. Hostilities with whites dwindled as communication between Vietnamese and whites improved. However, by the late 1990s, the heyday for shrimping ended. The large numbers of Vietnamese and other shrimpers led to consistent over-fishing; shrimp were being removed from the waters faster than they were being replaced. In the spring of 2000, the *Houston Chronicle* reported that the Texas Parks and Wildlife Department announced plans to retire some 50% of inshore commercial shrimp licenses. This was devastating to the Vietnamese families that relied on shrimping for their livelihood. Kim Nix, an advocate for Vietnamese shrimpers and fishermen along the Gulf Coast, lamented, "Many can't speak English and have no other skills. They are also having the worst shrimping year they have ever had. They have nothing to fall back on." Symbolic of their dedication to their Texas towns, Vietnamese coastal communities in the early 2000s lobbied the U.S. government to impose tariffs on foreign shrimp, including those from major shrimp exporter Vietnam.[18]

Throughout the decades, many of the first-generation Vietnamese Texan parents, aunts, and uncles persuaded the second-generation children to get out of the shrimping business and get an education. Chien Nguyen, whose father owned a boat docked in Galveston, said that his father and uncle told him that he needed to go to school because the shrimping business is such hard work:

> They tell me all the time, 'Shrimping is for stupid people like me who can't speak English and get an education. It's a hard life. You, on the other hand, have a chance to make a better life. You can be someone better than a shrimper."[19]

Tough As Nails: *Vietnamese Women in the Nail Salon Industry*

Just as Vietnamese men dominated the shrimp industry during the 1980s and 1990s, Vietnamese women during this time came to dominate the nail salon industry in Texas. Word had spread from southern California that work in the nail salon industry was easy to obtain. Rosie Nguyen came to Houston in 1979 from San Antonio. There was no work for her or her husband Anthony. They and their two children stayed with a friend for several months while they looked for employment in Houston. Rosie got a call from her friend Thi in Orange County, California. Thi said that she was making a very good living as a nail technician in a beauty salon, and that her license was easy to acquire. Rosie had worked in a salon in Vietnam and felt that her skills and knowledge could help her in America. She signed up for a cosmetology course and received her Texas license shortly thereafter. With $5,000 borrowed from friends, she rented a booth at a salon near her apartment. Rosie worked diligently and skillfully. In two months, she was able to pay back her loans. By the end of 1980, she had saved enough to open her own shop. Hers was one of the first Vietnamese nail salons in Houston. Rosie spread word of her success to other Vietnamese women, and as more and more Vietnamese women entered the nail industry, the clients became acquainted with the Vietnamese women's skillfulness. Huong Tran, a Vietnamese nail salon owner in Austin, explains:

> Our hands are smaller than the American so it was easier for us to do detail. We get more people request than the other workers did and so we made more money. I think the customer cares a lot about the quality of the work and we try to give them the best.[20]

In 1979, just as Vietnamese women were charging into the nail industry, Dr. Stuart Nordstrom, an American dentist, created the acrylic nail using a compound normally used in dental crowns. The acrylic nail is stronger and more natural looking than the conventional plastic nail tip. He launched Creative Nail Designs, Inc. in 1980, and promoted the new nails through free training kits. Because the acrylic application was also less expensive to use, it allowed Vietnamese manicurists to offer natural-looking, stronger nails for a lower price. Vietnamese manicurists took advantage of the new product to develop what is now known as the "discount nail salon." Historically in the United States, the nail salon industry provided services to wealthy, upper class white women and celebrities. Services started between $50 and $75, and required weekly to bi-weekly maintenance. The Vietnamese were willing to provide these services for less than half that price. The discount nail business opened up manicure services to the masses, so that women of all classes, and even teenaged girls, could afford to have their hands decorated not only for special occasions such as proms or weddings, but also for simple beauty pleasure.

Why did Vietnamese immigrants choose this particular industry? Difficulties immigrants face in the U.S. labor market included language problems, licensing restrictions, lack of information about the job mar-

Cindy Le began working as a nail technician in 1995, a year after arriving in Texas. Here, she demonstrated her skills in 2007 at Vidao Nails (Houston), owned by Pam Nguyen and husband Tony Chin, who said that 95% of the city's nail salons were run by Vietnamese.

Dat Nguyen played middle linebacker for both Texas A&M University and the Dallas Cowboys. He was a top tackler on both teams.

ket, and lack of degrees or non-recognition of their degrees and skills. Vietnamese immigrants overcame these handicaps by working in the nail salon industry. A license in the early 1980s required approximately 150 hours of schooling, and opening a salon required an average of $5,000 in capital. Addressing language barriers, Nguyen Cao My, a well known activist for the Vietnamese community, suggested to the Texas Cosmetology Commission that because so many Vietnamese wished to be manicurists, the commission should offer exams in Vietnamese. Acknowledging the rise in Vietnamese applicants, the TCC first allowed translators at the exams, and eventually offered the exam in Vietnamese. This assistance coupled with the burgeoning social networks that the Vietnamese community had developed created a surge in Vietnamese nail technician license ownership. By the end of the century, literally tens of thousands of Vietnamese immigrants in Texas were working in the nail salon industry.[21]

The 2000 *Greater Houston Southwestern Bell Yellow Pages* listed over 500 nail salons, a large percentage of them owned and operated by Vietnamese. In Texas, Vietnamese immigrants opened salons in both large cities and small towns. Clearly, Vietnamese immigrants transformed the Texas beauty industry. Nonetheless, successes offered challenges, as well. Relations between husbands and wives were sometimes strained by the wives becoming the major breadwinners through their nail work. And there is evidence that breathing the chemicals used in nail work hours each day causes life-threatening health problems.

The Rise in Population and Violence

Vietnamese Texans prospered from work on the Gulf, in nail salons, ethnic restaurants, ethnic services, and technical and blue-collar jobs. Although Vietnamese lagged behind other Asians in professional and managerial work during this time, they were doing particularly well in the technical field. According to Rice University's 1996 Houston Asian Survey, 49% of Vietnamese in Houston did technical work, which was comparable to the Chinese (51%), the Asian Indians (46%), and the Filipinos (59%). Many of these technical workers were second-generation

Vietnamese Texans holding degrees in computer science and engineering. Government agencies such as NASA provided employment to many Vietnamese as well. One notable Vietnamese NASA employee is Mr. Tinh "Eugene" Tien Trinh. He became the first Vietnamese American astronaut and was awarded NASA's Inventor of the Year award in 1992 for his research team's invention of the Bioreactor, which helps prolong the life of tissue in space.

As companies like Compaq, Texas Instruments, Shell, and Texaco hired Vietnamese programmers, engineers, and information systems specialists, Vietnamese were encouraged to migrate to Texas, and second-generation Vietnamese Texans advanced their families' wealth. With more economic stability, Vietnamese Texans sponsored family members through family reunification programs. Housing and commercial real estate were much more affordable in Texas than in California. Home ownership was on the rise for Vietnamese Texans, and agencies like the Texas Department of Homeowners Insurance released a brochure in Vietnamese to help Vietnamese attain home insurance. All these factors contributed to the Vietnamese population in Texas more than doubling to 69,634 by the 1990 Census.[22]

As the Vietnamese population rose in Texas, so did crimes committed by Vietnamese against other Vietnamese. While many Vietnamese succeeded in adjusting to their new country, others did not. Many of the young—mostly boys who arrived as teenagers, without parents, without an education, and without direction—found themselves in a lot of trouble. Those who did come with their parents often felt disconnected from their traditional Vietnamese parents and alienated from family, schools, their American community, and their own Vietnamese community. They were sometimes the victims of racial harassment and discrimination. The St. Joseph apartment homes were a part of the Vietnamese ghetto along Park Place and Broadway boulevards approximately five miles south of downtown Houston. Poorer Vietnamese immigrants gathered here to purchase cheap apartment homes from a Vietnamese owner. The housing project was intended to help the struggling immigrants as they searched for good paying jobs and a better life. Times continued to be tough for many of these immigrant parents who worked ten or twelve hour shifts at low wage jobs. As a result of long-term poverty and children being left unattended by working parents, the neighborhood deteriorated into a haven for Vietnamese gangs.[23] Duc Dang was 13 when in 1982 he and his parents moved into the St. Joseph apartment homes. Dang recollected his downward spiral in life:

> It started bad at school. I was 13 years old and didn't know any English. They put me in an ESL class, and it was hard. The teacher don't care if we did good or not. My English got better, but a lot of those Mexican and black kids kept calling me chink, "ching chang." Me and my friend Trung got so pissed off we just want to beat the shit out of them. I got kicked out. Both my mom and dad were pissed when I got thrown out. My dad took the broom and beat me like crazy shit. It was depressing. My grades sucked because I just didn't like school anymore. In high school I met some other Vietnamese kids who went through the same thing. We just hang out, smoke, drink, and talk about girls and making money. Then we got a plan to steal some money from this family. [My friend] heard from his mom that the family was keeping a lot of cash at home. They just bought a new car, too. We broke in, found the cash under a drawer, and boom! We each had four or five hundred dollars. We thought it's so easy. So we kept doing it.[24]

The burglaries turned into robberies when they no longer cared if anyone was home. So entrenched in taking easy money, their desperation overcame their sense of humanity.

As semi-loose gangs formed within the Vietnamese communities, home invasions and robberies rose dramatically. By 1987 crime in Houston's Vietnamese community had been steadily on the rise; other Texas cities saw similar trends in the 1980s. The Vietnamese gangs attacked Vietnamese more than other ethnic groups, and they also tended to attack other Asians, such as Chinese and Koreans. Vietnamese Texan communities were terrorized for years, especially during the late 1980s and early 1990s. Vietnamese gangs ambushed and robbed families outside their homes and extorted money from Vietnamese businesses. Home invasions involved breaking into people's homes while they were inside, terrorizing them, stealing their valuables, and committing acts of violence against them. Vietnamese gangs earned reputations, especially in Texas, as being particularly violent. Vietnamese criminals preferred Vietnamese victims because they tended to keep large sums of money in their homes; they often distrusted banks, had difficulty communicating with bank officials, avoided paying taxes, or avoided reporting income to continue receiving social welfare aid. Vietnamese victims often did not report crimes to police because of immigration issues or fear of retaliation. Many of the criminals knew their victims; some were even family members.

Gang members sometimes killed each other. Unlike some other gangs, such violence was not part of turf wars or conflicts over illicit drug markets, but a matter of disrespect and who was "badder" than the other. These kinds of attitudes led to shootings in pool halls and restaurants in Texas's Vietnamese business areas. In December 1986, two gunmen opened fire into the Tam Game Room, a Port Arthur pool hall frequented by Vietnamese, killing two and injuring three others. The pair then went to an adjoining Vietnamese restaurant and shot another man in the face, killing him instantly. The two gunmen were apprehended seven months later in California. Thien Nguyen pled guilty to the murders and was given two life sentences. Hai Vuong, the other gunmen, tried to fight the case. In May 1988, Vuong, a Vietnamese refugee and shrimper, was sentenced to death on capital murder charges. On December 7, 1995, he was put to death by lethal injection in Texas. He was the first Asian to be executed in the United States since the 1976 Supreme Court decision to recommence the death penalty.[25]

The public shootings were not limited to small towns. On January 30, 1989, downtown Houston's Little Saigon business district became a battle ground of gunfire and dead bodies. Two men were killed and three injured that afternoon when a gang of Vietnamese men sprayed bullets into Givral's Sandwich Shop. Witnesses described the sounds like firecrackers and the scene like war. People were screaming and running from the restaurant while the victims fell one by one. Police went on a manhunt for several members of a Vietnamese gang. Its leader, Duy "Tony Playboy" Nguyen, was featured on television's *America's Most Wanted*. He, along with five gang members were arrested and found guilty of the downtown shootings.[26]

In the late 1980s, an increase in crimes spurred Texas law enforcement agencies to provide their officers special training in working with the Vietnamese community. Police departments in major cities like Houston and Dallas and smaller towns like Port Arthur and Beaumont educated their officers in basic communication in the Vietnamese language as well as in Vietnamese cultural norms and traditions. Vietnamese community leaders and local media urged the Vietnamese people to cooperate with law enforcement. Police departments recruited Vietnamese and other Asian officers. Cities published flyers and pamphlets in Vietnamese about the American legal system. Law enforcement officials feel that the outreach programs have certainly helped. Home invasions and robberies dwindled in the 1990s, and in 2004, those kinds of criminal activities were almost non-existent in the Vietnamese community; on average, Vietnamese Texan youth in the new millennium may also be more Americanized, less alienated, more integrated into the middle class, and better educated.[27]

Vietnamese Texans suffered from other forms of violence, as well. One of the earliest unusual murders in the Vietnamese communities occurred on August 24, 1982, when Dam Phong, the editor of a Vietnamese-language newspaper in Houston, was apparently assassinated outside of his home. Phong had three weeks earlier published an article in his 30,000-circulation paper that called anti-Communist Vietnamese groups fronts for gangsters and extortionists. Next to his body, police found a note listing other journalists the group planned on killing. While other Vietnamese American journalists were indeed killed, political violence and political conflict of this kind was more intense in Southern California than in Texas.[28]

On August 9, 1990, two teen-aged Neo-Nazis beat and kicked Hung Truong on the streets of Houston. "God forgive me for coming to this country," said the fifteen year-old Truong as he was kicked with a steel-toed boot, "I'm so sorry." When paramedics arrived, according to witnesses, Truong had difficulty standing up, but a paramedic decided not to take Truong to the hospital, saying that he would simply have "a hell of a headache" tomorrow. The police did not escort him home or call his parents. He avoided going home and spent the night at a friend's house. By the next morning, Hung Truong was dead. Derek Hilla, an 18 year-old, 6-foot-6-inch white supremacist "skinhead" was convicted of murder. The murder shook up the Asian Texan community.[29] Even as gang violence and racial violence ravaged Vietnamese Texan communities, its brutality hardly rivaled that of the Vietnam War; nevertheless, Vietnamese Texans sought to live more peaceful lives, as they had left their homelands for better times.

Vietnamese Texan Struggles with the Black Community

Although California had a long history of anti-Asian American riots and Texas did not, the Black-Asian conflicts leading up to and extending through the Los Angeles riots of 1992 were paralleled by related tensions in Texas. For instance, according to a Vietnamese Texan whose Arlington convenience store was located in a black neighborhood:

> They complain so loudly that the prices were too high. Kids steal candy. I catch them and yell at them, but I never pressed charges. I think many black women are rude and question my staring at them. I watch to make sure that no one steals anything because they do it a lot. When they hang around my store, I get nervous. I don't know if something might happen like a fight or a shooting.[30]

Black customers' complaints mirrored those of blacks in Los Angeles:

> The problem I have with these Asian store owners is that they always think a black man is trying to steal. They look you up and down and that makes me uncomfortable. Also, they never smile or say hello to greet the customer. That's why some of us blacks don't give them no respect.[31]

Just five months after the 1992 Los Angeles riots, African American Houstonian Eric DeLeon Hicks, 22, stole beer from a Vietnamese-owned store in east Fort Bend County and was preparing to leave. The son of the store-owner, Hung Nguyen, 18, tried to stop Hicks from leaving. Hung told his father to put away the gun because it was unnecessary. Hicks rampaged through the store and attacked Hung, breaking his foot and giving him a concussion. As Hicks left, Hung shot at him twice, supposedly as a warning, but one bullet, shot into Hicks's back, killed him. Immediate protests in front of the Nguyen store forced them to close it permanently, and they eventually planned on moving away from Houston. Three grand juries were formed to decide on an indictment of Nguyen. The first was disbanded because the black community protested that it included no African Americans. Rep. Al Edwards, D-Houston, argued that Nguyen should be tried for murder. The second grand jury which included six blacks returned a murder indictment but it was thrown out because the jury included no Asian Americans. The third grand jury, which included four whites, two blacks, two Asians, and four Hispanics decided that Nguyen should not be indicted. The young Hung Nguyen was haunted by his own actions, and apologized to the Hicks family.

During the protests in front of the store, Hicks's mother stated publicly through her pastor at New Faith Church that the boycott of the Nguyen store was not "constructive to the healing." Helen Hicks's reconciliatory words likely served to calm the potentially volatile situation, and perhaps as a result, the non-indictment of Hung Nguyen did not cause a major protest.

Nevertheless, when cultural misunderstanding, shoplifting, disrespect, alcohol, guns, and fear are all present in a convenience store, controversial racial incidents are almost inevitable, and less serious incidents continued to damage Asian American-African American relations in Texas. In response, Vietnamese communities in Dallas, Fort Worth, and Arlington worked with their city officials. They held meetings on how their communities could better work with African American communities. They worked alongside African Americans to educate each other about cultural differences. In Houston, the Sunnyside Task Force was created in 1997. Officials from the mayor's office, the office of U.S. Representative Sheila Jackson Lee, the police department, churches, and Asian American businesses attended the meetings to better understand underlying tensions. Since those meetings, incidents of violence between the two groups have abated.[32]

Vietnamese Texan Enclaves, Political Power, Survival, and Prosperity

The turn of the new millennium marked twenty-five years since the first arrival of Vietnamese immigrants to America. In the year 2000, the Census recorded nearly 140,000 Vietnamese in the Lone Star State. The Vietnamese Texan population is the second largest Vietnamese population outside of Vietnam, behind only California. Vietnamese communities in Texas recreated a home away from home and have built some of the largest ethnic enclaves in America. Vietnamese Texans have depended heavily on support networks to ease the experience of settling into a foreign land. One major form of support in the early years was the religious institution. The majority of people in Vietnam are Buddhist, but the first-wave immigrants were mostly Catholic. When communities were being formed in Texas, churches and temples were some of the first organizations established. Religion played a role in the settlement process. Catholic charities helped with the sponsorship of immigrants from the first wave. Vietnamese churches and Buddhist temples helped subsequent waves of immigrants through social support programs that helped them find housing, fill out paperwork, learn about other social agencies, and find employment. The Vietnamese Martyrs Catholic Church in San Antonio is the heart of that Vietnamese community, where people come to worship, socialize, and celebrate Vietnamese cultural traditions such as the Lunar New Year.

The Queen of Vietnamese Martyrs Catholic Church is the cornerstone of the Vietnamese community in Port Arthur, Texas. It began with help from Anthony Pendleton, who started the Refugee Self-Sufficiency Program. This program stemmed from the Catholic Diocese of Beaumont, which helped settle nearly 150,000 Vietnamese immigrants in 1975. The Port Arthur church annually lights over 200,000 Christmas lights as a symbol of peace and gratitude to the community at large for helping them in their resettlement in the area. The church has about 4,000 members from Port Arthur and the surrounding area. The majority of Vietnamese in Port Arthur are Catholic, and their church was the first Vietnamese Catholic Church in the nation.

In the 1990s, churches and temples, in addition to helping Vietnamese in Texas, reached out to help the needy in Vietnam. Religious institutions in Houston became the preferred conduits for Vietnamese to donate money to help disabled, homeless, and needy people in Vietnam. Large Buddhist pagoda-styled temples have changed the architectural face of Texas cities and towns.

Vietnamese business districts have also changed the face of Texas. The Vietnamese-owned Hong Kong Mall is one of the most notable ethnic markets in Texas, catering to Vietnamese and Asian Houstonians who come from all over the Houston area to eat ethnic foods, buy ethnic clothes, meet recognizable faces, and feel a sense of belonging.

Houston has the oldest established Little Saigon in Texas. It is located in downtown Houston, and although it is not as busy as it was in the early 1980s, it has become a landmark that city officials have recognized as the Vietnamese Business District. In the early years of the Vietnamese community, Houston's Little Saigon was where people could eat at Vietnamese restaurants; shop for Vietnamese groceries, music, books and videos; and find Vietnamese attorneys, doctors, and jewelers. One specialty shop that was frequented by early Vietnamese Houstonians was the *dich vu*. These shops offered postal services where Vietnamese immigrants could send goods home to family and loved ones in Vietnam. Today, these shops have become like Western Union, where Vietnamese can send cash remittances to family and friends in Vietnam. In Austin, Vietnamese and their businesses concentrated on the north side of the city. In the Dallas area, Vietnamese business districts flourished in Garland, Richardson and Arlington.[33]

Because of the tremendous growth of the Vietnamese Houstonian community, and because some Vietnamese achieved great wealth, some expected by the early 2000s that the Vietnamese Houstonian community was destined to follow Chinese Houstonians into local political offices. One early candidate, Andrew Tran, lost in 2002 the race for District 149 State Representative. In 2004, real estate developer Hubert Vo, a Democrat, launched an underdog campaign against Talmadge Heflin, a highly influential Republican representing District 149 in Southwest Houston. Vo won the election by thirty-two votes. After two recounts, Vo's mar-gin of victory increased to thirty-three votes. Heflin requested that the Republican-controlled Texas House of Representatives investigate the legality of the votes cast in the election, the implication being that Vietnamese supporters of Vo voted in the wrong district or were not U.S. citizens. Vo campaign consultant Mustafa Tameez stated that the investigation could intimidate Asian Americans from political participation. Asian Americans throughout the nation lent their monetary support to help Vo retain his seat. Long-time activist Rogene Gee Calvert, who was president of the Asian American political action committee, 80–20 of Houston, organized a rally at the state capitol upon Vo's swearing-in on January 11, 2005. The Texas Capitol had never seen so many Asian Americans on its steps. The crowd of hundreds was perhaps one-third Asian, and within that group, two-thirds Vietnamese. The other two-thirds were white, African-American, and Hispanic. Chanting "We want Vo!" the crowd erupted in cheers as Vo stepped out of the statehouse. "This is not a victory as much as it is a challenge," Vo said, repeating his campaign concerns on education and health care. On January 27, the House of Representatives investigative committee announced that Hubert Vo had won the election fairly, and Texas's first Vietnamese American state legislator began voting on state bills.[34]

The Vietnamese Texan community demonstrated charity, organization, and heroism when Hurricane Katrina struck Louisiana, Mississippi, and Alabama in August 2005. As the federal government failed to rescue thousands of people in and around New Orleans, many Vietnamese in the area struggled to survive, often injured, sick, and trapped in floodwaters, inside or atop buildings. About three hundred Vietnamese of the Queen Mary of Vietnam church in Versailles, Louisiana, located in east New Orleans, were trapped in neck-high floodwaters. Rescue helicopters flew nearby but did not rescue the Vietnamese who had gathered for safety at the church. Trang Nguyen of Arlington, Texas learned of their plight and launched a massive lobbying effort involving phone calls, internet postings, and encouraging others to contact government officials. After days of being trapped, the Versailles Vietnamese were rescued.[35]

Trieu Giang, who headed Austin's Vietnamese American Katrina Relief Efforts, began preparing for possible Vietnamese hurricane evac-

Texas State Representative Hubert Vo spoke at a raucous rally on the steps of the Austin Capitol after he was sworn in. Supporters demanded that the state cease the vote recount aimed at unseating Vo. He is surrounded by his wife, children, and father.

Lai Thi Tran of the Austin Police Department and Tina Bui of the City Public Information Office were two of the City of Austin's only Vietnamese-speaking employees and worked hard to help Hurricane Katrina evacuees at the Austin Convention Center in August 2005.

uees even before the hurricane hit the Gulf Coast. When Vietnamese evacuees began arriving before, during, and after the hurricane, the Austin Vietnamese community was prepared and found housing for at least eighty Vietnamese American evacuees and helped them obtain government aid, translated for them, provided Vietnamese food, and kept their spirits up. The Vietnamese communities in Houston and Dallas were hard-working and heroic in helping Asian evacuees. Thousands, possibly ten thousand or more Vietnamese, may have initially evacuated to Houston, where Vietnamese volunteers helped process their aid applications, provided food, clothing, and petty cash, and even provided health care. Because of a lack of Vietnamese-speakers, Vietnamese evacuees sought help from other Vietnamese in Texas. Kim Vo and her family found shelter at the Austin Convention Center (see p. 386). She said that her home was underwater and that her Versailles community was scattered throughout the nation. "I feel bad," she stated, "I cry everyday." For refugees of the Vietnam War, it was at least their second time losing everything. "They came here with empty hands," said Giang. "Suddenly they lost everything they work so hard for. And then that puts them in a really tragic shock." Some evacuees found permanent homes in Texas, but most returned to New Orleans, where the undaunted Vietnamese rebuilt their community in quick fashion.[36]

Just weeks after Katrina, Hurricane Rita ravaged the Vietnamese-heavy Port Arthur-Beaumont area, devastating the lives of many Vietnamese Texans, especially fishermen whose boats were damaged or destroyed. But the local Vietnamese rebuilt, much like the first Vietnamese refugees secured new lives on the Texas coast in the 1970s. Since their arrival in Texas, the Vietnamese have overcome tremendous hardships, and they have done so, necessarily, through various means. Out of the tumult, the Vietnamese have established a thriving, prominent, and permanent Vietnamese Texan community.

ENDNOTES

1   Darrel Montero, *Vietnamese Americans: Patterns of Resettlement and Socioeconomic Adaptation in the United States* (Boulder, CO: Westview Press, 1979).

2   Nancy Viviani, "The Long Journey," *Vietnamese Migration and Settlement in Australia* (Melbourne University Press, 1984); Paul James Rutledge, *The Vietnamese Experience in America* (Bloomington and Indianapolis: Indiana University Press, 1992).

3   Khoi Tran, interview by Thao Ha, June 20, 2002.

4   Dallas-Fort Worth SMSA figure, from 1980 U.S. Census, Vol. 45; Thao Ha, "Asian American Communities in Houston: Vietnamese Americans," Working Paper Series from the University of Houston Center for Immigration Research, June 2001.

5   Fred R. von der Mehden, "Indo-Chinese in Houston" D National Endowment for the Humanities: Houston Center for the Humanities 1982.

6   *The KKK and Vietnamese Fishermen*, in DIVERSTORY (working title) (Frank Wu, ed., forthcoming).

7   Chanh Nguyen, interview by Thao Ha, July 13, 2002.

8   Irwin Tang, "Still Shrimping: Vietnamese American shrimpers 25 years after the second wave," *AsianWeek*, Aug 29, 2003.

9   Ibid.

10 Ibid.

11 Ibid.

12 Mai Do, interview by Thao Ha, July 13, 2002.

13 Nancy Truong, interview by Irwin Tang, August 14, 2005.

14 Tang, "Still Shrimping…"

15 Vietnamese Fishermen's Association v. Knights of the Ku Klux Klan, 518 F. Supp. 993, 1010 S.D. Texas 1981.

16 U.S. Census 1980.

17 Irwin Tang, "Nguyen Blitzes the NFL," *AsianWeek*, Sep 5, 2003.

18 Kim Nix, interview by Thao Ha, May 21, 2002.

19 Chien Nguyen, interview by Thao Ha, May 23, 2002.

20 Huong Tran, interview by Thao Ha, January 9, 2000.

21 My Nguyen, interview by Thao Ha, January 12, 2000.

22 US Census 1990a. Characteristics of Population, 1960, 1970, 1980, and 1990.

23 Thao Ha, "Asian American Communities in Houston: Vietnamese Americans."

24 Duc Dang, interview by Thao Ha, August 11, 2000.

25 Michael Graczyk, "Texas inmate is first Asian to be executed," *Houston Chronicle*, Dec. 8, 1995.

26 John Maekig and Eric Hanson, "Seven indicted in Vietnamese Gang Slayings," *Houston Chronicle*, April 19, 1989.

27 Hai Ho, interview by Thao Ha, July 18, 2000.

28 William Kleinknecht, "Journalists at Risk," *American Journalism Review*, December 1999, accessed at *http://www.ajr.org/Article.asp?id=766*, Jun 14, 2004.

29 Eric Hanson and Tara Parker Pope, "Skinheads charged in teen's death," *Houston Chronicle*, Aug 11, 1990; Kelly Rucker, "'We just came here to be happy'/Father mourns slain Asian teen," *Houston Chronicle*, Aug 13, 1990.

30 Triet Le, interview by Thao Ha, October 7, 2000.

31 Kevon Marks, interview by Thao Ha, October 8, 2000.

32 My Nguyen, interview by Thao Ha, October 1, 2000.

33 Vi Diep, interview by Thao Ha, June 13, 2000; site studies conducted by Thao Ha, June 4, 2000.

34 Irwin Tang, "Hubert Vo Victory in Texas May not Last," *AsianWeek*, Dec 24, 2004; Irwin Tang, "Victories and Challenges: State Legislators Hubert Vo and Van Tran Expand the Universe of Vietnamese American Political Representation," *Nha*, Mar/Apr, 2005.

35 Irwin Tang, "Hurricane Katrina victims recover from 'tragic shock,'" *AsianWeek*, Sep 16, 2005. Irwin Tang and Carla Williams-Namboodiri, "Vietnamese Community Hard-Hit," *AsianWeek*, Sep 9, 2005.

36 Irwin Tang, "Hurricane Katrina"; Tang and Williams-Namboodiri.

———————— ★ ————————

CHAPTER THIRTEEN

CAMBODIAN TEXANS, LAOTIAN TEXANS, HMONG TEXANS, THAI TEXANS, AND BURMESE TEXANS

Sophia Hong, Vynarack Xaykao, Pat S. Charnveja, and Irwin A. Tang

The Cambodian Texans

by Sophia Hong

Three Waves of Immigration

Prior to 1975, fewer than 1,000 Cambodians lived in the United States, very few of them in Texas. Fifty to sixty Cambodian Navy men studied English at San Antonio's Lackland Air Force Base from 1972 to 1973, according to Navy man Sywong Ngin, who was among them. Although they all returned to Cambodia, events led some back to Texas. In April 1975, the Khmer Rouge, a Communist Cambodian group led by Pol Pot, took over Cambodia. The Khmer Rouge forced Cambodians into rural concentration labor camps and murdered dissidents, ethnic minorities, monks, professionals, and intellectuals. From 1975 to 1979, two million Cambodians died from starvation, execution, torture, and malnutrition.[1] Survivors witnessed the killing of their families and the destruction of their villages.

This first wave of Cambodian refugees to the United States consisted mainly of westernized and educated Cambodians and former Cambodian military personnel escaping from the Khmer Rouge. Sywong Ngin, Sambath Chan, and Channy Soeur were all members of the defeated Cambodian Navy:

> We heard that the Khmer Rouge started killings of high ranking officers and anyone who worked in the government, or any military. Now we started to get together the idea of where we gonna go and what we're gonna do. And we heard news, worse and worse, so we left the swiftboats and got on a big boat. I say, maybe 300 to 500 people on 3 big boats, and we planned to go to Singapore.

About 2,000 military personnel landed at Subic Bay Naval Base in the Philippines; roughly 200 of them eventually settled in Texas. Civilians also fled. Theav Hong, an employee of the relief organization CARE, gathered his family and fled to a Thai refugee camp. From there, many Cambodian refugees were sent to Camp Pendleton, San Diego, whereupon they were resettled throughout the United States. U.S. servicemen in Texas who had befriended Cambodian military men during the Vietnam War sponsored some Cambodian refugees. Ngin, Soeur, and the Hongs all resettled in San Antonio. Some refugees attended Texas universities, and many migrated to Houston and Dallas, seeking better economic opportunities.[2]

The Cambodian Texan community was deeply depressed during the reign of the Khmer Rouge. "Most Cambodians are very sad because we lost some family members that we don't know [if] they kill by Khmer Rouge, starved, dead, or missing, because we have no communication or news from our mainland," said Lay Kheang Chheng, a former Cambodian fighter pilot who resettled in Houston in 1975. Ngin lost his entire family, and Soeur lost his entire family except for two sisters. This tragic history unified Cambodian Texans. Peng Hong, Theav Hong's brother-in-law, who resettled in San Antonio in May 1977, observed, "Because we lost family, we were very sincere and happy to see each other at gatherings . . . even though we don't know each other."[3]

Cambodians arriving in Texas before 1979 had difficulty finding jobs. "Mostly labor jobs, not easy to find office jobs in a country you don't even speak English with," said Peng, whose first job involved making sandwiches for vending machines. In 1977, a handful of former Navy men were sponsored by Butler Brick Company in Elgin. They eventually moved to Austin. About 90% of Cambodians in Houston in 1978 earned money by picking up trash along local freeways. "They got paid like $30 per day, and one of the Cambodians was killed by doing that," remembered Theav Hong.[4]

The second wave of immigrants, consisting of 10,000 refugees, arrived in the U.S. in 1978–1979 as the Khmer Rouge gradually fell from power. Seam Kheng Hong, Peng Hong's wife, arrived in Texas in August 1979. She had endured four years in a concentration camp and lost her entire family except for two brothers. Flown to a state previously unknown to her, Seam then endured a twenty-three hour van trip. "I was so scared at that time," she recalled, "[we] didn't know where they take us to . . . a little small town named Mineral Wells. They put us in a house, like a old military base, but we just don't know."[5] Traumatized Cambodians feared uncertain situations.

In late July 1979, seventy-one Cambodians were resettled in Mineral Wells, Texas, west of Dallas. Housed in former Army duplexes, they worked at a factory making Army cots. "In Mineral Wells, [Americans] came to teach us [English] where we live. We go to school and work at the same time," Mrs. Seam Hong described. Most of these 200 or so Cambodians saved money and moved to Houston or Dallas. In the Dallas/Fort Worth area, four agencies resettled about 100 Cambodians between 1975 and 1980.[6]

The majority of Texas's second-wave immigrants settled in the Houston area. Peng Hong estimated that in 1979 there were about 400 to 500 Cambodians in Houston, including former Cambodian Head of State (1970–1972) Cheng Heng. In 1975, Heng flew to Paris to negotiate peace with the Khmer Rouge, but before making contact with them, the Khmer Rouge had already seized Phnom Penh. Unable to return home, in 1979 Heng became a caseworker for the Houston YMCA Indochinese Refugee Services Center, which opened in October 1978. This, the largest U.S.

YMCA refugee center, provided temporary housing, relocation services, English classes, cooking classes, and lessons on the American lifestyle.[7]

The Refugee Act of 1980 allowed for resettlement of 50,000 Cambodians in the U.S. each year through 1983, increasing Cambodian immigration to Texas. In 1978, only 17% of the refugees resettled by the Houston YMCA were Cambodian, but by 1981, the number grew to 50%. In 1981, about 800 Cambodian refugees were resettled in East Dallas, and about 100 in Fort Worth.[8] Sam Tek Ly endured four years of the Khmer Rouge and six months in a Thai refugee camp. Upon arriving in Fort Worth in September 1981, Ly's sponsor arranged housing for him, his brother, and their families. "A two bedroom house with eight people," Ly said. Ly's sponsor also arranged employment for him as a mall janitor. "There was like five Cambodian families in Fort Worth," recalled Ly, "and every one of them is scared because nobody can speak English." Agencies settled many Cambodian immigrants in low-income apartment complexes fraught with crime and poor facilities. Most of the 700 refugees in the Dallas area in 1982 were resettled in East Dallas, where a low-income Southeast Asian community known as Little Asia grew quickly. In Houston's Fourth Ward, many Southeast Asians were settled in Allen Parkway Village. One Cambodian Texan said, "We came to America and just asked for a place to survive, so we don't want to complain. We're lucky just to be here."[9]

Trauma, Mutual Support, and Economic Establishment

"Even though I come to this country, every time I close my eyes, I have nightmares about the time I was in Pol Pot. I dream about the Khmer Rhouge, I dream about my [late] family," Seam Hong said, having lived in Texas for over twenty years. "I have never had any kind of dream about my life here in America."[10] Dealing with past trauma severely hindered Cambodians in their efforts to establish new lives in Texas, but Cambodians helped each other. The Cambodian Association of Houston (CAH) was started by Sokhaum Khoy and Chheng Heng. After President Lon Nol left Cambodia on April 12, 1975, Sokhaum Khoy became the interim President of Cambodia. However, his family encouraged him to escape Cambodia, anticipating the coming of the Khmer Rouge. Thus, Sokhaum

Khoy and his family left Cambodia and made their way to America, where they eventually resided in Houston.[11] By speaking at churches, the CAH raised hundreds of dollars for Cambodians struggling in Thai refugee camps. Like other such organizations, the CAH assisted incoming refugees by taking their children to the hospital, translating at government agencies, and acting as liaisons between communities.[12]

"[In the early years], not many Khmers in Houston," recalled Seam, "so, soon as they heard a Cambodian arrived in Houston, they helped each other get a job." In 1975, Lay Kheang Chheng was the first Cambodian employed at Houston's Intercontinental Airport. "My supervisor see that I work very good," remembered Chheng, "he want to hire some more Cambodians." By 1982, approximately 100 Cambodians worked at Houston's two airports. In 1984, Yani Rose Keo established Cambodian Gardens, Inc., which bought farmland in Rosharon, south of Houston, and provided jobs for Cambodian immigrants, including former farmers. The farms sold their produce to local wholesalers and supermarkets Fiesta and Whole Foods. By 2000, thirty farms generated millions of dollars in income. By 1989, Dallas Semiconductor in Carrollton-Farmers Branch employed about 250 Cambodians, who had spread word about the firm's immigrant-friendly attitude.[13] And, having learned the trade from successful Cambodian Californians, Cambodian Texans opened so many doughnut shops that by 2000, they owned a major portion of Texas doughnut shops.

Better-educated Cambodian Texan immigrants often took professional jobs. Channy Soeur graduated in 1984 from UT-Austin with a degree in petroleum engineering. Because of racial discrimination, he could not find a job in his field. Working in government instead, Soeur rose to the position of Assistant Director of Solid Waste Services, becoming the first Asian American executive in the City of Austin.[1]

Peace and the Second Generation

The overthrow of the Khmer Rouge did not bring peace to Cambodia, as remnants of the Khmer Rouge and two other Cambodian factions continued a civil war against the Vietnam-backed government. The civil war continued to kill Cambodians. In 1988, Sywong Ngin, Channy Soeur, and Pheng Kol (all living in Austin) met at Kol's house and worked for three days to draw up a peace plan based on "co-existence." They realized that the Khmer Rouge, backed by powerful China, would have to be allowed to continue as a political organization. Most Cambodians objected to allowing the Khmer Rouge any legitimacy. "But how else could the Khmer Rouge be convinced to put down their arms, and how else could Cambodians finally live in peace?" Ngin and Soeur asked.[15]

In 1989, the group organized an international conference of Cambodians at Austin's Hyatt Hotel. Three to four hundred Cambodians from around the world attended to discuss how to end the civil war. Emotions ran high as many Cambodians refused to support any plan allowing the Khmer Rouge to continue existing. "We told them that we have to let karma take care of the Khmer Rouge," said Ngin, "we have to stop the suffering of the people." The Texan trio organized further discussions in California and Washington State. The Texans' efforts may have influenced the peace negotiators, as the final U.N. peace plan incorporated their ideas. The implementation of the U.N. peace plan in the 1990s brought some peace to Cambodia, and Cambodian Texans, in turn, could focus their attention on their lives in the United States.[16]

"Srey Thom," a Cambodian-American teenager from Houston, described the cultural gap between her and her refugee parents: "[My parents] say, 'you know when I was in Cambodia during Pol Pot, I used to scavenge for food and eat bugs and got like no rice, got barely anything.' And I'm sitting here complaining about wanting McDonald's." But the second-generation did deal with serious issues, including joining Cambodian gangs, which sometimes robbed and killed other Cambodians. Cambodian youth joined gangs to protect themselves in school and on the streets. They felt alienated in school and were addicted to the bounty of crime.[17]

To maintain traditional culture, many Cambodian Texan youth, like Srey Thom, participated in traditional dance demonstrations. "It's fun, and it's a way for me to hold on to the culture and learn more about it."[18] Their parents' resiliency and perseverance motivated Cambodian American children to pursue success through higher education. Many earned university degrees, assisted with managing family businesses,

Laura Cole Soeur and Channy Soeur at a Vietnamese-Cambodian restaurant in Austin, 2005.

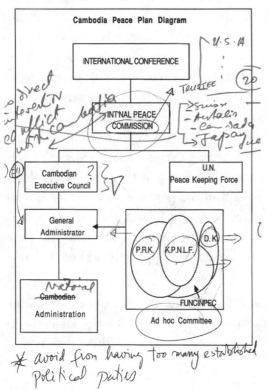

Notes and preliminary diagram of a Cambodian peace plan drawn up by Channy Soeur, Sywong Ngin, and Pheng Kol in Austin, Texas.

and worked as professionals in corporations and government, enabling their families to attain stability, success, and a prosperous future.

Laotian Texans

by Vynarack Xaykao

Texas is home to the second largest Laotian population in the United States. After the Communist takeover of Laos in 1975, thousands fled the country out of fear of persecution and imprisonment. Most escaped by crossing the Mekong River to Thailand. The Mekong River could take their lives or carry them to safety; it was in this body of water that they staked their futures. Thousands of ethnic lowland Lao as well as tribal minorities such as Khmu, Hmong, Yao, and Tai crossed it. At least 5,000 Laotians died while attempting to escape.[19]

On November 26, 1975, Sang Seunsom decided to swim across the river with his son, Souraphanh, and police sergeant, Khambot Thongsavanh.[20] He had been scheduled to attend a reeducation "seminar" with the other directors in the Ministry of Education on the previous day. Seunsom had been a civil servant, a group especially targeted by the Communist Pathet Lao who now ruled the nation. Believing that the seminar would lead to certain death, he decided to risk swimming to freedom. As he prepared to swim across the Mekong, a bird swooped down in front of him, a bad omen. Thinking he would drown, 48-year-old Seunsom stuffed his money (200,000 kip and 4,000 baht) into his pants and tied them around his teenage son's neck, placing his hopes for the family with his son. About 100 feet into the swim, Souraphanh began struggling from the weight of the gold. Seunsom unloaded the money and untied the pants from his son's neck. They swam back to Laos to rest before attempting the one-kilometer swim again. This time, Thongsavanh found a piece of wood that kept the three afloat as they swam to Thailand.

Once they reached Thailand, most refugees were placed into camps administered by the United Nations High Commissioner for Refugees (UNHCR), primarily at Nong Khai and Ban Napho. There they applied to be resettled in a third country and underwent interviews with the Joint Voluntary Agency (JVA) to determine if their cases matched the interests of the U.S. Of the voluntary agencies (volags) in Texas, the UNHCR primarily worked with the United States Catholic Conference (USCC) and the International Rescue Committee (IRC), who found sponsors willing to support families for a short time. Most Lao refugees did not know what different states in the U.S. were like and arrived in Texas by chance. The volags employed a scatter approach, hoping that the refugees would assimilate faster into U.S. culture if they did not live near each other.[21]

Adjustment to Life in Texas

Kham-Hou Boussarath was head of the first Laotian family to arrive in the Dallas-Fort Worth area in August 1975. His seventeen-member extended family was sponsored by Boun-Nheuang Outhavong, his brother-in-law who had moved to Plano after attending college in Missouri. In order to enroll them in school, Boussarath, like many other Laotian refugee families, lowered his teenage children's ages in the resettlement paperwork. In Laos, Boussarath had been a general in the Royal Lao Army. He had also attended universities in Vietnam and France, but his skills did not transfer easily to his new situation in Texas. Though the family had little sewing experience, he started Boussarath Sewing Company and made clothes for companies that supplied them to JC Penney and other stores. Several years passed before the Boussarath family met other Laotian families in the area. The majority arrived between 1979 and 1981. At one point, Boussarath tried to rally the Laotian community to return to Laos as guerilla fighters and reclaim the country from the Communists, but his plan lacked enough support.[22]

Many Laotians who arrived prior to 1989 were placed in east Dallas in an area that came to be called Little Asia.[23] Its affordable housing and public transportation system made it easier for the newcomers to adjust to living in Texas. But the high concentration of refugees in the area led to crime problems. Laotians have been slow to accept authority structures in the U.S. because they had bad experiences with uniformed communist officials in Laos. They are reluctant to ask the police for help or to report crimes and would rather settle matters among themselves by seeking the advice of community leaders. Responding to their hesitation, police officer Ron Cowart established the East Dallas Community Police and Refugee Affairs Center in 1985 as a place the refugees could go for help. The police storefront provided job referrals, clothing donations, crime prevention, and counseling services to refugees.[24]

Another organization that provided assistance to refugees was the IRC. Seunsom was hired as an IRC caseworker two months after his arrival and kept the job until its Indochinese refugee program ended in 1986. The IRC provided an apartment and a living allowance until families could stand on their own feet. The average Laotian refugee had eight and a half years of education, so they tended to qualify only for manufacturing positions. The 1994 Texas Refugee Study found that 39% of Laotians in the Houston area were employed in manufacturing, 14% did technician work, and 9% worked in auto repair or transportation.[25] Many companies were happy to have Laotian employees because they worked hard, were honest, and did not talk back to their supervisors.

Several Houston and D/FW electronics companies such as Compaq and Excellent Diskettes have hired Laotians.[26] These jobs were affected by the recessions of the 1980s and 2000s and the outsourcing of labor to foreign nations. Being self-sufficient, though, is important to Laotians, and they often network with one another to find jobs in companies where other Laotians already work. Though Waste Management of Houston has gone through multiple management and name changes over the years, its many Laotian employees have stayed and risen through the ranks. Most Laotians who rely on welfare have moved to states with more generous benefits such as California.

Laotian Villages

As early as 1977, the IRC noticed that refugees were moving to Texas from their original resettlement states. This pattern was attributed to better employment opportunities in Texas. The USCC also observed similar movements among the families it had helped and began to move families to these burgeoning ethnic communities rather than scattering them as they had done previously. The 2000 U.S. Census counted 10,452

Laotians living in Texas. The highest concentration of Laotians live in D/FW, and the Houston area has the second largest community.[27]

As the Laotians became more established they eventually moved to the suburbs of Dallas and Fort Worth. In April 1982, a Laotian man named Kamsee bought twenty acres of farmland in an unincorporated area in Saginaw with the intention of starting a farm.[28] Thai Buddhist monks convinced him to use some of the land to build a *wat*, a Buddhist temple. Three other families purchased land from him and donated some of it to the wat, giving it a total of four acres. The families themselves lived on their own land in mobile homes at first, and added on to these homes until they resembled permanent houses. Some also constructed houses from scratch with the help of relatives and friends. Because they did not have to follow building codes or hire licensed contractors, they were able to save money.[29] Most of the houses are large two-story brick structures on ½-acre to 2-acre lots that can accommodate several generations of a family. The Laotians built their own infrastructure including roads, power lines, and an artesian well. Much of the village's construction and site design was done by the monks living there. The Saginaw village now consists of approximately 300 families.[30]

Other smaller Laotian villages have sprung up in Texas. Some Laotian families live on farms in Rosharon, where Cambodians were the first to establish farms. They sell their watercress, peppers, and bok choy to Asian grocery stores. Dozens of Laotian families bought farmland in Venus (south of Dallas), where they built Wat Chunramany. At a forty-acre Lao settlement in Keller, families donated parts of their lots to Wat Buddharatanaram.[31]

The Wat as Center of Life

The wat serves as a center for the Lao communities in Texas because Buddhism is a way of life. In all their actions, Laotians try to achieve merit. That is why they give money and land and volunteer their time to the needs of the temple and the monks. Because the wats are part of larger communities, some have earned merit by donating to local charities that help non-Laotians. Before they were able to build their own wats, Laotians attended Thai temples. Wat Lao Siribuddhavas, the first major

Laotian Texans at a soul calling ceremony called "baci," which is held to celebrate births or help people heal after illness. During baci, participants tie cotton threads around each others' wrists and wish each other good luck.

Hmong Texan girls wearing traditional garb in a field dotted with bluebonnets in Dallas. Their necklaces are made of pure silver and typically weigh 4-5 pounds.

Lao wat in Texas, was built in Irving in the early 1980s. The membership grew so much that in the mid-1990s it was moved to a sixty-acre lot in Royse City. Pra Pho Linh is the chief monk presiding there. Wat Lao Thapnimith Saginaw started out as a shed made of four wooden poles and a plastic roof. Monks brought over from Thailand lived in tents while the wat and their homes were being constructed. By 1986 the wat buildings rested on twelve and a half acres. Seunsom was the first chairman of Wat Phouthasamakhy in Houston and oversaw its initial construction in 1987. Recalling mishaps at the wat, Seunsom said, "Two fires have destroyed our warehouse, but they have not destroyed our faith in religion." The newest Lao Buddhist temple was inaugurated on June 19, 2004, in Fort Worth.[32] The chief monk is Acharn Thay, a former colonel in the Royal Lao Army. In Austin, the Lao worship at Wat Buddhananachat, a Thai temple also attended by Cambodians.

Laotians generally form temple associations with respected community members serving on the board. These associations are responsible for managing construction projects, planning events, and raising and managing money. The decorations for the temples are often flown over from Thailand or Laos. The major Lao wats all have giant golden Buddhas as centerpieces in their altars. In June 1983, Thai Buddhists brought large Buddha and Sangha statues to the Saginaw wat.[33] The temple associations must also sponsor ordained Lao or Thai monks to live and work at the temples.

Lao refugees build temples to reconstruct their ethnic identity. The younger generations growing up in Texas do not understand the Buddhist teachings as much as their parents and grandparents. Many only attend during celebrations to socialize with other Laotians. Some temples hold youth classes on Buddhist teachings and Lao culture such as dance and writing. Even the approximately 10% of Laotians who are not Buddhist go to the wats for the same reasons.[34]

The progression of the Laotian Texans is reflected in their religious structures. They build slowly with their own hands, spending only what they can afford. They work as a team. Several Texas wats are now undergoing expansion. The wats, whose foundations lie deep within the Texas soil, are now an unmistakable part of the Texas landscape just as the Laotians have become an integral part of the Texas community.

Hmong Texans

by Vynarack Xaykao

For centuries the Hmong people have moved from place to place in search of a permanent home where they could live peacefully and raise their families. From the Middle East to China to Laos, this ethnic group has had to flee war and famine with no country to call its own. Continuing their nomadic history, many of them were forced to flee their mountainous abodes in Laos for the plains of Texas in the late 1970s because they sided with the United States during the Vietnam War.[35]

Escape From Laos

The Hmong people lived in the mountains of northeast Laos and provided the country's first line of defense against the advancing Vietminh. The U.S. feared the domino effect of Communism spreading from Vietnam to Laos. The CIA secretly trained Hmong Special Guerilla Units (SGU) led by General Vang Pao, a Hmong serving in the Royal Lao Army. They established the Auto Defense Community (ADC) consisting of Hmong farmers who stayed behind to defend their villages. Most Hmong males fourteen or older served in one of these units.[36]

The Communist Pathet Lao took control of Laos in spring 1975. American pilots transported from Long Cheng to Thailand over 12,000 Hmong in danger of persecution. Other Hmong found covert means of fleeing Laos. Many families spent thousands of kip hiring smugglers to transport them across the border to Thailand. Mrs. Va Vang Yang, whose family was the fifth Hmong family to move to Dallas-Fort Worth, recalls paying Lao taxi drivers a total of 165,000 kip to drive her family to Tha Bo on the Mekong River, where the family of five squeezed into a small boat and rowed to Thailand.[37]

Tou Ger Lo and his family, who arrived in D/FW just before Yang, set out for Vientiane from Ban Xone and were stopped at Hinh Heup

Bridge after having walked for two days.[38] The Communist troops demanded to see Vientiane resident identification cards, so they walked back to Ban Xone to obtain ID cards before returning to Vientiane. Lo then hired a smuggler to help his family cross the Mekong River for 100,000 kip.

Once in Thailand, most Hmong refugees were placed in UNHCR camps at Ban Vinai and Nong Khai. Those seeking resettlement in the U.S. were interviewed by INS and CIA officials. Preference was given to those with higher military rank and those who served in the war.[39]

Primary Resettlement in Texas

The voluntary agencies (volags) most active in resettling Laotian refugees in Texas were the United States Catholic Conference (USCC), Church World Services, and the International Rescue Committee (IRC). Agencies placed refugees all over the U.S. to minimize the burden on agencies in local communities. Despite the large Hmong families, the agencies tried to keep them intact. The third Hmong family to arrive in D/FW was led by Doua Hang and consisted of his wife, nine children, and three brothers (a total of fourteen). The sponsors who helped Hmong refugees resettle prepared everything a family needed in advance. Upon arrival the families were taken to apartments or houses furnished with beds, chairs, tables, kitchen supplies, and food. Hang's son, Vang Jeff Hang, is grateful for the generosity of the Shady Oaks Baptist Church in Hurst, which had prepared his family's house with five bunk beds to accommodate all the children. Cher Pao Thao's family was the first Hmong family in D/FW, arriving on May 6, 1976. The IRC gave his family a twenty-five pound bag of rice, two chickens, and $16 per week to purchase food and supplies for his family of three.[40]

Sponsor support and orientation was very important in ensuring successful acculturation to U.S. life because the Hmong had little previous exposure to the modern world in their isolated mountain villages. They were accustomed to hunting for food in the jungles, raising poultry and pigs for consumption, and growing their own vegetables. Thao's sponsor helped his family adapt by showing them how to buy groceries in a store. Yang's sponsor taught her safety measures as well as how to use ovens and toilets.[41]

The sponsors' most important role was to find companies that would hire the new settlers so that they could, in time, become self-sufficient. Due to their limited education, most Hmong people took blue-collar jobs in manufacturing plants or provided custodial services. All family members who were capable of working had to find jobs, including women whose traditional role in Laos was caring for the family. Thao's wife, Mab Hawj, emphasized that refugees use what wits they possess to function on the job, "I feel good about myself. I don't know how to write and read. But I use my strength(s). I look at (other people doing the work) and my hand(s) do it."[42] She has risen through the ranks to reach level six out of eight levels since becoming a machine operator at Sweetheart Cup in 1981.

Some Hmong left high-ranking positions to become ordinary citizens of the United States. Thao was the director of the provincial veterinary clinic in Long Cheng.[43] Considered highly educated in Laos, his first job in Texas involved assembling picture frames at Dallas Woodcraft, where several other Hmong subsequently found employment. Continuing his education at Mountain View College, he now works as an assistant production manager.

Continuance of Hmong Traditions

Hmong people rely on a system of clan membership in which each clan has its own religious traditions, leaders, and support networks. The clans represented in Texas in 2004 are: Vang, Vue, Moua, Yang, Xiong, Lo, Ly, Kue, Hang, Her, and Thao.[44] Each clan selects a leader who has good morals and leadership skills. The leader serves as a mediator who resolves traditional and cultural problems within the clan as well as with other clans.

To preserve clan unity, Hmong people tend to listen to their leaders and to follow them wherever they go. Though Hmong families were initially scattered around the U.S., they later clustered in areas where their leaders resided. By the early 1980s, several leaders decided to reunite the clans in the San Joaquin Valley in California. As a result, nearly 100 Hmong families in Houston and several families in D/FW left without informing their employers or sponsors. Generous welfare policies in other states may also have contributed to the Hmong exodus.[45]

The presence of a strong leader in D/FW was one of the reasons some Hmong families chose to remain there and others eventually returned. As the oldest Hmong person to settle in Texas, Neng Chue Thao Xaykao was a role model. He was a colonel in the Royal Lao Army and the provincial military governor of Xieng Khouang.[46] His wife, Cha Vang, was General Vang Pao's younger sister. In D/FW Xaykao worked as a machinist and served as the community's shaman.

He practiced shamanism until he died of cancer in 1991, and Nao Cha Lo assumed the role. Most Hmong are animists who worship their ancestors as well as nature's spirits. They believe that a shaman can communicate with these spirits. When people become sick, their souls leave their bodies. A shaman can heal them by calling the souls back. The shaman also knows how to conduct traditional weddings, funerals, and New Year ceremonies, which have been simplified due to limited time and knowledge.

Some Hmong also practice Christianity. The First Baptist Church Hmong Mission in Irving was led by Deacon Kai Moua and is now under Deacon Va Meng Vang. In North Richland Hills, Pastor Pa Chay Her, one of the first Hmong to settle in Houston, heads the Hmong Alliance Fellowship. In Fort Worth, Hmong families worship at St. George Catholic Church.[47]

Secondary Resettlement in Texas

The Hmong American Planning and Development Center, Inc. (MAPDC), was established in 1985 to help Hmong and Laotian refugees from other states relocate in D/FW and achieve self-sufficiency. Though they fought for the U.S., the Hmong do not receive veterans' benefits because their service was secret. MAPDC Executive Director Thao Phia Xaykao estimates that 60% of his clients moved from California's central valley, 30% from Wisconsin, and 10% from Minnesota. Land is cheaper in Texas than in those other states, allowing families to buy their own homes after an average of two years. Additionally more blue-collar jobs are available in D/FW than in the farming areas where the clients were first resettled.

The twenty families per year assisted by the program tend to be young, but some older couples relocate to D/FW to shield their children from bad influences.[48]

Since its peak in the late 1970s the Hmong population in Texas has remained relatively stable. The number of Hmong in Texas nearly doubled from 176 in 1990 to 347 in 2000, but it must be noted that the Census undercounts the Hmong due to their lack of participation. Most Hmong live in Dallas and Tarrant counties. Success stories of Hmong Texans have attracted Hmong from other states to move to Texas. No Hmong families in Texas are on public assistance, and most of their children graduate from high school and attend college. The host communities have also been receptive and actively helpful. Yang has received help from her sponsor Peggy Cox for almost thirty years and considers her to be her mother.[49] Established families have, in turn, sponsored new arrivals and provided strong support networks.

Many Hmong families finally found a permanent residence in Texas. They bought their own homes and raised children who achieved more than their parents could have imagined in Laos. While most Hmong in Laos could not attend schools in the cities, their children have had greater educational opportunities in the United States. The Hmong's success in Texas can be attributed to the work of the state's resettlement agencies and sponsors as well as to the Hmong's own hard work and strong ties of kinship.

Thai Texans

by Pat S. Charnveja

The history of Thai Americans in Texas can be traced back as far as the early 1950s. The first Thai man to settle in Texas was a former Royal Thai Air Force pilot, Prachan "Charlie" Sthapitanonda. He returned to Amarillo, Texas in late 1953 and settled down with his American wife, Joan Thompson, in 1954. Charlie was the only Thai man living in Amarillo until his oldest daughter, Prapatip (Pat S. Charnveja), came from Bangkok, Thailand to live with him and his family. Today, there are approximately seventy Thai Texan families living in Amarillo in both Potter and Randall Counties.[50]

In early 1958 Arun Pvongnak came to Houston from Thailand and lived with a naval officer's family. Now in his seventies, Arun was the first Thai immigrated to the Texas Gulf Coast area. Around the time Pvongnak came to Houston, Tongake Sookma immigrated to Dallas, becoming one of the earliest Thais to live permanently in the area. A soldier in Thailand, Sookma was invited to immigrate to the United States by a military family. Sookma became a plumber, and his two daughters joined the U.S. military. More Thais immigrated to Texas in the early 1960s, and a major portion of the early Thais were medical doctors seeking specialized training in U.S. residency programs. David Pita was one such doctor in the mid-1960s in Chicago before he and his wife, Alice (a white American), moved to Dallas, where, in 1971, there were about fifty Thai families. Dr. Pita became a leader among the Thai community, speaking out on issues like Asian gang violence and serving as president of the Thai Community Center of North Dallas.[51]

Many Thais moved to Houston and the Gulf Coast area beginning in the early 1970s. These individuals were professionals from the fields of medicine, nursing, engineering and architecture. Few owned small grocers and restaurants. During that time, many undergraduate students came to the Gulf Coast area to study. Some studied engineering at Lamar University, University of Texas, and University of Houston while others pursued business and medical degrees. During the late 1970s and early 1980s, the oil and gas industries were booming in Houston. The majority of Thais relocating to the Gulf Coast area came from Los Angeles, San Francisco, New York, and Chicago to seek greener economic pastures or escape the cold weather. Some Thais, upon earning graduate degrees, opened businesses.[52]

The Thai Community Today

Before the end of the Vietnam War, Thai Texans likely were the second largest Southeast Asian ethnic group in Texas (the Filipinos being the largest). However, their growth since 1975 has been slower than that of many other Asian groups. In 1990, the Census counted 5,816 Thai Texans, and that number increased 27% to 7,384 in 2000, making Texas home to the second-largest Thai population in the nation, the largest being in California. According to the 2000 census, 2,707 Thais live in the Dallas-Fort Worth area counties of Dallas, Tarrant, Denton, and Collin; the Houston area's Harris, Fort Bend, Nueces, Jefferson, Galveston, and Montgomery counties were home to 1,832 Thais. The Thai community of the Gulf Coast region was most heavily concentrated in the Southwest Houston area— Sugar Land, Missouri City, and Stafford. The Thai population was substantially undercounted; in 2006, David Pita estimated between 18,000 and 20,000 Thais in the Dallas-Fort Worth region. It is estimated that 5,000 Thais/Thai-Americans live in the Gulf Coast area. The 2000 Census counted 1,510 Thais in the Austin and San Antonio vicinity.[53]

Ninety percent of Thai Texans hold undergraduate or graduate degrees. Most of them are small business owners. They are in real estate, accounting, law, private medical practices, printing and copying, travel agency, convenience stores, gems and jewelry, international trade and business consulting, and the restaurant business. They usually rely on themselves or the help of their friends to get established. Thai Texans do experience discrimination, glass ceilings, and inequality at their workplaces. "A person with any ethnic background will likely be passed up any promotions in favor of a white person," commented Yongyuth Ruchirushkul, a Thai Houstonian leader. "Your neighbors may not be too happy to see a non-white neighbor who tries to fit in, but it's very rare compared to discrimination at workplace."[54]

Eighty-five percent of the Thai community in the Houston area are Buddhists, 8% are Christians, and the rest are Muslims and other religions. There are several Thai Buddhist temples in Harris and Fort Bend Counties. The largest temple, Wat Buddhavas of Houston, was established in 1982, and shortly thereafter the wat requested a monk from the Sangha Supreme Council of Buddhist Monks in Bangkok. In 1983, a temple building opened in northwest Houston, and Abbot Prachan Kamchan arrived to serve as the temple's first monk. The temple was the Houston area's first Thai (Theravada) Buddhist temple and served, in the beginning, sixty or seventy families of Thai, Laotian, and Cambodian descent. By 1996, there were five Thai monks at the temple. The first Thai

In 1969, Bootsabar Wilson came to Dallas to study English, planning to return to Thailand and teach the language in her village. She married Mark Wilson and stayed in the United States. One of the earliest Thais in Dallas, she remains faithful to Buddhism and often visits the local Thai temple, The Buddhist Center of Dallas.

temple in Dallas was the Buddhist Center of Dallas, which opened its doors in March 1982. In 1983, the temple bought 103 acres in North Dallas, where today's temple was built and expanded. By the mid-2000s, five monks lived at the Buddhist Center of Dallas. By 2006, Thai Buddhist temples stood in many Texas cities, including Killeen and Portland (near Corpus Christi); the presence of U.S. military bases in Thailand resulted in some Thais immigrating and settling in or near Texas military bases, such as Fort Hood, near Killeen.[55]

Thai Texan social and community organizations were established as early as 1975, when Thailand's Queen Sirikit visited Dallas. A committee of local Thais, including Dr. David Pita, organized a reception for the Queen. Out of this committee grew the Thai Association of North Texas. Since then, Thai Texans have very much been a part of the political process by voting, volunteering, and serving on the boards and committees of city governments and civic and political organizations. Issues such as the welfare of seniors and youth, education, health care, insurance, housing, transportation, gang prevention, and language barriers are of concern in the Thai community. Even as younger Thai Texans assimilate into a multicultural society, many also maintain their Thai culture by participating at Thai Buddhist temples, Thai Arts and Culture of Houston, Heritage of Thailand, Thai Performing Arts Group, and Thai student associations. Important umbrella organizations are the Thai Texas Association (Houston) and the Thai Association of North Texas.

The first Thai restaurant in Ft. Bend County, Fu Lu Su, was opened in 1978 by Surin and Choochuen Anomaiprasert. The Anomaipraserts have since opened the Thai Pepper, Teala's, and Baroque restaurants. Soon after the opening of Fu Lu Su, Houston had its first Thai restaurant, Thai Rama. In 1983, Bangkok Inn, one of Dallas's first and more successful Thai restaurants, opened, and by 1986, there were a handful of Thai restaurants in Houston. The popularity of Thai food grew rapidly in the 1980s, and by 1991 even Amarillo had three or four Thai restaurants. In 2004, there were over sixty Thai restaurants in Harris, Ft. Bend, Montgomery, and Galveston Counties. Restaurant owners are among the most successful of Thai Texan entrepreneurs.[56]

In 2005, Houston's Thai medical community consisted of approximately fifteen physicians and dentists and one hundred nurses and medical technicians. Among these professionals was Dr. Prapand Apisarnthanarax, a well-respected dermatologist in Houston, who became the first Thai faculty member of the University of Texas Medical Branch at Galveston in 1973 and an associate professor with tenure in dermatology in 1978. Also prominent was Dr. Tasnee Chonmaitree, an internationally recognized researcher and professor of Pediatrics and Pathology at the University of Texas Medical Branch at Galveston. Many Thai physicians trained each year in Texas, and they participated in local Thai community functions.[57]

The Thailand-Houston connection is very strong in part because of Thai Prime Minister Dr. Thaksin Shinawatra (2001–2006). He lived in Houston during the 1980s while studying for his Ph.D. in Criminology at Sam Houston State University (SHSU). In October 2002, SHSU awarded Dr. Thaksin its prestigious Humanitarian Award for the work he has done for Thailand and its people. During his visit, Prime Minister Thaksin was reunited with his former classmates, and he proudly proclaimed Houston as his second home.[58] For most Thai Texans, Texas is their first home.

The Burmese Texans[59]

by Irwin A. Tang

In 1962, Norman Zaw Wong was a Burmese citizen studying economics at Ohio's Wesleyan University. That year, Burmese general Ne Win staged a coup d'etat and replaced the Burmese government with a military council. Movement into and out of the nation was strictly controlled, and Norman Zaw Wong became one of many Burmese in the U.S. unable to return to Burma. Among them, few had ever lived in Texas. The unknown territory was far from the Pacific Coast. Wong, whose father was involved in the Burmese oil industry, worked in the summers from 1961 to 1964 as a seismic assistant for oil companies along the Texas and Louisiana coast. Wong learned the rough language of the oil workers, but his visa expired, and he became an illegal immigrant, like many other Burmese "stuck" in the United States.

In the early 1960s, Wong remembered, fewer than twenty Burmese families lived in Texas. But the population grew as professional Burmese working in engineering, architecture, computer sciences, medicine, and other trades migrated from other states and from Burma to the state of Texas. Like other Burmese political refugees, Wong sought legal residency. He found a job working for his father's friend as an oil tool salesperson, and, like many other Burmese, gained political asylum status from the U.S. government. Most Burmese migrating to Texas chose to live in Houston, and in the 1970s, fewer than 100 Burmese families lived in the city.

Aye Aye Kye's parents were employees of the Burmese government that preceded the coup. In 1964, the military government arrested and imprisoned them for political reasons. Aye Aye Kye, only two years of age then, was cared for by her grandparents for four years. In the 1980s, facing national economic stagnation and impoverishment, the military government allowed more Burmese to migrate to other nations, to increase the inflow of hard currencies. "Those who had connections, brains, or sheer will to survive" left Burma for Pakistan, the Middle East, East Asian nations, and North America, said Kye. In part because of this migration, the number of Burmese in Houston increased to 100–200 in the 1980s.

By 2004, Burmese Texans lived mostly in Houston and Austin, where the computer industry hired many of them. In 1988, a violent crushing of the opposition movement in Burma resulted in the imprisonment of Nobel Peace Prize winner Aung San Suu Kyi, as well as the fleeing of hundreds of thousands of Burmese (including many of the minority Karen people) into Burmese jungles and other nations. Between 1988 and 2004, some refugees immigrated to the United States either through third nations or through Catholic Charities. Some re-settled in Texas, whose warm climate was familiar. They live throughout the state, including El Paso, where some work at a meat packing plant. The post-1988 immigrants tend to be less educated and speak less English than their predecessors. Aye Aye Kye, after witnessing the 1988 violence, left Burma in 1989 for graduate school in Texas.

The 1988 uprising united Burmese Texans in opposition to the military government. They raised money to support the opposition forces and felt a camaraderie with each other that has since dissolved to some degree. In 1989, Norman Wong and others helped form the Burmese American Association of Texas. The BAAT remained a social organization and avoided politics. By doing so, Burmese in Texas felt free to join the organization without fear of repercussion to their families in Burma. With the military government still a threat to Burmese Texans' immediate and extended families in Burma, and with the extreme poverty resulting from totalitarian rule, Burmese Texans are among the Asian ethnic groups most focused on their nation of ancestral origin. They work to improve conditions in Burma, and their relations with other Burmese are influenced by their politics and relation to the government.

In recent years, the Burmese Texan population has increased tremendously. In 2007, approximately 1000 Burmese, most of them refugees, lived in Dallas alone, according to Ceu Lian Thang, a Burmese Baptist minister there. A 2007 Burmese government crackdown on antigovernment forces contributed to the recent influx of Burmese refugees, who belong to numerous ethnic and language groups.[60]

Among the Burmese are those of Burman, indigenous Burmese, Chinese, and Indian descent. While most Burmese Texans are Buddhist, some are Muslim, Hindu, and Christian. In 1996, the Venerable Ashin Nyanissara, the Sitagu Sayadaw of Burma, founded in Austin a Buddhist temple called Sitagu Vihara. In 2003, the Vihara served about 120 Burmese, Sri Lankans, and Westerners. The monks also visited Houston every month. Services are conducted in Pali, and a Children's Dhamma School teaches children about Theravada Buddhism. The Vihara sits on sixteen rural acres west of Austin, and this Buddhist community plans to build a full Burmese-styled stupa, or Buddhist monument.[61]

ENDNOTES

1   Sucheng Chan, *Survivors: Cambodian Refugees in the United States* (Urbana: University of Illinois Press, 2004), 81–82; Eric Lai and Dennis Arguelles, eds., *The News Face of Asian Pacific America: Numbers, Diversity & Change in the 21st Century* (San Francisco: AsianWeek, UCLA Asian American Studies Center Press, 2003), 94–95.

2   Usha Welaratna, *Beyond the Killing Fields: Voices of Nine Cambodian Survivors in America* (Stanford: Stanford University Press, 1993), 166; Sambath Chan, interview by Sophia Hong, Pflugerville, Texas, October 9, 2004; Theav Hong, interview by Sophia Hong, Houston, Texas, July 20, 2004; Channy Soeur, interview by Irwin Tang and Sophia Hong, Austin, Texas, March 23, 2005.

3   Lay Kheang Chheng, interview by Sophia Hong, Houston, Texas, January 10, 2005; Syvong Ngin, interview by Irwin Tang and Sophia Hong, Austin, Texas, March 23, 2005; Soeur, interview; Peng Hong, interview by Sophia Hong, Houston, Texas, June 28, 2004.

4   Peng Hong, interview; Theav Hong, interview; Sambath Chan, interview.

5   Nancy Smith-Hefner, *Khmer American* (Berkeley: University of California Press, 1999), 8; Seam Hong, interview by Sophia Hong, Houston, Texas, September 15, 2004.

6   Smith-Hefner; Seam Hong, interview; Sucheng Chan.

7   Mitch Lobrovich, "In the YMCA, a Chief of State," *Dallas Times Herald*, February 25, 1979; Stephen Johnson, "Cambodia Refugees: Laotians Face Far Fewer Problems in Adapting to Life in U.S.," *Houston Chronicle*, June 7, 1981.

8   Ibid; Sucheng Chan, 118.

9   Sam Tek Ly, telephone interview by Sophia Hong, January 22, 2005; on Little Asia see Sucheng Chan, 118; Phillip Seib, "Life in Dallas' Little Asia Remains Hard but Promising," *Dallas Morning News*, February 10, 1988, Viewpoints section.

10 Seam Hong, interview.

11 Peng Hong, interview.

12 Theav Hong, interview.

13 On quotes, see Seam Hong, interview; Chheng, interview; on farms, see Sucheng Chan, 119; Cathy Gordon, "Cambodians Grow Unusual Vegetables on Tomball Farm," *Houston Chronicle*, October 22, 1989; Melissa Hung, "Cambodian Queen," *Houston Press*, April 13, 2000. On Carrollton, see Kathy Jackson, "Settling In: Job Opportunities, Safe Neighborhoods Lure Cambodians to Carrollton, FB," *Dallas Morning News*, September 18, 1989.

14 Soeur, interview.

15 Ngin, interview; Soeur, interview.

16 Ibid.

17 "Srey Thom," phone interview by Sophia Hong, Houston, Texas, August 2, 2005; Sucheng Chan, 218.

18 Bong Srey, phone interview by Sophia Hong, Houston, Texas, August 2, 2005.

19 Jeremy Hein, *From Vietnam, Laos, and Cambodia: A Refugee Experience in the United States* (New York: Twayne Publishers, 1995), 35.

20 Sang Seunsom, interview by the author, Houston, TX, June 1, 2004.

21 Hein, 39; Ines M. Miyares, *The Hmong Refugee Experience in the United States: Crossing the River* (New York: Garland Publishing, 1998), 12.

22 On Boussarath, see Arouny Joy Boussarath, telephone conversation with author, June 8, 2004; Arouny Joy Boussarath, personal e-mail, June 7, 2004; on "the majority" see Sadhon Bhookong, "A Laotian Refugee Community: Its Impact on Adaptation," Texas Women's University Ph.D. dissertation, 62–63.

23 Lori Stahl and Anh Do, "Loss in Little Asia: Middle-Class Families Move; New Refugees Settle," *Dallas Morning News,* July 10, 1989, 17a.

24 Bobette Riner, "Offering Immigrants a Hand: Police Open up Storefront to Serve Asian Community," *Dallas Morning News,* Nov. 22, 1985, 29a; Lori Stahl, "Finding A Purpose: Dallas Officer Builds One-Man Bridge To Asian Community," *Dallas Morning News,* Oct. 18, 1987, 29a.

25 Eric H. Taylor and Lisa S. Barton, *Vietnamese, Laotian, Ethiopian, & Former Soviet Union Refugees in Texas: Findings From the Texas Refugee Study,* Texas Office of Immigration & Refugee Affairs, 1994.

26 Ed Timms, "Refugees Find Help At Center: Agencies Fighting Increasing Problems," *Dallas Morning News,* Dec. 27, 1988, 15a.

27 On IRC, see HEW Refugee Task Force, *Report to the Congress,* Mar. 21, 1977, 15; for census figures, see U.S. Census Bureau, *Census 2000*; on the rest, see Miyares, 28.

28 Bhookong, 66–75.

29 Bryan Woolley, "Laos On The Prairie: Three Hundred Laotian Families Try To Keep Their Culture Alive While Settling Outside Forth Worth," *Dallas Morning News,* Nov. 12, 1995, 1f.

30 Thao Phia Xaykao, telephone conversation with author, June 10, 2004.

31 On Rosharon, see Seunsom, interview; on Venus, see Thomas Huang, "Race In America: Choosing Self-Segregation," *Dallas Morning News,* Aug. 2, 1998, 36a; on Keller, see Amy Roquemore, "Place of Worship: Buddhists Create Home Near Keller To Follow Culture, Religious Practices," *Dallas Morning News,* Aug. 30, 1998, 1s.

32 On first and newest wats, see Xaykao; on Saginaw, see Bhookong, 71–76; Seunsom.

33 Bhookong.

34 On identity, see Penny Van Esterik, *Taking Refuge: Lao Buddhists in North America* (Tempe: Arizona State University, 1992), 88; see also Taylor and Barton.

35 Fungchatou T. Lo, *The Promised Land: Socioeconomic Reality of the Hmong People in Urban America (1976–2000)* (Bristol, IN: Wyndham Hall Press, 2001), 22; Keith Quincy, *Hmong: History of a People* (Cheney, WA: Eastern Washington University Press, 1988), 26.

36 "Hmong Were the Closest Allies With the United States During the Vietnam War," Lao Veterans of America [website]; Available from *http://www.laoveter-*

ans.com/refugee1.html; accessed May 29, 2004; on Hmong males, see Thao Phia Xaykao, interview by the author, Grand Prairie, TX, May 28, 2004.

37 Lynellyn D. Long, *Ban Vinai: The Refugee Camp* (New York: Columbia University Press, 1993), 36; Mrs. Va Vang Yang, interview by the author, Fort Worth, TX, May 29, 2004.

38 Tou Ger Lo, interview by the author, Fort Worth, TX, May 29, 2004.

39 On UNHCR, see Long; on the rest, Lo, *The Promised Land*, 85.

40 On volags, see Lo, *The Promised Land*; on Hang family, see Vang Jeff Hang, interview by the author, Grand Prairie, TX, May 29, 2004; on Thao family, see Cher Pao Thao, interview by the author, Duncanville TX, May 29, 2004.

41 Thao, interview; Yang, interview.

42 Xaykao interview; Thao interview.

43 Lo, *The Promised Land*, 22.

44 Ibid, 26; on Texas, see Xaykao, interview.

45 On San Joaquin Valley, see Xaykao, interview; on Houston and D/FW see Sang Seunsom, interview by the author, Houston, TX, June 1, 2004; on final sentence, see Thao, interview.

46 Xaykao, interview.

47 Xaykao, interview; on Fort Worth see Lo, interview.

48 Xaykao, interview.

49 U.S. Census Bureau, *Census 1990 Summary Tape File 1 & 3*; U.S. Census Bureau, *Census* 2000; Yang, interview.

50 Charnveja, Pat, author's personal knowledge.

51 Charnveja; David Pita, interview by Irwin Tang, January 2006.

52 Charnveja, personal knowledge.

53 U.S. Censuses 1990 and 2000; Terri Williams, "Thai-Americans retain culture," *Dallas Morning News*, Aug 14, 2000;

54 Yongyuth Ruchirushkul, interview by Pat Charnveja, Houston, September 22, 2004.

55 Richard Vara, "Songkran Day," *Houston Chronicle*, Apr 13, 1996; Charnveja, personal knowledge.

56 Charnveja, personal knowledge; *Houston Chronicle*, "Restaurant review: Thai Lotus," August 28, 1986; Kim Pierce, "Thai Nipa," *Dallas Morning News*, May 11, 1990; Crider, "Texas Eating Style," *Austin American-Statesman*, Apr 3, 1991.

57 Charnveja, personal knowledge.

58 Charnveja, personal knowledge.

59 Section is based on interviews with Norman Zaw Wong and Aye Aye Kye in 2004.

60 Kovach, Gretel, "For minister, work is part of mission," Texas Cable News, Aug 25, 2007, see *www.txcn.com/sharedcontent/dws/news/longterm/stories/082607dnentrefugees_ceulian.ec76be.html*, accessed Dec 15, 2007.

61 *http://www.sitagu.org/*, accessed on January 26, 2006, website of the temple.

★

CHAPTER FOURTEEN

THE PAKISTANI TEXANS, BANGLADESHI TEXANS, SRI LANKAN TEXANS, NEPALESE TEXANS, AND TIBETAN TEXANS

Irwin A. Tang, Melissa Masoom, and Dr. Harishini Ernest

The Pakistani Texans

by Irwin A. Tang

According to the 2000 Census, the state of Texas is home to the nation's second largest Pakistani American population. While the 2000 Census counted about 20,000 Pakistanis, there may have been, in 2004, as many as 100,000 Pakistanis living in Texas, according to community leaders. The majority of Pakistani Texans live in Houston. The estimated 50,000 or 60,000 Pakistani Houstonians constitute one of the largest Pakistani city populations in North America.[1] Other major centers of Pakistani Texan population are Dallas-Fort Worth and Austin.

Around the late 1960s, the United States became the most popular destination for Pakistani graduate students studying abroad. In these early years, Pakistani migration to Texas consisted largely of graduate students and professionals in the fields of engineering, computer science, and medicine. Texas A&M University, UT-Austin, and the University of Houston educated most of the Pakistani students. Houston's association with space exploration lent both the city and UH prestige. The many employment opportunities in the sprawling city also offered Pakistani students ways to supplement their income. After graduation, Pakistani students from throughout the United States sought work in Houston's oil and energy industries. In 1980, when Masrur Javed (M.J.) Khan arrived from New Rochelle, New York with wife and son to work for the energy company, Brown and Root, Khan estimated there were less than 1,000 Pakistanis living in Houston.[2]

While Houston may have always been the most popular Texas destination for Pakistani immigrants, many others settled in Dallas where, in the late 1970s, the Pakistani community centered around Arlington and Grand Prairie, a suburb where the community established a mosque. When in 1980 Rashid Qureshi moved to Austin to work as an engineer for Advanced Micro Devices, he noted only six Pakistani Texan families and about two hundred Pakistani international students. The local mosque was located at a Nueces Street house near the University of Texas, and worshippers were mostly Arab and Asian students.[3]

Born in Karachi, Pakistan in 1950, M.J. Khan earned his M.A. in Civil Engineering from the University of Illinois at Urbana-Champaign. Married before moving to the United States, M.J. and wife Attiya gave birth to son Faraz in New Rochelle. Upon moving to Houston, M.J. Khan spent a great deal of time helping to develop the social organizations of the Pakistani Houston community. When M.J. Khan first arrived to Houston in 1980, there were no mosques run by Asian or Arab Muslims. A few dozen Pakistani professionals and Arabs met at a house on Richmond Avenue to worship. While many Pakistanis migrated to Houston during the oil boom of the 1970s and early 1980s, the oil bust of the mid-1980s resulted in the exodus of some Pakistani Houstonians. In response to unemployment during the oil bust, many Pakistani professionals opened small businesses. Running businesses allowed Pakistanis greater control over their families' destinies, according to Rashid Qureshi, who opened in the mid-1990s the first of three automobile oil change centers in Austin. As an engineer, he had grown wary of the three-year boom and bust cycle of the high-tech industry and considered running one's own business "an American dream."[4]

The Pakistani Texan community transformed in the 1980s from a population made up largely of engineers, computer experts, and doctors into a population dominated by small business owners. Running convenience stores became the most popular commercial venture among Pakistani Texans, while others opened retail stores, restaurants, motels, and hotels. One source of the increase in Pakistani immigrant workers and entrepreneurs was the increase in Pakistani "family reunification" immigrants—siblings and parents of Pakistani Texans who had attained citizenship. As the population increased, Pakistani Texans established formal associations to help each other and to represent the local Pakistani communities to larger society. The Pakistani Association of Greater Austin, for instance, helped newly-arrived Pakistani international students adjust to American culture and to ameliorate homesickness.[5]

In the early decades, single Pakistani men in Texas often returned to Pakistan to find a wife and marry because of a lack of Pakistani women in Texas. Some Pakistani men married Pakistani and non-Pakistani women already living in the United States.

Amidst the oil bust and the plummeting of real estate prices, few Houstonians seemed to care that two Pakistanis in Houston were arrested in 1984 for attempting to export krytons, extremely high-speed switches that can be used to detonate nuclear weapons. One Pakistani was convicted and deported to Pakistan. Although some in the Pakistani community were aware of the arrests, those arrested were not members of the mainstream Pakistani community, and the arrests were not a major event.[6]

The honeymoon for Pakistani Texans ended on June 14, 1985 when Shiite Muslim Lebanese extremists hijacked TWA Flight 847 and had it flown to Beirut, Lebanon. There the hijackers killed a U.S. Navy diver. As the hostage crisis dragged on and the Muslim holy month of fasting known as Ramadan ended, three Houston men on June 22 threw a pipe-bomb into the largely Pakistani Dar Us Salam mosque (in southwest Houston) just minutes after fifteen or twenty Muslims had left the mosque. Because the bomb did not detonate, the bombers (who were not Muslim or Pakistani) retrieved the bomb and re-set its detonation. The bomb exploded and caused $50,000 in damages, but no one was injured.

The Pakistani and Muslim communities of Houston were shocked by the bombing and realized that their community was being blamed for acts of violence committed by Muslims on the other side of the world. Receiving threatening phone calls, Muslim leaders cancelled a celebration set for the end of Ramadan. Initially, police department officials downplayed the possible connection between the bombing and the hijacking, but statements by the three bombers—including a wheelchair-bound university student—revealed that they indeed bombed the mosque in retaliation for the hijackings.[7]

In response to the bombing of the mosque, the Islamic Association of Houston, led by M.J. Khan, met with Mayor Kathy Whitmire and the Houston police department to ensure that protection of the city's Muslims was a priority. Because of the mosque bombing and because of unrelated hate crimes against Jewish and Christian houses of worship, local Muslims, Jews, and Christians met in 1990 to discuss hate crime prevention.[8]

Nonetheless, vandalism and threats against mosques and Muslims, including Pakistanis, continued from the late 1980s through the years following the terror attacks of September 11, 2001. Vandals repeatedly attacked Houston's Mosque Mohammed and turned over and burned the mosque teacher's car in 1988-1989. Saeeda Khan, the Pakistani teacher told the *Houston Chronicle*, "It does not make sense because we are U.S. citizens and proud of that. And Pakistan has nothing to do with the Middle East." Texans' hostilities toward Shiite Muslims overseas had translated to vandalism against the largely Sunni Muslims of Houston. Most Pakistani Texans are Sunni Muslims, and a portion are Shiite Muslims. Pakistani Muslims in Houston are so numerous that they may constitute as much as a majority of the Muslims in Houston, a city considered the second largest in U.S. Muslim population.[9]

In 1986, the Pakistan Association of Greater Houston collected donations as small as five and ten dollars from Pakistani Houstonians to establish a merit-based scholarship at the University of Houston. Today, the endowed scholarship supplies $1000 each semester to four students. Over the years, the scholarship likely helped to improve the image of Pakistanis in Houston.[10]

After Houston emerged from the oil bust in the late 1980s, tens of thousands of Pakistanis immigrated to the Houston area during the 1990s. Like other immigrant communities, word spread among Pakistani Americans and prospective Pakistani immigrants that Houston was a good environment for Pakistanis, Muslims, and entrepreneurs. Pakistanis saw in the growth of the Houston population opportunities to run small businesses. In the 1980s, Pakistani Texan entrepreneurs grew in numbers and became the majority among Pakistani Texans. As Pakistanis established homes and businesses throughout the city, especially in southwest Houston, they also built mosques. When Pakistanis move to a neighborhood, "the first thing they do is build a mosque," according to M.J. Khan. Today there are eighty-four mosques and places of Muslim worship throughout greater Houston, in large part due to Pakistani worshippers.[11]

Whereas in Dallas and Austin, Pakistani Texans lived in more evenly dispersed places, the Pakistanis in Houston tended to concentrate geographically. Many of the Pakistanis in Houston have located their businesses and homes in Southwest Houston, Sugarland, and Fort Bend County, where many other Asian Americans live. The intersection of Bissonet and Kirkwood is the center of the largest Pakistani commercial district in Texas, as well as the location of the offices of the Pakistani Association of Greater Houston.

Pakistani Texans, especially convenience store owners, have struggled with crime. Convenience store clerks and owners are everyday at risk of being robbed or murdered, and in the 1990s and 2000s, many Pakistani Texans have been killed. The murder of ten Asian American convenience store owners and clerks (plus one Lebanese American) in a period of six months in the year 2000 in Houston threw the Pakistani Houstonian community into turmoil. The murdered were mostly Pakistani and Indian Houstonians. "Anything that affects the convenience stores affects the community," said M.J. Khan in retrospect. "Every one of the murdered were good friends of the community. One of them was a good friend of mine." Having been elected as president of the Pakistan Association of Greater Houston in 1986, Khan was a respected leader. He met with the Houston Police Department to ensure that the safety of convenience store workers was a top priority, and he also helped to produce a videotape that demonstrated simple ways for Pakistani convenience store workers and owners to protect themselves from crime.[12]

While there were fewer murders of Pakistani convenience store workers in subsequent years, the Pakistani Texan community was again thrown into great turmoil when Muslim terrorists attacked the United States on September 11, 2001. M.J. Khan remembered the community reaction to the attacks:

> [Pakistani Texans] were shocked, horrified, and angry. They were shocked that something like this could happen. This was the first time in the history of America we had a attack like that. Every community lost. [We were] angry because [the attacks] gave a bad name to the entire Muslim community. How dare these people claim to be Muslim and do something like this, which has no place in any religion, especially Islam?[13]

Muslims and Pakistanis throughout the state worked in the aftermath of September 11, 2001 to mend the image of their communities and to help fellow Muslims struggling to deal with the ramifications of the U.S. "War on Terror." In Austin, for instance, Pakistani Texan Mosin Lari helped to form Muslim Community Social Services. Besides offering scholarships to Muslims, the organization helped war refugees seeking medical care in Austin.[14] Pakistani and Muslim Texans went out of their way to show their patriotism by displaying American flags at their homes and businesses.[15] Pakistani Texans typically did not fear terrorist sleeper cells or auxiliary organizations because they did not knowingly associate with terrorists or their supporters. Many Pakistani Texans, however, did fear the U.S. federal government because it had targeted some Pakistanis in Texas who were known to be upstanding residents. Pakistani Texans became extremely concerned about being deported, wrongly accused, or illegally detained by the government. Many Pakistani Texans who had questionable or illegal immigration statuses returned to Pakistan or sought sanctuary in Canada, from which they often returned to Pakistan anyway. The most disturbing post-September 11 actions taken against South Asians came in the form of violence.

Houston City Council member M.J. Khan poses in 2004 with young constituents.

Sri Lankan Austinites honored those who died in the 2004 Indian Ocean Tsunami.
Above the table is the flag of Sri Lanka, and on the table sit numerous lit candles.

Nationwide, government investigations and public suspicion caused a broad withdrawal of Pakistanis from public life. When, in 2003, M.J. Khan ran for and won the District F seat on the Houston City Council, it signaled a return of Pakistanis and Muslims to public life and a reinvigoration of the Pakistani Texan community. The fact that Khan was elected just two years after September 11 signified that Houstonians, and perhaps Texans, had accepted Pakistanis as Texans and Americans.

Bangladeshi Texans

by Melissa Masoom

The War for Liberation and Search for a Better Life

In 1966, the country now known as Bangladesh (then known as East Pakistan) took their first step towards independence. Bangabandhu Sheikh Mujibur Rahman, known as the "Father of the Nation," was urged by Bengalis in a time of political and economic deprivation to put forward the Magna Carta. The document contained Bangabandhu's historic six points and was the foundation for East Pakistan's future independence. In March of 1971, Bangabandhu held a meeting at the Ramna Race Course. Two million Bengalis showed up. The move towards rebellion prompted the Pakistani army to launch one of history's worst genocides. The war for liberation had begun.

By the end of the year, after the deaths of an estimated three million people, the new sovereign state of Bangladesh had been born. Yet the economy and political climate suffered. As a result, a number of Bangladeshis had already begun searching elsewhere for a better education and a better life. Middle-class Bangladeshis at the time could not afford to send their children to the United States for undergraduate university educations. Thus, the first individuals to migrate to the United States were mostly male graduate students on scholarship, as well as professionals such as engineers and doctors.

Starting around the late 1960s, a few hundred graduate students and professionals made their homes in New York, Texas, and California.

Mostly bachelors or husbands whose wives had remained in Bangladesh, these men assimilated into the American middle-class without drawing too much attention to themselves. For instance, they tended to avoid participating in the 1960s civil rights movements. It is important to note that these early Bangladeshis did not come as an immigrant group with collective goals, but rather as individuals with personal reasons for being in the United States.

Texas was the second most popular state for the settlement of Bangladeshis in the 1970s and early 1980s. The Bangladeshi immigrants at this time clustered around college towns and large cities such as Houston, Dallas-Fort Worth, and Austin. College Station, home of Texas A&M University, became a popular destination for Bangladeshis because the university provided many South Asian agriculture or engineering graduate students with scholarships and assistantships, allowing them to bring their wives and families to Texas after a short time.

The earliest Bangladeshi organizations were formed by students, and these organizations expanded as the students graduated and began their careers. These organizations were successful in helping the Bangladeshi freedom movement after 1971, as well as raising money for refugees of the war with Pakistan. These organizations also protested the Nixon administration's pro-Pakistani tilt and its ignoring of Pakistani war atrocities. Dr. S.S. Newaz, President of Polyorganix, Inc., in Houston, has been in Texas since 1969. For him, the early Bangladeshi Texans were extraordinary in their ability to organize and create a movement to benefit those they had left behind. He recalls his involvement in beginning one such organization:

> I was the president of Pakistan Student Association at the University of Houston in 1971—at the beginning of the Bangladesh movement. There were 3 members of Bangladesh origin like me, out of like 100 members. When the war broke out in East Pakistan, and the freedom was declared for independent Bangladesh, Pakistani members were outright hostile to the role of these three-four minority members. We consistently gave interviews on TV, newspapers and other media highlighting the plight of millions of suffering people and describing the atrocities of the Pakistani army. So many of the people we

The Bangladeshi Students Association of UT-Austin at a festival of student organizations in March 2007. In front are organization president Azrin Amin and her sister, Tasrin Amin. Behind the table are Natalie Hossain, Fahmida Ferdousi, and Mustafa Jamil.

knew personally were freedom fighters. It was not too long before I was stripped of my office of the Pakistan students' association.[16]

The Bangladeshi students formed a Bangladesh Students Association, but because the university required ten members for any given organization, Newaz recruited friends from India, Japan, and elsewhere to join. Newaz served as the president of the Bangladesh Students Association, even before Bangladesh became an independent nation. After some members of the association graduated, they formed the Bangladesh Association of Houston. Dewan Aftab Ahmed was the founding chairman. Most of the early Bangladeshi Texans subsisted rather comfortably as a result of their professions. Therefore, they had time to form small local organizations to promote the culture and traditions of Bangladesh, as well as a political agenda.

A Metamorphosis

According to Dr. Newaz, after the 1970s, the Bangladeshi Texan population went through an "astonishing metamorphosis." As the first immigrants became citizens, they were able to sponsor their family members and bring them back to Texas from Bangladesh to settle. Wives, children, and even parents flocked to Texas where their husbands, fathers, and children had already adjusted to American life.

Furthermore, the implementation of OP-1 and Diversity Visa (DV) programs changed the nature of Bangladeshi immigration. The new Bangladeshi immigrants and Bangladeshis from other states settled throughout Texas, including San Antonio, El Paso, and Laredo. A large number of these new immigrants fit into a lower income bracket than their predecessors because of their lack of education. Many of them opened up shops and restaurants. Others worked minimum wage jobs in fast-food restaurants and other businesses.

The family life of this new wave of Bangladeshi Texans consisted of upholding the culture as best they could in a new country, yet it was rather private and remained in their own homes. Quite a number of the wives from Bangladesh held college degrees of their own. Many women, like their husbands, held jobs in colleges and universities. Others, however, stayed home to be traditional housewives. All these women shared a common feeling of loneliness, for their husbands had already adjusted to this new land.

Like other South Asians and Muslims, Bangladeshis struggled with the post-September 11 backlash of violence and vandalism. But Bangladeshi Texans, like other Asians, have also dealt with anti-Asian and anti-immigrant discrimination. In 2004, a Bangladeshi family living in student housing at Texas A&M University complained several times to the university that there was a gas leak in their house; the university ignored them, and the subsequent gas explosion that summer killed a young Bangladeshi girl and her grandmother and critically injured two other members of the family.[17]

The children of Bangladeshi immigrants attended Texas public schools and usually excelled. As a result of successful South Asian students, the idea of the "model minority" included all Asians. These children faced the obstacles of balancing the differences between their traditional Bangladeshi parents and the American lifestyle they led outside their homes. However, the language of Bengali was not completely lost. This new generation of Bangladeshi-Americans in Texas spoke primarily Bengali with their parents.

The primary religion of Bangladeshi Texans was Islam. Throughout the years, as the number of Bangladeshis increased in Texas, they formed religious organizations. Bangladeshi Texans joined other Muslims, including Pakistanis, in building and worshipping at local mosques. The 2000 Census counted 2,620 Bangladeshis in Texas.

Sri Lankan Texans

by Dr. Harishini Ernest

Overview and Early History

Sri Lanka is a small island-nation lying off the southern tip of India. Sri Lanka's two main ethnic groups are the Sinhalese, most of whom are Buddhist, and the Tamils, most of whom are Hindu. Other groups are the Muslims, the Burgers (most of whom are Christian), and the indigenous

Veddas.[18] Five hundred thirty-one Texans identified themselves as Sri Lankan in 1990, compared to 1,195 in 2000, representing a 100% increase in ten years. The 2000 U.S. Census counted the largest numbers of Sri Lankans in the cities of Houston (200), Austin (133), Plano (73), Dallas (47), Arlington (40), Fort Worth (32), Irving (31), Richardson (23), and Garland (12). When informally polled, Sri Lankan elders estimated about 250 Sri Lankans in the Austin area, indicating a Census undercount.

The majority of Sri Lankan immigrants to the United States came after the 1965 immigration reform. The first wave of these Sri Lankan immigrants settled in California. The next wave went to New York, Illinois, Texas, and New Jersey. Many of the Sri Lankans interviewed for this chapter spent time in Minnesota prior to coming to Texas. Between 1965 and 1975, most Sri Lankan immigrants were graduate students and professionals, many of whom descended from socio-academic elites in Sri Lanka. To this day, Sri Lankan Americans tend to work in technical fields such as engineering, web development, and medicine. A large portion work in education: early childhood, public K-12, and tertiary education.

Irangani Weerasuria was the first Sri Lankan in Texas. She arrived in Austin in August 1965 "when Austin was a little country town." She came to Austin because a UT professor and a priest wrote to the Sri Lanka Training Center in Colombo, requesting a teacher to demonstrate the Montessori method. Weerasuria was granted an American SOS visa (as-soon-as-possible visa) in three days and came alone, leaving her husband and son in Sri Lanka. Weerasuria's impression of Austin in 1965 was that there were ranches everywhere and that Texans were wonderful people. The UT professor and the priest got permission to use a wing of St. Peter's Apostle Church to house the Montessori School. She started with a few professors' children. With limited funding, Weerasuria made, or bought with her own money, much of the Montessori equipment. A few years later, she opened in Austin the International Montessori House of Children, which she ran until 1989. Being the only Sri Lankan in Austin, Irangani Weerasuria was considered a novelty. People were struck by the saris she wore, and some even thought that Montessori was a cult. She appeared on the local Cactus Pryor and the Buelah Hodge television shows and eventually ran four Montessori schools.[19]

The second Sri Lankan Texan, Amitha Chandrasoma, came to Austin in 1975 and opened three Montessori schools. Chandrasoma first immigrated in the mid-1960s on an invitation to promote Montessori education in Minnesota. She sponsored many of her relatives to work in her schools and recruited as many as twenty Sri Lankan teachers. Dilum, her son, estimated that she sponsored 100 to 200 people over the course of twenty years.[20] Dilum noted that his deceased mother was community-conscious and helped her relatives find homes, finance a family car, and find jobs. The relatives sponsored their spouses and children. Other Sri Lankan Montessori pioneers in Texas, both being women, were Shireen de Silva and Antoinette Gomez. The Sri Lankan pioneers either started their own Montessori school(s) or took over ownership of a school from another Sri Lankan. Weerasuriya and Chandrasoma encouraged and trained other Sri Lankan women in the Montessori method. The number of Sri Lankan-run Montessori schools in Austin rose to seven in the 1990s before falling to five by 2005. Sri Lankan Austinites are still largely concentrated in Montessori education.

After the escalation of ethnic violence against Tamils in Sri Lanka in 1971, many Sri Lankan Tamil refugees migrated directly to the United States, while others migrated to the U.S. through Europe, Africa, or Australia. Also, after the 1983 anti-Tamil riots, more than 800,000 Tamils fled to India, Europe, Canada, and the United States. Such migrations increased the numbers of Sri Lankans in Texas.

The Sri Lankan Community in Houston and Other Cities

Houston has a large community of Sri Lankans. They belong predominantly to two associations, split along ethnic lines. The Ilankai Tamil Sangam of Texas (ITST) is composed mainly of Tamils and Hindus and was formed in the late 1980s and early 1990s. The Sri Lankan Association of Houston (SLAH) is mainly composed of Sinhalese and Buddhists. Both organizations do a great deal of community work with goals to maintain culture and roots.

The Ilankai Tamil Sangam of Texas holds events celebrating Pongal, New Year, Deepavali, Christmas, and in July, members go to Dallas for the Metroplex Tamil Sangam's cultural event. The ITST also raises funds for the non-profit Manithaneyam and for Tamil refugees in Sri Lanka and the United States. Since the members are mainly Hindu, the organization celebrates the Hindu festivals even though the current (2005) ITST president is a Tamil Christian. Likewise, The Sri Lankan Association of Houston has organized variety shows and a fundraiser for Lak Daruwo (a children's organization in Sri Lanka), in addition to cultural events. Some of the members of the SLAH were instrumental in forming the Buddhist Vihara in Houston.

Artist Nelum Walpola and her husband have lived in the Dallas area for three years. They note that although about 250 families live in the area, there is no formal Sri Lankan organization there. Further, the Sinhala and Tamil community do not interact frequently. Buddhists worship at the Thai or Vietnamese Buddhist temples while Hindus attend Irving's Hindu temple.[21]

Sri Lankan Religious Practices in Texas

While in Sri Lanka, the religious breakdown is Buddhist (70%), Hindu (15%), Christian (8%) and Muslim (7%), the proportions are likely different in Texas. There are five Buddhist centers in Austin, five in Houston, five in Dallas, six in Irving, and two in San Antonio. However, only one of Austin's temples is Theravada Buddhist and only two of Houston's are. The rest are meditation centers and/or study groups for those who follow Zen, Zen-Soto, Shambala, or Mahayan Buddhism. The two main temples at which Sri Lankan Buddhists worship are The Houston Buddhist Vihara and The Austin Sitagu Buddhist Vihara. The Houston Vihara (the vihara is a Sinhala Buddhist temple) was built in 1988 using donations largely from local Sri Lankan Buddhists. Bhante Pannila Ananda is the founding President and Abbot of Houston's Vihara. In Sri Lanka, he is the Sangha Chief, or Nayaka Thera, of the Attanagalla Rajamaha Vihara, which carries on the Theravada Buddhist traditions in Southeast Asia. The Sitagu Buddhist Vihara in Austin was founded in 1996 by the Venerable Ashin Nyanissara, Sitagu Sayadaw of Burma. Both the Houston and Austin viharas host several monks. The Austin vihara is shared with local Burmese Buddhists.

Sri Lankans of the Hindu faith in Texas sometimes conduct pujas or bhajans in their homes. Some hold prasad services in halls rented from universities. In Houston, many worship at the Sri Meenaskhi Temple.

Others go to the Hindu Temple of San Antonio, the Omkranath Temple at College Station, the Hindu Temple at Temple, and the DFW Hindu Temple. Generally, Hindu Tamil Lankans do not frequent North Indian Hindu temples or those geared for non-Asians.[22]

Christian Sri Lankans, the majority of whom are Catholic, worship at local parish churches, and the handful of Muslim families worships at local mosques. For the few Sri Lankan families who follow Sai Baba,[23] Austin's Sathya Sai Baba Center serves as a locus. Sai's believe in all religions, do not discriminate, and are committed to selfless humanitarian service.

September 11, 2001 and December 26, 2004

In 2003, Faz'le Yousuf, then president of the Houston South Asian Chamber of Commerce, was among six area leaders who met with Sri Lankan attorney, George Willy, to discuss the impact of the war on terrorism on businesses owned by South Asians and other immigrant entrepreneurs. "Even though our community had nothing to do with it, we felt as though we had to defend ourselves" said one Sri Lankan interviewee. When Plano artist, Nelum Walpola, immigrated to the U.S. in 1986, she thought she had left behind terrorist attacks. The horror of September 11, 2001 impelled her to paint "Freedom will Prevail," a water color painting showing the Twin Towers in flames with the American flag flying proudly on one tower.[24]

On December 26, 2004, Sri Lankan Texans were horrified to see on television a massive tsunami crashing upon Sri Lanka and other Asian nations, killing hundreds of thousands. Those Texas ethnic groups most affected—Sri Lankans, Indonesians, Indians, Thais, Cambodians, and others—flew into action within hours, raising relief funds at temples, organizations, universities, and businesses. In Houston, the Buddhist SLAH organization and Hindu Sri Lankans raised significant funds for tsunami relief and long-term development in tsunami-ravaged areas. A January 2005 fundraiser luncheon raised over $25,000, and in March 2005 Sri Lankan Houstonians, students included, organized "The Run for Tsunami Relief."[25] A Dallas memorial service honored volunteers who did tsunami relief work in Asia. Devastated emotionally, some Sri

Lankans held candlelight vigils. The tragedy brought together the Sri Lankan Texan community, Hindus and Buddhists alike.

Nepalese Texans[26]

by Irwin A. Tang

Kamal Adhikary was born in 1944 in the town of Tansen, Nepal. His father was an educated property manager and a farmer, and his mother was a housewife. Adhikary earned a degree in English from the top Nepalese university, Tribhuvan University in Katmandu. English being a difficult major, those with English degrees obtained jobs easily. After teaching at Tribhuvan University, studying in England, and working in the nation of Yemen, Adhikary eventually made his way in 1982 to the University of Texas at Austin to study English education. Upon arrival, there were only three Nepalese in Austin, but more in Houston, and even more in Dallas. By 2004, according to Adhikary, about 1,000 Nepalese Texans lived in Dallas, 200 to 250 in Houston, about 125 in Austin, about 30 in San Antonio, and a few students at each of the Texas A&M universities. Although there are thirty-six different ethnic groups among the Nepalese people, they can roughly be divided into two groups—those of Sino-Tibetan descent and those of Indian descent—each of approximately equal population in Texas.

Between 1960 and 1990, most Nepalese who migrated to Texas originally came to the U.S. as graduate students, earning degrees in computer science and engineering. By the 1990s, more Nepalese became familiar with the diversity visa lotteries held by the U.S. government, and many more Nepalese workers began immigrating. The 1990s to the early 2000s represented the heaviest period of Nepalese immigration to Texas. According to Adhikary, Nepalese Texans tend not to open small businesses and do tend to work in government jobs. One of the most accomplished Nepalese Texans is Rajendra Bhattarai, City of Austin wastewater regulatory manager.

Like other immigrants, early Nepalese immigrants spread news of their lives in Texas, and later immigrants often settled where earlier ones had established themselves. Among Texas cities, Dallas became by far the most popular destination. The city had an international airport, at least two major universities, and it was also home to a major flying school. Some Nepalese went to Dallas to learn to fly planes in their mountainous home country, but after news of the school spread, some Nepalese began attending the school to find employment in the U.S. and earn permanent residency status.

The Maoist insurgency in Nepal played a role in motivating Nepalese to immigrate to the United States, as some young men have been pressured by the rebels to join their military group. Another major event in Nepal, the 2001 murder of members of the Nepalese royal family, had little effect on the lives of Nepalese Texans.

Transported to Texas, Nepalese culture transformed. In part because the population of Nepalese Texans was so small (less than 2,000), Nepalese Texans allowed caste differences in large part to dissipate. Nevertheless, caste differences continued to influence marriage and courtship choices, even as marriage to a white Texan likely did not provoke family conflict. Nepalese tend to be Hindu and Buddhist, with the line between the two religions often blurred. In Texas, the Nepalese attend Indian Hindu Temples and Asian Buddhist Temples for prayer, worship, and important life events such as marriage. Nepalese Texans do not strongly distinguish themselves from each other by religion.

Having a rather quiet history in Texas, the biggest events for the Nepalese Texans have been the annual Dashain celebrations held wherever Nepalese live. During this fifteen-day Hindu celebration, Nepalese "go home," and every home is open to all. Guests are fed special foods, all enmity is forgotten, and relationships are sometimes mended during this time. Adhikary remembers how in the early days, Nepalese Austinites gathered at a home for Dashain, but by 2004, the important 10th day of Dashain was held at a community hall.

A great concern among Nepalese Texan immigrants is the maintenance of their culture and language. Because there are so few Nepalese Texans, few opportunities to speak Nepalese exist outside the home, and while Nepalese youth can learn Sanskrit at Indian Texan language schools, Sanskrit is similar but not identical to Nepalese. Helping to maintain the Nepalese language in Texas, Dr. Adhikary, while earning his doctorate in anthropology, taught Nepalese at the UT-Austin Center for Asian Studies from 1986 to 1993.

Tibetan Texans[27]

by Irwin A. Tang

Of the estimated forty-six Tibetan Texans in 2004, forty-four of them lived in Austin, Texas. About eight of the Tibetan Texans were born in Nepal, and the rest were born in India and Tibet. Outside of one American-born child, the rest of the Austinites immigrated to Texas from India and Nepal.

In 1959, the People's Republic of China's military invasion and bombing of Tibet caused a mass exodus of Tibetans to India and Nepal. Lobsang Tenzin was just one year old when he and his parents fled from Tibet to avoid both the violence and life under Communist Chinese rule. The Indian government set up villages for the Tibetan refugees, and Lobsang's family farmed a small plot of land in the southern Indian province of Karnataka; Lobsang's father also sold sweaters. In third grade, Lobsang moved to the Indian city of Bangalore to study at St. John's Catholic School. At seventeen, he returned to his family's land and worked on the farm. After arguing with his family about it, he joined in 1975 an Indian military regiment known as Establishment 22 (officially known as Special Frontier Forces), which consisted of Tibetan soldiers. The group was originally formed by the Indian government with help from the United States CIA in order to battle the People's Republic of China during the Sino-Indian War of 1962, but the force was used instead in the Indian-Pakistani war over East Pakistan in 1971. Lobsang never saw combat, and Establishment 22 never attempted to liberate Tibet from China.

In 1978, Lobsang fell in love with Tsetan Chodon, and a year later the couple (never formally married) gave birth to daughter Dickey Dolker and then in 1980 to son Namgyal Tsultsin. Lobsang quit Establishment 22 in 1983. In the early 1990s, the Dalai Lama and the United States organized a "green card" lottery to allow 1,000 Tibetan heads of families to immigrate to the United States. Paying a twenty-five rupee application fee, Lobsang won a green card.

Meanwhile in the United States, the government had agreed to resettle Tibetans in U.S. cities only if there was no cost to U.S. taxpayers. An Austin Tibetan resettlement organization applied to help, but it was informed that other cities—including New York City; Boulder, Colorado; and Minneapolis—could support the 1,000 Tibetans without Austin's participation. Weeks later, the 200-volunteer strong Austin organization was informed, according to Dick Patton (the Austin resettlement program's ESL director), that twelve "lower-income" Tibetans needed to be settled in Austin because the other cities were reluctant to accept them.

The twelve Tibetan heads of families arrived in Austin throughout 1993, and they immediately began learning from the Austin Tibetan Resettlement Project the basics of American living, including driving and the English language. The Tibetans found jobs in the growing Austin economy of the 1990s. They worked at service-industry jobs, especially selling carpet (because of retailer Floor King's employment of Tibetans). In later years, the heads of the Tibetan families were allowed to bring their families to the United States, and in 1999, Lobsang was re-united with his wife and two children.

Life in India and Nepal tended to be slower and more self-paced than the "crazy" and "busy" life in Texas, where work supervisors dictated schedules. Lobsang stated that he reminds himself that he is in the U.S. to allow his children better educational and employment opportunities. Tibetan refugees were not granted citizenship status in India. His daughter, Dickey Dolker (Tibetans do not employ surnames and each name is given by the parents or the Dalai Lama), now works as a medication assistant at a nursing home.

Austin is the smallest resettlement community of Tibetans in the nation, and although many Austinites were interested in Tibet and Tibetan culture, there is no Tibetan Buddhist temple in Austin. Instead, families worship at home, at their own altars to the Dalai Lama. On some Saturdays, families gather to pray for the Dalai Lama and for "all sentient beings." While Tibetan Texan parents are trying their best to pass on the Tibetan culture, younger children often speak little Tibetan. Generations raised in India and Nepal speak Hindi and Nepalese and remember those countries as their original homes. Lobsang, for instance, wishes he "had three houses, one in Tibet, one in India, and one in the United States."

Tibetan Texans are united by their desire for a Tibetan nation independent of China. Every March 10, Tibetan Austinites, along with some university students, protest for Tibetan independence at Houston's Chinese Consulate. A number of Tibetans also protested in Crawford, Texas when Chinese President Jiang Zemin visited President George W. Bush's ranch there. Meanwhile, Tibetan Texan children carve out their own identities in Texas.

ENDNOTES

1   U.S. Census 2000; M.J. Khan, interview by Irwin Tang, 2005.

2   Khan, interview.

3   Qureshi, Rashid, interview by Irwin Tang, Austin, 2005.

4   Khan, interview; Qureshi, interview.

5   Khan, interview.

6   Larry Pressler, "The Restraint of Fury: US Non-Proliferation Policy and South Asia," *http://www.fas.org/news/pakistan/1994/940705.htm* accessed on Nov 7, 2005; Khan, interview.

7   Steve Friedman, "Islamic leaders meet with mayor, police chief on security measures," *Houston Chronicle*, Jun 25, 1985; Friedman, "Investigators probe mosque explosion," Jun 24, 1985; Eric Hanson, "2 arrested in bombing of mosque," *Houston Chronicle*, Jun 29, 1985; "Houstonian sentenced for bombing mosque," *Houston Chronicle*, Oct 26, 1985.

8   Khan, interview.

9   John Williams, "Vandals attack local mosque, teacher's car," *Houston Chronicle*, Jan 26, 1989; Williams, "Local mosque hit four times by vandalism," Jan 26, 1989; "Vandals mar dream of Mosque," *Dallas Morning News*, Jan 27, 1989.

10 Khan, interview.

11 Ibid.

12 Ibid.

13 Ibid.

14 Qureshi, interview.

15 Nadia Ali, conversations with Irwin Tang, Austin, 2004.

16 S.S. Newaz, interview by Melissa Massoom, 2005.

17 Allan Turner, "A&M workers' inaction a key factor in fire," *Houston Chronicle*, Jan 28, 2005.

18 Harishini Ernest, "Language Planning in Sri Lanka," (unpublished Master's thesis, University of Texas: Austin, TX: May 1984); Sri Lanka Virtual Library, *www.lanka-library.com*, accessed 2005; The World Factbook, *http://www.cia.gov/cia/publications/factbook/geos/ce.html*, accessed 2005.

19 Irangani Weerasuria, interview by Harishini Ernest, 2005.

20 Interview with son, Dilum Chandrasoma and daughter-in-law, Surangi Wijaratne Chandrasoma, January 2005.

21 Nelum Walpola, who lived many years in Plano, interview by author, Feb 2005.

22 A List of Hindu Temples in USA and Canada, *http://www.geocities.com/Athens/5180/temple1.html*, accessed 2005.

23 Sathya Sai Baba Center of Austin, *www.sairegion10.org/texassaimeeting.html*, accessed 2005.

24 *The Houston Chronicle*, "Group Aims to give a Link to South Asia: Global Trade is the Main Focus of Local Chamber," *http://www.sarid.net/archives/2005-february/050216-south-asia-chamber.htm*, accessed Feb 16, 2005; Lei Zhang, "Plano artist paints tribute to Sept. 11 victims," *Plano Star Courier* Nov 7, 2001, *http://www.paintingsbynelum.com/inthenews.htm*.

25 Rachel Graves, "Sri Lankans plan tsunami aid event, Lunch is one of many fundraisers being organized by Houstonians," *Houston Chronicle*, Jan 22, 2005; Edward Hegstrom and Jason Spencer, "Asians in Houston anxiously await word. Groups working to raise relief funds for victims," *Houston Chronicle*, Dec 28, 2004.

26 This entire section is based on an interview with Kamal Adhikary conducted in Austin, Texas, Oct 14, 2004.

27 This history is based on interviews with Lobsang Tenzin, Dickey Dolker, Dakpa Tisang, and Dick Patton, by Irwin Tang, Oct 8, 2004, Austin, Texas. Quotes come from those interviews.

━━━━━━━━━━━ ★ ━━━━━━━━━━━

CHAPTER FIFTEEN

THE INDONESIAN TEXANS, MALAYSIAN TEXANS, SINGAPOREAN TEXANS, AND PACIFIC ISLANDER TEXANS

Irwin A. Tang and Keng-Loong Yap

The Indonesian Texans[1]

by Irwin Tang

The earliest large group of Indonesians to live in Texas was a group of more than 300 Indonesian sailors removed from a Dutch ship in New York City during the final year of World War II. The sailors were taken by the U.S. government to Crystal City Internment Camp where Japanese from throughout the Western Hemisphere had been imprisoned. The Indonesians were interned at Crystal City for "protective custody" until the end of the war, according to a Japanese internee, Edison Uno, who recalled the Indonesian men:

> Only a few could speak sufficient English so the sailors designated a spokesman for the group in any negotiations with camp authorities or other internees.

> These sailors were not allowed to mingle with other groups in the camp. Yet, due to their Muslim religion, diet and their cultural differences, they were quite content to be left alone. Their imprisonment

was a solitary one. They had very little recreation or work to keep them occupied. Their only pleasure seemed to be watching American movies, which they could not understand; however they always enjoyed the westerns and as I recall, became quite boisterous over typical Hollywood love scenes.[2]

It is unclear if any of these Indonesian sailors stayed in the United States beyond World War II; the federal government likely forced them to return to Indonesia. Their stays, then, were relatively short, much like the work and education stints of many Indonesians, until 1965.

The children of wealthy and educated Indonesians often received their college and postgraduate educations in the Netherlands and the United States, including Texas. Some of the native Indonesian students in the 1960s and 1970s were sponsored by the Ford Foundation, which sought better relations with the Indonesian government. Indonesian employees of U.S. oil companies drilling in and around Indonesia often made their way to work in Houston and Dallas. A major portion of them were geologists.

Among the students and professionals in Texas, the native Indonesians tended to return to Indonesia, while the Chinese Indonesians tended to stay in Texas. Although Chinese Indonesians made up only about three percent of the population in Indonesia, they made up a majority of the permanent Indonesian Texan population. Native Indonesians made up the second largest group, and a small number of Dutch and Indian Indonesians also lived in Texas. The total number of Indonesian Texan long-term residents in 2004 may have been as high as five to ten thousand, even though the 2000 U.S. Census counted only 2,861 (more than 20% of whom considered themselves biracial). Almost all of the Chinese Indonesian Texans are Christian, Buddhist, or non-religious, and almost all native Indonesian Texans are Muslim. The vast majority of Indonesian Texans are college educated. And although the Chinese in Indonesia control much of that nation's commerce, the Chinese Indonesian Texans have largely avoided opening businesses and have instead worked almost entirely as professionals.

Houston is home to the largest number of Indonesian Texans and Indonesian visiting workers in Texas. Houston has attracted Indonesians because of its professional opportunities in oil, energy, computer technology, and engineering. Also attracting Indonesians to Houston was the establishment in 1980 of an Indonesian Consular Office. The consular office today serves as a center of community activity for local Indonesians, and the expansive compound includes a museum, a library, and a mosque. Among about 400 native Indonesian Texans, about 300 of them live in Houston, according to the consulate.

In addition to professional native Indonesians, there are native women who have married non-Indonesian American men and settled in Texas after marriage. Some of these women married Muslims, such as Pakistanis, and others married non-Muslims, such as whites. There is also a substantial number of native Indonesian male sailors who "jumped ship" from international vessels and became illegal immigrants in Texas until they married American women who had citizenship.

While most native Indonesian Muslims worship at the consulate, Chinese Indonesian Christians worship at both non-Indonesian Christian churches and the four Indonesian Chinese churches in Texas, including Houston's First Baptist Indonesian Church, established in 1985. On a typical Sunday, less than 100 Chinese Indonesians attend each of these churches, including the Indonesian Catholic Community Church.

Born in 1931 in Batavia (Jakarta), Indonesia, William Kwie was one of the first Indonesians to settle permanently in Texas. His parents, both Chinese, immigrated to Indonesia, and in 1950, upon the transfer of governance from the Netherlands to an independent Indonesian government, Kwie chose to become an Indonesian citizen, even as other Chinese decided to become Dutch citizens, or moved to the People's Republic of China and the Republic of China. Some refused Indonesian citizenship and did not obtain any other citizenship; they became stateless people carrying red passports.

In 1955, Kwie earned a master's degree in chemical engineering from the Technical Institute of Bandung. After receiving a scholarship from an unnamed American source, Kwie in 1958 earned a Ph.D. in chemistry from UT-Austin. In the 1950s, Kwie found in Texas one native Indonesian international student and one native Indonesian woman married to a non-Indonesian American in central Texas. Upon returning to Indonesia, Kwie found that his nation was at war with the Netherlands over possession of New Guinea; declining to fight for this purpose, Kwie returned to North America to work for chemical and pharmaceutical companies, as well as for the state of Texas. He worked in Austin, Mexico City, South Carolina, and Oklahoma.

Upon moving from Austin to Houston in 1976, Kwie found a permanent Indonesian community of less than fifty people. In 1977, the Houston Indonesian Club (formed in 1974), had about thirty regular members. In the 1980s, the Indonesian community expanded tremendously due to immigration through family reunification provisions. With three children who had been educated and found work in the United States, S.T. "Sean" Tjia moved to Houston in 1977 to retire and reunite with son Albert Shea (a different spelling of Tjia), who had recently graduated from the University of Houston. In Houston, S.T. Tjia worked in the information division of the Taipei Economic and Cultural office in Houston (formerly the consular office of the Republic of China).

Indonesian Americans were required to register with the government after the attacks of September 11, 2001. Eddy Poerwana of the Indonesian Consulate in Houston said that the community felt "stabbed in the back," especially considering that Malaysian Americans (also a largely Muslim community) were not asked to register; in 2004, the consulate did, however, appreciate the added security resulting from two Houston police showing up at every Consulate event since September 11, 2001.

Although the Chinese Indonesian Texans were motivated to immigrate to the United States because of anti-Chinese violence, persecution, and legislation in Indonesia, the Chinese and the native Indonesians of Texas get along "harmoniously." This is due in part to their small size as a community, intermarriage of native Indonesians with non-Indonesian Americans, and the willingness to keep political differences from preventing friendships.

The Malaysian Texans and The Singaporean Texans

by Keng-Loong Yap

The Malaysian immigrants to Texas are mostly descendants of Chinese and Indian coolies who first made their way to Malaysia (then known as Malaya) in the late 19th century during British colonial rule. These Malaysians immigrated to the U.S. to escape the institutionalized discrimination against ethnic Chinese and ethnic Indians in Malaysia. The discriminatory system of employment and education was codified into the Malaysian constitution following a deadly ethnic riot in 1969 between the indigenous Malays on one side and the ethnic Chinese and ethnic Indian Malaysians on the other side. The roots of the enduring ethnic antagonism between the indigenous Malays and the non-Malays lie in the ethnic division of labor established by British colonial rulers, as well as cultural differences between the Malays, who must observe the Islamic faith by law, and the Chinese and Indians, who are predominantly Buddhists, Hindus, and Christians.

The earliest settlement of Malaysians in Texas occurred in the early 1960s, shortly after the British granted independence to Malaysia in 1957. These early immigrants were a small group of middle-class professionals who originally worked at Shell Oil operations in Malaysia and who were subsequently transferred to Shell operations in Houston. They were part of a larger group of British-educated Chinese- and Indian-Malaysians who had decided to leave Malaysia for the U.K., the U.S., and elsewhere soon after Malaysian independence. These Chinese and Indians felt disenfranchised with the Malaysian constitution because it did not provide equal citizenship rights and status to Chinese and Indians.[3]

The largest wave of Malaysian immigration to Texas occurred in the 1990s at the height of Texas's booming information technology (I.T.) economy. Surging employment opportunities brought scores of I.T. professionals from Malaysia to work in the I.T. sectors in Dallas, Houston, and Austin. Most of these I.T. workers worked for American I.T. companies in Malaysia, namely Motorola, Intel, and Texas Instruments, before being transferred to the companies' U.S. operations in Dallas, Houston, and Austin. Besides those who came to Texas via job transfers, many

Malaysians settled in Texas after completing their college education in the United States. Many of them chose to settle down in Texas owing to its growing I.T. sector.[4]

While Malaysian Texans are highly concentrated in the I.T. sector, there is a great deal of diversity within the small Malaysian community. Among sixteen Malaysian Texans interviewed between 2002 and 2005, there were also accountants, florists, realtors, business executives, medical technicians, consultants, entrepreneurs, and church pastors. And while most of them have settled in the major cities of Dallas, Houston, and Austin, there were Malaysians living in Brownwood in central Texas, as well as in the border city of Laredo. And while the vast majority of Malaysian Texans are of Chinese and Indian descent, there is in Texas a minority of Malaysian Texans of ethnic Malay descent.[5]

Most Malaysian Texans share a common pursuit of the American dream's promise of freedom of expression, freedom of religion, and equal rights. They were drawn to America for its democratic ideals and its system of meritocracy. For Mr. Thomas Tan, an engineer who lives in Austin, America is where he can "secure a bright future for his children" because America symbolizes a place of boundless potential where anyone "can have a decent living if he or she works hard for it." And for Jimmy Khoo, a computer consultant who lives in Dallas, America "symbolizes all that Malaysia is not," because America discriminates not on the basis of race but rather on the merits of one's performance.[6]

While the majority of the interview respondents contend that minorities in the U.S. do not yet have equal rights and status, they consider America to be much more equal compared to Malaysia, and "is a close second to heaven," according to Amy Lee, a business executive who lives in Dallas.[7]

Much like the Malaysians, most of the Singaporean immigrants are descendants of Chinese laborers who came to Singapore in the late 19th century during the British colonial period. Unlike their Malaysian counterparts, the Chinese-Singaporeans are the majority ethnic group in Singapore and, hence, were not motivated to leave Singapore due to anti-Chinese discrimination. Rather, most of them have immigrated to the U.S. and elsewhere because they feel stifled by the authoritarian regime that has ruled Singapore with an iron-clad authority for over forty years, ever since Singapore gained its independence from the British in 1959.[8]

The earliest immigrants to Texas were mostly middle-class, British-educated professionals who had previously worked at multinational energy companies based in Singapore. They had come to the U.S. in the mid-1970s and settled in Texas to work in the booming energy industry in Houston. Nevertheless, few Singaporeans joined the millions of Asians immigrating in subsequent decades, and the Singaporeans remain one of the smallest ethnic groups among Asian Americans nationally and in Texas. Demographically, they tend to be middle-class, Christian, English-educated professionals, and they are mostly concentrated in the major metropolitan cities of Dallas, Houston, and Austin. Among the seven Singaporean Texans interviewed between 2002 and 2005, there were business executives, consultants, academicians, classical pianists, as well as two individuals who married Americans and subsequently immigrated to the U.S.[9]

Most left Singapore because they felt disheartened with the lack of basic citizen's rights there, and they opted to come to the U.S. because they believed in the American democratic ideal that espouses freedom of expression, assembly, and religion. Jessica Chan of Austin explained that, although "America isn't the most democratic place," she can express her political views freely here. Singapore's paternalistic laws governing daily life tend to repress free speech. On the other hand, most of the respondents still hold Singapore dearly in their hearts and visit Singapore regularly. In fact, Rachel Chia of Houston, a former business executive, considers the violent crime in the U.S. appalling and still prefers the orderly society of Singapore. Rachel thinks of herself as an "accidental immigrant," who would not have settled down here if she had not married a Texan whom she met during a flight stopover in the U.S. en route to Singapore following a business conference in the U.S. While most Singaporean Texans came to the U.S. for greater civil liberties, Allison Chew of Houston, a former business executive and now a socialite, cited age discrimination in the workplace as her primary reason for leaving Singapore. She said that the she felt "compelled" to leave her job several years ago, after she was passed over for numerous promotions. She chose to immigrate to the U.S. because she felt that, "America does not discriminate based on age but the merits of your work performance."[10]

The Hawaiian Texans, The Tongan Texans, and Other Pacific Islander Texans

by Irwin A. Tang

Texas is home to the largest native Hawaiian population east of the Rocky Mountains, and it ranks fourth among all states outside of Hawaii. According to the 2000 U.S. Census, 7,750 Texans claimed to be of native Hawaiian descent. This number does not include those whose ancestors lived in Hawaii but who possessed no *indigenous* Hawaiian blood. Among Hawaiian Texans, the largest ethnic grouping is comprised of those with native Hawaiian blood mixed with Asian and/or white blood. Because so few "pure" Hawaiians exist anywhere in the world, there was not in 2004 a single Hawaiian Texan of *only* native Hawaiian ancestry.[11]

The first Hawaiians to come to Texas were associated with the U.S. military. Louis Andrew Keau'luhiole McCabe was born in Koolaupoko of Oahu Island in Hawaii on November 8, 1929. His father worked as a civilian rigger at the U.S. naval base at Pearl Harbor. During the Japanese attack on Pearl Harbor on December 7, 1941, McCabe's father, maternal uncle, and two maternal cousins were killed. Civilian workers were called to work at the base as it was besieged by Japanese warplanes. Following in the footsteps of two older brothers who had served in World War II, McCabe joined the military in 1948. Young native Hawaiian men often joined the military to "get off the rock" (leave the islands); the economy and society were racially stratified, with whites at the top, Asians in the middle, and native Hawaiians "at the bottom of the totem," as McCabe put it.

After basic training, McCabe was stationed at Fort Hood in Killeen, Texas, where he ran into a handful of Hawaiians, all in the military. Spending most of the 1950s stationed elsewhere, McCabe was stationed at San Antonio's Fort Sam Houston from 1960 to 1962. There were less than one hundred Hawaiians in San Antonio, consisting almost entirely of single military men; there were few married military men or Hawaiian women who had married Texan soldiers stationed in Hawaii. McCabe's home served as a gathering place for Hawaiians seeking to congregate with other Hawaiians, eat Hawaiian food, eat rice, play Hawaiian music, and dance Hawaiian hula dances.

After serving in Brownwood, Texas (where there were no Hawaiians) and serving two tours in the Vietnam War, McCabe returned to San Antonio in 1976 to discover that about fifty or seventy-five Hawaiian families had settled permanently in San Antonio, making it the largest Hawaiian community in Texas. Most were retired military men and their families, and some were currently involved with the military. The state's first Hawaii Club was formed in 1974 in San Antonio in order to maintain Hawaiian culture, socialize, and "be good ambassadors for the state of Hawaii." Hawaiian communities also developed around military bases in Killeen, El Paso, Corpus Christi, and Wichita Falls, as well as the large cities of Houston and Dallas-Fort Worth. As a result of the Vietnam War, many Hawaiians joined the U.S. military. Many of those servicemen were stationed in Texas, and some settled there. According to McCabe, the 1970s saw the heaviest migration from Hawaii to Texas.

Word of mouth spread the news that Texas was a good place to retire because of the low cost of living, especially compared to Hawaii, and the benefits of living near military hospitals. Many of the retired military personnel found jobs with the federal government in Texas, making the government one of the top employers of Hawaiian Texans. Furthermore, public education in Texas, considered below average among the "lower 48" states, was seen as far better than the public education in Hawaii. Economic opportunities in Texas were considered better than those in Hawaii. Many Hawaiians, Samoans, Tongans, and others from Pacific Islands found jobs at the American Airlines hub in Dallas-Fort Worth, while some engineers of Hawaiian descent found jobs at NASA near Houston.

Hawaiians anywhere outside of Hawaii tend to find each other and form collective *ohana*, or family. Attempting to re-create and pass on Hawaiian culture to their children, Hawaiian Texans formed cultural and hula dance organizations. Many of these organizations performed their dances for ethnic and mainstream community gatherings like the Texas Folklife Festival of San Antonio. Some, like Na Pua O Hawaii, formed by McCabe in 1978, performed for free (for nursing homes), before becoming commercial ventures. In many ways, it is through Hawaiian music and dance that Hawaiian Texans have most affected Texas.

In 1994, a Hawaiian man named Frank Keli'i Chang (III) settled in Euless among the Pacific Islander community there. Chang was of Hawaiian, Chinese, Samoan, Tongan, and Spanish descent, and he was a teacher of Hawaiian, Tongan, Samoan, and Maori chants and dances. This *kumu hula*, or teacher of the hula, "changed our lives," according to McCabe. The history of Hawaii and its people is told through chants and hula dances. Chang invigorated the practice of Hawaiian culture in Texas by founding a nonprofit school for Pacific Islander culture in Dallas in 1994 and then two other schools in San Antonio and Houston in 1998. In 2000 and 2001, a Texas hula dance group taught by the school was the first so far east to be invited twice to the Merry Monarch Hula Festival in Hawaii, the most prestigious Hula competition in the world.

Tongan and Samoan Texans

By 2004, the Tongan American community centered around Euless, Texas had grown to 4,000 or more, making the Hurst-Euless-Bedford area between Dallas and Fort Worth the sixth largest Tongan American community in the nation. Tongans first arrived in the Euless area in the 1970s, and perhaps as early as the 1960s, to work as missionaries for the Church of Jesus Christ of Latter-Day Saints. While some Tongans came to the area on work visas sponsored by the church, others came on visitors' visas and overstayed.[12]

By the early 1980s, there were about thirty or so Tongans living in the Euless area. They formed a church known in the Tongan language as "Tongan United Church." In English, the Church was known as "First Tongan United Methodist Church" even though Mormon, Protestant, and Catholic Tongans all met at the church. "It didn't matter what faith you belonged to, they all went to this one church," noted Ilaiasi Ofa, a local Tongan community organizer. The church allowed Tongans to worship in the Tongan language. The church, located at the intersection of

The Hawaii Club, formed in 1974, offered opportunities for Hawaiian Texans to practice traditional dances and to socialize. This photo was taken at an early gathering. Lou McCabe stands at the far right.

Pipeline and Main, marked the center of the Tongan community. As the number of Tongans belonging to non-Methodist denominations grew, they formed separate congregations. In the late 1980s, four hundred Tongans from the Tongan United Church broke away and formed a Tongan ward of the Church of Jesus Christ and Latter-Day Saints; another ward formed in the early 1990s. Plus, three other Tongan churches were established at Pipeline and Main. In 2004, the most common denominations among Tongan Texans were Mormonism, followed by Methodism, Catholicism, and the faith of the Free Church of Tonga, a uniquely Tongan form of Christianity.

In the early 1980s, a large number of Tongan Americans migrated from Salt Lake City and California to the Euless area in order to work for American Airlines, which runs a major hub at the DFW Airport. Working at loading cargo, cleaning and maintaining planes, and serving food, the Tongans found the airlines jobs attractive in part because employee ticket discounts allowed them to visit family in Tonga more often. Other Tongans immigrated directly to Euless through family reunification.

The Tongan Texan community grew tremendously in the 1980s and then nearly doubled between 1990 and 2000. It was estimated that within the Euless community, every Tongan family had at least one member working for American Airlines. With some cargo loaders earning up to $70,000 a year through overtime work, a great deal of money was sent from Euless back to extended family living in Tonga—such remittances being a major form of income for the resource-scarce nation. When the attacks of September 11 caused American Airlines to lay off a large portion of their workforce, Tongan Texans were disproportionately affected. Some lost their homes to foreclosure, others needed donated food, and still others moved to different cities to find employment.

Most first-generation Tongan Americans who migrated to Euless never went to college, and less than half graduated from high school. They came with high expectations from their extended family in Tonga, where Tongan families value the idea of "What's yours is ours," and "What's ours is yours," according to community activist Ilaiasi Ofa. The Tongan Texans hoped to send large remittances back to Tonga. Nevertheless, they felt the American pressure to "keep up with the Joneses" through material possessions, and their children learned American values. With parents working two jobs, the generations often did not connect.

Ilaiasi Ofa was born in 1964 in Haapai, Tonga, and he earned a degree in accounting in New Zealand. He and his wife were the only Tongans in Little Rock, Arkansas when they met and married. Ofa and his wife moved to Euless in 1997 and formed the Voice of Tonga in the year 2000. The organization helps Tongans with immigration, health, family, and employment issues. Ofa directed a local Tongan television show and answered questions about immigration and other issues on Tongan language radio shows broadcast throughout the world.

In 2004, a Samoan community numbering 400 to 500 lived in the Dallas-Fort Worth area, concentrated in Arlington. The Samoan community is similar socially to the Tongan community, and there are many social and religious relations between the two communities. Both communities contribute many football players to local high school football teams. A substantial portion of Tongan and Samoan Texan young men who attend college do so through football scholarships. Success in football has become a major source of pride, as parents, often rugby fans back in their native lands, cheer for their sons on Friday nights. In 2005, Pacific Islander Texan players helped propel Euless Trinity High School to a state championship.[13]

The most famous Pacific Islander Texan was Mark Pulemau Tuinei, who played as an offensive lineman for the Dallas Cowboys. Born in Oceanside, California and raised in Hawaii, Tuinei played left tackle on the offensive line for the Cowboys from 1983 to 1998. Tuinei was elected to the Pro Bowl twice and helped the Cowboys win three Super Bowls in the 1990s. A mentor for other Samoan players, Tuinei was a pioneer for Pacific Islander professional football players.

The Pacific Islander population in Texas also includes Guamanian, Fijian, Tahitian, and French Polynesian Texans.[14]

ENDNOTES

1 Most of this article is based on interviews with Eddy Poerwana on 10/23/2004 (by phone) and with William Kwie, S.T. Tjia, and Eddy Poerwana on 11/5/04 at the Indonesian Consulate in Houston.

2 Edison Uno, "Crystal City Internment," *Crystal City Internment Camp 50th Anniversary Reunion* (Monterey, California, 1993).

3 B. W. Andaya, and L.Y. Andaya, *A History of Malaysia, Second Edition*, (Honolulu: University of Hawai'i Press, 2001); E. T. Gomez, "Introduction: politics, business and ethnicity in Malaysia: a state in transition?" *The State of Malaysia: Ethnicity, Equity and Reform* (London: RoutledgeCurzon, 2004); K.H. Lee and Heng, P.K., "The Chinese in the Malaysian Political System" *The Chinese in Malaysia* (Kuala Lumpur: Oxford University Press, 1999).

4 K.L. Yap, "Ethnic identity of 'overseas Chinese' in Texas : a case study of re-migrants from Malaysia." (Austin, TX: M.A. Thesis, University of Texas at Austin, 2004).

5 Ibid.

6 Ibid.

7 Ibid.

8 K.L. Ho, "*Shared Responsibilities, Unshared Power: The Politics of Policy-Making in Singapore*" (Singapore: Eastern University Press, 2003); D. K. Mauzy, and R.S. Milne, "*Singapore Politics Under the People's Action Party*" (London: Routledge, 2002) ; H. Mutalib, "*Parties and Politics.*" (Singapore: Eastern University Press).

9 Jessica Chan, Rachel Chia, and Allison Chew, interviews by Yap Keng-Loong, 2002–2005.

10 Ibid.

11 The Hawaiian Texans section is based on an interview and conversations with Lou McCabe of San Antonio, Texas, by Irwin Tang, San Antonio, 2004.

12 The Tongan Texans section is based on phone interviews and emails with Ilaiasi Ofa of Euless Texas, by Irwin Tang, in 2004.

13 Ibid.

14 Ibid.

————————— ★ —————————

CHAPTER SIXTEEN

A BRIEF DEMOGRAPHIC PROFILE OF ASIAN TEXANS

Dr. Arthur Sakamoto, Hyeyoung Woo, and Keng-Loong Yap[1]

The Rapidly Increasing Size of The Asian Texan Population

Today there are more Asian Americans in Texas than in Hawaii. But while Asian Hawaiians are relatively well known, highly visible, and prominently figured in Asian American history, culture, and politics, the stories of Asian Texans are generally unknown. How did it come to be that that there are now more Asian Americans in Texas than in Hawaii? Demographically, who are the Asian Texans?

Table 1 shows the basic outline of the demographic statistics from the 2000 Census for the leading states with the largest Asian American populations including California, New York, Texas, and Hawaii. As shown in Table 1, California clearly has the most Asian Americans. In fact, the number of Asian Americans in California exceeds the populations of Asian Americans in New York, Texas, and Hawaii combined. When counting only single-race Asian Americans (i.e., not counting multi-racial Asian Americans who are of mixed racial ancestry such as being both Asian and white), Texas is third with an Asian American population of 562,319.² This figure is clearly behind New York's Asian American population of 1,044,976. On the other hand, Table 1 also shows that the population of single-race Asian Americans of Texas exceeds that of Hawaii (i.e., 562,319 versus 503,868, respectively). Hawaii exceeds Texas, however, when multi-racial Asian Americans are included in the figures (703,232 versus 644,193, respectively).³

California, New York, and Hawaii are often noted as states with high concentrations of Asian Americans. Why is Texas not noted in this regard when Texas has more Asian Americans than Hawaii (at least in terms of single-race Asians)? One major reason, we would suggest, is because Asian Texans are much more of a minority in their own state. As shown in Table 1, Asian Texans are numerous in absolute terms, but their total population is substantial mainly because Texas is a large and highly populated state. In fact, Texas is the second most populated state in the nation (with California being the most populated state). As a percentage of the total population of Texas, however, Table 1 shows that single-race Asian Americans are only 2.7%. In other words, Asian Americans in Texas are only a tiny proportion of the total population of Texas. Whereas single-race Asian Americans were 3.6% of the total population of the nation as a whole in 2000 (see Table 2), the percentage of Texans who are Asian is only 2.7% and is, therefore, actually below the national average.

Because Asian Americans are such a small proportion of the total population of Texas, they are easy to overlook as they do not stand out. By contrast, Table 1 shows that 41.6% of the population of Hawaii is Asian (and that figure increases to 58.0% when multi-racial Asians are included). In contrast to the situation of Asian Americans in Hawaii, the small proportion of Texans that are Asian means that they tend to lack political power, do not figure prominently in popular views of Texan society, and are probably more likely to be stereotypically imagined because social interaction with actual Asian Texans is less frequent for non-Asian Texans.

A second feature of Asian Texan demographics is that its large numbers are relatively recent. As shown in Table 2, there were only 20,641 Asians in Texas as late as 1970 (or about .2% of the total Texan population at that time).[4] In the Census before World War II (i.e., 1940), only 1,785 persons in Texas were Asian. Based on the total population size of Texas of about 6.4 million in 1940 (see Table 2), an Asian Texan population of 1,785 implies that only about one person in 3,600 Texans was Asian at that time. By contrast, Hawaii and California have had significant numbers and proportions of Asian Americans for over a century. In short, because the growth and large absolute numbers of Asians in Texas is a comparatively recent phenomenon, an Asian Texan is a relatively new concept for many people even among those who specialize in the study of Asian Americans.

Table 2 further shows that, in 2000, 7.4% of the total U.S. population lived in Texas (i.e., 20,851,820), but a somewhat smaller percentage (i.e., 5.5%) of all single-race Asian Americans did so. This indicates that, as was discussed above, the proportion of Asian Americans in Texas is less than the national average. A century earlier, in 1900, the total population of Texas was 3,048,710 or 4.0% of the total population of the U.S. At that time, Asian Texans numbered only 849 and that tiny figure comprised only .7% of the total Asian American population of 114,189. These results are another way of indicating that the Texan population grew substantially during the 20th century and that the growth was proportionately greater for Asian Texans.

Asian Ethnic Groups Among Asian Texans

Table 3 shows the population figures for specific Asian ethnic groups in Texas and in the nation as a whole based on the 2000 U.S. Census data. Also shown in Table 3 is the ethnic distribution among Asian Americans (in the columns labeled "% of Total") for Texas and for the nation as a whole. The column labeled "% of Group Total" refers to the percentage of the total U.S. population of the given Asian ethnic group that resides in Texas. For instance, the 133,752 Vietnamese Texans represent 20.69% of all Asian Texans, and those same Vietnamese Texans also represent 11.92% of all Vietnamese Americans. The 1,122,278 Vietnamese Americans represent 9.46% of all Asian Americans. So about 20% of Asian Texans are Vietnamese, and only about 10% of Asian Americans are Vietnamese.[5]

Table 1: Asian American Population in Texas and Other States, 2000 U.S. Census

	California	New York	Texas	Hawaii
Total Population	33,871,648	18,976,457	20,851,820	1,211,537
Total Asian Population	3,697,513	1,044,976	562,319	503,868
	[4,155,685]	[1,169,200]	[644,193]	[703,232]
Percent Asian	10.90%	5.50%	2.70%	41.60%
	[12.3%]	[6.2%]	[3.1%]	[58.0%]
Percent Bi/ Multi-Racial Asians among All Asians	11.00%	10.60%	12.70%	28.30%

Note: Numbers for "Total Asian Population" refer to persons who are single-race Asian Americans while the numbers in brackets refer to population figures that also include multi-racial Asians. Figures do not include Pacific Islanders because, in the 2000 U.S. Census, they are classified as constituting a separate racial category.

SOURCES
U.S. Census Bureau (2002), *The Asian Population: 2000,* Washington, D.C., U.S. Government Printing Office.

FOOTNOTES for Table 2 (right)
1 Based on the 2002 Current Population Survey which does not identify multi-racial persons. In this survey, multi-racial persons must choose only one racial group with which to identify.
2 Includes only single-race Asians based on the 2000 U.S. Census.
3 Includes both single-race and multi-racial Asians based on the 2000 U.S. Census.

SOURCES for Table 2 (right)
C. Gibson & K. Jung, 2002. Population Division: Working Paper No.56, Retrieved July 1, 2004, from http://www.census.gov.
U.S. Census Bureau, 2003. Statistical Abstract of the United States, 2003, Retrieved July 1, 2004, from http://www.census.gov.

Table 2: Asian American Population in Texas and the U.S. by Year

Census year	Total Population		Total Asian Population			Percent distribution of Total Population in Texas (Asian)
	U.S.	Texas	U.S. (%)	Texas (%)		
2002[1]	288,369,000	21,780,000	11,559,000 (4.0)	649,000 (2.8)		7.6 (5.6)
2000[2]	281,421,906	20,851,820	10,242,998 (3.6)	562,319 (2.7)		7.4 (5.5)
2000[3]	281,421,906	20,851,820	11,898,828 (4.2)	644,193 (3.1)		7.4 (5.4)
1990	248,709,873	16,986,510	7,273,662 (2.9)	319,459 (1.9)		6.8 (4.4)
1980	226,545,805	14,229,191	3,500,439 (1.5)	120,313 (0.8)		6.3 (3.4)
1970	203,211,926	11,196,730	1,538,721 (0.8)	20,641 (0.2)		5.5 (1.3)
1960	179,323,175	9,579,677	980,337 (0.5)	9,848 (0.1)		5.3 (1.0)
1950	150,697,361	7,711,194	321,033 (0.2)	3,955 (0.1)		5.1 (1.2)
1940	131,669,275	6,414,824	254,918 (0.2)	1,785 (-)		4.9 (0.7)
1930	122,775,046	5,824,715	264,766 (0.2)	1,578 (-)		4.7 (0.6)
1920	105,710,620	4,663,228	182,137 (0.2)	1,260 (-)		4.4 (0.7)
1910	91,972,266	3,896,542	146,863 (0.2)	943 (-)		4.2 (0.6)
1900	75,994,575	3,048,710	114,189 (0.2)	849 (-)		4.0 (0.7)
1890	62,947,714	2,235,527	109,527 (0.2)	713 (-)		3.6 (0.7)
1880	50,155,783	1,591,749	105,613 (0.2)	136 (-)		3.2 (0.1)
1870	38,558,371	818,579	63,254 (0.2)	25 (-)		2.1 (-)

Although not a large group in either absolute or proportionate terms in Texas, Pakistanis are the only other Asian ethnic group for whom a substantial percentage resides in Texas (i.e., 12.20% as shown in Table 3).

Table 3 shows that Asian Indians are a large group in Texas (i.e., 127,645) and are a close second to the Vietnamese Texan population. Asian Texans are disproportionately Indian. This characterization derives from the fact that the percentage of all Asian Americans that are Asian Indian (i.e., 13.83%) is significantly lower than the percentage of Asian Texans that are Asian Indian (i.e., 19.75%). Pakistanis are also overrepresented in Texas though not Bangladeshis or Sri Lankans.

The Chinese are the other large group in Texas with a population of 106,996. The Chinese are the largest Asian group nationally, however, so although the Chinese Texan population is large, it is not quite as large in percentage terms as for the nation as a whole. Nationally, about one in five Asian Americans is Chinese (i.e., 20.14%) while about one in six Asian Texans is Chinese (i.e., 16.55%).[6]

The next largest Asian groups in Texas include the Filipinos and the Koreans (59,763 and 45,659, respectively). In percentage terms, however, these groups are somewhat underrepresented compared to their national averages. The two groups that are the most underrepresented in Texas are the Japanese (2.58% of Asian Texans but 6.57% of Asian Americans nationally) and the Hmong (.22% of Asian Texans but 1.50% of Asian Americans nationally). Finally, Table 3 also indicates that the percentages of Asian Texans that are multi-ethnic Asians and multi-racial Asians are generally similar to the percentages for the nation as a whole.[7]

Social And Economic Characteristics Of Asian Texans

In Table 4, we show the averages for a number of social and economic characteristics of Asian Americans in Texas as well as for Asian Americans in the nation as a whole in 2000. For comparative purposes, the averages for non-Hispanic whites are shown in Table 4 as well. Due to space limitations, we do not consider other minority groups (such as African Americans), and Table 4 is also limited to persons who are at least 25 years of age.

The results in Table 4 show that Asian Americans are, on average, younger than whites. Further, Asian Texans tend to be slightly younger than Asian Americans as a whole. When compared to whites or other Asian Americans, Asian Texans are more likely to be enrolled in college or to be college graduates. Asian Texans are not more likely to be veterans or to be on active duty in the military.

Asian Texans and Asian Americans are much more likely than whites to be foreign born while Asian Texans are even more likely to be foreign born than Asian Americans as a whole.[8] Although not shown in Table 4, we note that the percentage of Asian Texans that is foreign-born is only slightly higher than in most other states. Table 4 does indicate, however, that among foreign-born Asian Texans, the average number of years of residence in the U.S. is 14.9 while it is 16.0 among foreign-born Asian Americans as a whole.[9]

In terms of family incomes, the median for Asian Americans is larger than that for whites. This racial difference is smaller in Texas, however, than in the nation as a whole. Furthermore, Asian Americans are known to have larger family sizes. The income-to-needs ratio refers to family income after adjusting for family size and composition. Taking the latter into account, the income-to-needs ratio is actually slightly smaller for Asian Americans than for whites (i.e., 3.4 versus 3.6, respectively) in both Texas and the nation as a whole. The smaller average income-to-needs ratio indicates that, generally speaking, Asian American households tend to have fewer dollars per person in the family.[10] Table 4 also shows that Asian Americans have higher poverty rates than whites.

Asian Texans In Metropolitan Areas

Generally speaking, Asian Americans tend to be more urban than whites. In order to consider the urban residence of Asian Texans more specifically, Table 5 shows the Asian American populations in the seven Texan metropolitan areas that have the largest numbers of Asian Americans. These figures refer to the populations of "Consolidated Metropolitan

Table 3: Distribution of Ethnic Groups among Asian Americans in Texas and the U.S.

Ethnic Groups	Texas			U.S.	
	Frequency	% of Total	% of Group	Frequency	% of Total
Vietnamese	133,752	20.69	11.92	1,122,278	9.46
Asian Indian	127,645	19.75	7.78	1,639,913	13.83
Chinese[1]	106,996	16.55	4.48	2,388,306	20.14
Filipino	59,763	9.24	3.16	1,889,453	15.93
Korean	45,659	7.06	4.25	1,074,871	9.06
Pakistani	18,674	2.89	12.20	153,085	1.29
Japanese	16,676	2.58	2.14	778,788	6.57
Laotian	10,327	1.60	6.76	152,414	1.29
Thai	7,651	1.18	7.43	102,997	0.87
Cambodian	7,355	1.14	4.06	181,232	1.53
Bangladeshi	2,167	0.34	4.54	47,734	0.40
Indonesian	1,747	0.27	4.61	37,907	0.32
Hmong	1,428	0.22	0.80	178,146	1.50
Sri Lankan	1,223	0.19	5.55	22,055	0.19
Malaysian	776	0.12	6.94	11,184	0.09
Other Asian, specified[2]	1,886	0.29	7.24	26,035	0.22
Other Asian, not specified[3]	7,007	1.08	5.93	118,168	1.00
Multi-Ethnic Asian[4]	9,675	1.50	4.29	225,377	1.90
Multi-Racial Asian[5]	86,044	13.31	5.04	1,708,159	14.40
Total	646,451	100		11,858,102	100

Note: For methodological reasons, the totals in Table 3 are not exactly the same as the corresponding totals in Table 2, but they are very close in percentage terms.

FOOTNOTES

1 Chinese includes Taiwanese.
2 "Other Asian, specified" refers to other particular Asian ethnic groups such as Mongolian and Burmese.
3 "Other Asian, not specified" refers to respondents that are simply given as "Asian".
4 "Multi-Ethnic Asian" refers to persons who are of mixed Asian ancestry such as Chinese and Japanese.
5 "Multi-Racial Asian" refers to persons who are of mixed racial ancestry that includes at least one Asian group and one non-Asian group (e.g., Chinese and White).

SOURCE

The Public Use Microdata 5% Sample for Texas and the 1% national sample from the 2000 U.S. Census.

Table 4: Averages on Selected Social and Economic Characteristics for Asian Americans and Non-Hispanic Whites in Texas and the U.S., 2000 U.S. Census

	Texas		U.S.	
	Whites	Asians	Whites	Asians
Age	49.7	42.4	50.4	44.6
Female	51.80%	52.00%	52.10%	53.20%
Married (or Widowed)	76.10%	78.70%	74.50%	75.80%
Enrolled in College/University	4.20%	10.90%	4.20%	10.00%
College Graduate	28.30%	40.40%	25.20%	37.70%
Active Duty in Military	2.90%	1.40%	2.90%	1.60%
Veteran	16.90%	3.20%	16.20%	4.50%
Foreign-Born	3.70%	92.10%	5.10%	83.90%
Foreign-Born, Non-Citizen	1.40%	44.00%	1.80%	37.20%
Years in U.S.	25.5	14.9	28.6	16.0
Median Family Income	$60,100	$61,700	$58,000	$63,500
Income-to-Needs Ration	3.6	3.4	3.6	3.4
Below Poverty Line	6.00%	10.10%	6.50%	9.90%
Self-Employed/Family Worker	13.40%	12.90%	12.50%	11.50%

Note: Figures for "Years in U.S." pertain only to foreign-born persons.

SOURCE

The Public Use Microdata 5% Sample for Texas from the 2000 U.S. Census.

Table 5: Asian American Population in Texas by Major Consolidated Metropolitan Statistical Areas (CMSAs): 2000 and 1990 Census

Metropolitan Statistical Areas	Asian Population		
	Census 2000	Census 1990	Changes (%)
Houston-Galveston	156,337	132,241	24,096 (18.22)
Dallas-Fort Worth-Arlington	133,824	98,247	35,577 (36.21)
Austin-San Marcos	28,237	18,985	9,252 (48.73)
San Antonio	18,277	16,080	2,197 (13.66)
Killeen-Temple	6,343	7,201	-858 (-11.92)
El Paso	5,094	6,485	-1,391 (-21.45)
Bryan-College Station	3,951	4,313	-362 (-8.39)

Note: Consolidated Metropolitan Statistical Areas include the surrounding suburban fringe areas and are not limited to the central city.

SOURCE

The Public Use Microdata 5% Samples for Texas from the 1990 U.S. Census and the 2000 U.S. Census.

Statistical Areas" which generally means that they include the counties that are adjacent to the particular central city.

Table 5 shows that Houston-Galveston has the largest population of Asian Americans in both 1990 and 2000. Its official Asian American population for 2000 is 156,337, which represents a substantial increase of 18.22% over the previous decade. The growth of the Asian American population between 1990 and 2000 was even greater (i.e., 36.21%) in Dallas-Fort Worth-Arlington, however, so that its 2000 Asian American population is catching up with that of Houston-Galveston. Austin-San Marcos is the metropolitan area that has the third largest Asian American population in Texas. Although the growth of its Asian American population between 1990 and 2000 was remarkable in percentage terms (i.e., 48.73%), in absolute terms the Asian American population of Austin-San Marcos in 2000 was 28,237 which is a distant third when compared to Houston-Galveston and Dallas-Fort Worth-Arlington.

The other metropolitan areas referred to in Table 5 include San Antonio, Killeen-Temple, El Paso, and Bryan-College Station. Although San Antonio is a larger metropolitan area than Austin-San Marcos overall, San Antonio has significantly fewer Asian Americans as its official Asian American population in 2000 was only 18,277. Still smaller are the Asian American populations of Killeen-Temple, El Paso, and Bryan-College Station (since each have Asian American populations that are well less than half that of San Antonio). What is distinctive about these smaller metropolitan areas is that their Asian American populations actually declined between 1990 and 2000. These declines in Killeen-Temple, El Paso, and Bryan-College Station suggest that Asian Texans have a proclivity for larger metropolitan areas that have greater educational and economic opportunities.

Conclusion

Asian Americans were once thought to be a phenomenon of mainly Hawaii and California, but the continued growth of the Asian American population is changing that view. Asian Texans as a significant demographic group appeared relatively late when compared to Asian

Hawaiians and Asian Californians. Asian Texans are, however, here to stay. Whereas Hawaii and California have become saturated with urban areas, congested highways, and exorbitant land prices, the Texan population and economy continues to grow and expand freely.[11] The Asian Texan population will likewise continue to grow and to receive increased recognition.

ENDNOTES

1 For research assistance, we thank Starling Pullum and the Population Research Center of the University of Texas at Austin.

2 Multi-racial Asians refer to persons who have some Asian ancestry and at least one non-Asian ancestry (e.g., Asian and African American). Single-race Asians refer to persons whose ancestry is entirely Asian.

3 U.S. Census statistics are typically subject to error which is usually believed to be relatively small at least in percentage terms. General patterns regarding state comparisons are unlikely to be affected by this error, however, unless the under-reporting is substantially greater in one state than in another.

4 Before 2000, U.S. Census statistics do not identify or distinguish single-race persons from multi-racial persons. The figures shown in Table 2 for 2002 are based on survey data (i.e., not Census data) that also do not distinguish single-race persons from bi/multi-racial persons.

5 Oklahoma and Louisiana are the two other states where the Vietnamese are the largest Asian group. These two states, however, have much smaller Asian American and Vietnamese American populations than does Texas.

6 These figures for Chinese also include Taiwanese.

7 Multi-ethnic Asians refer to persons who have more than one Asian ethnic ancestry (e.g., Chinese and Vietnamese) but who do not have any non-Asian ancestry.

8 The percentages of Asian Americans and of Asian Texans who are foreign born would be reduced when persons under 25 years of age are included in the analysis. Most native-born Asian Americans were born after the 1965 Immigration Act and a large proportion of native-born Asian Americans were children in 2000.

9 Due to its geographic isolation, its large proportion of Asians among all residents, and its lack of economic opportunities for migrants due to its stagnant economy, Hawaii stands out as the only state where the majority of adult Asian Americans are native born. Washington and California are the other two states where the percentage of native born among Asian American residents is significantly above the national average.

10 More exactly, the income-to-needs ratio refers to family income divided by the official U.S. Census poverty threshold for a family of the given size and number of children.

11 For example, Texas has recently surpassed New York as the second most populated state in the U.S.

★

CHAPTER SEVENTEEN

THE ASIAN TEXANS: A COMMON HISTORY

Irwin A. Tang with Roy Vu

Asian Texans began interacting across ethnic lines on a regular basis in El Paso. In fact, the first two recorded Japanese residents of El Paso lived in its Chinatown as early as 1885. By 1921 some hundreds of Chinese and 150 Japanese lived in the city, many of them running small businesses. Indians, Koreans, and Filipinos also lived or passed through El Paso in these years. Anti-Asian immigration laws and the Asian American underground railroad (see Chapters Two and Three) funneled tens of thousands of Asians, Asian Mexicans, and Asian Americans into and/or through El Paso. For those who settled in El Paso, racism, segregation, and the monitoring, harassment, searches, detainment, and deportation of Asian El Pasoans associated with immigration policies pushed Asians into a common social class with a common agenda. The most obvious result was that Asians worked across ethnic lines to circumvent immigration officials. Japanese El Pasoan Ging Hasekawa, for instance, "smuggled" Asian immigrants (likely Chinese, Japanese, Indians, and

Koreans) from Juárez, Mexico into El Paso, likely its Chinatown.[1] Jim Crow and segregation tended to force Asians of various ethnic groups into certain industries, lines of work, and neighborhoods. Asian Texans, across ethnic lines, were united by Mexican Texans and Mexican culture. Anti-miscegenation laws, the social sanctions against marrying white women, the lack of Asian women (this lack being exacerbated by the "wild west" nature of Texas), and the fact that many Asian Texans came from Mexico and spoke Spanish resulted in Asian Texans—across ethnic lines—marrying Mexican and Mexican American women, living among Mexicans, and working in businesses that serve Mexicans.

A number of factors shifted the center of Asian Texan inter-ethnic interaction from El Paso to San Antonio, starting around the Mexican Revolution (1910-1920). The Mexican Revolution forced Asians to leave Mexico while simultaneously discouraging Asian migration to that nation. Fewer Asian Mexicans meant fewer Asian immigrants entering at El Paso. In 1916, most of the 527 Chinese who escaped the revolution with John J. Pershing settled in San Antonio (see Ch. 5). Their successes attracted other Asians to the city. Stricter immigration policies may have also lowered the number of Asians migrating into El Paso. Furthermore, Texas's 1921 Alien Land Law discouraged Japanese from establishing farms in the Rio Grande Valley, and early Filipino migration centered around San Antonio. San Antonio's economy and population grew at a quick pace, likely attracting Asians wishing to start new businesses in growing neighborhoods. Between 1910 and 1950, San Antonio's population increased by over 310,000, while El Paso's grew by less than 100,000. A typical interethnic interaction in San Antonio involved Filipinos patronizing Chinese-owned grocery stores and gambling parlors, where Filipinos could find Asian food ingredients and satisfy gambling habits.

World War II tended to unite Asian Texans in their desire for an Allied victory and their opposition to anti-Asian harassment, as anyone who looked Japanese was in danger of being verbally or physically attacked. The "military period" of Asian Texan history saw Filipinos, Japanese, Koreans, Chinese, Thais, Pacific Islanders, and Vietnamese living on and around Texas military bases throughout the state, making these places, like Killeen, centers of inter-ethnic Asian Texan interaction. The

1950s saw an early example of the melding together of a multi-ethnic Asian identity. Japanese Texan waitresses, some of whom had married American GIs in Japan, served local politicians and other patrons at the Chinese-owned PolyAsian restaurant in Houston. Albert and Jane Gee's upper-end restaurant served Chinese, Japanese, and Polynesian food in its Kabuki Room.[2]

While the city of San Antonio continued to grow quickly during the post-1965 "diversification period" of Asian Texan history (see Historical Overview), so did Houston and Dallas. Unlike San Antonio, though, the latter two cities multiplied each decade the number of local opportunities in the fields of engineering, medicine, energy, computers, telecommunications, space technology, and finance. Because post-1965 immigrants and second-generation Asian Americans concentrated in these areas, Houston and Dallas became the centers of Asian Texan population and inter-ethnic community organization and politics. The number of multiethnic voting bloc organizations, social service organizations, student organizations, religious groups and institutions, and commercial groups accelerated quickly in Houston, Dallas, and university communities. They were fueled by both ambitious immigrants and second-generation Asian Texans who identified as Asian Americans.

During the "diversification" period of Asian Texan history, centers of interethnic interaction included energy and high-technology firms; hospitals and medical centers; Christian churches (some explicitly Asian American) and Buddhist and Muslim temples; community centers (some explicitly Asian American), schools, universities and military bases. The 1970s saw the development of Asian business districts and suburban enclaves. Asian Texans concentrated in certain suburbs in order to place their children in the best schools and to live around other Asians. Schools and universities became primary places where Asians interacted socially, romantically, and scholastically across ethnic lines and where Asian Texans began to see themselves as *Asians* and *Asian Americans*, even if those terms did not become popular until the 1980s.

The fact that some local Asian Texan populations were small often forced Asians together despite ethnic and political differences. Indians and Pakistanis ate at the same South Asian restaurants. Thai, Vietnamese, Laotian, and Cambodian Buddhists worshipped at the same Buddhist temples. Hong Kong and Taiwanese students joined the same student associations. As local populations expanded, specialization proliferated, but so did cross-ethnic organizing. For instance, Malayalam-speaking Indian Christian churches proliferated in Houston simultaneous to the establishment of multiethnic Asian organizations such as the 80–20 voting bloc organization.

Throughout their history, Asian Texans, across ethnic groups, considered certain issues crucial to their values, prosperity, and survival. These issues included education, small business success, crime, immigration, and racial discrimination. But as much as these tangible issues were important so too were dignity, pride, shame, and keeping or saving "face." Asian Texans had a collective sense that they could not rely on any government. Instead, they relied largely on ingenuity, hard work, and taking strategic risks. Dissatisfied with neighborhood schools, Asian Texan families moved to the best school districts. Concerned with crime and the KKK, some bought guns to defend themselves. Seeing that they might never earn a high wage, Asian Texans invested in their children's educations, so that they would not struggle similarly.

Asian Texans were highly mobile and highly flexible. They tended to move frequently to whichever markets provided the best opportunities. Because of recessions and booms—and in Texas there were many—Asians not only moved residence, they frequently moved from one class to another. Professionals worked jobs as dishwashers or started small businesses unrelated to their profession; store clerks saved enough to open their own stores. They sought solutions that worked for them and often "worked the system" as best they could—from petitioning local courts for citizenship, to buying land denied to them by putting the name of a white friend on the deed, to forming organizations to lend money to each other, to taking dangerously rickety shrimp boats out to sea in order to break into the business.

The Asian Texans that met the most tragic ends, of course, tended to be those with fewer skills and fewer opportunities. Since their arrival to Texas, Asian Texans have been highly concentrated in running Mom-and-Pop small businesses—from laundries to convenience stores. Running or working in small groceries and convenience stores has al-

Many Southeast Asian refugees, when first arriving in the U.S., concentrated in low-income apartment complexes such as this one in Southeast Houston (2004).

Houston's Wat Phouthasamakhy, a Lao Buddhist temple. The interior is adorned with sculptures of Lao and Buddhist deities. It stands next to an older Wat.

ways been dangerous because of the frequency of armed robberies. The dangers to business owners and to those living or working in high-crime neighborhoods spiked in the late 1980s and early 1990s. Organized Asian crime had deep roots in Texas, taking the form of Chinese "tongs" in the pre-World War II decades. After 1975 Southeast Asian gangs took over as the primary form of Asian organized crime. Although dominated by Southeast Asians, other Asians—Chinese and Koreans most notably—also participated in gang activities. Asian gangs were most active between the late 1970s and the mid-1990s. Couched in those years was the explosion of violence between street gangs (comprised of all racial groups) over local drug markets and "territory." Thus, Houston and Dallas-Fort Worth newspapers in the late 1980s and early 1990s regularly published articles noting the murders of Asians as a result of armed robberies, gang-styled shootings, or a new, terrifying crime known as the home invasion.

Others who struggled tremendously were immigrants stuck in a cycle of poverty. They tended to lack capital, support from extended family, English skills, formal education, political power, standard housing, and safe living environments. These Asians tended to concentrate in certain neighborhoods and apartment complexes. "Little Asia" was a multiethnic neighborhood in East Dallas which sprung up in the late 1970s. Upon arrival to the area, many Cambodian, Laotian, and Vietnamese refugees crowded into dilapidated apartments. By 1985–86 some 4,000 Southeast Asian refugees were crowded into a neighborhood barely a quarter of a square mile. Crime, segregation, and low wages made it extremely difficult to move out of this neighborhood, but most eventually did.[3]

Asian Texans in Elected Office

During the racial-caste period, Chinese communities were often self-policing and left to help and punish their own. Oftentimes a "mayor" of Chinatown represented the Chinese and those associated with them in relations with others. For instance, in 1911, Chinese El Pasoan leader Mar Wing Kee asked Mayor Charles Kelly to stop the production of a four-act play entitled "The Chinatown Trunk Mystery." Mar stated that the play presented "an improper reflection upon the Chinese."[4] As late as the 1950s, Albert Gee was considered the "mayor" of Houston's Chinese community. These leaders and community organizations lobbied, protested, petitioned, and donated funds in order to achieve their ends. Perhaps recognizing that lobbying the government is never as effective as *being* the government, Asian Texans began in the 1960s an accelerating ascent into elected office.

Many Asian Texan politicians have been Chinese Texans whose families ran grocery stores and restaurants in Black and Hispanic neighborhoods. Thomas J. Lee grew up in a restaurant speaking Spanish and Chinese to his parents and customers. In 1964, San Antonio voters elected him to the Texas House of Representatives, making him the first Asian Texan to hold political office. Lee, a lawyer who did "almost all of the legal work for the Chinese in the city" held the office for one term.[5]

David Wellington Chew, a descendant of Herlinda Wong Chew, served as an El Paso city council member from 1989 to 1991. In 1994, he was elected as a Justice to the Texas 8th Court of Appeals, and in 2007, he became the court's first Asian American chief justice. While Chew's ancestry was Chinese and Hispanic, Asian Houstonian activist Glenda Kay Joe's was Chinese and Irish. In 1991 she ran for an at-large seat on the Houston City Council on a crime and economic development platform, and she lost. That same year, Governor Ann Richards appointed Houston lawyer Robert Gee to be the first person of color to serve on the state Public Utility Commission. Because of in-fighting among Republicans, Democrat Gee quickly rose to head the commission. This marked the first public service of a member of the Gees, an influential Chinese Houstonian family united by surname. In 1993 conservative Republican Martha Jee Wong, also a Gee, won the District C seat on the Houston City Council and held it for three terms, serving until 1999. Wong, who had been Texas's first Asian school principal, helped increase Asian Houstonian representation in various city offices, including the police department. In 2002 Houston's District 134 elected Wong to the Texas House of Representatives, making her the first Asian American woman to serve in the Texas legislature. She was re-elected in 2004.

Chinese Texan Gordon Quan was the son of Chinese Americans who ran a grocery store in an eastside Hispanic neighborhood in Houston. "We attended a Chinese Baptist church, which was really more like a

Born in Pakistan, Mustafa Tameez served as an important political consultant for Vietnam-born Hubert Vo, as Vo was elected to the state legislature in 2004.

Jennifer Kim, of both Korean and Chinese descent, was elected to the Austin City Council in 2005.

community center," writes Quan in a short biography. After teaching at a predominantly black school and then practicing immigration law for twenty years, Quan won a seat on the Houston City Council in the year 2000. In 2002 he was unanimously elected as Houston's Mayor Pro-Tem. As a councilmember, Quan has been involved in every major issue and controversy involving Asian Americans; but, as he points out, "I make it a point to reach as many non-Asian American events as possible, too. I'm in the Hispanic community, the African-American community."[6]

In 1999 David Chiu was elected mayor of San Marcos; he was the first Asian American mayor of a Texas city. When he ran for re-election in 2002, the "San Marcos Citizens for Traditional Values" sent a mass mailing to residents stating that Chiu "claims to be a refugee from communist China, but his governing style is straight out of that oppressive regime." The letter also implied that Chiu supported homosexuality. Chiu lost the election by 23 votes.

While Dallas has lagged behind Houston in electing Asian Americans, its suburb of Addison elected Chinese American restaurant owner Joe Chow to its city council in 2002 and then as mayor in 2005. Other Dallas-Fort Worth suburbs have elected Asian council members as well. In the new millennium, Texas elected its first Indian, Pakistani, Korean, and Vietnamese Texans to city and state office. Pakistani Houstonian M.J. Khan was elected to the Houston City Council in 2003. A Houston district elected Vietnamese Texan Hubert Vo to the Texas House of Representatives in 2004. That same year, Indian Texan Thomas Abraham was elected to the Sugar Land City Council. In 2005 Jennifer Kim, a Chinese-Korean Texan, was elected to the Austin City Council as a left-of-center pro-growth representative in a city with a relatively small Asian American population.

Texas, despite its year 2000 population being only 2.7% Asian American, elected more Asian Americans to public office in the 1990s and 2000s than New York State, with its population consisting of 5.5% Asian Americans. Why? Perhaps while Asian Americans built political momentum and positive cache in Houston in the 1980s and 1990s, places like New York City and Los Angeles struggled with popular anti-Korean movements led by high-profile figures like New York City's Rev. Al

Sharpton. New York City, with its nearly 10% Asian population in 2000, did not elect its first Asian American city council member until 2001, and New York State did not inaugurate its first Asian American lawmaker until 2004. Houston, with its 5.3% Asian American population, beginning in 1993, elected three Asian American city council members and two Asian American state legislators.[7] The city elected a Muslim (M.J. Khan) to its city council just three years after the terror attacks of September 11, 2001.

Relations with Other People of Color

Perhaps no two racial groups in Texas have had a more mutually beneficial relationship than Asian Texans and Latino Texans, specifically Mexican Texans. During the "racial caste" period of Asian Texan history, a plurality, (or even a majority), of Asian Texans, in many years, came to Texas from Mexico. They tended to speak Spanish and adapted aspects of Latino cultures. Many arrived with Mexican wives. Asian Texan men who married women they met in Texas married Mexican American women more so than Asian, white, or black women. Asian Texans often lived among Mexican communities, worked with Mexican Texans, and ran businesses serving Mexican Texans. And there is no evidence that these two groups had anything but harmonious relations.

While Asian Texans were not as closely tied to Mexican Texans during the "military period" of Asian Texan history, the opening of hundreds of thousands of Asian Texan businesses during the "diversification period" brought Asian Texans and Mexican Texans into a symbiotic economic relationship. The primary facet of this relationship was the hiring of Mexican immigrants and Mexican Texans by Asian Texan business owners. A typical business owned by Asian Texans hired, for the most part, two groups of people: Asians belonging to the same ethnic group as the owners and Mexicans. For example, a typical Thai restaurant hired Thais and Mexicans. It did not typically hire Filipinos or Pakistanis or other non-Thai Asians. As a result, Mexican workers were hired by *every* Asian ethnic group, but Asian workers tended to be hired only by *their own* ethnic group. Asian Texan businesses, then, employed *by far* more Mexicans and Mexican Americans than any other ethnic group. Low-wage Asian and Mexican immigrant labor allowed many Asian Texan businesses to make a profit and to succeed. While the economic relationship was necessary for many Asians and Mexicans to remain in the United States, Asian and Mexican Texans also had generally amiable interpersonal relations.

Despite the "replacement worker" status under which the Chinese rail and plantation workers originally came to the South in the 1860s and 1870s, Black-Asian relations were generally harmonious, even if those relations, taken in aggregate, were not as close or complex as Asian-Mexican relations in Texas.

Asian-owned stores were a major nexus of interaction between Asians and other people of color. The Chinese-owned grocery stores of the twentieth century were amazing places. Before the advent of the convenience store, these small groceries were located primarily in black and Hispanic neighborhoods. They carried freshly cut meat, produce, and seafood. They often served as micro-lenders and hang-out places simultaneously. Nevertheless, as early as 1920, blacks complained of mistreatment and abuse at a Chinese-owned store in Texas and organized a protest outside of that store.[8]

By the 1970s, three major developments changed the nature of interactions at these stores. First, freeways divided neighborhoods; created a "car culture" rather than a more pedestrian one; and alienated people from each other. Second, convenience stores and supermarkets replaced the vast majority of small grocers. Finally, second- and third-generation Chinese Texan groceries were replaced by convenience stores run by first-generation Asian Americans—mostly Koreans, Vietnamese, Indians, and Pakistanis. Language barriers and cultural differences between newly arrived immigrants and store patrons resulted in alienation, misunderstanding, and conflicts.

Despite the fact that Asian store owners were generally well-liked throughout Texas, animosity towards these store owners was intensified by anti-Korean movements on both the west and east coasts. These movements of the 1990s were rooted in in-store conflicts between patrons and Asian store owners and the notion that Asian stores were draining money from and exploiting black communities. The 1992 Los Angeles Riots, inspired in part by anti-Korean anger, amplified tensions between blacks and Asians throughout the nation. At the height of gang violence in the United States, Asian Texan convenience store owners had also purchased guns to protect themselves. In 1994 a Korean Texan convenience store owner shot and killed a black man in retaliation for shoplifting (see the Korean Texans chapter). Also that year, a Vietnamese Texan store owner fatally shot a black man who had drawn a gun in an argument in Houston's Fifth Ward neighborhood. In protest, the store was picketed. It was also heavily damaged in a fire whose source was unknown. In 1997 a Vietnamese store owner in Houston's Sunnyside neighborhood, in an altercation, shot a teenaged black boy in the ankle after a rock had been thrown through his store window. The store owner claimed he thought the rock was a bullet. After this incident, black pastor James E. Nash and Vietnamese Houstonian Dr. Tinh Tran formed the Sunnyside Asian/African American Task Force, which organized town meetings to air grievances, coordinate cooperation in parades and other cultural events, survey area crime, and produce a "statement of values and practices" to be displayed by Sunnyside's seven merchants, all immigrants in a predominantly black community.[9]

As Pakistanis and other South Asians owned more stores, they more often became the targets of armed robberies by people of all races. In 2000, amidst a string of ten slayings of Asian American convenience store owners in Houston in a period of six months, City Councilmember Gordon Quan, along with Pakistan Association of Greater Houston president M.J. Khan and Rev. James Nash, organized the Circle of Unity organization to prevent crimes against Asian store owners and improve relations between Asians and Blacks. "Last month, Houston's 10th store clerk was murdered," wrote Gordon Quan to community leaders. "This continued violence cannot be tolerated."[10]

The spate of murders finally made the concerns of Asian retail workers a major media issue in Houston. In a November 2001 *Houston Chronicle* article, Khalid Muhammad said, "I pray for another night of peace and that I'll return home to my wife and two babies safe in the morning." That month, Quan helped distribute a safety kit written in Hindi, Urdu, Korean, and Vietnamese to 500 of the 2000 Asian-owned convenience stores in the Houston area.[11] In a 2003 *Houston Chronicle* article, a Muslim convenience store owner told local New Black Panther Party leader Quanell X about the frustrations of dealing with daily insults, shoplifting, and the fear of robbery. The article referred to the store owners as "foreign," and quoted Rev. James Nash as saying that the African American community was divided 50-50 over whether Asian-owned stores should stay or go. Nash also stated that relations had improved greatly since 1998.[12]

Although store owners and clerks were killed every year, and although patrons had been murdered, there were no riots, racist songs, or widespread boycotts as had occurred on the coasts. Local black and Asian leaders helped to heal the wounds opened by both the Los Angeles Riots and by local shootings. Dr. Suzanne Ahn, M.D., and Congresswoman Eddie Bernice Johnson worked together in Dallas (see Chapter Nine), and Councilman Gordon Quan, Dr. Tinh Tran, and Reverend James E. Nash worked together in Houston. They fought prejudice and misunderstanding through education and charity.

Education and Higher Education

Asian Texans have long been concerned about their children's education. In the days of segregation, Gong Lum, after losing his Supreme Court battle, moved his family from Mississippi to Houston so that his children would be allowed to attend white schools (See Ch. 10). Other Asian families likely acted out of the same motivation. In the 1980s and 1990s, however, Asian Texans struggled with a different problem. Rather than being categorized with blacks under segregation, in the age of affirmative action programs, Asian Texans were classified with whites.[13]

In 1989 teacher Betty Waki of the Sharpstown area of Houston was laid off as part of an affirmative action program aimed at increasing the number of "minority" teachers. Although Waki was Japanese American, she was not considered a minority. Glenda Joe and Michael Chou, co-founders of Council of Asian American Organizations, led Asian

Houstonians in pressuring the school board to re-hire Waki, and she was subsequently reinstated, but Asians were still considered "white" in the education system.[14]

In the 1990s, Asian Texans sometimes moved both very short and very long distances so that their children could attend the best schools. Sometimes, Asians even changed jobs or the locations of their businesses to do so. Or they sent their children to private, often religious, schools, even if their children did not belong to that religion. Many Asian families, then, likely moved out of the city of Houston when the Houston Independent School District (HISD) implemented an affirmative action program that placed caps on the number of students from each racial group enrolled in HISD "gifted and talented" programs. Whites and Asians combined were allowed 35% of available seats. The program was designed to increase black and Hispanic enrollment in HISD magnet schools, known as Vanguard schools. Although whites and Asians combined made up less than 14% of the student population, some argued that some students were being denied slots in favor of less-qualified students. In 1997 two white fifth graders filed a racial discrimination law suit against the school district, and concerned parents, such as Chinese Houstonian Bobby Moon, lobbied and spoke out against the affirmative action program. In 1998, HISD responded by switching to a system that only added points to the entrance eligibility scores of low-income black and Hispanic students.[15]

In 1996 a ruling by the 5th U.S. Circuit of Appeals ended affirmative action in college acceptance criteria in Texas, Mississippi, and Louisiana. Because affirmative action programs typically made entry more difficult for Asian American applicants, its elimination was expected to increase Asian American acceptance rates. However, in 1997 Texas passed the "10% rule" which required universities to admit all high school students who graduated in the top 10% of their class. Because many Asian Texan families enrolled their children in the best Texas high schools, the 10% law prevented some of those previously deserving children from attending UT-Austin. After all, it was much more difficult to graduate in the top 10% from, say, Bellaire High School or Plano High School, than to do so at most Texas schools. By 2002 about 70% of all freshman slots were taken up by "top 10%" students. Aliyah Khan, who graduated in the top 13% of her Plano High School class, wrote in a 2004 *Dallas Morning News* opinion piece that after realizing she would have gained admittance into UT-Austin if only she had gone to high school in Frisco, Texas, "it frustrated me that only a difference of a few miles stood in the way of my automatic admission." The 10% law, however, did allow Asian Texans attending less challenging high schools to more easily gain entrance to the best Texas universities, perversely encouraging Asian Texan parents to keep their children in those less challenging schools.[16]

In 2003 the U.S. Supreme Court ruled that certain forms of affirmative action in higher education were legal. The University of Texas re-instated race-based entrance criteria while Texas A&M University opted not to do so. Despite many policy changes, Asian American attendance at UT-Austin has increased steadily since 1974, matching the growth in Asian Texan population. It is unclear how many more or less Asian Americans would have attended UT-Austin if there were no programs designed to increase diversity. It is clear, however, that Asian Texans have largely shunned a comparable university—Texas A&M University—largely because of its lack of Asian Americans, its relatively rural location, and its perceived "redneck" (racist) culture. In that way, "race" still highly influenced university attendance. By 2001 Asian Americans made up about 19% of the first-time freshmen at UT-Austin but only about 3% of such freshmen at Texas A&M University. As UT-Austin and Texas A&M grew, so did their foreign Asian student populations, but those numbers peaked in the early 2000s, with 4730 total foreign students attending UT-Austin in 2002.[17]

In spring 1995, in part because of Houston City Councilmember Martha Wong's efforts, the University of Houston inaugurated its Asian American Studies Center. The University appointed Dr. Yali Zou as the Center's permanent director; the program offered a minor in Asian American Studies. Also in the spring of 1995, UT-Austin students lobbied for the establishment of a Center for Asian American Studies. The lobbying effort was organized by the campus group Asian Relations Committee, led by graduate student Irwin Tang and Dr. Andrew Chin of UT's LBJ School of Public Policy. After a semester-long campaign and a formal meeting between students and the university administration, UT-Austin committed itself to establishing the Center for Asian American Studies (CAAS). Delays in implementation resulted in student protests in 1998, led by the Asian American Relations Group. These protests led to another meeting between students and administration, which resulted in the administration again committing the university to the establishment of the CAAS. Interim directors were hired, classes began, and an Asian American Studies major was offered.

In May 1999, students protested the UT administration's preferred choice for the permanent director of the program, some implying that the university disliked the students' preferred candidate, Dr. Tom Nakayama of Arizona State University, because he was gay. Ten protesting students, known as "The UT-10," were arrested and charged for refusing to leave the central administration building. The Center did not hire a permanent director until 2003, when it hired Dr. Rowena Fong. She resigned after one year as director, and in 2005, the Center then hired as permanent director Dr. Madeline Hsu, an Asian American historian. The UT and UH Centers represented major successes in Asian Texan activism in a region of the nation—the Deep South and Plains States— where very few academic resources had been dedicated to Asian American Studies.[18]

Asian Texans in NASA

Many of the scientists and astronauts at the federal space agency, NASA, have been Asian Texans. In the 1960s long-time Chinese Houstonian Frederick Dawn invented a material known as the Beta Fiber, which was used to make space suits and, later, stadium domes. The Beta Fiber made possible the landing of humans on the moon.[19]

Some of the first ethnic Chinese, Japanese, Vietnamese and Indian astronauts trained and lived in Texas. The first ethnic Chinese astronaut, Taylor Wang, originally of Shanghai, served as scientist-astronaut on a 1985 Space Shuttle Challenger flight. Mamoru Mohri became the first Japanese to enter space on a Space Shuttle mission in 1992. The second Indian and the first Sikh to fly in space was Kalpana Chawla, who died on her second flight, when the Space Shuttle Columbia disintegrated upon re-entry to Earth. Chinese American Leroy Chiao moved to the Houston area in 1989, when he began his astronaut training. He flew on space shuttle flights in 1994, 1996, and 2000 before serving in 2004–2005 as the commander of the International Space Station. "By our nature, human beings are explorers," said the first Asian commander of the space station. "We're curious. We need to see what's on the other side of the mountain."[20]

September 11, the Asian Tsunami, Hurricane Katrina, and Beyond

In the weeks after the terrorist attacks of September 11, 2001, Asian Texans witnessed a spike in hate crimes against South Asian Texans and Muslim Texans. Waqar Hasan, 46, was subjected to ethnic and religious insults from customers as he helped his brother establish a convenience store named "Mom's Grocery" in Dallas. On September 15, Mark Stroman, 33, asked Mr. Hasan for a sandwich, then shot Hasan in the head, killing him. One week later, in Pleasant Grove (a Dallas neighborhood) Stroman shot gas station attendant Rais Bhuiyan in the face, blinding him in one eye. On October 4, in Mesquite (a Dallas suburb), Stroman uttered "God bless America," before firing his .44 caliber gun into the chest of gas station owner Vasudev Patel—killing him.

Hassan was Pakistani, Bhuiyan was Bangladeshi, and Patel was a naturalized Indian American. Hassan and Bhuiyan were both Muslims, and Patel was of the Hindu faith. Hassan had lost his brother and father to murderous kidnappers in Pakistan, and he had sought to live in a "civilized" society by moving his family to the United States. At the time of his death, his wife and four daughters were living in New Jersey, waiting for Hassan to establish himself in Texas; after his death, Congressman Rush Holt (D-New Jersey) sponsored a 2004 private relief bill granting legal residency to the Hassans, preventing their deportation.[21] Vasudev Patel, while living in the United States, married wife Alka in 1983, and they moved in 1992 to Mesquite, Texas to run the Big Town Shell store. The couple had two children, and Vasudev often provided help to customers in need. After Vasudev's murder, their son became

Asians and Asian Americans continue to seek refuge or new homes in Texas. Kim Vo's East New Orleans neighborhood had been flooded by Hurricane Katrina when she arrived at the Austin Convention Center for shelter.

Asian Texans of all ethnic groups united in times of need. Here, Asian Texans worked the phone lines for a Tsunami telethon in Austin, Texas.

despondent and questioned aloud why he should continue living. Meanwhile, Alka Patel worked sixteen hour shifts at the convenience store to keep the business alive. One man who came to the aid of the Patels was Sam Hashmi, a Pakistani Texan.[22]

September 11 united Asian Texans through common experiences of tragedy, anti-Asian backlash, and post-September 11 investigations, deportations, and constricted immigration policies. Among Asian Texans, Pakistani Texans suffered the worst of the backlash, but Pakistani, Indian, and other South Asian Texans worked together through the crisis, ameliorating some of the effects of the violence and immigration crackdowns. South Asian Texans showed that the religious and political divisions that existed in South Asia do not necessarily prevent them from working together for the common good in the United States.[23]

Stricter immigration criteria lowered the number of Asian students and workers migrating to Texas and increased the numbers of detentions and deportations of Asians. Some Asian Texans protested the new immigration rules. Lawyer Gus Mercado and other Filipino Dallasites fought in vain against the deportation of ten Filipino airplane mechanics whose visas had expired. Many post-September 11 events brought together Asians across ethnic group, whether those events were fund-raisers for September 11 victims or protests of unconstitutional detentions.

On December 26, 2004 Asian Texans were again united by tragedy. A devastating tsunami hit Indonesia, Sri Lanka, India, Thailand, Cambodia, the Philippines, and other nations, killing hundreds of thousands. Asian organizations and places of worship flew into action immediately. Buddhist, Hindu, Muslim, Protestant, and Catholic places of worship became centers for collecting millions of dollars in relief and re-development funds. Secular organizations also raised funds; in Austin, the Austin Asian American Chamber of Commerce organized a television telethon. Non-Asian organizations joined the efforts; a Houston-based group organized a benefit concert featuring "gangster" rapper Scarface. Asian Texans again worked together across ethnic and religious lines.

Asian Texans continued to raise tsunami relief and re-development funds well into the summer of 2005, but these efforts were interrupted by the news that Hurricane Katrina would likely hit the southern coast of the United States. Given this warning, Asian Texan organizations again flew into action. Before knowing exactly when, where, and how Katrina would make landfall, some Vietnamese organizations, for instance, prepared to receive Vietnamese evacuees from other cities and states. When Hurricane Katrina struck Louisiana, Mississippi, and Alabama on August 29, 2005, tens of thousands of Asian Americans, many of whom had lost all they owned, evacuated to Houston, Dallas, San Antonio, Austin, and other places, seeking shelter and aid. Many of them specifically sought help from other Asians; in Houston, Vietnamese gathered at the Vietnamese-owned Hong Kong Mall, and Chinese went to the Chinese Community Center. Asian Texans also sought out Asian victims to provide aid. Dozens of Filipino Houstonians offered their homes to Filipino Americans and others.

Language barriers were a major issue. Because government agencies and national aid organizations had on staff very few Asian language interpreters, evacuees often could not communicate their needs. When Asian evacuees began arriving in Austin, for instance, City Council member Jennifer Kim was asked in the middle of the night to find Vietnamese interpreters. Yi-Noo Tang was drafted into the effort because the Chinese Community Center needed a Cantonese speaker. As various organizations provided ethnic-specific aid, the Asian Pacific American Heritage Association coordinated overall activities in Houston.

Less than a month later, Hurricane Rita hit Texas at its Louisiana border. The large Vietnamese community of Port Arthur, among other Asian communities, was devastated. It was the final blow to some Vietnamese shrimping businesses, many of which closed shop after their boats and docks were destroyed.

Like so many Asian Texans in years past, many Asian Katrina evacuees, having lost much, arrived in Texas with little and decided to stay here. Like so many before them, Asians found sanctuary among Asian Texan communities. Just as in the days of Exclusion and the Great Depression, Asian Texans relied on each other when government failed or betrayed them. And like the Chinese Galvestonians responding to the Great Storm of 1900, some Asian Texans acted heroically in response to tragedy.

Over a century passed between those two hurricanes. Today, we look back on over 160 years of Asian Texan history, a history as long as that of Texas herself. The struggle for acceptance, prosperity, and identity runs the length of that history. Today, Asian Texans are integral to every facet of Texas society. Indeed, Asian Texans have added new facets of culture, myth, and glory to the state. Asian Texans are grandparents, parents, children and everything in between. Asian Texans are rich and poor, highly educated and not, Democrat, Republican, and independent. Some work together as Asians; others have nothing to do with larger Asian communities. Asian Texans have successfully fought for their right to live with dignity as individuals, groups, and families. They identify as Asian Americans, Asians, Americans, Texans, and Asian Texans.

Our histories shape our lives, even as we continue to make history.

ENDNOTES

1   Romo, David Dorado, *Ringside Seat to a Revolution: An Underground Cultural History of El Paso and Juárez: 1893–1923* (El Paso: Cinco Puntos Press, 2006), pp. 198–201; see also Indian Texans chapter of this book.

2   Gee, Jane Eng, interview by Irwin Tang, 2005.

3   Marvel, Bill, "Century of Newcomers: Immigrants from as far away as Milan, Moscow and Monterrey have helped shape Dallas' history," *Dallas Morning News*, Oct 30, 1995.

4   See Romo, p. 199.

5   Tolbert, Frank, "T. J. Lee: He Speaks Everyone's Language," *Dallas Morning News*, Jan 17, 1965.

6   Public Television, U.S., "Gordon Quan," retrieved on Oct 20, 2005 at *www.pgs. org/searching/aap_gquan.html.*

7   Martha Wong was elected to both city council and the state legislature.

8   Beeth, Howard and Cary D. Wintz, eds., *Black Dixie: Afro-Texan history and culture in Houston*, Texas A&M University Press (College Station, Texas: Texas A&M University Press, 1992).

9   Bryant, Salatheia, "Communities work on healing, ending feuds," *Houston Chron-*

icle, Nov 9, 1997; Kolker, Claudia, "Coalition's ethnic action plan lauded: Justice agency chief calls effort 'realistic'," *Houston Chronicle*, Mar 18, 1998.

10 De Mangin, Charles, "Quan seeks to decrease tensions among convenience store owners," *Houston Chronicle*, Aug 2, 2000.

11 Zheng, Chunhua Zen, "Area convenience store workers get safety plan," *Houston Chronicle*, Nov 29, 2001.

12 Hegstrom, Edward, "Working to build bridges," *Houston Chronicle*, Nov 10, 2003.

13 On Gong Lum, see Chapter 10 of this book.

14 Vu, Roy, "History of Asian Pan-ethnicity Movements in Houston," unpublished manuscript, 2004.

15 Markley, Melanie, "Suit cites unfair admission rules," *Houston Chronicle*, Oct 19, 1997; Tedford, Deborah, "2 white students claim HISD discrimination," *Houston Chronicle*, Apr 22, 1997; Markley, Melanie, "Minority children sought for gifted-student schools," *Houston Chronicle*, Sep 8, 1998; Markley, Melanie, "'Our goal is education': HISD sees rise in gifted programs after fall of racial quotas," *Houston Chronicle*, May 28, 2000; interview with Bobby Moon, by Irwin Tang, 2003.

16 Khan, Alyah, "The Ten Percent Divide: System penalizes accomplished students at rigorous high school like Plano," *Dallas Morning News*, Jun 20, 2004; Elliott, Janet, "UT wants to modify top 10% legislation," *Houston Chronicle*, Oct 9, 2004.

17 UT-Austin Office of Institutional Research; Texas A&M University Office of Institutional Studies and Planning; Dillon, Sam, "Foreign students looking beyond U.S.," *Austin American-Statesman*, Dec 21, 2004.

18 Tang, Irwin, personal knowledge.

19 *http://www.dpo.uab.edu/~svan/Re-Appropriating.html* as retrieved on Oct 17, 2005.

20 *http://www.nasa.gov/vision/space/preparingtravel/exp10_next_crew.html* as retrieved on Nov 6, 2005; see astronaut biographies at nasa.gov.

21 Trejo, Frank, "Slain clerk's family gets residency," *Dallas Morning News*, Nov 5, 2004; Southern Poverty Law Center, "Intelligence Report, *http://www.splcenter.org/intel/intelreport/article.jsp?pid=247* as retrieved on Oct 30, 2005.

22 Bell, Cherie, "Widow struggles after 9-11," *Dallas Morning News*, Oct 13, 2002.

23 See the South Asian Texan chapters of this book.

Photograph and Image Credits

Page 34 Document image available from the Daughters of the Republic of Texas Library and UT-San Antonio's (UTSA's) Institute of Texan Cultures, both in San Antonio.

Page 37 Photos courtesy of Charles Sadberry, Dallas-Fort Worth. Drawing (bottom) available from *Harper's* magazine.

Page 39 Photos courtesy of Joe Lung, Jr., Austin, Texas.

Page 41 Photos courtesy of Joe Lung, Jr., Austin, Texas.

Page 52 Photo from University of Texas at El Paso, Special Collections.

Page 61 Photo from University of Texas at El Paso, Special Collections.

Page 65 Both photos from University of Texas at El Paso, Special Collections.

Page 69 Photos by Irwin Tang.

Page 97 Photo (top) from UTSA's Institute of Texan Cultures, No. 068-2994. Photo (bottom) from UTSA's Institute of Texan Cultures, No. 086-0260.

Page 102 Photo (top) from UTSA's Institute of Texan Cultures, No. 068-3002, courtesy of Taro Kishi. Photo (bottom) from UTSA's Institute of Texan Cultures, No. 100-0699, courtesy of Tom Shelton.

Page 117 Photo (top) from UTSA's Institute of Texan Cultures, No. 068-02965. Post card (bottom) from Carter Rila Collection, Special Collections and University Archives, San Diego State University.

Page 124 UTSA's Institute of Texan Cultures, No. 075-1052, courtesy Sonny Lew, San Antonio.

Page 127 Photo (top) from UTSA's Institute of Texan Cultures, No. 076-0491, courtesy Virginia Wong. Photo (bottom) from UTSA's Institute of Texan Cultures, No. L-3605-B, San Antonio Light Collection, courtesy of the Hearst Corporation.

Page 137 Photo (top) from UTSA's Institute of Texan Cultures, No. L-2894-I, San Antonio Light Collection, Courtesy of the Hearst Corporation. Photo (bottom) from UTSA's Institute of Texan Cultures, No. L-2867-C, San Antonio Light Collection, Courtesy of the Hearst Corporation.

Page 146 Photo (top) from UTSA's Institute of Texan Cultures, No. 071-0160, courtesy of Sam P. Nesmith. Photo (bottom) from UTSA's Institute of Texan Cultures, No. 079-0139, courtesy of R.C. Tate.

Page 161 Photo from UTSA's Institute of Texan Cultures, No. 083-0199, courtesy of Virginia San Luis Dizon, San Antonio.

Page 164 Photo (top) from UTSA's Institute of Texan Cultures, No. 083-0 courtesy of Virginia San Luis Dizon, San Antonio. Photo (bottom) by Irwin Tang, Austin.

Page 170 Photo (top) from UTSA's Institute of Texan Cultures, No. L-3624-C, *San Antonio Light* Collection, Courtesy of the Hearst Corporation. Photo (bottom) by Irwin Tang.

Page 175 Photo (top) courtesy of Virginia San Luis Dizon, San Antonio. Photo (bottom) from UTSA's Institute of Texan Cultures, No. 075-1214-B.

Page 184 Photo (top) courtesy of Punjab Sekhon. Photo (bottom) courtesy of Sam Kannappan.

Page 187 Photo (top) courtesy of Sam Kannappan. Photo (bottom) courtesy of Tracy Thottam.

Page 199 Photo (top) courtesy of NASA. Photo (bottom) courtesy of Mike Ghouse, Dallas.

Page 209 Photo (top) courtesy of Sunny Cho, Austin, from her film, *K-Town*. Photo (bottom) by Irwin Tang.

Page 214 Photo (top) courtesy of Michelle Cho, Dallas. Photo (bottom) courtesy of Savannah Choi.

Page 224 Photo (bottom): UTSA's Institute of Texan Cultures, No. G-220-4. Photo (top) courtesy of Dr. Chai Ho Ahn, Dallas.

Page 237 Photo (top) courtesy of Jane Gee, Houston. Photo (bottom): UTSA's Institute of Texan Cultures, No. 068-2955, courtesy of Harry Gee, Jr.

Page 249 Photo (top) by Irwin Tang. Photo (bottom) courtesy of Taiwan Semiconductor, Taiwan.

Page 261 Photo by Irwin Tang.

Page 268 Both photos by Trang Duong, Austin.

Page 275 Photo (top) by Irene Tang, Houston. Photo (bottom) by Trang Duong, Austin.

Page 286 Both photos by Irwin Tang.

Page 297 Photo by Irwin Tang. Document courtesy of Channy Soeur.

Page 302 Both photos courtesy of Vynarack Xaykao, Dallas-Fort Worth.

Page 311 Photo courtesy of Bootsabar Wilson, Dallas-Fort Worth.

Page 325 Photo (top) courtesy of M.J. Khan, Houston. Photo (bottom) courtesy of Harishini Ernest, Austin.

Page 328 Photo courtesy of Azrin Amin.

Page 351 Photo courtesy of Lou McCabe, San Antonio.

Page 373 Photo (top) by Van Pham, Houston. Photo (bottom) courtesy of Vynarack Xaykao, Dallas-Fort Worth.

Page 376 Photo (bottom) by Irwin Tang. Photo (top) courtesy of Jennifer Kim, Austin.

Page 386 Both photos by Irwin Tang.

Index